FOOD FOR ALL IN AFRICA

FOOD FOR ALL IN AFRICA

Sustainable Intensification
for African Farmers

**Gordon Conway,
Ousmane Badiane, and Katrin Glatzel**

COMSTOCK PUBLISHING ASSOCIATES
AN IMPRINT OF CORNELL UNIVERSITY PRESS
ITHACA AND LONDON

First published 2019 by Cornell University Press

Library of Congress Cataloging-in-Publication Data

Names: Conway, Gordon, author. | Badiane, Ousmane, author. | Glatzel, Katrin, author.
Title: Food for all in Africa : sustainable intensification for African farmers / Gordon Conway, Ousmane Badiane, and Katrin Glatzel.
Description: Ithaca : Comstock Publishing Associates, an imprint of Cornell University Press, 2019. | Includes bibliographical references and index.
Identifiers: LCCN 2019012611 (print) | LCCN 2019016997 (ebook) | ISBN 9781501744426 (epub/mobi) | ISBN 9781501744419 (pdf) | ISBN 9781501743887 | ISBN 9781501743887 (pbk.)
Subjects: LCSH: Food security—Africa, Sub-Saharan. | Agricultural intensification—Africa, Sub-Saharan. | Sustainable agriculture—Africa, Sub-Saharan. | Produce trade—Africa, Sub-Saharan. | Farms, Small—Africa, Sub-Saharan.
Classification: LCC HD9017.A3572 (ebook) | LCC HD9017.A3572 C66 2019 (print) | DDC 338.1/967—dc23
LC record available at https://lccn.loc.gov/2019012611

To the memory of Calestous Juma,
a smart, dedicated man with a delightful sense of humor

Contents

Figures

Tables

Foreword

Nearly twenty years ago Sir Gordon Conway was my president at the Rockefeller Foundation, where we worked together as colleagues. We were focused on developing new institutions and processes for agricultural development in East Africa, notably, village-level agrodealers, local seed companies, and the creation of bank guarantees for agricultural loans.

Conway wrote about these innovations in his classic book *The Doubly Green Revolution* and in a subsequent textbook, *One Billion Hungry*. For this new book he is joined by two co-authors: Ousmane Badiane, the director for Africa of the International Food Policy Research Institute at Dakar, Senegal, and a noted authority on the political economy of agricultural development in Africa; and Katrin Glatzel, program head of the Malabo Montpellier Panel, and a visiting researcher at Imperial College London.

Food for All in Africa is a deliberately optimistic book. As the authors say in the introduction, even though most African farmers are smallholders, with no more than two hectares of land, many have demonstrated that with the right advice and inputs they can feed their families and create sustainable livelihoods. The challenge is to bring these achievements to scale by linking them to modern and effective food value chains.

At the African Development Bank, we aim to strengthen agriculture and food security through an integrated value chain approach that can improve the livelihoods of Africans who live in rural areas. Many are reliant on subsistence farming, and a sizable proportion are chronically vulnerable to climatic uncertainty. Africa lives off its land, and more than 70 percent of Africans work on the land, an enterprise that too often fails to meet their needs. By continuing to invest in agricultural technologies and rural infrastructure, including rural roads, irrigation, electricity, storage facilities, access to markets, conservation systems, and supply networks, the African Development Bank will help countries to increase agricultural productivity and competitiveness.

The African Development Bank is investing US$24 billion in agriculture over the next ten years to help turn agriculture into a business for creating wealth and lifting millions out of poverty.

We are pleased to collaborate with the Federal Ministry of Economic Cooperation and Development in Germany and the Department for International Development in the United Kingdom in funding the new Malabo Montpellier

Panel, co-chaired by Ousmane Badiane and Joachim von Braun. This is a successor to the original Montpellier Panel, chaired by Sir Gordon Conway, whose members included both African and European experts in agricultural development and whose aim was to demonstrate to European donors how to target European investment in Africa more effectively.

The successor, the Malabo Montpellier Panel, has a predominantly African membership and is based in Dakar. It produces periodic reports on key issues of interest to African government, non-government, and private sector leaders. The first two reports, published in 2017 and 2018, are titled "Nourished: How Africa Can Build a Future Free from Hunger and Malnutrition" and "Mechanized: Transforming Africa's Agricultural Value Chains." The reports have helped to raise awareness of the importance of these topics in regard to agriculture in Africa.

As we continue to tackle the challenges of transforming Africa's agriculture, I look forward to reading more such insightful reports in future.

Akinwumi A. Adesina
President of the African Development Bank

Acknowledgments

Much of this book is based on our work, as well as that of our colleagues, under the auspices of Agriculture for Impact, the Montpellier Panel, and its successor the Malabo Montpellier Panel.

Agriculture for Impact (A4I) (2010–16; www.ag4impact.org; www.canwe feedtheworld.org) was an independent advocacy initiative based at Imperial College London. A4I encouraged European decision-makers to provide more effective support to sustainable, productive, equitable, and resilient agricultural development for smallholder farmers in Africa. A4I convened the Montpellier Panel (2010–16), a group of European and African experts in the fields of agriculture, trade, ecology and global development.

The Montpellier Panel's successor, the Malabo Montpellier (MaMo) Panel (2017–; www.mamopanel.org), is facilitated jointly by the International Food Policy Research Institute, Imperial College London, and the Center for Development Research at the University of Bonn. It convenes leading African and international experts in agriculture, ecology, nutrition, and food security to guide policy choices by African governments to accelerate progress toward food security and improved nutrition.

We have also greatly benefited from the inputs of the staff and members of the panels. We would like to thank them for their considerable expertise, innovative ideas, and important insights, without which the work of the panels and this book would have been much poorer.

Acronyms

AGRA   Alliance for a Green Revolution in Africa
AGRODEP   African Growth and Development Policy
APRM   African Peer Review Mechanism
CA   conservation agriculture
CAADP   Comprehensive Africa Agriculture Development Programme
CGIAR   Consortium of International Agricultural Research Centers (previously Consultative Group on International Agricultural Research)
CIMMYT   International Maize and Wheat Improvement Center
CO_2 carbon dioxide
COMESA   Common Market for Eastern and Southern Africa
CSA   climate-smart agriculture
DAP   diammonium phosphate
ECOWAS   Economic Community of West African States
EU   European Union
FAO   Food and Agriculture Organization of the United Nations
FAW   fall armyworm
GHGs   greenhouse gases
GHI   Global Hunger Index
GMOs   genetically modified organisms
GPS   global positioning system
HGSF   Home Grown School Feeding
IFPRI   International Food Policy Research Institute
IPM   integrated pest management
ISM   integrated soil management
IWRM   integrated water resource management
MDGs   Millennium Development Goals
N_2O nitrous oxide
NDVI   normalized difference vegetation index
NEPAD   New Partnership for Africa's Development
NGO   non-governmental organization
OECD   Organisation for Economic Co-operation and Development
OPV   open pollinated varieties
PRSP   Poverty Reduction Strategy Programs

ReSAKSS   Regional Strategic Analysis and Knowledge Support System
SADC   Southern African Development Community
SDGs   sustainable development goals
SI   sustainable intensification
SOC   soil organic carbon
SPO   smallholder producer organization
SSA   sub-Saharan Africa
WFP   World Food Programme
WHO   World Health Organization
NERICA   new rice for Africa

FOOD FOR ALL IN AFRICA

A BOOK FOR OPTIMISTS

This is a book for optimists. Even though most African farmers are smallholders, with less than two hectares of land, we believe they can feed themselves and their families, and that they can generate enough income from their crops and livestock to send their children to school and to purchase medicines when they get sick, as well as have funds to invest in improving their farms.

Why do we hold this conviction? Partly because we know many farmers throughout the continent who have produced four, five, or six tons of maize per hectare, whereas in the past their yield was as little as 750kg. They have accomplished this with drought-tolerant maize seed combined with the application of blended fertilizer appropriate for their locality plus a much-needed soil ingredient, such as boron in southern Ethiopia or lime in Mozambique. In other communities similar massive increases in yields are possible for rice.

The challenge is to bring these achievements to scale. Many African economies have experienced unprecedented rates of economic growth, and agricultural growth has averaged about 7 percent per annum since 2005. Thanks to these achievements, African countries have started to reduce poverty, hunger, and malnutrition. Populations are rising, which presents both challenges and opportunities. By 2050 over half of the African population will be living in urban areas; both urbanization and urban incomes are rising fast, a consequence of migration from rural areas. As a result, Africa's demand for food is projected to more than double by mid-century, owing partly to demands for more food staples, more varied and nutritious foods, and more processed food and partly to improved intraregional trade. This is generating a pull factor that reaches down the value chain to smallholder farmers.

A Doubly Green Revolution

Twenty years ago, one of us published a book entitled *A Doubly Green Revolution: Food for All in the Twenty-First Century*.[1] The original Green Revolution of the 1960s and 1970s was highly successful, increasing yields and production of staple crops to such a vast degree that famine in Asia and Latin America was averted. Yet in its wake the revolution brought serious environmental problems as well. We argued then for a new revolution that could be both applicable under highly diverse conditions and environmentally sustainable. In effect, we needed a Doubly Green Revolution, one that would prove to be even more productive than the first Green Revolution, even more green in terms of conserving natural resources and the environment, and even more effective in reducing hunger and poverty.

In the intervening years much has been achieved. Attempts are now being made to reduce the excessive use of agrochemicals, such as fertilizers and pesticides. More attention is paid to environmental threats like soil degradation and especially to the consequences of global warming and climate change. Almost everywhere in Africa there are small projects funded by governments or NGOs that create sustainable approaches to food and fiber production—approaches based, for example, on conservation agriculture, agroforestry, crop rotation using legumes, crop-livestock integration, or fully organic systems.

Doubly Green Value Chains

How do we take what we have learned and bring it to scale? At the outset we recognize that African smallholder farmers are not interested just in "hanging in," that is, subsisting on the edge of poverty. They are businesspeople who want to "step up," who want not only to feed their families but also to make a modest income that enables them to send their children to school or buy much-needed medicines. And the most entrepreneurial engage in an effort to "step out," connecting to input and output markets that transform their productivity and their income-earning capacity.[2]

Inevitably this means linking farmers to markets where they can buy appropriate, environmentally friendly inputs and transform them through value chains into profitable and sustainable incomes. Value is generated along value chains from research and development at the base, through seed and fertilizer companies, village agrodealers, and farming practices, to storage, agroprocessing, urban retailing, food services, and agricultural trade. In Africa around 20 percent of gross domestic product is generated by such agribusiness and food-related business. Some of this value extends down to small and medium enterprises and to the farm and rural households. With government support, farmers will create a trillion-dollar food market by 2030.

At the same time, imports of raw and processed foods have increased to about US$35 billion per year and are estimated to rise to about US$110 billion by 2025. Many of these imports could be produced in Africa. According to one estimate, if Africa was more intensively farmed, the continent could easily produce another one hundred million tons of grain equivalent—as much as is produced in the US corn belt. And Africa could become net agricultural exporter.

The Virtuous Circle

It is possible to envisage a virtuous circle generated by agricultural development. As agriculture develops, resulting in greater yields for both subsistence and cash crops, farmers become more prosperous, and the rural poor, whether landless or on smallholdings, benefit through wage labor. Chronic hunger decreases. The rural economy also grows through the creation of small rural businesses, providing more employment and improved rural facilities, especially schools and health clinics. The development of roads and markets allows the rural economy to connect efficiently to the urban economy and the growing industrial sector. Free trade offers opportunities for expanding imports and exports, especially high-value agricultural exports like coffee, cocoa, and cotton as well as fruits and vegetables. Better infrastructure, free trade, and growing urban demand for food can accelerate investment in agricultural development, further intensifying the virtuous circle.

It is a circle that recognizes the interconnections with other virtuous cycles, conceived in a similar fashion. In each cycle a problem solved leads to a subsequent problem that, on the basis of the first solution, is more easily solved, and so on. In total through the cycles' interactions they form the basis of a sustainable future for Africa and, indeed, for our world.

Our Aim

This book is a discussion of how Africa's farmers can be helped not only to feed themselves and their families but also to gain income by producing food and other crops as well as livestock products for sale to growing urban and export markets. For this to happen we believe Africa requires a new agricultural transformation that is appropriate for Africa and one that recognizes the continent's great diversity of environments, climates, histories and cultures.

Part 1 describes the key challenges African farmers face and some of the opportunities for progress.

Chapter 1. African Farms and Farmers. Over 80 percent of African farmers are smallholders, and in many respects they are highly efficient. At the same time, medium-scale farms, those between five and one hundred hectares, account for a rising share of total farmland. Nevertheless, African populations are growing extremely fast, and in many countries smallholder farm sizes are shrinking and land is becoming more intensively and extensively cultivated, leading to further degradation. The way forward lies in farmers developing resilient livelihoods that encompass sources of income off farm. Diversity in the livelihood includes rural women, young people, and other disadvantaged people, all of whom need to integrate with agricultural and agribusiness value chains.

Chapter 2. Hunger and Malnutrition. Despite significant advances, severe hunger and malnutrition are all too common. Detailed nutrition and food security surveys can provide valuable information on how to reduce vulnerability and food insecurity. Undoubtedly the most shocking statistic of all is the incidence of child malnutrition, often referred to as "hidden hunger," which measures the lack of essential micronutrients. This complex challenge involves distinct disciplines and agencies, but in recent years there have been successes by experts in health, nutrition, and agriculture working together over the life of the child to intervene in various ways and at different stages in the child's life.

At the same time, Africa is urbanizing rapidly. A steep surge in the growth of the African middle class has taken place, especially in the 2000s. The effect of such an increase is rising urban demand for more and better food, which provides opportunities to increase and diversify food production in rural areas, resulting in greater value capture and rising incomes for smallholder farmers.

Chapter 3. The Threats to Food Security. Although chapter 2 ends on an optimistic note, many challenges arising from a range of threats external to the farm household lie ahead. Severe biological threats from pests, disease, and weeds continue. Healthy, fertile soils are the cornerstone of food security and rural livelihoods, but African soils are degrading. Water is just as important for the productivity of plants. Agriculture uses over 90 percent of freshwater withdrawals in SSA but only about 6.5 percent of the cultivated land is irrigated. Lack of water leads to chronic and acute stress.

Africa is already battling the impacts of climate change. Rising temperatures and variable rainfall are increasing the exposure of smallholders to drought, famine, and disease. Agriculture is an important emitter of greenhouse gases (GHGs), not only carbon dioxide but also such powerful gases as methane and nitrous oxide. In addition, there are often severe socioeconomic challenges, including unstable and high prices of basic commodities. Finally, conflicts cause disruption to food security.

Chapter 4. Resilient Farmers. We define *resilience* as the capacity of an agricultural value chain and its elements to withstand or recover from stresses and shocks and thus bounce back to the previous level of growth and development. Resilience can be strengthened in many ways and at different levels in the value chain through political, economic, sociological, and technological interventions.

Magic bullets do not exist, but there are solutions that combine a range of sustainable inputs, including organic technologies and limited amounts of selective synthetic inputs, combined in an integrated fashion appropriate to the local conditions. These include integrated pest management, integrated soil management, and climate-smart agriculture. Higher up the value chain are technologies for resilient storage and resilient markets. An opportunity also exists for businesses to invest in resilience technologies. African smallholders are businesspeople capable, at least potentially, of making profitable returns from their smallholdings.

Part 2 presents the concepts and practices of sustainable intensification as an answer to these challenges and opportunities.

Chapter 5. Sustainable Agriculture. We propose that the way forward will be a prosperous and sustainable agriculture sector deeply rooted in the concept of sustainable intensification (SI): producing more with less, using inputs like seeds, fertilizers, and pesticides more prudently, adapting to climate change, reducing GHG emissions, improving natural capital such as soil moisture capacity and the diversity of pests' enemies, and building resilience.

One approach to SI is to employ precision agriculture, ensuring that inputs—whether nutrients, pesticides, seeds, or water—are used in a precise, sparing, effective, and strategic way in order to minimize their environmental impact. Thus microdosing permits the prudent, targeted use of inputs such as fertilizers, thereby improving soil quality and moisture while reducing the environmental impact that excessive use can cause. It also reduces costs and helps improve nutrient use efficiency and protection against drought.

Precision farming focuses on just one aspect of SI. More generally, it is a concept that includes three mutually reinforcing pillars: ecological intensification, genetic intensification, and socioeconomic intensification.

Chapter 6. Agriculture and Ecology. Ecological intensification involves the use of ecological processes more intensively and in a sustainable manner. The aim is to use land, water, biodiversity, and nutrients ecologically efficiently and in ways that minimize negative environmental impacts. Such systems can conserve and utilize natural capital, thus improving the quality and quantity of food production. Conservation agriculture is one such integrated system of soil, water, and biological resource management, combined with carefully selected external inputs. This and similar systems can reduce GHG emissions from agriculture.

Biodiversity is a key factor in maintaining stable, resilient agroecosystems. Included in conservation agriculture are various forms of intercropping that utilize the mutually beneficial ecological relationships arising when two or more crops are grown in association, either as mixtures or rotations. This serves, for example, to reduce pest and disease attack. Organic farming also aims to mimic nature by making use of natural ecological processes and resources. The potential increase in yields and farmers' incomes sustainably is considerable in developing countries, especially in those areas faced with degraded soils, lack of capital, and low product prices. But care needs to be taken in determining where organic agriculture can contribute to sustainability and productivity and where it might have the reverse effect.

Chapter 7. The New Genetics. Genetic intensification consists of developing crop and livestock crosses that contain genes capable of producing improved yields on a sustainable basis. These crosses often show increased vigor, such that they tend to outperform both parents, although for reasons that are not fully clear. Today, hybrids and crosses are the basis for most improved crop and livestock breeds, including wheat, rice, maize, and dairy cattle.

Nevertheless, as has been long recognized, conventional breeding techniques have practical limitations. The application of modern cellular and molecular biology is pursued through four practical techniques: marker-assisted selection, cell and tissue culture, recombinant DNA, and gene editing. We examine the extent to which these interventions contribute to SI: improving nutrition, increasing resilience to pests, diseases, and climate change, and improving nitrogen fixation.

Chapter 8. Value Chains. The third pillar of SI focuses on the development of sustainable socioeconomic intensification. It encompasses the intensification of the relationships between farmers, which results in the development of innovative and sustainable institutions on the farm, in the community, and across regions and nations as a whole. Part of the response of rural people to the isolation they experience is to create associations, such as savings and loans associations and formal cooperatives.

The critical question is how these institutions can be taken to scale. We argue that the successful transformation of African agriculture lies in the effective integration of smallholder farmers into modernizing value chains. A food value chain describes the complicated process of transformation involving a sequence of events from the molecular product of one or more genes in crops or livestock, through intermediate stages of husbandry, harvesting, processing, marketing, and consumption, to the final molecular changes in the human who consumes the food product. Each component of the value chain, each structure or process has its distinctive characteristics, especially its own capacity to generate value.

Part 3 is about the technology and processes of agricultural transformation.

Chapter 9. Digital Farmers. There are numerous technologies and practices available to increase agricultural production and food security in a sustainable fashion; the challenge is to achieve this rapidly and at scale, efficiently, sustainably, and inclusively. There are experiences and tools at hand. Foremost among these are digital technologies, both hardware and software. The explosion in the number of cell phones in Africa is, in some respects, astonishing. Africa is going digital, enabling millions of Africans to connect for the first time. The effect is to revolutionize the lives of African farmers—by overcoming isolation, by speeding up change, and by taking success to scale.

Digital connectivity has enormous implications for agriculture and nutrition. It is already being used to disseminate information on nutrition and health, providing timely information on everything from weather predictions, crop selection, and pest control to management and finance. Technologies include the analysis of big data, using machine learning and blockchain technology applications that help to produce and analyze digital soil maps, to provide sophisticated insurance and faster breeding cycles for traditional African crops.

Chapter 10. Transforming Agriculture. Charting a course for a successful agricultural transformation leading to broad-based employment and income growth starts with a good understanding of the history of agricultural dynamics and the factors underlying it. The first decade of independent Africa was marked by strong overall economic growth, but things started to deteriorate rather rapidly in the following decade. The biggest impact on smallholders emanated from the far-reaching interventions by governments aimed at organizing nearly all activities in the agricultural sector.

Only in the last two decades have African economies experienced a remarkable recovery in economic and agricultural growth. Rapidly modernizing agribusiness value chains, in particular the staple foods processing sector, have provided a major opportunity for labor-intensive industrial development, including a large source of employment for youth and women. Rising incomes are driving rapid transformation in diets and thus staples value chains, with a rapid increase in processed foods. The fundamental changes in the quality of sector governance and increased public sector investment in the last two decades have to be sustained to bring about real transformation of African economies.

Chapter 11. Leadership and Performance. Africa, unlike any other developing region, has struggled for decades to find the proper strategic approach and direction for economic policy design and sector governance. The lack of leadership by African governments and constituencies in policy and strategy formulation in the agricultural sector has led to widely shifting policies, rules, and regulations that made it extremely difficult for smallholders to work productively.

Not until the beginning of the millennium did a series of developments on the continent create the conditions for the establishment of real African leadership. The agenda for the agricultural sector was articulated in the Comprehensive Africa Agriculture Development Programme (CAADP), a continent-wide framework for agriculture-led growth and development with clear targets. However, there are risks of policy reversal. Mutual accountability processes are crucial to increasing cooperation and coordinating action among multiple stakeholders—for example, governments, farmers, input suppliers, processors, and donors—in solving issues that no single group can address alone. Such review and dialogue platforms are all-important building blocks for more effective African leadership and improved policy processes and outcomes in the future.

The Basis for Optimism

We believe Africa requires a new agricultural transformation that is appropriate to Africa and that recognizes the continent's great diversity of environments and climates and its histories and cultures. In this book we describe, with examples from African practices and experiments, how this can be achieved. We do not pretend it will be easy, but the physical, biological, economic, and social tools for achieving it are available, and this offers us a broad basis for optimism. By combining the ingenuity of farmers and scientists we believe we can achieve sustainable food production and access for Africa's growing population.

Part 1

CHALLENGES AND OPPORTUNITIES

AFRICAN FARMS AND FARMERS

Sylvester and Beatrice Namarunda farm a hectare of poor, eroded land in western Kenya. They have four children, two boys and two girls, all under the age of twelve. They share the farm work, but Beatrice is also responsible for producing food, fetching water, gathering fuel, ensuring the children go to school, and looking after them when they are ill. They face shortages of almost everything. Their soil is exhausted from many years of continual cropping. They also lack access to money for investment. As a consequence, they often can't provide the youngest children with food they need, so they go hungry and are frequently ill.

Maize is their traditional staple crop, but they also plant small amounts of bananas or cassava and, occasionally, beans and some vegetables. Fertilizers and seeds are expensive where they live, and they can't get credit. The seed they sow is acquired locally; the maize is a poor, open pollinated variety (OPV) that yields about two tons per hectare in a good year. Like most farmers in Africa they must contend with pests, diseases, and weeds that attack their crops and cause severe damage, sometimes wiping them out altogether. The farm also faces periodic drought that greatly reduces yields. At the end of each season they usually harvest less than one ton of maize, an amount insufficient to feed their family (figure 1.1).

The Namarundas' farm is just one of millions in Africa of a similar size and in a similar precarious position but existing in differing climates and environments and subject to different cultural, economic, and political circumstances.

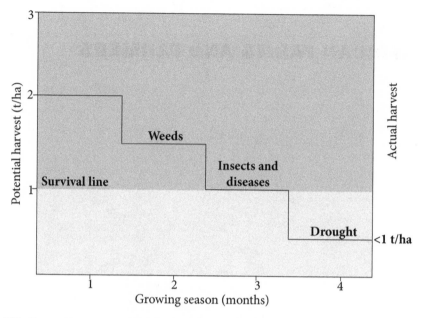

FIG. 1.1. An insecure farm in Africa

Source: Gordon Conway and Gary Toenniessen, "Science for African Food Security," *Science* 299, no. 5610 (February 21, 2003): 1187–88, https://doi.org/10.1126/science.1081978. Reprinted with permission from AAAS.

Africa is extraordinarily diverse: one only has to look at a map of the soils to see this. They range from highly acidic and harshly weathered to dark, moderately leached soils with rich organic topsoil. Even western Kenya, where the Namarundas live, contains a considerable diversity of soils.

On top of this the climate is equally characterized by extremes of rainfall and growing periods. In the Democratic Republic of Congo, the rainfall is nearly year-round, and cropping of annual crops is almost continuous. At the other extreme, along the southern fringe of the Sahara and at the borders of southern Africa, rainfall is barely enough to grow a single crop. In between, going north and south of the equator, rainfall varies from two crops a year toward the equator to one crop more distant. There are also short growing seasons in the Horn of Africa, in Ethiopia and Kenya. In the deserts of northern and southern Africa crops can be grown only with irrigation, if it is available.

This intersection of soils and climate determines the natural biomes and ecosystems of Africa as well as the human-crafted agroecosystems. African farmers are thus often faced with challenging environments in which to create a decent livelihood. Yet, against the odds, millions of small farmers do just that. In this book we describe how they manage to overcome the constraints impeding them, both natural and those caused by cultural and economic diversity and by political boundaries.

The Size of Farms

The Namarundas are not typical farmers, but they represent many millions of poor farmers who live in Africa. Over 80 percent of farmers in sub-Saharan Africa (SSA) are smallholders, defined as farmers with less than two hectares of land.[1] But this reality is changing: much of SSA is experiencing new land ownership patterns that may contribute to greater agricultural productivity. A study by Thomas Jayne of Michigan State University and colleagues has assessed changes over the past decade in the farm size distributions of Ghana, Kenya, Tanzania, and Zambia.[2] Medium-scale farms, of between five and one hundred hectares, account for a rising share of total farmland (figure 1.2).[3]

Medium-scale farms are likely to become the dominant size of farming in many African countries. About half of these farmers are members of urban and rural elites who obtained their land later in life, purchased by non-farm income. Such farms can be a source of dynamism, technical change, and commercialization of African agriculture. But this process of land acquisition may increase land scarcity. A positive example is the experience of Ghana where these medium sized

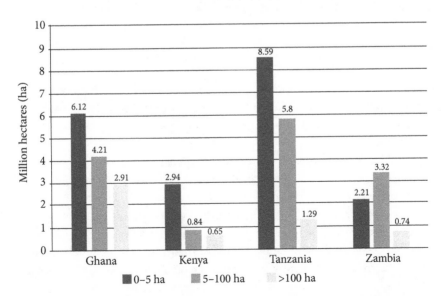

FIG. 1.2. Total area by size class for four countries in sub-Saharan Africa

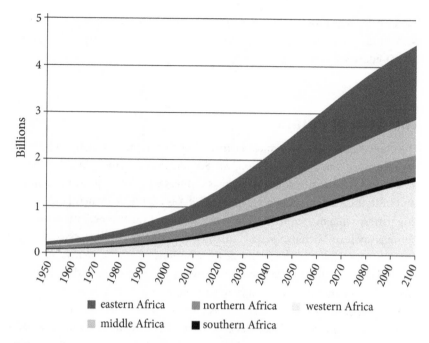

FIG. 1.3.   Rapid population growth in Africa

Source: Population Division, "World Population 2012," (New York: United Nations Department of Economic and Social Affairs, August 2013), http://www.un.org/en/development/desa/population/publications/pdf/trends/WPP2012_Wallchart.pdf. Recreated from data in United Nations, Department of Economic and Social Affairs, Population Division, *World Population Prospects: The 2017 Revision* (2017), custom data acquired via website. Used with the permission of the United Nations.

holdings are owned by farmers who started out with fewer than five hectares and then acquired more land. Their total landholdings exceed the total holdings of those with fewer than five hectares, and they are contributing substantially to food production.[4]

At the same time, African populations are growing extremely fast (figure 1.3). By 2050 roughly half of all the added population in the world will be living in SSA. Moreover, the rural population will be nearly 50 percent larger in 2050 than it is now.[5] Over 60 percent of the rural population will be under twenty-five years of age. By mid-century there will be as many rural people in Africa as in China and southeast Asia combined.[6] China is already experiencing declining rural populations, but Africa is in the early stages of its demographic transition, characterized by a rapid decline in mortality, particularly child mortality, followed by a rapid decline in fertility.[7] Child mortality rates are declining quickly in most countries. Women's fertility is also declining where schooling is improving.[8] We also know that the fertility rates desired by African women decline sharply and significantly in countries where population density is increasing. Thus in a high-density country like Rwanda women desire about 1.5 children, compared with 6 children in a low-density country such as Tanzania. Nevertheless, there appears to be an unmet demand for contraception, resulting in a higher birth rate than is desired. Probably the most effective policy for reducing birth rates is to couple the availability of family planning with improved female education and empowerment.[9]

Box 1.1. The consequences of Africa's demographic transition

[In most countries of SSA] fertility rates and youth dependency rates . . . are among the highest in the world. . . . [As a consequence, SSA has] higher poverty rates, smaller investments in children, lower labor productivity, high unemployment or underemployment, [extensive land cultivation,] and the risk of political instability. But demography need not lead to disaster. . . .

The prospects for Africa may be positive. Declines in fertility automatically raise income per capita in the short run and have the potential to bring further gains in savings and investments in the long run. With prudent policies, African countries can reap the benefits of this demographic dividend. Policy choices and actions can transform the population of a nation into a healthy, educated, empowered labor force that can contribute to real and sustained economic growth that lifts people out of poverty. . . .

Child mortality rates, the leading edge of the demographic transition, are declining quickly in a majority of countries in the region. . . . [Moreover,] the rapid expansion of school enrollments in the region makes it likely that the total fertility rate of the school-age cohort will be lower than that of previous cohorts. And once a substantial fertility decline gets under way, feedback loops can accelerate the process.

Source: Reproduced from David Canning, Sangeeta Raja, and Abdo Yazbeck, eds., *Africa's Demographic Transition: Dividend or Disaster?* (Washington, DC: World Bank, 2015), 1–2.

Nevertheless, the current rapid population growth, along with the practice of dividing the parents' land among the children, have produced immediate and far-reaching consequences: in many countries smallholder farm sizes are shrinking, land is becoming more intensively cultivated, leading to further degradation, land rents and costs are rising, and agricultural growth is becoming less inclusive.[10] Much, however, depends on whether the country is high density, land constrained, or low density, where there is abundant arable land that is poorly productive. In high-density countries farm sizes have shrunk by 30–40 percent since the 1970s but have stayed the same in low-density countries.[11] Twelve African countries, including large ones such as Nigeria and Ethiopia as well as Uganda, Kenya, and Malawi, have rural population densities above one hundred people per square kilometer. Collectively they contain about 60 percent of SSA's rural population.[12] Several countries have abundant land, among them the Democratic Republic of Congo, Congo Republic, Gabon, and Cameroon, which have large areas of unutilized arable land; most of this land, however, is under dense tropical rain forest, an important regional and global resource.[13] If it were to be cleared for agriculture, much of the planet's biodiversity would be lost, and climate change would become even more devastating in effects than it is now.

In some land-constrained countries, larger farm sizes come about through the integration of farms within farm associations. In Senegal most crops are rainfed, and water availability is one of the country's biggest agricultural challenges. Droughts and floods are frequent. Yields have declined as soils have become degraded and eroded from waterlogging. But providing new sources of water can create new opportunities for smallholder associations (box 1.2).

Box 1.2. A sixty-hectare farm in Senegal

In Senegal we visited a sixty-hectare farm, Ngomène, near Dakar created through the pooling of the land of members of the local farmers' association. It is supported by the government's National Agency for Agricultural Integration and Development. Ngomène has a central well provided by the agency and is equipped with electric pumps, transformer cabins, pumping stations, and drip irrigation technology. It currently employs 125 local men and women who are divided into 5 groups of 25 people each tending to 5 or more hectares of land.

Ngomène has three cropping seasons per year. In the two dry seasons the farmers grow vegetables and fruits, either for export or for the Senegalese market, while during the third, rainy season they grow grain crops for families working on the farm. Many benefits are derived from the collective action of the members of the farming association: women make their own income, giving them more autonomy and allowing them to invest in their children's education, in health, and in the production of nutritious food. Before the farm was established, the area suffered from rural exodus. Now, farmers have access to jobs, earn an income, and can send their children to the village's new school. The well-being and livelihoods of the farmers and their families are much improved.

Senegal is in a good position to benefit from export crops. It takes just four days for a ship carrying refrigerated containers to reach Europe from Dakar, satisfying the increasing demand in Europe for Senegalese fruit and vegetables.

Source: Reproduced from Katrin Glatzel, "Unlocking Senegal's Agricultural Potential," *One Billion Hungry: Can We Feed the World?* (blog), June 25, 2015, https://canwefeedtheworld.wordpress.com/2015/06/25/unlocking-senegals-agricultural-potential/.

Over the past decade both foreign and national investors have purchased large tracts of land in Africa in so-called landgrabs.[14] According to a recent comprehensive study, about twenty-three million hectares of arable land, or about 10 percent of SSA's total cultivated area, have been acquired in this way, mostly by foreign investors.[15] The purchases are concentrated in just six countries, Ethiopia, Ghana, Madagascar, Mozambique, South Sudan, and Zambia, and cultivation is dominated by oilseeds (60 percent), timber and pulpwood (15 percent), and sugar crops (13 percent) rather than by basic food crops.

The Ethiopian government claims such land deals will bring in much-needed foreign currency and facilitate technology transfer from large agribusinesses to smallholder farmers. Yet while local communities can benefit from these developments, access to land crucial for food security may be taken from local people.[16] Although large areas of land look empty, they are not. Often local communities have a range of traditional rights over the land, and many countries do not have legal or procedural mechanisms to protect these rights. Large-scale acquisitions can also create environmental conflicts if such incentives as priority rights over water are offered to encourage investment or if inappropriate resource-intensive farming practices are employed over large areas. Furthermore, a lack of transparency and regulation can foster corruption.

Much has been written about landgrabs, a great deal of it anecdotal.[17] Yet it is difficult to find good research on specific instances and information detailing the consequences, good and bad. One example of a bad outcome in Mali is described in box 1.3, although this is by no means a typical Foreign Direct Investment (FDI) project. These projects come in all shapes and sizes with differing forms of investment and land use and diverse outcomes for the indigenous people.

Box 1.3. A case of land acquisition in Mali

Mali has a relatively reliable rainy season and a large area around the Niger River that is arable and potentially irrigable. The government has prioritized agricultural development there and is additionally looking to attract FDI in modern production as well as biofuel crops. By 2009 FDI had applied for about 170,000 hectares of this land, with 140,000 hectares for food crops and the rest for biofuel production. One large-scale deal, a fifty-year renewable lease on 17,000 hectares of land, was struck to form a public–private partnership called the Markala Sugar Project. It included three components:

- A private entity called SoSuMar, whose shareholder is a South African sugar company, Illovo, a subsidiary of Associated British Foods.
- A public company called CaneCo owned by the Malian government, cultivating and processing sugarcane to produce both needed sugar for the Malian market and the by-product ethanol for local electricity generation.
- A third arm, CommCo, responsible for developing a portion of the land entirely for community development.

The project's aim was to create five thousand direct and twenty thousand indirect jobs as well as to bring additional infrastructure. But it also entailed the displacement and resettlement of sixteen hundred people and the clearing and conversion of a large area of natural vegetation to create sugarcane plantations.

As of 2012 the project was not fully implemented. Illovo discontinued their involvement with the project largely due to political risk and also funding difficulties. Local people still cannot farm the land because it remains fenced off, and they continue to protest against industrial farming in the region.

Sources: Aly Diallo and Godihald Mushinzimana, "Foreign Direct Investment (FDI) in Land in Mali" (Eschborn, Germany: Deutsche Gesellschaft für Technische

Zusammenarbeit GmbH, 2009); Environmental Justice Atlas, "Markala Sugar Project: SoSuMar/Illovo Sugar Refinery in Cercle de Segou, Mali | EJAtlas," accessed April 17, 2018, https://ejatlas.org/conflict/markala-sugar-project-sosumar-illovo-sugar-refinery-in-cercle-de-segou-mali; Olivia Kumwenda, "Illovo Pulls out of Mali Sugar Project," *Reuters*, May 28, 2012

Africa urgently needs financial investment in its agricultural development, but such projects must be implemented with care, avoiding exploitation of either people or their rights and ensuring environmental protection and resilience. Joachim von Braun and Ruth Meinzen-Dick of the International Food Policy Research Institute (IFPRI) have proposed a code of practice for land acquisition consisting of the following elements:

1. Transparency in negotiations, with local landholders being informed and involved in negotiations over land deals.
2. Respect for existing land rights, including customary and common property rights, with compensation to an equivalent livelihood.
3. Sharing of benefits, including with the local community.
4. Environmental sustainability: creation of sustainable agricultural production practices.
5. Adherence to national trade policies: priority for domestic supplies when food security is at risk.[18]

If this code is adopted it will make an important difference, but it will probably need more teeth if it is to be effective.

Smallholders

Despite the trend toward larger farm sizes in Africa, achieving food security for all on the continent will largely depend on smallholder farmers, at least for the next one to two decades. As has long been recognized, smallholders are in many respects highly efficient.[19] On the one hand, small farms produce more per hectare than large farms: many studies have shown there is an inverse relationship between farm size and production per unit of land. On the other hand, the development economists Paul Collier and Stefan Dercon of Oxford University point out that this connection may be true of small versus large farms, that is, one hectare versus ten hectares, but not small farms versus *very* large farms, that is, one hectare versus hundreds or thousands of hectares.[20] In Africa, where labor is relatively cheap and capital relatively expensive, there are few economies of scale.

Household labor is the key to smallholder production. The farm usually consists of a family with long experience of the local environment and knowledge of what works and what does not. Since the labor is readily available, motivated and, most important, flexible, it can respond immediately to the variable climate. It is also adaptable to the frequent crises such as pest and disease outbreaks, droughts or floods or slumps in market prices.[21]

The majority of African smallholders who typically farm fewer than two hectares possess these characteristics. Such smallholders can create food security, but it is not easy. It requires not only care and labor but also the adoption of new technologies plus access to both input and output markets together with an ability to secure loans and insurance. For example, a modern drought-tolerant maize hybrid can yield up to four to five tons per hectare when combined with the application of a fertilizer blended to the local soil conditions plus addition of an element such as boron or lime that may be inadequate in that location.

Living off an Acre

In the case of very small farms, for example, less than an acre (0.4 hectare), families are able to subsist, but it is difficult. Many experts believe that a farm of this size is simply not viable in Africa and that the priority should be to amalgamate such farms. However, a non-profit organization known as the One Acre Fund (OAF) is demonstrating that with careful attention they are viable (box 1.4).

Box 1.4. Viable one-acre farms in Rwanda

Rwandan farmers have farm holdings that are just half a hectare in size, spread over several locations. The flatter land is often used to grow crops for sale at local markets, and the steeper, sloping land that is more difficult to farm is allocated for food for household consumption. However, as the population swells, people move on to even steeper slopes which are even more demanding to farm, and where shallower soils are more prone to erosion and landslides.

The farmers are fortunate to have at least two and sometimes three growing seasons, allowing them to survive on their small plots and even make a surplus for sale. OAF works with over 125,000 Rwandan farmers, providing them with a bundle of goods and services on credit, including financing for inputs, access to seed and fertilizers, training in agricultural techniques, market facilitation to maximize profits from harvest sales, and crop insurance. The package costs about US$80 per farmer, and farmers are responsible for paying it back during the course of the agricultural season; the repayment rate is very high, 98 percent.

As in the case of larger smallholders, access to modern OPVs of maize and hybrids, as well as fertilizers appropriate for local soil types, can lead to an increase in average yields to three tons per hectare. On average these small farmers make a gain of 53 percent in income, taking them beyond the subsistence level so that they can pay back their loans and cover other costs such as education and health care.

Source: Agriculture for Impact, "Off the Ground: Investing in Rwanda's Agriculture Value Chains," Briefing Paper (London: Agriculture for Impact, May 2016), https://www.mamopanel.org/media/uploads/files/OFF_THE_GROUND-_INVESTING_IN_RWANDAS_AGRICULTURE_VALUE_CHAINS_2016.pdf.

In Kisumu in western Kenya, where OAF also works, the challenge is tougher. There is a second rainy season there, but it is weak. Women farmers claim that with an acre or less they cannot feed their families. Sometimes what makes the difference is husbands who work in the larger cities of Nairobi or Mombasa to earn additional income. Nevertheless, as many of the women are single mothers (HIV and AIDS have caused many deaths in the district), it is difficult for them to survive. OAF provides farmers with insurance that pays out in the dry years. More generally the answer lies in farmers developing resilient livelihoods that encompass other sources of off-farm income.

The Nature of Livelihoods

A livelihood can be simply defined as the means whereby members of a farm household secure a living, but this definition embraces a great diversity of enterprises. In developed countries a household's livelihood is typically the product of one or two adults working a set number of hours for an employer and, in return, receiving a set wage. By contrast, for rural people living in the developing countries a livelihood is often constructed from a range of production and income-earning opportunities, on and off the farm. Farming may be at the core, but non-agricultural activities may play a critical role. An overview of the range of rural livelihoods that exist in Africa emerges from the 2009 Rwandan Comprehensive Food Security and Vulnerability Analysis and Nutrition Survey described in box 1.5.

Box 1.5. Rural livelihood strategies in Rwanda

For the nearly fifty-five hundred households surveyed, ten categories of livelihood were discernible (figure 1.4).

"Agriculturalists" depend almost exclusively on agriculture for their livelihoods and have the lowest average number of income-generating activities. Three groups (low-income agriculturalists, agrolaborers, and marginal livelihoods) are especially vulnerable. A high proportion have poor access to land (mostly less than 0.1 hectares), fertilizers, and credit. Their households are often headed by a woman or an uneducated person

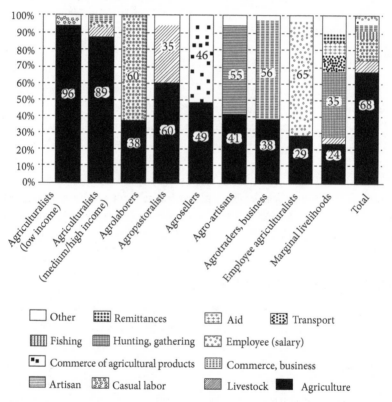

FIG. 1.4. Activities of Rwandan farmers in each livelihood group

Source: WFP, "Rwanda: Comprehensive Food Security and Vulnerability Analysis and Nutrition Survey, July 2009 (Data Collected in February–March 2009)," VAM Food Security Analysis (Rome: WFP, July 2009), http://documents.wfp.org/stellent/groups/public/documents/ena/wfp210888.pdf.

or both, and they have over 50 percent occurrence of stunting in children. In the other livelihood groups, families assemble a wider range of activities and may be more resilient as a result.

It is clear that agriculture alone is rarely sufficient to provide a productive and healthy livelihood. In the next chapter we look at the nutritional consequences of the different groups in these surveys.

Source: WFP, "Rwanda: Comprehensive Food Security and Vulnerability Analysis and Nutrition Survey, July 2009 (Data Collected in February–March 2009)," VAM Food Security Analysis (Rome: WFP, July 2009), http://documents.wfp.org/stellent/groups/public/documents/ena/wfp210888.pdf.

Diversity in the livelihood, on and off the farm, is manifestly a strategy for enabling farm households to cope with challenging, risk-prone environments as well as with social and political pressures. Periodic disasters happen frequently enough to make resilience a major objective of African farmers (see chapter 3).

Women Farmers

A woman's day in rural Africa "starts when the babies cry and need food before dawn, when the cow needs to be milked, when breakfast is cooked, when the children are dressed to go to school, and it continues after a full day in the field when she fetches water and firewood and food for the evening meal, and cooks the meal, milks the cow, and tends to her children and husband."[22]

It is an obvious point, but not all African farmers are men. Yet in policy and practice this fact is often overlooked. Agricultural extension workers are commonly male and interact only with men. In SSA about half of the agricultural labor force is female, and 60 percent of female labor is in agriculture.[23] Often a high proportion of small farms are headed by women, like Beatrice Namarunda.[24] Their crop yields are often low; not surprisingly, she and her children are often hungry. A large number of the poorest and most disadvantaged and marginalized people in SSA are women, and some of the poorest households are headed by women.

As a result, women play a crucial role in generating sustainable rural livelihoods: they are farmers and businesswomen in smallholder agricultural production, they manage household nutrition as mothers, and they are innovators and educators. Indeed, these roles span the entire value chain.[25] Yet when it comes to policy making and equally so in policy implementation, women are invisible at every level: from the household, to the community, to the private sector, to research, and to local, regional, and national governments.[26]

The gender gap in agriculture translates into a lost opportunity to improve the quality and quantity of the world's food supply.[27] Agnes Quisumbing and her colleagues at IFPRI distinguish three principal contributions women make to food security: food production, access to food, and nutrition:[28]

- In SSA women's labor accounts for as high as 75 percent of food production, the men concentrating their efforts on cash crops.[29] African women are also responsible for 90 percent of the work involved in processing food.
- Access to food depends on income. There is a close relationship between women's income and calorie consumption in the household, even though women earn considerably less than men.[30] Lack of income for women crucially affects children's access to food since women typically spend a high proportion of their income on food and health care for children.[31]
- Children are also better nourished when breastfeeding is practiced and attention is paid both to providing nutritious food for weaned infants and to maintaining good hygiene. These tasks are predominantly and often exclusively carried out by women; yet if they are active as farmworkers or earning off-farm income, there are severe constraints on their time.[32]

Women could increase yields on their farms by 20 to 30 percent if they had the same access to and control over productive resources as men. Total agricultural output in developing countries would rise by 2.5 to 4 percent, in turn reducing the number of hungry people in the world by 12 to 17 percent, or 100–150 million people.[33]

At the same time, we know women's empowerment can make a profound difference to health, education, and overall economic development. Nearly half of the decreases in the prevalence of underweight children between 1970 and 1995 have been due to improvements in women's education.[34] For example, work by the Helen Keller International Program in Burkina Faso showed that using women extension agents to educate women in farming households led to increased dietary diversity and decreased wasting, anemia, and diarrhea. Moreover, when girls are educated they have fewer children than their uneducated sisters. Their maternal mortality declines, and their children have better nutritional and general health outcomes and are also more likely to attend school. Most important, because educated women are more productive farmers, their economic opportunities and lifelong earnings increase. Yet there are still fewer girls than boys in schools.[35]

Catherine Bertini, a former head of the World Food Programme (WFP), concludes her essay on invisible women by stating,

> for women to be seen and heard, and for society to benefit from their knowledge, changes must occur, including:
>
> - Educating girls
> - Starting research with women's needs in mind
> - Enhancing women's health support
> - Supporting breastfeeding
> - Improving women's literacy
> - Creating agricultural extension programs that include women
> - Expanding micro-bank loans and insurance
> - Creating legal rights for women to own and inherit land
> - Considering societal gender roles in all development thinking

She concludes, "Visible women can change the world."[36]

Youth

The number of people in Africa who are between the ages of ten and twenty-four surpasses three hundred million and will grow to over four hundred million by 2025.[37] These numbers represent about a third of the African population. This is a much higher percentage than in any other continent and will remain unusually high for the next several decades. By 2040 the total labor force will be one billion strong, making it the largest and youngest worldwide. Furthermore, the rural population in SSA will grow by 6 percent.[38] This forecast is widely seen as presenting a growing crisis, but it does not have to be.

Rural youth are typically either farm laborers or landless. Young people often see agriculture as being outdated, unprofitable, and requiring hard work. Yet this outlook is not necessarily accurate. Agriculture is a dynamic sector offering a multitude of opportunities for entrepreneurship along the entire agribusiness value chain. This is true of the rural and food sectors such as agricultural supplies and innovation in farming technologies. Opportunities also occur in the information and communications technology sector or working in a commodities market. Attractive careers for young people also arise from employment in processing, transport, marketing, and retailing along the agribusiness value chain.[39]

"Young people are often dynamic, inquisitive, and challenging. Everywhere in the world they create a distinctive culture, are innovative, and often invent new forms of independent work. Young entrepreneurs are also more likely to hire fellow youths and pull even more young people out of unemployment and poverty. They are particularly responsive to new economic opportunities and trends and are active in high-growth sectors. Further, entrepreneurship offers unemployed or discouraged youth an opportunity both to build sustainable livelihoods and to integrate into society."[40] A good example is the story of a young Ethiopian called Tuna (box 1.6).

Box 1.6. The story of Tuna, a young entrepreneur in Ethiopia

Tuna Geda, 30, is busy in his onion farm located near Lake Zway in the eastern Shoa province of Oromia Regional State of Ethiopia. Like tens of young farmers who are now working for him, he is also a son of poor farmers who rely on rain-fed agriculture farming on a plot of 0.25 ha. In order to support his family, Tuna began working for other farmers as a daily labourer when he was 15. Including the half hectare of land he got from his family after his father died a few years ago, he now produces fruits and vegetables on 25 hectares and cereals on another 12 hectares. "I decided to quit school at sixth grade after I began working for a very hardworking rich farmer in our neighbourhood," he says. "Then I say to myself 'one day I will have tractor like him and become a rich farmer.' When my father died, I realised that it is time for me to act." Tuna then began using groundwater, renting a water pump for growing vegetables on his family's plot. After he bought one water pump, Tuna began renting idle plots from the neighbourhood to expand his agriculture.

Source: Reproduced from Felicity Proctor and Valerio Lucchesi, "Small-Scale Farming and Youth in an Era of Rapid Rural Change" (London, The Hague: International Institute for Environment and Development, HIVOS, 2012), http://pubs.iied.org/pdfs/14617IIED.pdf.

Yet people like Tuna encounter many barriers and pitfalls. They have low levels of skills and education as well as limited access to finance, and few market opportunities. They also lack broader institutional support and hence suffer if their businesses get into difficulties. For young women, the lack of access to educational opportunities prevents the pursuit of an entrepreneurial career.

A good example of a program that successfully overcomes these barriers is run by TechnoServe, an NGO in Rwanda. It focuses on investment in agricultural value chains through strong vocational and business management training for young people and women as well as affordable financing for starting and growing enterprises (box 1.7).

Box 1.7. The STRYDE program in Rwanda

Between 2011 and 2014 the programme helped over 3,500 young people in rural areas in Rwanda get their business ideas off the ground and become successful entrepreneurs. It provides a 3-month intensive training program [for secondary school leavers] covering business management skills, financial literacy, personal development, and confidence building exercises. Upon completion of the training, TechnoServe supports the STRYDE graduates to develop sound business plans and facilitates access to loans. . . .

The 'Association pour la vision des Élèves de Nyonirima' (AVEN), is a group of twelve young people who decided to form a cooperative following their STRYDE training. AVEN's main business is in producing improved seed potatoes in partnership with Musanze Catholic University, which provides them with quality seeds and access to their greenhouses. AVEN received an initial loan of US$2,000 to start their potato business. With their profits, the group now aims to acquire more land, increase their harvest to up [to] 45 tonnes per season and build a warehouse to store their crops before they sell them at local markets. Each member also now runs a small business on the side, [using further loans. The businesses range] from growing and selling garlic and tree tomatoes, owning a bar, providing mobile banking services, running a rabbit-rearing business to selling the services of their bull for cattle insemination.

Source: Reproduced from Agriculture for Impact, "Off the Ground: Investing in Rwanda's Agriculture Value Chains," Briefing Paper (London: Agriculture for Impact, May 2016), https://www.mamopanel.org/media/uploads/files/OFF_THE_GROUND-_INVESTING_IN_RWANDAS_AGRICULTURE_VALUE_CHAINS_2016.pdf.

These examples illustrate part of the solution, but the challenge is to take them to scale. For this to happen, rural women, young people, and other disadvantaged people need to integrate with agricultural and agribusiness value chains. Collier and Dercon argue for development strategies that shift the emphasis and resources away from small farmer (and small trader) models to the opening up of new forms of commercialization. They recognize that this will not happen soon enough through the amalgamation of farms or through the landgrabbing of large state-led farms or geopolitically motivated megafarms. So, what is the alternative? They argue for the creation of opportunities for serious larger-scale commercial investment in agriculture and hybrid models in which smallholders interact with larger farmers and vertically integrated enterprises upward in the value chain.[41] Going to scale is thus not about the size of farms but about the size and configuration of value chains (see chapter 7).

Isolation

Policymakers need to recognize that most poor and food-insecure farmers suffer from isolation. They live far from cities and towns, and their isolation is partly created by poor roads. Markets that provide inputs or purchase outputs may be many kilometers away and essentially inaccessible. When we went to Manica Province in Mozambique, not far from the Zimbabwe border, to visit farmers working with Alliance for a Green Revolution in Africa (AGRA) we drove for thirty-five kilometers along a muddy track for two and half hours to Boavista village, having to stop along the way to dig our vehicles out. The villagers were pleased to see us and proudly showed us their experimental plots, where they had achieved high yields of maize using blended fertilizers and a treatment of lime. But in the absence of help from AGRA it would have been difficult for them to obtain inputs or market their harvests.

One answer to isolation lies in encouraging farmers to come together and form farmer associations. These can provide support to farmers by helping them to secure inexpensive inputs and good returns from markets, providing savings and loan facilities, reinforcing/strengthening extension services, and organizing collaborative, often mechanized, field operations. Farmer associations foster resilience, affording mutual support and encouraging self-help. Effective associations need to be open, inclusive, and fully participatory via fair and transparent government. They come in many forms, including cooperatives, out-grower groups, and others, often with distinct cultural identities.

Isolation can also be overcome through digital technology, using mobile telephones, satellites, supercomputers, and the software that accompanies them.[42] Technology has the potential to effectively shorten the distance between previously isolated smallholders and the other components of the food value chain:

- It can speed up the supply of farm inputs through e-vouchers and real-time tracking of inventory.
- Local access to credit can be made more timely and more efficient, as can access to microinsurance.

- Breeding processes, which rely on digital-based identification of genomic structures, can greatly shorten the time for new crop varieties and livestock breeds to be produced.
- New digital possibilities can also make the process of innovation more participatory, a change that should dramatically increase adoption of new technologies.[43]

"As connectivity increases and the flow of information and ideas gets faster, a positive feedback system is created with smallholders at the center. They can get better access to inputs that are provided quickly while they also gain wider access to markets to sell their crops on more favorable terms. Each link in the chain is easier and faster, and so the feedback loop speeds up. It is then easier to get farmers' feedback and also to collect data on their situations, resulting in better tailored recommendations and services than before. Smallholder farmers gain the negotiating power, confidence, and readiness to adopt new technologies and processes and engage with the wider community."[44]

Hanging In, Stepping Up, and Stepping Out

From the examples given in this chapter it is clear that the economic, social, and technological development of farm households can be characterized in a number of ways. Fundamentally, however, that development involves decreasing isolation and the vulnerability of rural livelihoods while at the same time making livelihoods more productive, partly by increasing the importance of non-farm activities. In summary, rural peoples' livelihood aspirations are, first, to maintain and protect their current wealth and welfare and, second, to advance their wealth and welfare.

Andrew Dorward of the School of Oriental and African Studies at the University of London argues for three broad types of livelihood strategy or transformation:

- Hanging in strategies, concerned with maintaining and protecting current levels of wealth and welfare in the face of threats of stresses and shocks.
- Stepping up strategies, involving investments in assets to expand the scale or productivity of existing assets and activities.
- Stepping out strategies, with accumulation of assets to allow investments or switches into new activities and assets.[45]

These strategies are explicitly bottom-up, as illustrated by farm households that keep livestock (box 1.8).

Box 1.8. Livelihood strategies for livestock farm households

In contributing to a "hanging in" strategy, livestock keeping . . . has four important functions: providing for subsistence consumption (through home consumption of meat, milk, eggs, or fiber); supporting complementary (commonly cropping) activities (providing draught power and/or manure); buffering against seasonality in income from other activities (for example, cropping activities or seasonal labor); and providing some assets for insurance against unpredictable demands for cash. Beyond these minimal maintenance functions, livestock keeping may enable advancement through accumulation either of more productive animals (the "stepping up" strategy) or of a set of assets that hold value as savings to be used to "buy in" to other assets needed to gain entry to other livelihood activities (the "stepping out" strategy).

What determines which of these livestock contributions are important . . . [is determined] by the technical, institutional, and market opportunities and constraints people face, and these in turn depend upon . . . [rural] peoples' access to assets and . . . upon the social, economic, and natural environment in which people are located.

Source: Reproduced from Andrew Dorward et al., "Hanging In, Stepping Up and Stepping Out: Livelihood Aspirations and Strategies of the Poor," *Development in Practice* 19, no. 2 (April 2009): 240–47, https://doi.org/10.1080/09614520802689535.

The advantage of this simple categorization of livelihood strategies and their potential transformations, as illustrated in box 1.8, is that it provides a powerful framework. It enables a clearer and more communicable understanding of the dynamic processes of livelihood growth, poverty reduction, and development as well as the opportunities that exist for change—a theme that runs throughout this book.

The Opportunities

In this chapter we have discussed many challenges that African smallholders face: tough climates and degraded soils, small farm sizes, growing populations, land-grabs, and rural isolation. These hurdles are especially high for rural women and young people. But we have tried to identify where meaningful opportunities lie, openings that can enable farm families not only to hang in but also to step up and step out.

The very high proportion of smallholder farmers in Africa will remain for some time to come, but a largely positive trend can be found in the growth of medium-sized farms. Such farms can be a source of dynamism, technical change, and commercialization. Providing they are not landgrabs, they can, as in Ghana, produce significant amounts of sustainable crop production. There are, as we have described, examples of pooling of land through farm associations, especially for the production of export crops.

Very small farmers find it tough to make a living through farming alone, and the answer to that dilemma lies in developing resilient livelihoods that encompass off-farm income. Women, as farmers and businesspeople, can play a crucial role in generating sustainable livelihoods, providing they can gain control over key resources. Young people are often not only dynamic but inquisitive and challenging. We describe examples in which their entrepreneurial spirit is harnessed within value chains. We have also noted that rural isolation can be overcome, in part by the creation of farmer associations and by the greater use of cell phones by farmers, in both cases enhancing the linkages to value chains and markets.

In the next chapter, we discuss the extent and impact of hunger and malnutrition in Africa. It primarily affects the poorest individuals, especially those farm households that are *hanging in*. Once they are able to step up and step out, their access to adequate food supplies improves.

HUNGER AND MALNUTRITION

In Illeu, a small town in Eastern Equatoria State [of South Sudan], Anorina Kabaka first had to bring a bucket full of sorghum grain to be ground into flour. While waiting for the sorghum to be ground she plucked tamarind nuts, which she would soak in water to flavour the meal. Once she had returned home, she lit a fire, set a pot of water to boil, and mixed the flour into a thick porridge.

In spite of her efforts, meals like this barely sustain her family of nine children.

"What we cultivate in the garden is not enough to take care of these children," said Ms. Kabaka. She wiped sweat from her face and continued. "Sometimes we go and cut firewood and take it to the market to sell. In case we get some money, we will buy food from the market. We don't have any other work."

Not too long ago Kabaka's 3-year-old daughter suffered from severe malnutrition. With treatment she has recovered, but still needs follow-up care. That morning Ms. Kabaka went to the local health post, which is also an outpatient therapeutic feeding centre [funded by UNICEF], and collected more than 20 packages of ready-to-use therapeutic food (RUTF) for her daughter's treatment.[1]

What Is Hunger?

Hunger is an evocative old Germanic word meaning "unease or pain caused by lack of food, craving appetite, debility from lack of food."[2] In developed countries it is a feeling of slight discomfort when a meal is late or missed. By contrast, television images from developing countries convey the realities of hunger: emaciated and starving children in war-torn countries or in the aftermath of droughts, floods, or other calamities. Yet hunger is also a chronic problem. For over 800 million people in the world—men, women, and children—hunger is a daily occurrence, both persistent and widespread. Of this number, over 200 million live in SSA.[3]

One of the targets of the Millennium Development Goals (MDGs) set in 2000 was to halve, between 1990 and 2015, the proportion of people who suffer from hunger. This has nearly been achieved for developing countries as a whole, thanks to considerable reductions in hunger in China and Southeast Asia. But in SSA the proportion has dropped only from 33 percent to 23 percent, while the number of hungry people has increased from 175 million to 220 million.[4] Overall SSA has a higher level of hunger than any other region in the world.

By 2015 Ghana had halved the number of hungry people; considerable progress had also been made in reducing the proportions of stunted, wasted, and underweight people.[5] Three countries, Angola, Malawi, and Rwanda, have achieved the target, and six others are on track to do so.[6] Many countries were making notable progress from 2000 to 2007, when the food and economic crises struck, sending millions of people back into a state of starvation.[7]

Progress has not been as good as was hoped, slowing for a variety of reasons: volatile commodity prices, higher food and energy prices, rising unemployment and underemployment rates, and, above all, the global economic crises. Increasingly frequent extreme weather events and natural disasters compound political instability, large-scale migration, and conflict. The consequence has been disruption to human lives and livelihoods, creating economic damage and food insecurity.[8] According to the Food and Agriculture Organization of the United Nations (FAO), conflict and political instability are poised to be the central cause of further deterioration and a reversal of the progress made in reducing hunger.[9]

South Sudan

These challenges, at their most extreme, afflict South Sudan, a country that has vast oil reserves and comprises one of the richest agricultural areas in Africa but suffers from the worst food insecurity in the world. Across South Sudan, the youngest nation in the world, hunger is a daily reality for many children. More than a quarter of South Sudanese children under the age of five are moderately or severely underweight, a result of food insecurity coupled with poor water, sanitation, and hygiene as well as unhealthy feeding practices. Moderate or severe stunting affects nearly a third of children under five years of age[10] (box 2.1).

Box 2.1. Food insecurity in South Sudan

South Sudan achieved independence from the Republic of Sudan in July 2011. Although its independence was celebrated around the world with great hope, South Sudan is poorly developed and has very little basic infrastructure for education, health, transport, safe water, and markets. About 80 percent of the population live in rural areas and rely on livestock and subsistence farming to survive.

South Sudan's hard-won celebration of independence was short-lived. The Sudan People's Liberation Movement, the ruling political party that originally led the way for independence, is now divided and fighting over power. In December 2013 political infighting erupted into violence in the streets of the capital, Juba.

The fighting has continued, becoming increasingly brutal and affecting nearly the entire country. On top of these unpredictable attacks, the country's economy is in crisis, as the South Sudanese pound has declined in value and the cost of goods and services has skyrocketed. Food prices are at a record high. Grace, thirty-five, a mother of four, explained that "my cost of living in Juba has almost doubled . . . in December 2014 I could sell one of my goats and buy seventy-one kilos of maize flour, now it is only thirty-eight kilos. Now I am spending all my income on food."

Despite poor infrastructure and a lack of technology, South Sudan has the potential to develop a strong agricultural sector. However, it has not been straightforward to grow enough food in this young nation emerging from decades of struggle. Although food security was starting to improve soon after independence, a new conflict erupted, disrupting farming and eroding hard-earned gains. Farmers were forced to abandon their land and hide from the violence, thereby missing the spring planting season. In 2013 harvests of staple crops like millet, maize, and sorghum were 20 percent higher than the previous five-year average. As conflict continues, few families have returned to their home to plant seeds, prepare land, or harvest their crops. In the northern parts of the country a severe drought damaged the sorghum crop in late 2016, compounding farmers' woes.

Food stores are running out, and many markets are empty. Traders are also hesitant to purchase food from safer areas in case of further attacks. What little food is available has soared in price, and most displaced families have no money to buy any goods. Over eight million South Sudanese in total are facing some degree of food insecurity; three quarters of the population, or 4.8 million people, are facing *severe* food insecurity.

Sources: Ben Parker, "Extreme Hunger in South Sudan," *IRIN*, July 2016, https://www.irinnews.org/maps-and-graphics/2016/07/08/extreme-hunger-south-sudan; Action Against Hunger, "South Sudan," 2017, https://www.actionagainsthunger.org/countries/africa/south-sudan; AFP, "Drought, Hunger Add to South Sudan's Woes," *News24*, October 20, 2016, 24, https://www.news24.com/Africa/News/drought-hunger-add-to-south-sudans-woes-20161020; FAO, "Sky-Rocketing Food Prices in South Sudan Are Deepening Food Insecurity and Raising New Vulnerabilities," FAO in Emergencies, 2015, http://www.fao.org/emergencies/fao-in-action/stories/stories-detail/en/c/296963/; "FAO/WFP Crop and Food Security Assessment Mission to South Sudan," special report (Rome, Italy: FAO and WFP, February 2014), http://www.fao.org/docrep/019/i3652e/i3652e.pdf; "Quick Facts: What You Need to Know about the South Sudan Crisis," Mercy Corps, February 23, 2017, https://www.mercycorps.org.uk/articles/south-sudan/quick-facts-what-you-need-know-about-south-sudan-crisis.

Undernourishment

In South Sudan and elsewhere hunger comes in many forms:[11]

- *Malnutrition* means "badly nourished" and is a general term for a condition caused by improper diet or nutrition. It includes both a lack of and an excess of nutrients but goes beyond a simple measure of how much people eat or fail to eat. Malnutrition results from inadequate or unbalanced intake of protein, calories, and micronutrients and is characterized by frequent infections and disease. Most important, it prevents people from functioning normally.
- *Undernutrition* describes the status of people whose food intake does not include enough calories (energy) to meet minimum physiological needs for an active life.
- *Starvation* is an extreme form of these conditions, characterized by a state of exhaustion of the body caused by lack of food. When starvation is accompanied by an epidemic of mortality, we describe it as a famine.

All of these conditions occur in Africa; in some countries and during some periods they are more common than others. Hunger is difficult to measure, so indicators that simply measure the height or weight of an adult or child and compare it with a standard have been devised. Three such measurements—stunting, wasting, and underweight—are commonly used. In practice, they are relatively accurate reflections of hunger (box 2.2).

Box 2.2. Practical measures of hunger

- Stunting or low height for age, is caused by long-term insufficient nutrient intake and frequent infections. Stunting usually occurs before the age of two, and its effects are largely irreversible. These include delayed motor development, impaired cognitive function, and poor school performance.
- Wasting or low weight for height is a strong predictor of mortality among children under five. It is usually the result of significant acute food shortage and/or disease and reflects a recent substantial weight loss. Child wasting tends to be a consequence of disasters because it measures intermittent, short-term, acute undernourishment.
- Underweight for age of a child. The deaths of many millions of children under the age of five are associated with the underweight status of the children themselves or of their mothers.

Sources: WFP, "Zero Hunger," 2018, http://www1.wfp.org/zero-hunger; "Progress for Children: A World Fit for Children Statistical Review" (New York: UNICEF, 2007), https://www.unicef.org/publications/files/Progress_for_Children_No_6_revised.pdf.

The media reports on the consequence of disasters like drought, floods, war, or earthquakes, but famine resulting from such disaster actually accounts for only 8 percent of hunger-related deaths; 92 percent result from chronic and recurring hunger.[12]

The Food We Need

In simple terms, hunger occurs because we do not receive the amount and quality of food we need. First, we need calories, the energy for us to live. There are several sources of food energy:[13]

- Carbohydrates are the main source of food energy. The World Health Organization (WHO) guideline states that carbohydrates should provide 55 to 75 percent of total energy.
- Fats, comprising saturated fats, monounsaturated fats, and polyunsaturated fats, are the second major source. Some fats are essential for proper growth and development in early life. Dietary guidelines backed by scientific studies recommend that a diet high in saturated fats will lead

to increased blood cholesterol levels and a higher risk of heart disease.[14] Ideally fats should provide 15 to 30 percent of total energy.

- Proteins are vital to both maintenance and growth.[15] The amount and quality of protein intake promote good muscle and bone growth and overall optimal human health.[16] Some of the amino acids in proteins cannot be synthesized in the body and must be in the diet. Ideally protein should provide 10 to 15 percent of total energy.

Individuals differ greatly in the calories they need depending on their age, gender, body size, and other factors. Adult men tend to require more calories than women. Children have much lower requirements, but they increase with age and peak around adolescence. Adults over the age of sixty also have lower requirements (table 2.1).[17]

From these individual needs it is possible to use a country's population composition broken down by age, gender, body size, activity level, and pregnancy status to work out its overall needs. The FAO does this by determining the Minimum Dietary Energy Requirement (MDER) for each country. MDER is the amount of energy needed for to engage in light activity and to maintain a minimum acceptable weight for attained height. The numbers of the hungry are those who get less than this amount.[18]

The Per Capita Food Supply can also be estimated. It is the amount available for consumption for each country in any year and is determined from the following:

- The Domestic Food Supply—national food production plus imports and changes in food reserves.
- *Less* the Domestic Food Utilization—food exports, food lost to pests and diseases, spoilage, and other wastage, and food used for non-human consumption.[19]

The MDER for most countries in SSA, other than South Africa, lies between eighteen hundred and nineteen hundred calories per person.[20] On this measure most, if not all, African countries have enough food for everyone, although the

TABLE 2.1. Dietary needs in calories per day

AGE	MEN/BOYS	WOMEN/GIRLS
0–12 months	518–775 (beginning and end of range)	464–712
1–18 years	948–3410	865–2503
18–30 years	2100–4500 (depending on weight and activity)	1650–3850
30–60 years	2100–4200	1750–3400
Over 60 years	1700–3600	1550–3150

Source: Adapted from FAO, UNU, and WHO, eds., "Human Energy Requirements: Report of a Joint FAO/WHO/UNU Expert Consultation: Rome, October 17–24, 2001," FAO Food and Nutrition Technical Report Series (Rome: Food and Agricultural Organization of the United Nations, 2004).

amounts are only just above the MDER. But the reality is different, as the amount of hunger depends on many factors, including the nature of the food, how it is processed, and how equitably it is distributed and accessed.

The Global Hunger Index

It has long been felt that the FAO calculations present only a partial picture of the extent of hunger. A new Global Hunger Index (GHI), introduced in 2006, combines the FAO percentage of population that is undernourished with other measures of child malnutrition and child mortality produced by the WHO and other agencies (figure 2.1).

Yet this analysis too is far from satisfactory because it still relies on the percentage of undernourished estimated from a normal distribution of food intake.

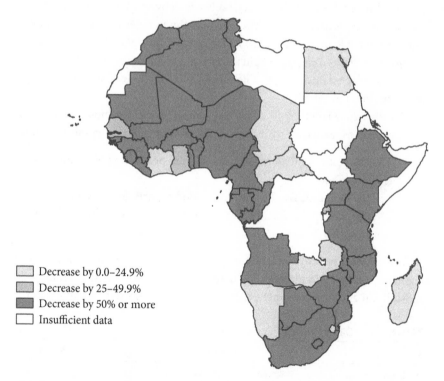

Decrease by 0.0–24.9%
Decrease by 25–49.9%
Decrease by 50% or more
Insufficient data

FIG. 2.1.   The Global Hunger Index scores for sub-Saharan Africa in 2016

Sources: Adapted from Klaus von Grebmer et al., *2016 Global Hunger Index: Getting to Zero Hunger*, figure 2.2 (Bonn, Germany: Welthungerhilfe; Washington, DC: IFPRI, and Dublin, Ireland: Concern Worldwide, 2016), http://www.ifpri.org/topic/global-hunger-index. Adapted and reproduced with permission from the International Food Policy Research Institute, www.ifpri.org. The original report in which this figure appears is available online at http://ebrary.ifpri.org/cdm/ref/collection/p15738coll2/id/130707.

Household Hunger

A more revealing approach is to conduct detailed nutrition and food security surveys of individual households. Inevitably, they are conducted on only
a sample of households, but they can provide valuable information on who
the food insecure and vulnerable people are, where they live, and why they are
food insecure. They provide more direct and revealing measures of hunger,
and, most important, they can offer clues as to how to reduce vulnerability and
food insecurity.[21]

One example of this approach is the series of surveys carried out by the WFP
in partnership with the Rwandan Ministry of Agriculture and the National
Institute of Statistics in sample villages in every district of Rwanda.[22] In each
survey, carried out over a six-week period, village heads and other key informants
in each of the sampled villages were questioned, as were sample households.
Starting in 2006, the surveys have been conducted every three years, although
not in the same households. The households are characterized in two ways: first,
in terms of six livelihood groups (see chapter 1) and also in six categories of
poverty and hunger (table 2.2).

TABLE 2.2.   Household categories in Rwanda by poverty, hunger, and resources

CATEGORY	DESCRIPTION	AS REPORTED BY HOUSEHOLDS (%)
Abject poverty (Umutindi nyakujya)	Need to beg to survive; no land, no livestock; lack shelter, adequate clothing, and food; often sick, no access to medical care; cannot afford for children to go to school; children malnourished	4
Very poor (Umutindi)	No land or very small holdings, no livestock; physically capable of working on others' land	13
Poor (Umukene)	Some land and housing; live on own labor and produce; no savings; can eat but food not very nutritious; no surplus to sell; children do not always go to school; often no access to health care	44
Resource poor (Umukene wifashije)	Like poor but have small ruminants and children go to school	14
Food rich (Umukungus)	Larger fertile landholdings; enough to eat; livestock, often paid jobs, and can access health care	1
Money rich (Umukire)	Land and livestock; good housing, often own a vehicle; have paid jobs; can access healthcare	0

Source: Adapted from WFP, "Comprehensive Food Security and Vulnerability Analysis and Nutrition Survey:
Rwanda 2012 (Data Collected in March–April 2012)," VAM Food Security Analysis (Rome: United Nations World
Food Programme, 2012), http://documents.wfp.org/stellent/groups/public/documents/ena/wfp255144.pdf?_
ga=2.187122856.1062231754.1523981558-1272296001.1523981558.

According to Rwanda's 2012 Comprehensive Food Security and Vulnerability Analysis and Nutrition Survey by WFP,

> Food insecure households are typically poor and rural, their members living in small, crowded homes and depending on low-income agriculture or casual labor. They rely on a small number of livelihood activities; often they have no kitchen garden, and their food stocks are not sufficient enough to last through the lean season until the next harvest. The farther households are located from a main road or market, the more likely they are to be food insecure. And food insecure households are more likely to be headed by a lowly educated, elderly person. Those that are involved in agriculture and land cultivation usually farm plots of land of less than 0.5 hectares. They comprise the top 17 percent of table 2.2.
>
> Conversely, households relying on more diversified activities, especially urban households not involved in agricultural production, are better off in terms of food security. The more crops a farming household cultivates and the more livestock it owns, the more likely it is to be food secure.[23]

More generally, the 2012 survey provided a positive view of the country's food security. Food production is increasing, markets are functioning relatively well, and food is flowing easily within and outside the country, thanks to the well-connected road network and market infrastructure. Almost 80 percent of households had acceptable food consumption and could be considered food secure, an improvement over the 2006 and 2009 surveys. These outcomes are the fruit of strong targeted government policies and programs implemented by partnerships between government, the private sector, and NGOs.[24]

Nevertheless, more needs to be done:

- Some type of difficulty in accessing food in the year preceding the survey is reported for more than half of all households
- One-fifth of all households report seasonal food access problems, usually in the run-up to the seasonal harvests, when food prices are higher and opportunities for casual employment are lower (figure 2.2).
- 17 percent of households experienced unusual "acute difficulties" in accessing food at some point in the year preceding the survey.
- 14 percent of Rwandan households have usual and almost year-round "chronic difficulties" in accessing food for their families.

On the basis of these findings, the analysis concluded with a set of practical recommendations, of which the following are a selection:[25]

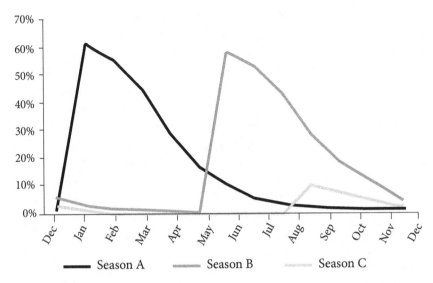

FIG. 2.2. Levels of household food stocks, relating to the three growing seasons

Source: WFP, "Comprehensive Food Security and Vulnerability Analysis and Nutrition Survey 2012: Rwanda (Data Collected in March—April 2012)," VAM Food Security Analysis (Rome: WFP, 2012), http://documents.wfp.org/stellent/groups/public/documents/ena/wfp255144. pdf?_ga=2.187122856.1062231754.1523981558-1272296001.1523981558.

- Expand social safety nets to reduce exclusion of malnourished and food insecure households.
- Scale up and implement seasonal interventions.
- Support household productivity to increase the time household food stocks last.
- Encourage kitchen gardens and diversity in crop and livestock production.
- Increase local agricultural production, sales of agricultural produce and marketing.
- Promote best productive and sustainable practices, for example, soil fertility enhancement and anti-erosion measures.

Hidden Hunger

Food security is not only about having enough calories or even protein. Undoubtedly the most shocking hunger statistic of all is the incidence of child malnutrition in SSA. In 2013 over 3 million under five-year-old children died, equivalent to 92 per 1000.[26] Linked to severe malnutrition are diarrhea, measles, respiratory infections, intestinal worms, and malaria. Well-fed children can fight them off;

the poorly nourished will succumb. Moreover, lack of critical micronutrients in the diets of children under the age of five leads to stunted development.

According to the Micronutrient Initiative, "For several decades it has been known that micronutrient deficiency—the lack of key vitamins and minerals—brings anemia, cretinism and blindness to tens of millions of people. But the news of the last decade is that these manifestations are but the tip of a very large iceberg. Levels of mineral and vitamin deficiency that have no clinical symptoms, and that were previously thought to be of relatively little importance, can and do impair intellectual development, cause ill health and early death on an almost unthinkable scale, and condemn perhaps a third of the world to lives lived below their physical and mental potential."[27]

We now know that the primary cause of stunting is a lack of critical micronutrients and minerals. Although these are present in very small amounts they are crucial if the body is to sustain essential cellular and molecular processes. The deficiencies are not necessarily detectable—hence the term *hidden hunger*—but they can have severe impacts, especially on pregnant women and children under five (figure 2.3).

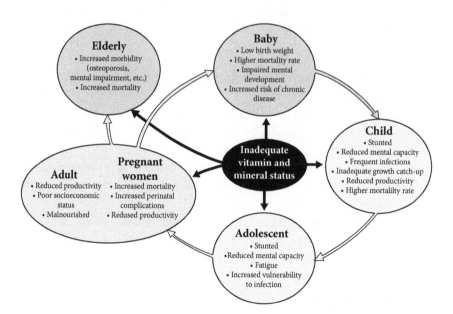

FIG. 2.3. The cycle of consequences of micronutrient deficiencies across the human life span

Source: Reproduced from ACC/SCN, *Fourth Report on the World Nutrition Situation* (Geneva: ACC/SCN in collaboration with IFPRI, 2000). The figure was adapted in R. L. Bailey, K. P. West Jr., and R. E. Black, "The Epidemiology of Global Micronutrient Deficiencies," *Annals of Nutrition and Metabolism* 66, suppl. 2 (2015): 22–33, doi: 10.1159/000371618.

The most critical micronutrient deficiencies are in vitamin A, iron, zinc, and iodine (box 2.3).

Box 2.3. Four of the most critical micronutrients to counter child malnutrition

- *Vitamin A* plays multiple roles in the body. Its deficiency is widespread in Africa, ranging from 20 to 40 percent, and nearly all countries have levels greater than 20 percent in children under five. As has been well established, lack of vitamin A can cause eye damage. In many countries a proportion of these cases become partially or totally blind each year, and many subsequently die. Lack of vitamin A has an even more serious and pervasive effect on the immune system, reducing a child's ability to cope with infections such as measles, diarrhea, and malaria.
- *Iron.* Lack of minerals in the diet can have equally severe effects. Iron deficiency, common in SSA, is the leading cause of anemia, that is, a reduction in the number of red blood cells to below normal levels. Anemia afflicts nearly 50 percent of women of childbearing age (fifteen to forty-nine years of age) and nearly 60 percent of all pregnant women in Africa. Iron-deficient anemic women tend to produce stillborn or underweight children and are more likely to die in childbirth. In the countries of SSA over 40 percent of preschool children are anemic.
- *Zinc* is a key mineral in the diet. A lack of zinc increases the severity of diarrhea, pneumonia, and possibly malaria and also causes stunting. In several SSA countries the deficiencies are over 30 to 50 percent.
- *Iodine.* Lack of iodine is the single greatest cause of preventable mental retardation: severe deficiencies of this mineral cause cretinism, stillbirth, and miscarriage; mild deficiency can significantly affect the learning ability of populations. Over 260 million people in Africa suffer from iodine deficiency.

Sources: Regan L. Bailey, Keith P. West Jr., and Robert E. Black, "The Epidemiology of Global Micronutrient Deficiencies," *Annals of Nutrition and Metabolism* 66, no. 2 (2015): 22–33, https://doi.org/10.1159/000371618; Hannah Ritchie and Max Roser, "Micronutrient Deficiency," Our World in Data, August 2017, https://ourworldindata.org/micronutrient-deficiency; Bruno de Benoist et al., "Worldwide Prevalence of Anaemia 1993–2005 : WHO Global Database on Anaemia" (Geneva: WHO, 2008), http://apps.who.int/iris/bitstream/handle/10 665/43894/9789241596657_eng.pdf?sequence=1; Solo Kuvibidila and Mbele Vuvu, "Unusual Low Plasma Levels of Zinc in Non-Pregnant Congolese Women," *British Journal of Nutrition* 101, no. 12 (June 2009): 1783, https://doi.org/10.1017/S0007114508147390; Bruno de Benoist et al., "Iodine Status Worldwide : WHO Global Database on Iodine Deficiency" (Geneva: WHO, 2004), http://apps.who.int/iris/bitstream/handle/10665/43010/9241592001.pdf?sequence=1.

As can be seen in figure 2.4, the incidence of hidden hunger in most countries of Africa has severe or alarmingly high scores.

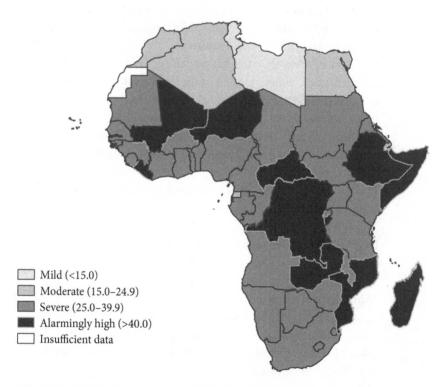

Mild (<15.0)
Moderate (15.0–24.9)
Severe (25.0–39.9)
Alarmingly high (>40.0)
Insufficient data

FIG. 2.4. Hidden hunger scores, 2011. The Hidden Hunger Index (HHI) uses indicators of iron-amenable anemia, vitamin A, and zinc.

Source: From Julie C. Ruel-Bergeron et al., "Global Update and Trends of Hidden Hunger, 1995–2011: The Hidden Hunger Index," ed. Stephen L. Clarke, *PLOS ONE* 10, no. 12 (December 16, 2015): e0143497, https://doi.org/10.1371/journal.pone.0143497.

The First Thousand Days

The grim reality of hidden hunger is described by Robert Thurow in his book *The First Thousand Days*. In the book a midwife in Uganda named Susan Ejang is quoted as talking to three dozen mothers-to-be and new mothers: "This time is very important to you as mothers and to your children. The time of your pregnancy and the first two years of your child's life will determine the health of your child, the ability to learn at school, to perform at a future job. This is the time the brain grows most . . . just 1,000 days from the beginning of your pregnancy to your child's second birthday."[28]

It is in these one thousand days when stunting, mental or physical or both, begins. As described in box 2.2 above, stunting is simply measured by the height of a child for his or her age. For children under five, a low height indicates that he or she is likely to be, or will become, stunted in their growth. The number of stunted children in SSA has risen from forty-four million to fifty-five million

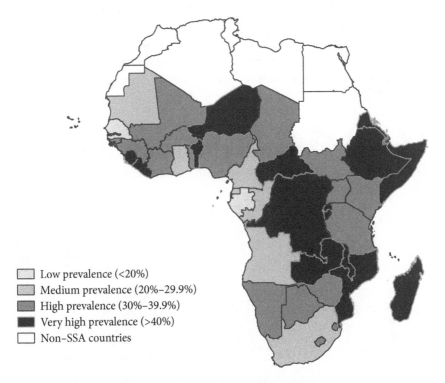

Low prevalence (<20%)
Medium prevalence (20%–29.9%)
High prevalence (30%–39.9%)
Very high prevalence (>40%)
Non–SSA countries

FIG. 2.5. Prevalence of stunting in sub-Saharan Africa

Source: Reproduced with permission from Food and Agriculture Organization of the United Nations, "Regional Overview of Food Insecurity Africa: African Food Security Prospects Brighter than Ever" (Accra: FAO, 2015), http://www.fao.org/3/a-i4635e.pdf.

between 1990 and 2015, although the proportion has decreased to about 35 percent of the under-five population.[29] In some countries the proportion is over 40 percent (figure 2.5).

On the face of it, the solution to hidden hunger is relatively simple. Children in the crucial first one thousand days of life and thereafter need to be provided with a diet that includes these four critical micronutrients and others in sufficient amounts to prevent stunting and to enable them to live healthy, productive lives. The nutrients can be supplied via breast milk, in supplementary feeding during weaning, and in the food of pre-school children.

There are several magic bullets: vitamins, iron, and zinc can be supplied as supplements and iodine by means of iodized salt. Alternatively, and in some respects preferably since it can be sustainable, is the process of biofortification. Biofortification uses breeding to build essential micronutrients into crop plants, for example, in the creation of golden rice or orange-fleshed sweet potatoes. For it to be sustainable, however, biofortification has to be contained in integrated programs of intervention that combine both health and agriculture interventions, as outlined in figure 2.6.

Health-based interventions, as noted, are crucial in the first thousand days. After birth the child has to be breastfed. WHO recommends exclusive breastfeeding for the first six months of an infant's life.[30] Thereafter infants should

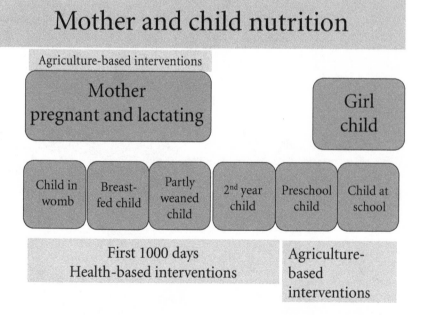

FIG. 2.6. Timing of health- and agriculture-based interventions to reduce stunting

receive complementary foods with continued breastfeeding up to two years of age or even beyond. When the child is weaned, that is, partly or fully taken off breast milk, she or he needs specially formulated feed that contains carbohydrates, protein, and the critical micronutrients.

In reality, African mothers often try to wean their infant babies by feeding them on the local staple crop. They may boil rice and use the liquid from the rice; it may look like milk, but it contains few or none of the critical micronutrients. Mashed-up maize, cassava, and bananas are also inadequate. Specially prepared infant foods are much better but may be costly. In Rwanda, where the incidence of stunting in children under five is nearly 40 percent,[31] the government is engaged in a joint venture with a Dutch company to produce infant foods by sourcing locally grown maize and soya beans that are milled and then blended with a micronutrient pre-mix, skim milk powder, and soy oil.[32]

In addition, agriculture-based interventions play a critical role, providing ingredients for infant foods and improving the diets not only of pregnant and lactating mothers but also of pre-school and school-age children, especially girls.

The challenge of the first thousand days is complex, involving various disciplines and agencies, but in recent years successes have been achieved by experts in health, nutrition, and agriculture working together. These are reported in the Malabo Montpellier Panel's report, "Nourished: How Africa Can Build a Future Free from Hunger and Malnutrition."[33]

Based on the report, seven countries—Senegal, Ghana, Rwanda, Togo, Cameroon, Angola, and Ethiopia—were able to substantially reduce the level of malnutrition between 2000 and 2016. For some of these countries, malnutrition was previously high due to conflicts and socioeconomic instability. Since then, these countries have benefitted from improved political and economic stability. Their governments have also committed to programmatic and institutional reforms which have played a key role in improving the nutrition status of their citizens. In addition, many countries have now created units specifically tasked with reducing malnutrition levels rather than relying wholly on the health sector tackle malnutrition. In Senegal the Cellule de Lutte contre la Malnutrition (CLM) provides technical assistance in the definition and implementation of the national nutrition policy (box 2.4).[34]

Box 2.4. Senegal's progress in reducing undernutrition

The Cellule de Lutte contre la Malnutrition (CLM) was created in 2001 within the prime minister's office.... It coordinates its activities with seven ministries—Health, Education, Economy and Finance, Decentralization, Trade, Industry, and Agriculture—and the National Association of Rural Advisors and civil society organizations. The main function of the CLM is to:

- Assist the prime minister in defining national nutrition policy and strategies;
- Review and agree on proposals for collaboration from the technical ministries in the implementation of the program;
- Facilitate a framework for consultation between technical ministries, nutrition policy entities, NGOs, and grassroots community organizations;
- Develop good synergy with other programs to fight poverty in general;
- Foster a policy to promote communication for behavioral change and good practices in the fight against malnutrition; and
- Contribute to the strengthening of national capacities for the effective conduct of nutrition programs.

In 2002, the Programme de Renforcement de la Nutrition (PRN) was launched by the CLM . . . to implement and evaluate nutrition interventions:

- A monthly weighing of the child from birth to age three, followed by advice given to the mother.
- Treatment of moderate cases of malnutrition through the distribution of fortified food and awareness activities for mothers, with severe cases referred to health services for treatment.
- Community-based distribution of products and medicines (mosquito nets, iron, vitamin A supplements).
- Information, Education, and Communication (IEC) and Communication for Behavior Change for the promotion of key family practices.
- Support for community initiatives (such as mills and market gardening). and
- Provision of potable water.

In 2006 an evaluation of the impact of [the program] was carried out [in three villages]. . . . It was found that between 2004 and 2006 wasting rates decreased significantly more in the intervention villages (−34 percent) than in the control villages (−21 percent).

Sources: Reproduced from Malabo Montpellier Panel, "Nourished: How Africa Can Build a Future Free from Hunger and Malnutrition" (Dakar: Malabo Montpellier

Panel, 2017), https://www.mamopanel.org/media/uploads/files/RPT_2017_Ma
Mo_web_v01.pdf; République du Sénégal PRIMATURE, "Enquête d'évaluation
de l'impact de l'intervention du Programme de Renforcement de la Nutrition en
milieu rural dans les régions de Fatick. Kaolack and Kolda," 2006, https://crdhvi
sion.com/docs/prn2006/prn2006.pdf.

In Senegal and other African countries the health sector leads in tackling malnutrition. There is evidence, however, that making agriculture more nutrition-
sensitive can improve nutrition outcomes. A study among pastoralists in northern
Senegal has shown that the introduction of a micronutrient-fortified yogurt has
led to a decrease in the prevalence of anemia from a very high 80 percent to close
to 60 percent.[35]

Another intervention in Senegal, Yaajeende (Abundance), has been developing biofortified varieties of millet, beans, and sweet potato. This project addresses
micronutrient deficiencies, including iron, zinc, and vitamin A. It is also promoting the adoption of conservation agriculture and sustainable land management
techniques. According to a mid-term evaluation, the program already led to a
drop in stunting by more than 4 percent.[36]

Livestock as a Source of Nutrition

Probably the most consequential, yet still controversial, benefit of livestock is
their contribution to the human diet. Animal source foods (ASFs) have several
unique characteristics.[37] They are energy-dense and are good sources of protein
and of many key micronutrients. ASF can enhance nutritional quality in diets.
This is especially true for young children and pregnant and lactating women.
Often nutrients in ASF such as iron and zinc exhibit greater bioavailability than
those from plant sources. Meat and fish are also sources of heme-iron, which is
absorbed better than the non-heme found in fortified cereals and plants such as
lentils and beans.

There is consensus in international dietary recommendations that animal
source foods form part of a healthy, balanced diet. However, the evidence for the
contribution in practice is rather thin. One classical experiment was carried out
on schoolchildren in Kenya (box 2.5).

Conducting trials of this kind is difficult owing to many compounding factors, including the health status of the children, the quality of the school, and the
influence of the parents. Nevertheless, the results proved clear enough for the
authors to conclude that "in developing countries where food security is low and

Box 2.5. Effects of animal source food on Kenyan children

Twelve rural Kenyan schools in Embu District were selected, and 554 children were randomized to four feeding interventions using a local vegetable stew. The groups were designated as "meat" (daily supplement of two ounces of meat), "milk" (a cup of milk each day), "energy" (oil supplement of equivalent energy), and "control" (no school intervention feedings). Feeding was carried out on school days for seven terms over twenty-one months, and the measurements of each child were repeated at intervals over two years.

The outcomes

Growth—all the supplements increased weight gain, and the addition of meat increased the lean body mass of all children: "The meat group had 80 per cent more increase in muscle mass over the two years of the study, and the milk and energy group had 40 per cent more increase."

Cognitive development—all children with meat supplementation significantly outperformed on a cognitive test that measures on-the-spot reasoning and problem-solving ability. The children "were more active in the playground, more talkative and playful, and showed more leadership skills." There were no group differences on tests of verbal comprehension.

Source: Shannon E. Whaley et al., "The Impact of Dietary Intervention on the Cognitive Development of Kenyan School Children," *Journal of Nutrition* 133, no. 11 (November 1, 2003): 3965S–3971S, https://doi.org/10.1093/jn/133.11.3965S.

children are mild to moderately undernourished with multiple micronutrient deficiencies, agricultural interventions to assist families in raising small animals for family consumption are likely to have positive impacts on children."[38]

Yet there is a growing argument that a meat-eating diet is unsustainable and will add to the pressure on land and other resources. A meat diet is likely to be more demanding of land, water, and energy than a vegetarian plus milk and eggs diet, but by how much is not clear.

Home Grown School Feeding

Home Grown School Feeding (HGSF) programs can be particularly effective in reducing malnutrition (box 2.6).[39] They require cultivation and husbandry of a greater diversity of nutritional crops on African farms, such as pulses and brassicas in addition to the staples as well as a diversity of farm animals providing meat, milk, eggs, yogurt, and cheese. Crops and livestock rich in the key micronutrients are often available, while in other situations varieties and breeds can be improved by crossbreeding to improve their nutritional quality.

Box 2.6. A pilot Home Grown School Feeding (HGSF) program in Zanzibar

In early 2014 the Partnership for Child Development (PCD), working with the government of Zanzibar, launched an HGSF pilot program in communities with some of the lowest levels of food security, child nutrition, and school enrollment. The two entities were feeding 5,250 schoolchildren with ingredients sourced from 200 local smallholder farmers and prepared by 26 local cooks.

The key elements are:

- A varied and nutritionally balanced school menu using locally grown cowpea, a good source of protein; sorghum, containing high levels of fiber, iron, and B vitamins; and orange-fleshed sweet potatoes, containing high-levels of vitamin A. These were rotated on a daily basis to combat micronutrient deficiencies.
- Smallholder training on how to cultivate and trade orange-fleshed sweet potatoes and in the latest harvesting and storage techniques, thus increasing the potatoes' shelf life and providing school meals for the entire school year.
- Local communities' construction of food storage units and kitchens, provision of water and firewood, and hiring of cooks.
- Strengthening market confidence by providing forward contracts that fix the price and quantity of the foodstuffs and hence give the smallholder farmers a secured future income and the assurance to enable them to invest and build up their own farms.

Source: Partnership for Child Development, "Annual Report 2013–2014" (London: Partnership for Child Development, School of Public Health, Imperial College London, 2015), http://www.schoolsandhealth.org/Shared%20Documents/PCD%20Annual%20Report%202013%20-%202014.pdf.

The HGSF pilot program will afford the Zanzibar government a base of evidence on how to develop and implement a sustainable school feeding program that not only meets the nutritional needs of local schoolchildren but also ensures a stable market for local smallholder farmers. In many respects HGSF is a win-win-win investment: child malnutrition is notably reduced, farmers and the cooks receive fair payment, the local community is engaged, and the range of stakeholders builds resilience and sustainability.

Overnutrition

Malnutrition encompasses not only a lack of the right foods but also situations in which children and adults are overweight. Unlike micronutrient deficiency, being overweight or obese is an obvious condition. Moreover, its incidence in both developed and developing countries is on the rise. According to data compiled by WHO, the prevalence of overweight/obesity in South Africa is over 25 percent for men and nearly 40 percent for women.[40]

Overweight and obesity are defined as abnormal or excessive fat accumulation such that an energy imbalance exists between calories consumed and calories expended. This imbalance comes about because of two factors: increased intake of energy-dense foods that are high in fat, physical inactivity owing to the increasingly sedentary nature of many forms of work, changing modes of transportation, and greater urbanization.[41]

Obesity is a complex condition involving both genetic and environmental factors.[42] Studies of twins show a correlation of the body mass index of over 60 percent. One hypothesis is that genes, selected in human history, enable individuals to turn food into fat deposits during periods of food abundance, thus storing food for use in later periods of food shortage.[43] Nevertheless, there is also a strong link between obesity and diet, exercise, and other environmental factors.

The consequences of obesity are increased risk of

- cardiovascular diseases;
- diabetes;
- musculoskeletal disorders, especially osteoarthritis, a highly disabling degenerative disease of the joints;
- some cancers, including endometrial, breast, ovarian, prostate, liver, gall bladder, kidney, and colon.

Childhood obesity is associated with a higher chance of obesity in adulthood, premature death, and disability. Obese children may also suffer from breathing difficulties, increased risk of fractures and hypertension as well as adverse psychological effects.

Obesity was previously considered a condition of developed countries and urban lifestyles. But many countries in Africa are now experiencing a so-called double burden of disease: while continuing to deal with the problems of infectious diseases and undernutrition, they are also experiencing a rapid upsurge of obesity and overweight, particularly in urban settings. It is not uncommon to find undernutrition and obesity co-existing within the same country, the same community, and the same household.[44]

Urban, and to some extent rural, children are increasingly exposed to high-fat, high-sugar, high-salt, energy-dense, and micronutrient-poor foods. These tend to be lower in cost but also lower in nutrient quality. When combined with lower levels of physical activity these dietary patterns result in sharp increases in childhood obesity and disease, such as type 2 diabetes. The estimated prevalence of children (seven to eleven years of age) overweight in Africa increased from 4 percent in 1990 to 7 percent in 2011. It is expected to reach 11 percent by 2025. The percentage of children under five who are overweight varies between 4 percent in West Africa and 15 percent in southern Africa.[45] The rise in the number of children who are both stunted and overweight is worrying. Most health care systems are ill-equipped to manage malnutrition.[46]

The number of supermarkets in Africa is expanding, but the evidence of their effects on consumer diets and nutrition is thin. One study has shown that shopping in supermarkets contributes to higher consumption of processed and highly processed foods and lower consumption of unprocessed foods.[47] This practice can improve food security and nutrition for very poor populations. But in general the retail environment affects people's food choices and nutrition, the effects depending on the types of foods offered, how they are displayed, and their price. Rather than thwarting modernization in the retail sector, policies that incentivize the sale of more healthy foods, such as fruits and vegetables, in supermarkets may be more promising in promoting desirable nutritional outcomes.

Malnutrition and Poverty

Many African farmers are both poor and hungry. Indeed, the afflictions of poverty and hunger are interlinked in a vicious circle. Food insecurity is intimately linked to poverty. Poor people have few or no assets, are unemployed, or earn less than a living wage and thus cannot produce or buy the food they need. At the same time, hunger renders them less able to productively farm or work at other

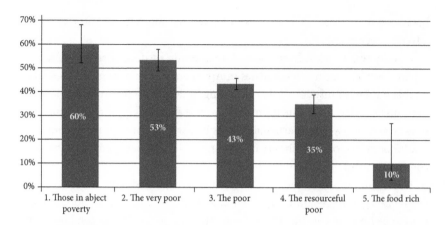

FIG. 2.7. Proportion of Rwandan households with children stunted (categories described in table 2.2)

Source: Reproduced with permission from WFP, "Comprehensive Food Security and Vulnerability Analysis and Nutrition Survey 2012: Rwanda (Data Collected in March—April 2012)," VAM Food Security Analysis (Rome: WFP, 2012), http://documents.wfp.org/stellent/groups/public/documents/ena/wfp255144.pdf?_ga=2.187122856.1062231754.1523981558-1272296001.1523981558.

jobs, trapping them in poverty. In Rwanda the proportion of children stunted is over 40 percent and highly correlated with poverty (figure 2.7).

As the Malabo Montpellier Panel concludes, "Agricultural and economic growth and transformation in Africa must be sensitive to nutrition and lead to sustainable food system development, creating jobs, improving livelihoods, and developing more diverse and nutritious diets. Without the political will to prioritize nutrition across all areas of government, including agriculture, health, and rural development, and without increased investments in infrastructure and public goods and services, malnutrition will persist, contributing to continued poverty and a reduced quality of life for millions of people across Africa."[48]

On the one hand, malnutrition not only causes ill health but also comes with a cost to African economies, averaging 11 percent of gross domestic product annually.[49] On the other hand the economic returns from investing in nutrition are high: for every US$1 invested, US$16 is generated.[50] Appropriate investments in the first one thousand days, that is, from pregnancy through the first two years, including prevention of low birthweight and early initiation of and exclusive breastfeeding will yield considerable benefits. This is true not only for a child's lifetime but also across generations. Nutrition-specific interventions that avert maternal and child undernutrition and micronutrient deficiencies cost US$370 per life-year saved. Nutrition-specific interventions need to be linked to nutrition-sensitive approaches: for example, women's empowerment, dietary diversity and food fortification, education, and social protection and safety nets. If this is done considerable reduction in rates of maternal and child undernutrition and mortality can be achieved. The benefits to global health and national economies would be even greater.[51]

Defining Food Security

Food security, which implies the absence of hunger, is an apparently straightforward concept that should be amenable to commonsense definition. But somewhat surprisingly it has been the subject of much debate. The controversy arises, in part, because food security operates at many levels and over different time scales: it can be viewed at the global level or as it applies to SSA or to an individual country, community, or household. These various levels relate only very loosely to each other. A country can be food secure but a household may not, or vice versa.

In the 1970s the emphasis was on the supply of food. But as Amartya Sen argued, food security is not simply about producing enough food. Sen concluded from his classic study of the Bengal and other famines that "starvation is the characteristic of some people not having enough food to eat. It is not the characteristic of there not being enough food to eat."[52]

This statement has been often quoted by activist groups arguing that there is plenty of food in the world; we do not need more food, according to this perspective, just better distribution of it. As we pointed out earlier, there is enough per capita calorie food supply in the countries of SSA that if it were divided equally among the population, each man, woman, and child would receive enough for a healthy lifestyle. To some extent it is a matter of political choice. In practice, food is not divided in this way (nor is income), and it is unrealistic to expect it will happen in the near, or even distant, future. All those people who cannot produce or afford the food they need could be given food. To some extent WFP does this, especially in humanitarian disasters. But if it were done on a universal scale it would undercut local markets and many farmers' efforts to produce more food for sale. Currently Africa imports over $40 billion worth of food and exports nearly $20 billion.[53] African farmers need to produce more food and help bring down its price, especially in local markets, so that rural households have ready access to the food they need. Because of the growing awareness of the interlinkage between poverty and hunger and the critical role of access to food, the United Nations' Committee on World Food Security in 2012 defined food security as "the condition in which all people, at all times, have physical, social and economic access to sufficient safe and nutritious food that meets their dietary needs and food preferences for an active and healthy life."[54]

In keeping with this definition Sen has identified three overarching entitlements by which individuals can establish ownership and command of food:

1. Endowment: labor power, wealth, land, and other resources.
2. Production possibilities: the ability to earn money to buy food or to grow one's own food.
3. Exchange conditions: the ability to buy and sell goods at fair prices.

Activists have also used the argument Sen made in the quotation above to argue against developing new and possibly hazardous agricultural technologies, but in a later book he added that access to technology was one of the entitlements of the poor.[55] Technology is part of the production entitlement: "This is where technology comes in: available technology determines the production possibilities, which are influenced by available knowledge as well as the ability of the people to marshal that knowledge and to make actual use of it."[56]

Technology, if used appropriately and wisely, can reduce both poverty and hunger, thus breaking the vicious cycle, but it has to be done alongside other forms of intervention, such as social support, improved land tenure, fair and better functioning input and output markets, efficient value chains and forms of governance that support the poor and give them voice and power. In addition to the potential of technologies, there are grounds for optimism arising from the increasing demand for food from the rapidly growing urban sector.

Urban Food Demand

Today, globalization and urbanization present African smallholders with considerably greater challenges than those faced by Asian farmers during the Green Revolution. Rapid urbanization can add stresses of many kinds, not least those arising from rural–urban migration. However, rising urban demand for more and better food can provide opportunities to increase and diversify food production in rural areas, resulting in greater value capture and rising incomes for smallholder farmers.[57]

Thomas Reardon and his colleagues at Michigan State and IFPRI argue that in the new era of urbanization a middle class is emerging, one that is creating a "Quiet Revolution in African food supply chains." This development is being led mainly by African entrepreneurs in tens of thousands of small enterprises, scores and, perhaps soon, hundreds of medium- and large-scale firms.[58] African food markets have expanded by six- to eight-fold over the past four decades, most of that growth occurring in the past two decades. One projection is that the food market will grow another six-fold in the next four decades.[59] Africa's urban areas now consume half or more of the overall food consumption. The food itself is changing rapidly, with a shift into non-grain foods like dairy, fish, meat, vegetables, fruit, and tubers as well as heavily into processed foods.

In the words of Reardon and his colleague,

> Supply chains are becoming two way super-highways—bringing food and fiber one way, and an "avalanche" of money back to the producers at every step in the chain—to the farmers, truckers and wholesalers, warehouse and cold store operators, and processors. This avalanche of income fuels grass-roots investments, much of it in rural areas or rural towns of small and medium farmers in the midstream and downstream segments of the rural–urban supply chains (such as investments in trucks), in farming (such as investment in pumps), and in the input supply chains. Rural households are also using this income to invest in education, housing, and rural nonfarm enterprises. This investment can lead to rural growth that spreads out in ripples to the poorest of those in the dynamic areas and also over time to the hinterlands. African policymakers have a major new opportunity in leveraging and encouraging this enormous development.[60]

They argue there are four key drivers of the expanding food market:

- First, Africa is urbanizing rapidly. The urban population growth is projected to increase by 3.7 percent per year compared to only 0.5 percent in rural areas. By 2020 the urbanization level will be 50 percent, and 65 percent by 2050.
- Second, because urban per capita food expenditure is high, urban food markets have become the dominant market for farmers. Thus while half the population is urban in West Africa, the urban share of the food economy is around three-quarters.
- Third, large cities are proliferating, yet small and middle-sized cities are growing faster than large cities.[61] Thus in West Africa, 40 percent of the urban population is in national metropolitan areas that are rapidly growing, while the remaining 60 percent is in secondary or tertiary cities. The rise of small and medium cities is a positive trend because they establish a much closer relationship with their surrounding rural areas.

- Fourth, there has been a steep surge in the growth of the African middle class, especially in the 2000s. The share of SSA population in the middle class (US$2–20 /day/capita at 2005 Purchasing Power Parity) rose from 24 percent in 1990 to 33 percent in 2008. Most of the expansion was in the so-called floating middle class, which had a purchasing power of US$2–4 day/capita that remains vulnerable to economic shocks.[62] Moreover, there is also growth in the rural areas.

Diets have also been changing:

- Women are increasingly working outside the home, and men are working farther from home, spurring the purchase of easy-to-process cereals, processed foods, and restaurant-prepared foods. Even the rural poor are buying some processed foods.
- There has been a huge increase in the food-processing sector in the past several decades as well as an emergence of the restaurant and fast food segment.
- Greater diet diversification means new and more sources of caloric energy but also of micronutrients.
- The development of rural non-farm employment and the gradual commercialization of agriculture have furnished cash incomes that are used in part to buy food. There are many net buyers of food in rural areas, not only among the landless but also among small farmers: in East and southern Africa countries, 95 percent of the rural poor bought at least 5 percent of their food.
- As a consequence of these developments there has been a substantial diversification of agriculture beyond grains and basic food tubers/roots into yams and potatoes, fruits and vegetables, poultry, beef, mutton, fish, dairy and eggs, and edible oils.
- This diversity results in major potential income gains for farmers: producing and selling their meat or dairy or fruit to urban areas results in five to ten times more income for farmers per hectare than grains.[63]

Overall, the rising urban food demand is becoming a major source of income for rural development. African smallholders now not only need to produce more efficiently but also to contend with far more complex and competitive markets. "Growing specialization, rapidly changing consumer preferences, and increasingly intricate technical specifications place significant demands on the average smallholder. Institutional and technical innovations, including better access to input and output markets, and enhancing rural–urban linkages constitute key components of future agricultural transformation strategies."[64] One consequence is the considerable incentive for the support of professional and business-like smallholder producer organizations (SPOs).

Nevertheless, achieving the "Quiet Revolution" at scale is not going to be easy, primarily because of the lack of infrastructure development. This sector needs increased investment in farms and rural small businesses, which requires loans from banks and other sources, the development of widespread small-scale food-processing, creation of efficient markets, and radical rebuilding of transport networks. The market will provide much of the necessary inputs, but government funding will be essential to building new and upgraded infrastructure.

The Opportunities

Hunger is one of the biggest challenges facing African households: there are over 250 million hungry people in Africa, nearly a quarter of the population.[65] While some of this is due to periodic famines and conflict, the greater part is chronic hunger. Most shocking is the incidence of child malnutrition in the form of stunting (see figure 2.5). Most African farmers are both poor and hungry; indeed, food insecurity is intimately linked to poverty.

In recent years considerable progress has been made in tackling African hunger. Part of the answer lies in such approaches as biofortification, that is, increasing the presence of genes that help crops provide much-needed micronutrients. A good example is the development of orange-fleshed sweet potatoes, which provide vitamin A. But in practice most progress is being made by integrated approaches, especially when governments create intersectoral committees—composed of nutritionists, agriculturalists, health experts, economists, planners, and so on—which meet on a regular basis and report directly to the president or prime minister and have the authority to design and implement programs. Many of these have already resulted in dramatic falls in child stunting.

Perhaps of greatest significance for the future are the changes generated by increasing urban populations, especially growing middle classes and their rising demand for foods, not just staples but more varied and nutritious foods. Diets are changing, and this results in major potential income gains for farmers. For example, in response to these changes, farmers are switching from low-value cassava and maize to high value poultry and horticulture. The consequent agricultural intensification is resulting in the growth of input supplies, for example, through agrodealers dealing in fertilizers and pesticides, especially herbicides. The effects are being felt in value chains, notably in storage, processing, and food preservation, especially in the demand for processed and convenience foods. Overall, the rising urban food demand is becoming a major opportunity for employment generation and a source of income for rural development.

This chapter thus ends on an optimistic note, but there are many challenges ahead arising from a range of threats external to the farm household. We examine these in the next chapter.

THE THREATS TO FOOD SECURITY

Hannas and Anna Matola farm a hectare of land in one of the poorest districts of southern Malawi. Weeds, including the notorious parasitic weed Striga, are their most persistent and pervasive problem. It takes Anna and her children forty to fifty days of weeding each crop to keep the weeds under control. They have tried cassava as an insurance crop, but it is attacked by a new, supervirulent strain of African cassava mosaic virus. The banana seedlings they bought from neighbors were infected with weevils, nematodes, and the fungal disease Black Sigatoka. Their beans, which are intended as a source of protein for the family and nitrogen for the soil, suffer from fungal diseases that rot the roots, deform leaves, and shrivel the pods.

On top of this they are trying to farm in one of the hotspots for land degradation, with the result that their yields without fertilizers are very low, even in a good year. They also suffer from acute crises caused by climate change. In 2016 the second year of a severe drought left them having to depend on handouts of food. Their youngest child, who is under five, is showing signs of stunting.

What Are the Threats?

In the first two chapters we described some of the formidable challenges a poor smallholder in Africa faces if he or she and their family are to be food secure and make a living. They include being able to grow or otherwise access the adequate and nutritious food they need. Moreover, they need to create a livelihood that enables them to earn cash to purchase essential household needs from the sale of crop or livestock produce or from the sale of their labor or their non-farm products. These challenges affect the whole household, men and women and youth, each often having distinctive skills and goals.

Most of these challenges are located on the farm or in the neighborhood and can be tackled by farmers, their families, and the local community, providing, of course, that governments create the investments in roads, irrigation, and other infrastructure as well as fair and efficient markets. Yet other, sometimes severe challenges are environmental or socioeconomic in nature and require an extra level of skill and expertise. Some, such as the depredations of pests and diseases and the constant battle against weeds, are immediate and obvious, while others, such as the gradual decline in soil quality, are ever-present but often slow to have an impact. In recent years there have also been extreme weather events caused by climate change. Finally, there are severe socioeconomic challenges ranging from the instability of commodity prices to the malfunction of value chains, the inadequacies of governance, and, in some countries, violent conflict. Farmers are increasingly aware of how serious these threats are, as are African political leaders.

Biological Threats

African farmers sometimes wake up in the morning, walk to their fields, and discover that their crops are almost totally destroyed, or their livestock are sick and dying. Overnight, farmers may have lost the basis of their livelihood and be reduced to prolonged poverty and hunger.

Locust Plagues

Descriptions of the locust plagues of antiquity convey the enormity of the threat. Exodus is one example: "The locusts went up over all the land of Egypt, and rested in all the coasts of Egypt: very grievous were they. . . . For they covered the face of the whole earth, so that the land was darkened; and they did eat every herb of the land, and all the fruit of the trees which the hail had left: and there remained not any green thing in the trees, or in the herbs of the field, through all the land of Egypt."[1]

Locust plagues were largely brought under control in the 1960s, but they have recurred with a vengeance in recent years. The most formidable locust in antiquity and today is the desert locust.[2] Locust populations alternate between a quiet period, known as a recession, during which they live in remote desert zones extending from North Africa to southwest Asia, and an invasion period, when they swarm over a larger area encompassing about fifty countries and reaching into SSA (figure 3.1).

From October 2003 to May 2005 West Africa faced the largest desert locust outbreak in fifteen years. It was triggered by anomalously very heavy rains in the western Sahel from July to September, favoring the transformation of solitary locusts into the first swarms. Further heavy rains caused population increases in Morocco, Senegal, and Mali.

An early warning system based on the monitoring of environmental conditions and locust populations was operational during the crisis. However, despite regular warnings issued by FAO the response by governments and donors was too slow to tackle the problem at the critical onset stage, when fewer pesticides were required and the probability of preventing the spreading of the outbreak was at its highest.

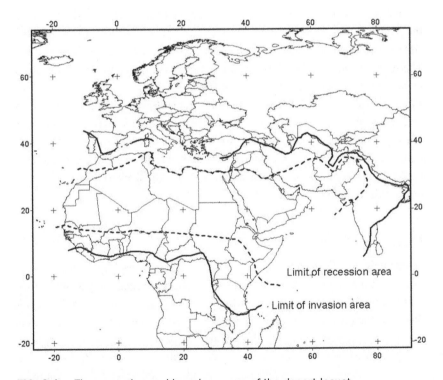

FIG. 3.1. The recession and invasion zones of the desert locust

Source: Pietro Ceccato et al., "The Desert Locust Upsurge in West Africa (2003–2005): Information on the Desert Locust Early Warning System and the Prospects for Seasonal Climate Forecasting," *International Journal of Pest Management* 53, no. 1 (January 2007): 7–13, https://doi.org/10.1080/09670870600968826.

Fortunately, lack of rain and cold temperatures in the winter breeding sites in early 2005 slowed the development of the locusts and allowed the locust control agencies to stop the cycle. During the upsurge nearly 130,000 km² were treated by ground and aerial spraying in more than twenty countries. The costs, estimated by the FAO, exceeded US$400 million, and harvest losses were valued at up to US$2.5 billion, with disastrous effects on the food security situation in West Africa.

The Toll of Weeds

Weeds also take their toll. Most farmers spend a great deal of time and effort trying to control weedy species. They are a perennial threat, as without weed control, production can fall by 50 to 90 percent. Moreover, fertilizer application without weed control is of little value; sustainable weed control thus becomes one of the central pillars of sustainable intensification.

Herbicides can be effective if they are applied selectively and do not harm the crop, but they are expensive and have to be applied carefully to avoid health risks. Hand weeding is often preferred because it is cheap, but it is hard work. The most serious weed of Africa is Striga (the most damaging species is *Striga hermonthica*), otherwise known as witchweed. It is a devastating parasite that siphons off water and nutrients from the crop plants, resulting in the characteristic witch appearance: the plants are stunted and withered. Striga seeds remain dormant and viable in the soil for up to twenty years. Striga causes yield losses in maize, sorghum, millet, and upland rice in SSA ranging from 30 percent to even total crop failure in a severe infestation. It affects the livelihoods of more than one hundred million people.[3]

Newcastle Disease

Fortunately, the devastating losses of cattle in Africa caused by rinderpest were finally eliminated in 2000, largely owing to an effective vaccine and a highly organized campaign by the FAO.[4] But other livestock diseases still occur. Newcastle disease is the most important viral disease of poultry. On the African continent the disease is endemic, and outbreaks are rampant.[5] On the one hand, large, highly professional commercial poultry farms, where Newcastle disease is readily controlled, are found in Nigeria, South Africa, and several other countries. On the other hand, Newcastle disease is more difficult to control among small, subsistence poultry farms. Yet this is the main source of high-quality protein for human consumption in Africa.

Newcastle disease is highly contagious and affects a wide variety of birds all over the world, but it is particularly damaging to domestic poultry. Early reports from Indonesia hypothesized it may have moved to poultry from wild forest birds. It was probably transmitted to Africa in the nineteenth century and today is widespread on the continent.

After a short incubation period, birds start to show respiratory problems and other symptoms, resulting in reduced egg laying and often death. The infected birds are highly infectious through respiratory droplets, feces, and other sources. Humans can sometimes be infected but with mild symptoms. In 2011 over thirty African countries reported the disease, and nearly half a million cases resulted in over three hundred thousand bird deaths.[6]

Fall Armyworm

Many new and unexpected epidemics, often caused by invasive species, also affect smallholders. A recent example is the fall armyworm, *Spodoptera frugiperda*, which arrived in Nigeria from the Americas in January 2016, possibly as a stowaway on commercial aircraft from the eastern seaboard of the United States or the Caribbean.[7] It has spread remarkably fast, affecting twenty-eight countries throughout SSA by August 2017. The moths are strong flyers and rapid breeders, the females laying in excess of one thousand eggs during their lifetime.

The armyworm larvae feed on maize, sorghum, and other cereals and grasses but also on a wide variety of other plants, over eighty in all. National mean losses, based on survey data in 2017, were 45 percent for Ghana and 40 percent for Zambia. For twelve selected countries, mean yield losses were over sixteen thousand tons and the economic losses between US$2.5 million and US$6.0 million.[8] The armyworms are having a serious effect on the livelihoods of smallholder farmers, as over two hundred million people are dependent on maize for food security in SSA. The arrival of the armyworm is a particularly heavy blow for southern Africa, which has been recovering from a severe drought.[9] They could soon arrive on the Mediterranean coast in Morocco, Algeria, Tunisia, and Libya, increasing the possibility of their spreading to Europe, and the high suitability of areas in Ethiopia could enable the pest to progress toward the Middle East and Asia.

Land Degradation

Healthy, fertile soils are the cornerstone of food security and rural livelihoods. A healthy soil is strong in structure and has an optimal mix of small and large particle sizes that give it good permeability and water-holding capacity. Highly fertile soil is rich with humus and has sufficient plant nutrients for high yields. It is also rich in soil biota and contains no pollutants.[10]

In some respects, the degradation of Africa's formerly healthy soils is the most fundamental problem African farmers face, partly because of its magnitude but also because it is not amenable to straightforward solutions. Africa's soils are very old and heavily weathered, but in recent years soil degradation has intensified in deeply complex ways that have intertwining and cyclical causes (box 3.1).

Box 3.1. Drivers of land and soil degradation

- Poor land management: Most African farms are rain-fed, dependent on increasingly erratic rainfall amounts and patterns; fertilizer, if available, is expensive; and farm labor, at critical times, is in short supply. Struggling to compete with these challenges, African farmers have steadily abandoned traditional practices that restore soil nutrients.
- Population pressure: The population of SSA is growing . . . [rapidly, and as a consequence] . . . arable land per capita is declining precipitously, thereby intensifying competition for land for food, rangeland, shelter, and other uses. [Nevertheless, agricultural land continues to grow, from 1.05 billion hectares in 1961 to slightly over 1.16 billion hectares today. Since 1980 the rate of growth appears to be even faster.]
- Insecure land tenure: Africa's lands are held under both statutory (individual) and the more widespread customary (collective) property ownership systems. Customary systems are often loosely defined and especially disadvantage women. When the terms are unclear [and] landholdings are small or fragmented . . . [there is little incentive to invest in land].
- Poor access to markets and services: Where markets are poorly developed or missing, farmers are more likely to make decisions determined by their basic subsistence needs, and make little use of modern inputs, such as improved seed varieties, fertilizers, or crop protection products that could otherwise create the time and resources needed for better land management practices.
- Climate change: Harsh growing conditions [and extreme weather events,] already experienced in many parts of Africa, are likely to

[reduce crop growth and exacerbate soil degradation]. . . . Climate change will [also] bring about higher levels of long-term stress, including desertification, and force large areas of cropland out of production.

Sources: Reproduced from Montpellier Panel, "No Ordinary Matter: Conserving, Restoring and Enhancing Africa's Soils" (London: Agriculture for Impact, 2014), https://www.mamopanel.org/media/uploads/files/NO_ORDINARY_MATTER-_CONSERVING_RESTORING_AND_ENHANCING_AFRICAS_SOILS_2014. pdf; Guy Blaise Nkamleu, "Extensification versus Intensification: Revisiting the Role of Land in African Agricultural Growth" (African Economic Conference 2011: Green Economy and Structural Transformation, Addis Ababa, Ethiopia, October 2011), 19, https://www.uneca.org/sites/default/files/uploaded-documents/AEC/2011/nkamleu-extensification_versus_intensification_1.pdf.

The drivers of soil degradation influence farmers' decisions, and as a result better land management practices are often sacrificed for short-term needs. If the causes are not addressed, farmers will continue to make the same choices, even at the expense of their future well-being. The cycle of poor land management will continue to restrict agricultural development for smallholder farmers and impede economic growth in Africa.[11]

Hotspots of Degradation

Land degradation broadly refers to a decline in the capacity of the land to supply human needs, whether of food or other services. Given such a broad definition, not surprisingly there is much controversy about its nature and extent. Early estimates were largely subjective, but advances in remote-sensing and satellite technologies have enabled efforts such as the Global Inventory Modelling and Mapping Studies to measure vegetative growth at a resolution of eight km^2. This technology has been calibrated for local conditions, by the team at the Center for Development Research (ZEF) at the University of Bonn, providing a worldwide measure of land degradation hotspots. The loss of biomass production is used as an indirect measure of the decline in particular of primary productivity (e.g., plant growth). Initial results show that land degradation hotspots stretch to about 29 percent of the total global land area.[12] In SSA land degradation hotspots are about 26 percent of land, affecting some 180 million people (figure 3.2).[13]

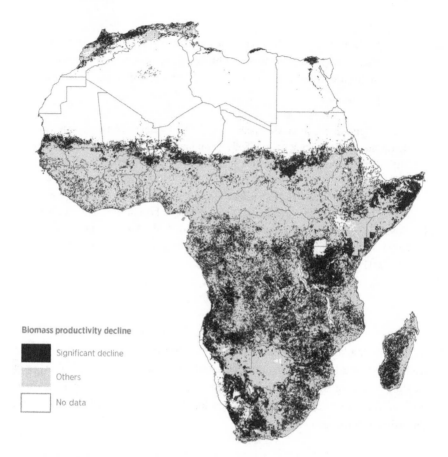

FIG. 3.2. Hotspots of land degradation

Source: Reproduced with permission from Quang Bao Le, Ephraim Nkonya, and Alisher Mirzabaev, "Biomass Productivity-Based Mapping of Global Land Degradation Hotspots," in *Economics of Land Degradation and Improvement—A Global Assessment for Sustainable Development,* ed. Ephraim Nkonya, Alisher Mirzabaev, and Joachim von Braun (Cham, Switzerland: Springer International, 2016), 55–84, https://doi.org/10.1007/978-3-319-19168-3_4.

Land degradation creates a vicious cycle in which negative effects build on each other.[14] The consequences are enormous environmental, social, and economic costs. In SSA the economic loss is estimated at $68 billion per year.[15] In some areas of Africa agricultural productivity declined by half between 1981 and 2003 as a result of soil erosion and related processes.[16]

While data at the national level are limited, they are striking where available. For example, in Ethiopia, over one-quarter of land is degraded, which affects about twenty million people, almost a third of the total population (table 3.1).

TABLE 3.1. Land degradation in Ethiopia

BASIC STATISTICS	HOTSPOT CHARACTERISTICS	ANNUAL COSTS
Total land area: 1.13m km²	High population pressure on lands and forest, farming on steep slopes, and frequent food crises caused by unreliable rainfall	Soil erosion and nutrient loss from farming and grazing: $106m
Average fertilizer use: 17kg/ha	Loss of top soil: 1b tons per year	"Deforestation": $23m

Degraded land area: 26%	Soil productivity losses:
	    at least 20%
		Loss of livestock capacity:
		    $10m

People affected: 21m = 29% of population		Total: $139m = 4% GDP

Source: Adapted from Montpellier Panel, "No Ordinary Matter: Conserving, Restoring and Enhancing Africa's Soils" (London: Agriculture for Impact, 2014), https://ag4impact.org/wp-content/uploads/2014/12/MP_0106_Soil_Report_LR1.pdf.

A Lack of Water

Water is as important to the productivity of plants as the provision of good soil structure and sufficient nutrients. A wheat grain may contain up to 25 percent water; a potato 80 percent. For rice, in particular, water is crucial; a gram of grain can require as much as fourteen hundred grams of water for its production.[17] Not surprisingly, water stress during growth results in major yield reductions for most crops.

Rainfall in Africa ranges from almost continuous in equatorial Africa to only a few days in the Sahel and in southern Africa. However, Africa has over fifty river water basins with extensive reach; the longest are the Nile, Congo, Niger, and Zambezi.[18] There are a number of large inland lakes as well. But the rainfall is highly variable. In the past twenty years available freshwater resources have been greatly reduced owing to severe, prolonged droughts. Furthermore, water pollution is affecting the quality and quantity of available water. Moreover, in Africa agriculture uses over 85 percent of freshwater withdrawals but only about 6.5 percent of the cultivated land is irrigated.[19] These various factors add up to a lack of water for many, if not most, African smallholders, preventing them from realizing their agricultural potential.

The Agricultural Demand

Crops require water—which is extracted from the soil through the plant root system—to grow, to be cooled, and to maintain turgor pressure, through which plants stay upright and direct their leaves toward the sun.[20] Crop water loss, known as evapotranspiration, consists, on one hand, of the water lost through evaporation from the soil and plant surfaces as well as that used for growth and, on the other, of the water lost by transpiration to the atmosphere through minute openings, termed the stomata, on the plant. From the roots, water moves to other parts of the plant, carrying minerals and chemicals such as glucose to where they are needed. Water is also required in photosynthesis, the process of the conversion of sunlight to usable chemical energy stored as sugars in the plant.

The amount of water a crop needs is affected by the growth stage, the amount of water in the soil, weather, and crop rooting depths.[21] For example, water needs are higher in a mature, fully grown plant than in a young seedling. If plants do not receive enough water to compensate for total evapotranspiration, they will yellow, their leaves will wilt, yield will decline, and eventually, if they remain without adequate water, will fail.

For rice in particular, the hazard of getting not enough or too much water is especially great because of the short stature of the new varieties. The young, transplanted seedlings may die for lack of water in the first few weeks and will drown under excessive flooding. Ideally, they need a constant flow of water at a depth of about 2.5 cm. Traditional rain-fed cultivation, which is subject to the vagaries of rainfall in the wet season, can rarely meet such exacting circumstances, and high yields require supplemental irrigation in most situations. In all modern cereal varieties, the potential to mature and produce grain irrespective of the season has placed a high premium on the provision of irrigation water in the dry season, when the potential yields are greatest.

Water Stress

The lack of water over much of Africa leads to chronic, acute stress. Large areas of northern Africa are being overexploited, and other areas in the Nile Basin and South Africa are being heavily exploited.[22]

Physical scarcity of water may be a fact of life in the most arid regions, yet it is heightened by policies that induce higher water use and the overdevelopment of hydraulic infrastructure.[23] In particular, the expansion of irrigated agriculture has often been at the expense of other water users and has damaged biodiversity, ecosystem services, fisheries and wetlands. The problem is compounded by bureaucratic rigidities and subsidized prices of water supplied to farmers. Managers in the government or private sectors have to make difficult decisions on water allocation, apportioning diminishing supplies between ever-increasing demands. Demographic and climatic changes further increase the stress on water resources. The traditional fragmented approach is no longer viable: a more holistic approach to water management is essential.[24]

A Rapidly Changing Climate

According to FAO, "climate change poses a major and growing threat to global food security. The expected effects of climate change—higher temperatures, more frequent extreme weather events, water shortages, rising sea levels, ocean acidification, land degradation, the disruption of ecosystems and the loss of biodiversity—could seriously compromise agriculture's ability to feed the most vulnerable, impeding progress towards the eradication of hunger, malnutrition and poverty."[25] There can be no doubt that our planet is warming. The trend is very clear. Since the industrial revolution in the nineteenth century it has warmed by over 1°C. The warming is uneven, but fifteen of the sixteen hottest years on record have occurred since 2001.[26] We know that the temperature for each year is affected by the phenomenon of El Niño and La Niña. The El Niño years tend to be the hottest, but each has been warmer than the one before (figure 3.3). If this trend continues unabated, we will reach 2°C above pre-industrial temperatures soon after 2050.[27]

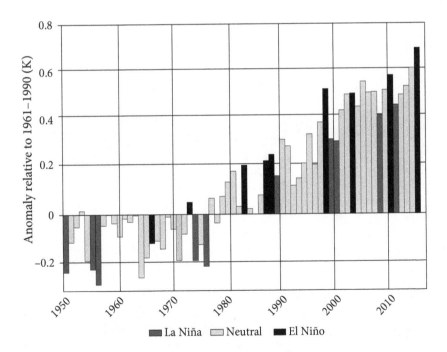

FIG. 3.3. Global warming over the past sixty-five years

Source: World Meteorological Organization, "Provisional WMO Statement on the Status of the Global Climate in 2016," press release no. 15, November 11, 2016, https://public.wmo.int/en/media/press-release/provisional-wmo-statement-status-of-global-climate-2016.

The central question here is what effect this warming trend is having and will continue to have on agriculture and food security, especially in the countries of Africa. There is not a simple answer. Africa's climates are diverse and also highly variable. This makes it difficult to separate the effects of natural variation from those produced by global warming. Nevertheless, there is growing evidence that climate change is having a significant and predominantly deleterious effect. The processes and their impacts differ from place to place in Africa and often in complex ways.

For example, the rainfall in the Sahel is naturally highly variable, experiencing decades-long phases of relatively high rainfall alternating with phases of drought (figure 3.4).[28] There was a nearly three-decade-long phase of devastating drought beginning around 1970, the longest drought of the century. One hypothesis is that oceanic warming around Africa may have weakened the land–ocean temperature contrast and consequently the monsoon. This caused deep convection to migrate over the ocean and engendering widespread drought over the Sahel.[29] From 2000 to 2010, however, rainfall increased notably, including heavy rains and flooding in 2007 and 2013. One theory suggests that the growing warming

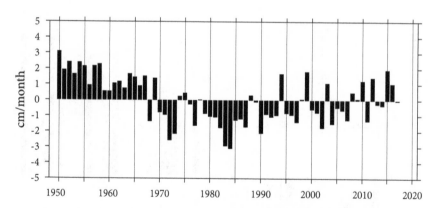

June through October averages over 20-10° N, 20° W-10° E. 1950-2017 climatology
Deutscher Wetterdienst Global Precipitation Climatology Centre data

FIG. 3.4.   Sahel precipitation anomalies, 1950–2017

Sources: Todd Mitchell, "Sahel Precipitation Index" (Joint Institute for the Study of the Atmosphere and Ocean, 1997), https://doi.org/10.6069/H5MW2F2Q; A. Becker et al., "A Description of the Global Land-Surface Precipitation Data Products of the Global Precipitation Climatology Centre with Sample Applications Including Centennial (Trend) Analysis from 1901–Present," *Earth System Science Data* 5, no. 1 (February 21, 2013): 71–99, https://doi.org/10.5194/essd-5-71-2013.

allows the atmosphere to hold more moisture, bring more rains, and shift winds, influencing the pattern of the West African monsoon.[30]

The Drivers of Change

Driving the African climate are several processes that are interrelated in complex ways not yet fully understood.[31] Two of these—tropical convection and the alternation of the monsoons—are regional processes that determine the regional and seasonal patterns of temperature and rainfall. A third—the El Niño–Southern Oscillation of the Pacific Ocean—is more remote in its origin but strongly influences the year to year rainfall and temperature patterns in Africa. The fourth comprises the jet streams (box 3.2; figures 3.5 and 3.6).[32]

La Niña and Rainfall

La Niña conditions in the tropical Pacific are known to shift rainfall patterns in many different parts of the world. Although they vary somewhat from one La Niña to the next, the strongest shifts remain fairly consistent in the regions and seasons shown on the map below.

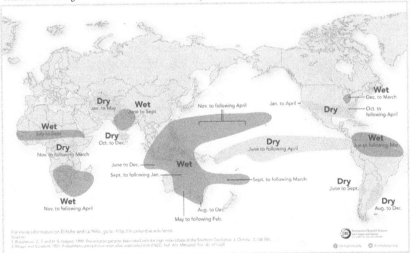

FIG. 3.5. The effects of a La Niña

Sources: C. F. Ropelewski and M. S. Halpert, "Global and Regional Scale Precipitation Patterns Associated with the El Niño/Southern Oscillation," *Monthly Weather Review* 115, no. 8 (August 1987): 1606–26, https://doi.org/10.1175/1520-0493(1987)115%3C1606:GAR SPP%3E2.0.CO;2; Simon J. Mason and Lisa Goddard, "Probabilistic Precipitation Anomalies Associated with ENSO," *Bulletin of the American Meteorological Society* 82, no. 4 (April 2001): 619–38, https://doi.org/10.1175/1520-0477(2001)082<0619:PPAAWE>2.3.CO;2; *La Niña and Rainfall* (Palisades, NY: International Research Institute for Climate and Society, Earth Institute, Columbia University, 2012), https://doi.org/10.4135/9781452218564. n384.

El Niño and Rainfall

El Niño conditions in the tropical Pacific are known to shift rainfall patterns in many different parts of the world. Although they vary somewhat from one El Niño to the next, the strongest shifts remain fairly consistent in the regions and seasons shown on the map below.

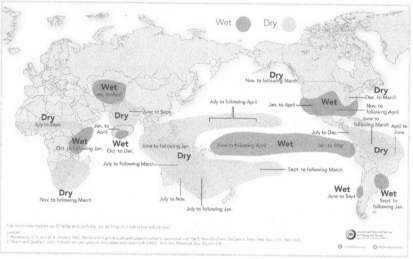

FIG. 3.6.   The effects of El Niño

Sources: C. F. Ropelewski and M. S. Halpert, "Global and Regional Scale Precipitation Patterns Associated with the El Niño/Southern Oscillation," *Monthly Weather Review* 115, no. 8 (August 1987): 1606–26, https://doi.org/10.1175/1520-0493(1987)115<1606:GAR SPP>2.0.CO;2; Simon J. Mason and Lisa Goddard, "Probabilistic Precipitation Anomalies Associated with ENSO," *Bulletin of the American Meteorological Society* 82, no. 4 (April 2001): 619–38, https://doi.org/10.1175/1520-0477(2001)082<0619:PPAAWE>2.3.CO;2; *El Niño and Rainfall* (Palisades, NY: International Research Institute for Climate and Society, Earth Institute, Columbia University, 2014), https://doi.org/10.4135/9781452218564.n384.

Box 3.2. The drivers of African climates

Tropical convection

Intense solar heating near the equator leads to rising warm, moist air and heavy rainfall. As the air rises it creates an area of low pressure at the surface, known for centuries by sailors as the Doldrums. The rising air moves north and south toward the tropics and eventually falls in the subtropics (about 30° N&S of the equator) as warm, dry air. From there it is carried back toward the equator by trade winds. Each year this so-called Intertropical Convergence Zone (ITCZ) moves north and south following the seasonal tilting of the globe toward the sun. There is some evidence that global warming is causing the range to expand by 2º latitude, thus increasing the range and aridity of desert areas.

The monsoons

The Indian monsoon is the most extreme form of monsoon, with a 180° reversal of the wind. The Indian south–west monsoon arises in spring and summer, followed by the north–east monsoon in winter, affecting the eastern margins of Africa. West Africa is affected by a south–west monsoon that arises in two phases. The first phase, April–June, centers on the Gulf of Guinea and appears to be influenced by sea-surface temperatures. Then, in a sudden event known as the monsoon jump, usually in early to mid-July, the rainfall maximum follows the ITCZ northward, bringing rainfall from May to September. So far there is no evidence of changes in the pattern of the monsoon due to global warming.

The El Niño–Southern Oscillation (ENSO)

The El Niño–Southern Oscillation is far distant from Africa, in the Pacific Ocean. It is characterized by an alternation between a phase known as La Niña and another called El Niño. During La Niña increasingly warm water moves westward from the high pressure of the Central Pacific to the low pressure located over Indonesia. Sea levels rise, accompanied by very heavy, extensive rainfall, while the eastern Pacific experiences relatively dry weather.

During El Niño there is a change in the prevailing pattern of ocean surface temperatures and pressures. The water flows reverse; rain falls in the east and droughts occur in Southeast Asia and Australia.

Although ENSO is primarily a Pacific Ocean process, the effects are felt as far away as Africa and, indeed, in most regions of the world. During an El Niño year, weather in December to February is usually wetter in eastern Africa but drier to the south, while La Niña produces the reverse. El Niño is also associated with a drier Sahel, while La Niña is correlated with a wetter Sahel and a cooler West Africa. There has been a tendency toward more prolonged and more frequent El Niños since the early 1990s. This has caused speculation that the change may be a consequence of global warming, but so far there is no evidence to substantiate the connection.

The jet streams are high-altitude, very strong winds that stream around the globe from west to east at speeds of more than 275 mph and at altitudes of four to eight miles above the surface. The polar jet streams form boundaries between colder and warmer temperatures. Because of the lower temperature differential north and south of the northern polar jet stream caused by global warming of the arctic and the melting of the ice the winds are now weaker, and they meander more, bringing colder air to the warmer south. In the northern hemisphere some of the recent weather extremes in the northern latitudes go beyond what would be expected from a simple increase in mean weather measurements. There is a strong likelihood that the changing behaviors of the jet streams are causing greater severity of extreme weather events in Africa as a result of interactions with the climate drivers described above.

Sources: Dian J. Seidel et al., "Widening of the Tropical Belt in a Changing Climate," *Nature Geoscience* 1, no. 1 (January 2008): 21–24, https://doi.org/10.1038/ngeo.2007.38; Guojun Gu and Robert F. Adler, "Seasonal Evolution and Variability Associated with the West African Monsoon System," *Journal of Climate* 17, no. 17 (September 2004): 3364–77, https://doi.org/10.1175/1520-0442(2004)017<3364:SEAVAW>2.0.CO;2; M. H. Glantz, ed., *La Niña and its Impacts: Facts and Speculation* (New York: United Nations University Press, 2002); "El Nino," Food and Agriculture Organization of the United Nations, accessed April 25, 2019, http://www.fao.org/el-nino/en/.; NOAA National Weather Service, "JetStream," JetStream—An Online School for Weather, accessed April 20, 2018, https://www.weather.gov/jetstream/; K. Kornhuber et al., "Evidence for Wave Resonance as a Key Mechanism for Generating High-Amplitude Quasi-Stationary Waves in Boreal Summer," *Climate Dynamics* 49, no. 5–6 (September 2017): 1961–79, https://doi.org/10.1007/s00382-016-3399-6.

Africa Is Warming Fast

Although these drivers are powerful global and regional forces, it is not yet clear the degree to which they are altered by global warming. What *is* certain is that global warming—expressed, for example, through higher sea and land-surface temperatures—is affecting their outcomes, increasing the incidence and severity of the droughts, floods, and other extreme weather events they produce.[33]

For the past fifty to one hundred years there has been an increase of 0.5°C or more in temperature across most parts of Africa. Africa is getting hotter very fast. Northern and southern Africa temperatures could be as high as 6°C above pre-industrial temperatures by the end of the century if there is no concerted effort to meaningfully reduce GHG emissions. This warming, expressed through higher sea and land-surface temperatures, is increasing the incidence and severity of droughts, floods, and other extreme weather events, as we are seeing for the El Nino years.[34]

Over the next one hundred years we can expect:

- Mean temperatures across Africa will rise faster than the global average.
- The drier subtropical regions will warm more than the moister tropics.
- The frequency of extremely dry and wet years will increase.
- Northern and southern Africa will become much hotter and drier.
- Rainfall will increase in East and West Africa.
- Sea levels will rise, with serious consequences for agricultural and urban land in the Nile Delta and certain parts of West Africa.[35]

The Consequences for Food and Nutrition

The key question is, *What effect might climate change have on agriculture and food and nutrition security in the countries of Africa?* There is no simple answer, but two risks to crop production are already affecting farmers:

First, growing seasons are becoming shorter, resulting in lower yields (figure 3.7a). For example, in northern Ghana the rainfall is erratic and has become increasingly so. In 2011 the rains were a month late and finished a month early, leaving only one hundred days to grow and mature a rice crop. Rice yields were low, and the hot weather meant the grains were likely to shatter on milling.[36]

Second, yields of maize in Africa are being severely affected by rising temperatures (figure 3.7b). Each "degree day" spent above 30°C reduces the final yield by 1 percent under optimal rain-fed conditions and by 1.7 percent under drought conditions.[37] More than 60 percent of current maize-growing areas in Africa will experience yield losses, and wheat production in northern Africa is also likely to be adversely affected.

Most livestock species are sensitive to temperatures over 30°C. They thrive in so-called comfort zones between 10°C and 30°C. Above this zone, animals reduce their feed intake by 3 to 5 percent for each degree rise in temperature.[38]

In the Sahel, the risk of heat stress by the end of this century will be so high that it may constrain people's ability to engage in any sort of agricultural practices at all.[39]

But global warming not only affects yields: it also damages food quality and safety and the reliability of its delivery to consumers. There is growing

FIGS. 3.7A AND B. *(left)* Anticipated reduction of more than 5 percent in the length of the growing period in Africa by 2050. *(right)* Areas where the average annual maximum daily temperature is projected to exceed > 30°C by the 2050s.

Source: Reprinted with permission from Polly Erickson et al., "Mapping Hotspots of Climate Change and Food Insecurity in the Global Tropics," (Copenhagen: CGIAR Research Program on Climate Change, Agriculture and Food Security, June 3, 2011), http://www.cumulativeimpacts.org/documents/ccafsreport5-climate_hotspots_advance-may2011.pdf.

evidence that micronutrient deficiency in important food crops, especially of zinc, iron, and protein, may also become worse as a result of elevated CO_2 concentrations in the atmosphere.[40]

Additional impacts affect livestock and fisheries:[41]

- Rangeland degradation and drought reduce forage productivity.
- Heat stress and lack of water reduce livestock production.
- Increased incidence of livestock diseases such as Rift Valley Fever.
- Declining fishery production in West and East Africa.
- Deforestation and forest degradation due to water scarcity.

Overall, agricultural losses in Africa will amount to 2 to 7 percent of GDP by 2100 because of climate change.[42] By 2050 hunger and child malnutrition could increase by as much as 20 percent as a result of climate change,[43] reversing the gains achieved through the MDGs process and jeopardizing the success of the Sustainable Development Goals (SDGs). Given the importance of agriculture as a revenue earner and the biggest employer in most African countries, the livelihoods of millions are at stake.

We know with a high degree of certainty why climate change is happening. Since the industrial revolution humans have been emitting CO_2 and other GHGs to the atmosphere. These gases form a layer over the earth's surface that traps an increasing proportion of the infrared radiation that would otherwise be radiated out to space, thus warming the land and the oceans beneath.

Since the industrial revolution atmospheric concentrations of CO_2 have increased by just over one-third from 280 parts per million (ppm) to 400 ppm now. Besides CO_2 there are five other GHGs, including nitrous oxide (N_2O) and methane (CH_4) that have three hundred times and twenty-one times the warming potential relative to CO_2, respectively. Adding these all together, total GHG emissions are now over 400 ppm of CO_2 equivalent.[44] CO_2 concentrations are predicted to reach 540–970 ppm by the end of the century.[45]

Alternative explanations for the rising temperature have been proposed. They include such phenomena as sunspot cycles and the effects of galactic cosmic rays, but, in the overwhelming majority of the scientific community, none are convincing.[46] The report of Lord Stern concluded, "The rising levels of greenhouse gases provide the only plausible explanation for the observed trend for at least the past 50 years."[47] Much is still unknown, however, and there are many uncertainties generated by complicated feedback loops and potential tipping points in the climate system. Needless to say, the current and impending impacts of climate change as well as their scale and potential irreversibility mean we do not have the luxury of understanding many of these uncertainties prior to taking action.

Agriculture is an important emitter of GHGs. The Intergovernmental Panel on Climate Change (IPCC) estimates that agriculture, forestry and other land use is responsible for just under a quarter (~10–12 GtCO$_2$eq/yr) of anthropogenic GHG emissions, mainly from deforestation and agricultural emissions from livestock, soil, and nutrient management.[48] However, most projections suggest declining annual net CO$_2$ emissions from agriculture in the long run, driven partly by technical change and partly by declining rates of agriculture area expansion.

As can be seen from figure 3.8, CO$_2$ emissions primarily come from the clearing of forest and other land for agriculture and from the burning of agricultural wastes. Nitrous oxide emissions from soils constitute around 40 percent of

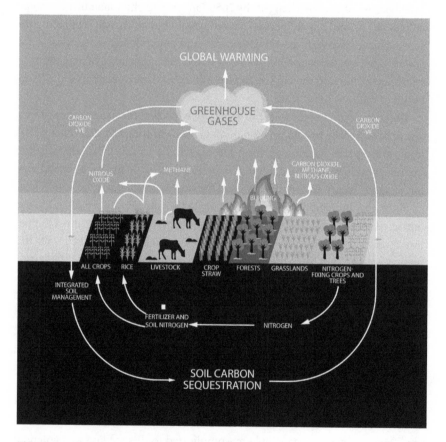

FIG. 3.8. Greenhouse gases and global warming

Source: Reprinted with permission from Montpellier Panel, "No Ordinary Matter: Conserving, Restoring and Enhancing Africa's Soils" (London: Agriculture for Impact, 2014), https://www.mamopanel.org/media/uploads/files/NO_ORDINARY_MATTER-_CONSERVING_RESTORING_AND_ENHANCING_AFRICAS_SOILS_2014.pdf.

non-CO_2 emissions and arise from the high levels of natural and synthetic nitrogen applied to the soils. Methane arises from enteric fermentation in livestock and from anaerobic rice cultivation.

Socioeconomic Threats

Severe socioeconomic challenges range from unstable and high prices of basic commodities to the malfunction of value chains and the inadequacies of governance. Rarely do poor people and especially poor farmers have any capacity to influence these conditions. They often simply have to suffer and cope, but good government policies can make a difference.

An example of a severe threat is the behavior of staple food prices. Starting in 1950 the real price of cereals steadily declined, and by 2000 global prices were 85 percent lower. But this decline was dramatically interrupted by the food price spike of 2008, when the international price of basic foodstuffs peaked at unprecedented levels. The spike was reflected in national and local food prices. One consequence was street demonstrations throughout Latin America, Africa, and Asia, many of which turned violent. The prime minister of Haiti was deposed following food riots there.[49]

Food prices fell at the end of 2008, but they were still 20 percent higher than earlier and growing, producing a new spike in 2012. Initially it looked like a new, maybe long-term trend, but since 2012 world prices have been on a downward trend, and real prices are now only about 10 percent above pre-crisis levels in 2002–4 (nominal prices are about 50 percent higher).[50] People in the developed countries felt the consequences, with higher food prices compounding the effects of the economic recession, but for the people of the developing countries the outcomes were devastating.

In Kenya grain prices remained high even after the peak and continued to fluctuate.[51] The price shock in 2011 was substantially greater than that in 2008 because of a major drought. Prices fell subsequently when the government imported large quantities of maize from neighboring Tanzania and Uganda; prices then rose again through most of 2015 (figure 3.9).

A report by Oxfam and the Institute for Development Studies has documented the impact of these high and volatile prices on both the urban and rural poor. What the researchers found was that people were living in a high degree of precariousness through fear caused by the cumulative effects of food price rises, inflation, and job losses. These were creating a sense of uncertainty. The authors record poor families coping by "removing a child from school, reducing food intake, stealing, sending family members away or begging."[52]

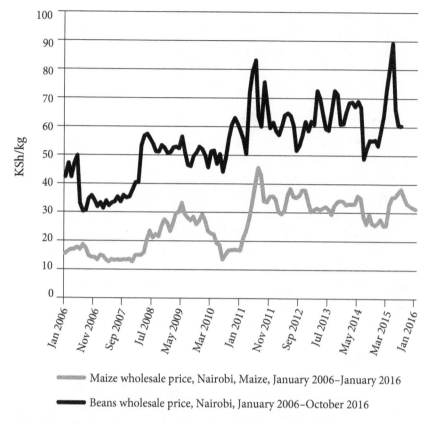

Maize wholesale price, Nairobi, Maize, January 2006–January 2016

Beans wholesale price, Nairobi, January 2006–October 2016

FIG. 3.9. Wholesale price of maize and beans in Kenya in recent years

Source: Reprinted with permission from P. Scott-Villiers et al., "Precarious Lives: Food, Work and Care after the Global Food Crisis" (Brighton, UK: Institute for Development Studies), September 8, 2016, http://www.ids.ac.uk/publication/precarious-lives-food-work-and-care-after-the-global-food-crisis.

Food prices may seem to be primarily an economic problem, but they are fundamentally one of political economy that considers political, technological, institutional, and behavioral factors. The operation of market forces alone, whether within a country or on a global scale, will not create food security.

Conflict

In recent decades the Sahelian region has experienced a number of conflicts, including large-scale interstate wars, civil wars, and localized conflict. There have been interstate wars primarily over land containing resources like natural gas and minerals. There have also been numerous internal conflicts and civil wars as well as social conflicts.[53] The latter include protests, riots, strikes, intercommunal conflict, government violence against civilians, and other forms of social strife.[54] The current major conflicts involve the Boko Haram insurgency in Nigeria and, in northeast Africa, major conflicts in the Sudan, South Sudan, Somalia, and across the Red Sea in Yemen.

Many factors contribute to these conflicts: historical tensions between ethnolinguistic groups and the legacy of colonial power, poor governance, marginalization of various social groups and corruption, and the proliferation of weapons and non-state militaries.[55]

Inevitably food and agricultural production suffers. Crops and livestock are destroyed, land is confiscated and often degraded, conflicts over water supplies are common, and, most important, the livelihoods of farm households are disrupted, and farmers and their families are killed or injured. One example is the role of migration as a source of tension between transhumant livestock breeders and inhabitants in pastoral areas, such as in Darfur (box 3.3).

Box 3.3. Famine and conflict in Darfur, Sudan

The Darfur region lies in the west of Sudan along the borders with Libya, Chad, and the Central African Republic. It has long been inhabited by two groups of people: 60 percent subsistence farmers and 40 percent nomadic or semi-nomadic herders of livestock. Traditionally they have lived together in relative harmony, the herders being allowed to cross the land of the subsistence farmers and use their wells.

The Sahel drought severely affected the Darfur region, culminating in the subsequent famine in 1984–85, when 95,000 people out of a total of some three million died (whether or not the drought was a product of climate change is debatable). The consequent shortages of food and water and the ensuing land degradation forced the herders to migrate southward, which increased competition for land and water between them and the subsistence farmers. This state of affairs was made worse by population growth. The conflicts escalated when the Janjaweed militia, with government support, began to force the farmers from their homes and take possession of the wells. The conflict subsequently escalated into a major war. The UN estimates that to date 450,000 people have died through violence and disease and as many as 2.5 million have been displaced.

Sources: Alex de Waal, "Tragedy in Darfur," *Boston Review*, October 5, 2004, http:// bostonreview.net/de-waal-tragedy-in-darfur; "War in Darfur," Wikipedia, accessed May 16, 2018, https://en.wikipedia.org/w/index.php?title=War_in_Darfur&oldid=841562445.

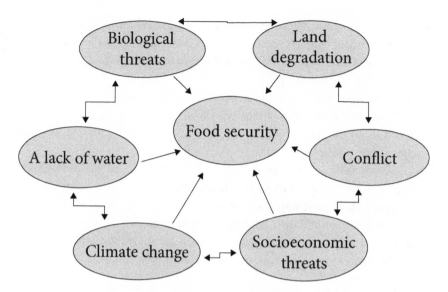

FIG. 3.10. The significant threats facing food security

The world as a whole faces numerous threats, most of which affect food security. We have selected the most important ones and schematically connected them (figure 3.10). All of these threats are becoming worse and increasingly interconnected.

In the next chapter we focus on the response to the challenges and the opportunities that are available.

RESILIENT FARMERS

In the village of Nwadhajane in southern Mozambique, the birthplace of the great Mozambique leader Eduardo Mondlane, the villagers are aware of climate change and its effects and have already taken significant measures to counteract the worst features. They have two kinds of land: lowland and highland. On the former, the crops are very productive but are washed out by periodic floods; in the highlands, they produce good crops in the flood years but poor crops during the droughts. The villagers' response has been to create several farmer associations that have reassigned the land so that each farmer obtains a portion of highland as well as some lowland. The farmer associations are also experimenting with drought-resistant crops.[1]

What is Resilience?

Resilience, like sustainability, is one of those terms that means all things to all people.[2] We define resilience as "the capacity of an agricultural value chain and its elements to withstand or recover from stresses and shocks and thus bounce back to the previous level of growth and development" (figure 4.1).[3]

As described by the Montpellier Panel, "A stress can be defined as a regular, sometimes continuous, relatively small and predictable disturbance, for example, the effect of increasing soil salinity or lack of rainfall or increasing indebtedness. Such stresses or chronic crises are directly damaging but sometimes slowly

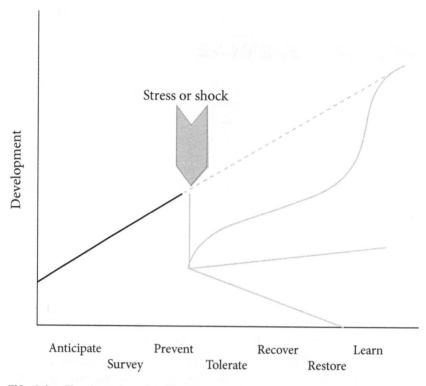

FIG. 4.1. The dynamics of resilience

Source: Adapted with permission from Montpellier Panel, "Growth with Resilience: Opportunities in African Agriculture" (London: Agriculture for Impact, 2012), https://www.mamopanel.org/media/uploads/files/GROWTH_WITH_RESILIENCE-_OPPORTUNITIES_IN_AFRICAN_AGRICULTURE_2012.pdf.

culminate to cause a shock or acute crisis. A shock is an irregular, relatively large, unpredictable disturbance, such as is caused by a rare drought or flood or a new pest outbreak, or when slow-onset disasters pass their tipping points and become extreme events. Many stresses and shocks are interlinked, for example, energy and input price volatility, extreme weather events and climate change, growing scarcity of natural resources and poverty and inequality."[4]

The following steps need to be taken to build resilience, as outlined in the 2017 Africa Agriculture Status Report (AASR):

1. The anticipation of the likelihood and location of a stress or a shock, through some form of survey, for example, the use of agroclimatic monitoring to inform famine early warning systems.
2. Preventative measures, such as building dams or sea walls, may allow agricultural development to continue unhindered.

3. Often, the best option is some form of tolerance that reduces the damage or allows rapid recovery.

4. Sometimes . . . damage is unavoidable, and the only response is to rebuild or restore the basis for growth.

5. Finally, building resilience is about learning from past experience. How did a value chain and its elements cope with a severe stress or shock? How can it do better in the future?

As a general rule, the more effort put into anticipating stresses and shocks and into designing preventative or tolerant responses, the lower the likely damage and costs of action will be.

At first sight the goal of resilience may seem at odds with growth and development of the value chain. Indeed, there is often a trade-off. It is possible to have a highly resilient but stagnant development or a rapid development that is destructive and highly volatile. The ideal is somewhere in between, at a point where appropriate resilience is built in at the outset in a way that exploits the synergies between development and resilience. Moreover, development is likely to be unpredictable unless resilience is built in. If growth is steady and assured it will encourage further investment, thereby creating a spiral of development.

Resilience is not only about acute crises with one-off solutions. Rarely does resilience depend on magic bullets. The lesson for practical resilience is that it has to consist of a system of interlinked components that reinforce each other. The challenge is to identify and preempt the risks arising in the value chain, analyze their causative factors, and determine components that, when combined, create a truly resilient approach.[5]

Integrated Pest Management

In the 1950s and 1960s, when it became apparent that the overuse of pesticides was polluting and making problems worse, the concept of integrated pest management (IPM) was created and applied in several environments.[6] IPM looks at each crop and pest situation as a whole and devises a program that integrates the various control methods in light of all the factors present. IPM uses a combination of biological and ecological control practices plus, where necessary, pesticides or vaccines that are targeted and highly selective and used as a minimum to get effective and cost-effective control. Today IPM is the ideal solution for many pest, disease, and weed problems.

Finding highly resilient approaches to insect, disease, and weed attack is not easy. Pesticides and vaccines can be very effective, in appropriate circumstances. Breeding for resistance to pests or diseases can give protection. But in certain circumstances such measures can have negative or even harmful effects. Moreover smallholder farmers may not be able to afford them. The ideal economic and sustainable approach is to combine these different approaches in an integrated fashion to suit the local ecological and socioeconomic conditions. Most important is the involvement of smallholder farmers in finding practical solutions.

Preventing Locust Plagues

The long remission in locust plagues since the 1960s had led both to complacency about such outbreaks and to a decline in support for the regional and national control bodies. The seasonal forecasts were accurate, but earlier forecasts giving even more warning are urgently needed. Prevention of outbreaks is better than cure. But to be effective it needs a sustainable approach, one focusing on satellite imagery and global positioning systems (GPS) to monitor outbreaks, to control operations, and, more important, to detect likely breeding sites and hence provide early warning of swarms. A pilot study in Mali has used a normalized difference vegetation index (NDVI) system to assess the vegetation (the same system used in detecting severe soil erosion), coupled with validation against in-situ data collection to identify the precise location of the breeding sites in the recession area.[7] But it is a challenging process since these areas are very sparsely vegetated.

There is heightened awareness of the economic and environmental cost of failure to prevent locust swarms, and this has led to a demand for an IPM solution. Chemical control of developing swarms is highly effective, and this should now be combined with oil formulations of mycopesticides, which contain the spores of *Metarhizium anisopliae,* a fungus that is lethal to the locusts but much less environmentally harmful, and release of the hymenopteran wasp egg parasitoids *Scelio* spp.[8]

Controlling Weeds

Herbicides can be effective against Striga, otherwise known as witchweed, provided they are selective and do not harm the crop. But, they are expensive and have to be applied carefully to avoid health risks. Hand weeding is cheap, but it is hard work. The alternative is an IPM approach referred to as push–pull, which relies on chemical signals to fool the invaders.[9] The signals are produced naturally by two plants that are sown among or around the crops of maize, sorghum, and rice:

- The push plant, a legume, *Desmodium*, is grown among the crop, repels the stemborer, and effectively suppresses Striga.
- The pull plant, Napier or another grass, is grown as a two-meter-wide border around the crop and attracts and traps the stemborer as well as being attractive to the natural parasites of the borer.

These two companion plants also provide nutritious animal fodder, while the intercrop push plant, often *Desmodium*, enhances fertility and reduces degradation of the soil.

The system was developed by the International Centre of Insect Physiology and Ecology in Kenya and Rothamsted Research in the UK. It is appropriate for Africa's mixed cropping systems and is based on locally available plants. Smallholders have seen yields rise from 1 ton/ha to 3.5 tons/ha. By 2017 more than 130,000 smallholders in Kenya, Uganda, Tanzania, and Ethiopia had adopted the system.[10]

Vaccinating against Newcastle Disease

Whereas the larger farms in Africa vaccinate their cattle against Newcastle disease, subsistence "backyard" farmers normally do not.[11] There is an effective vaccine against the disease that is used by commercial farmers, and a vaccine that is stable in hot conditions has been produced. But the challenge for smallholder farmer communities is to get the vaccination rate above 85 percent in order to achieve herd immunity, that is, the percentage cover sufficient to offer protection to individuals that have not been vaccinated. Some success has been achieved in implementing participatory epidemiology approaches. In Nigeria these have revealed a considerable depth of knowledge of the disease among farmers; for example, they clearly identify the syndromes of different forms of Newcastle disease.[12]

Countering the Fall Armyworm (FAW)

FAO warns that insecticide applications are costly, may not work because of resistance, poor application techniques, or low-quality pesticides, and will negatively affect the fall armyworm's (FAW) natural enemies.[13] Instead, FAO advocates the following IPM approach:

- Look for signs of presence of the FAW in the field and crush the egg masses and young larvae.

- Find out how and where the adult female moth lays her eggs. This helps determine where to plant mixed crops.
- Encourage beneficial insects such as tiny wasps that kill the eggs or larvae of the FAW.
- Encourage naturally occurring fungal and viral pathogens.
- Apply ash, lime, sand, or soil directly or other in local remedies to the infested plants.

FAW damage can look alarming, but maize plants have a good capacity to compensate for that damage, and often little yield is lost. Unfortunately, this does not add up to a sophisticated program of IPM. In South Africa farmers have been planting Bt maize against caterpillars since 2010, and this practice appears to be effective against the FAW.[14] However, a risk of this approach is that resistance may evolve.

Integrated Soil Management

Conventional means of soil management often cause more harm than good. An alternative is to use organic approaches. But this may require too much labor, and they may depend on scarce inputs. Moreover the yields may be too low. The solution is integrated soil management (ISM), which combines the best of organic and conventional approaches in a way that is environmentally appropriate and sustainable.

ISM can be defined as follows: "A set of soil fertility management practices that necessarily include the use of fertilizer, organic inputs, and improved germplasm combined with the knowledge on how to adapt these practices to local conditions, aiming at maximizing agronomic use efficiency of the applied nutrients and improving crop productivity. All inputs need to be managed following sound agronomic principles."[15] In practice this requires harnessing the skill and knowledge available in traditional farming, together with ecological approaches and precision farming using modern inputs.[16] ISM needs to go beyond purely organic or conventional approaches. It needs a fully integrated approach combining conservation farming with selective use of inputs. The aim is produce a climate-smart soil that both adapts to and mitigates climate change, thus ultimately intensifying agricultural production in a sustainable manner.

The benefits could be significant. The Economics of Land Degradation Initiative calculates that improved land management could deliver up to US$1.4 trillion globally in increased crop production or thirty-five times the value of estimated losses.[17]

What Can Farmers Do?

Many large-scale industrial farmers view the soil simply as a physical medium in which to grow crops. They sow the seed and apply synthetic fertilizers and other agrochemicals, often in abundance. They may get good yields in the short term, but the soil will organically degrade over the medium to long term. By contrast, most smallholders have an intimacy with their soil; they appreciate that it has a mix of particles and humus that nurtures their plants, and in a real sense they view their soil as a living entity, containing all manner of living organisms. They also recognize when their soil becomes infertile, producing sickly plants and poor yields. Inevitably the health and livelihoods of farm families will progressively suffer in this situation. Land degradation and the decline of soil fertility in Africa are deeply complex issues, with intertwining and cyclical causes. Without stemming the causes, farmers will continue to make the same choices, even at the expense of their future well-being.

One answer is the application of the principles of conservation agriculture (CA). These include a combined sequence of minimal soil disturbance, permanent soil cover, and crop rotations, including legumes. Other practices include intercropping with nitrogen-enriching legumes, mixing crops with livestock and trees, conserving water by building bunds and terraces, digging planting pits, and erecting windbreaks to minimize wind erosion can also be useful. But applying organic matter in the form of composts or mulches is hard work, and the returns to the investment may take years to appear. Moreover, if farmers do not own, or have reliable access to land, there may be little incentive to improve the land over the longer term.

Synthetic fertilizers may be part of the answer, but not, as is often the case in Africa, when a single compound, such as diammonium phosphate (DAP), is applied whether or not it is appropriate for the local soil conditions. More use needs to be made of blended fertilizer mixtures and specific micronutrients. This requires better and more extensive soil surveys and a greater reliance on agrodealers and extension agents in providing the right advice. Farmers may be able to invest in small-scale rainwater harvesting (e.g., placing plugs in gullies to conserve moisture), but large-scale harvesting may be too costly in time, labor, or materials. Moreover, access and right to land are pre-conditions for farmers to maintain or improve their soils. Too often farmers are forced to forgo better land management practices in lieu of more affordable, less labor-intensive uses of resources. As a result, the uptake of ISM practices in Africa remains low. Fundamentally, resilient ISM depends on governments establishing the appropriate incentive structures for sustainable land management.

Integrated Water Resources Management

Improved water use in agriculture will come about only through better management. A more resilient, holistic approach known as integrated water resources management (IWRM) has been developed.

IWRM is an empirical concept that has been built from the experience of practitioners on the ground.[18] Managers, whether in the government or private sectors, have to make difficult decisions on water allocation. More and more they have to apportion diminishing supplies between ever-increasing demands. Drivers like demographic and climatic changes further increase the stress on water resources, as described in chapter 3. Water activities are also often split among a number of ministries and departments, the fragmentation hindering attempts to produce an integrated management approach.[19] Such an approach is no longer viable; a more holistic model is essential. According to Global Water,[20] "IWRM is a process which promotes the coordinated development and management of water, land and related resources, in order to maximize the resultant economic and social welfare in an equitable manner without compromising the sustainability of vital ecosystems."[21]

In practice IWRM is a highly comprehensive and complicated approach encompassing basin- or watershed-scale management; integrating land and water activities; upstream and downstream areas; surface, ground, and coastal water resources; supply- and demand-side approaches; the various sectors and stakeholders involved in decision-making, including water users and marginalized groups; and effective integration of different levels of policy, institutions, and regulation.[22] Needless to say, it is a highly ambitious set of goals; the challenge is to find a management approach that is resilient to future climate changes and reflects both the priorities of the poor and the biophysical complexities and uncertainties.

The good news is that, in general, lessons from the experiences of the past thirty years indicate that small irrigation systems designed and managed by the community are more likely to deliver sustainable water supplies than a top-down approach. In many parts of the world and especially in much of Africa there is no other option; while the total area of irrigated land in northern Africa is 28 percent, only 4 percent in SSA is equipped for irrigation.[23] Over much of the continent, the environmental conditions are not suitable for large-scale irrigation systems. The future lies in small-scale systems like those developed in South Asia and, in the drier regions, in ingenious systems of water conservation and harvesting based on a micro-catchment approach.[24]

Notwithstanding the ingenuity of engineers, planners, and farmers themselves, water for agriculture is going to be in increasingly short supply. Perhaps the most resilient solution is to breed into crop plants (and livestock) the capacity to make much more efficient use of limited water.

Climate-Smart Agriculture

Climate-smart agriculture (CSA) depends on governments, development partners, the private sector, and farmers themselves to increase the resilience of their agricultural systems to withstand and adapt to climatic stresses and shocks. As with other risks, there are no magic bullets. A truly resilient approach has to integrate a range of technologies, tools, and processes. Central to CSA are three pillars as outlined by the Research Program on Climate Change, Agriculture and Food Security:

- Productivity: . . . Sustainably increase agricultural productivity and incomes from crops, livestock, and fish [to improve food security and nutrition outcomes], without having a negative impact on the environment. . . .
- Adaptation: . . . Reduce the exposure of farmers to short-term risks, while also strengthening their resilience by building their capacity to adapt and prosper in the face of shocks and long-term stresses. . . . [This involves] protecting the . . . services which ecosystems provide to farmers and others. These services that are essential for maintaining productivity and our ability to adapt to climate change.
- Mitigation: Wherever and whenever possible, [aiming to] help to reduce and/or remove greenhouse gas (GHG) emissions. This implies . . . [reducing] emissions for each calorie or kilo of food, fibre, and fuel . . . [produced]. . . . [Means include avoiding] deforestation from agriculture . . . [and managing] soils and trees . . . [to] maximize their potential to act as carbon sinks and absorb CO_2 from the atmosphere.[25]

In summary, this approach is defined as climate-smart agriculture (box 4.1).

Box 4.1. Climate-smart agriculture

Climate-smart agriculture aims to:

- Provide adaptation and resilience to stresses and shocks.
- Generate adaptation and mitigation as co-benefits.

- Take a location-specific and knowledge-intensive approach.
- Provide integrated options that create synergies and reduce trade-offs.

Source: Reproduced from Montpellier Panel, "Farmers on the Climate Frontline: Six Recommendations for Addressing Agriculture in the UNFCCC Negotiations" (Agriculture for Impact, 2015), https://www.mamopanel.org/media/uploads/files/FARMERS_ON_THE_CLIMATE_FRONTLINE-_SIX_RECOMMENDA TIONS_FOR_ADDRESSING_AGRICULTURE_IN_THE_UNFCCC_NEGOTIA TIONS.pdf.

What Can Farmers Do?

Farmers throughout Africa are adapting to climate change. If you visit a village and ask the farmers whether the climate and weather are changing, they will say, "Yes!" And if you ask how, they will have a clear sense of what is happening. If you ask if they are doing anything about it, they will say, "Yes, of course!" and tell you what they are doing.

In a survey of eleven African countries farmers were reported as growing different varieties and modifying planting dates and practices to account for shorter growing seasons.[26] Farmers faced with the threat of drought may plant a new drought-tolerant maize variety or a new flood-tolerant rice variety (box 4.2). They may try out the technique of CA or plant a greater diversity of crops. Mulch may be applied to stabilize and enrich the soil or terraces built on the contour to prevent erosion. More generally the answer lies in creating more diverse livelihoods so that other sources of income will offset the losses from drought or flooding.

Box 4.2. Drought affected Malawi farmers getting drought-tolerant maize

Hannas and Anna Matola, like many millions of Malawi farmers, have been affected by the drought of 2016 induced by El Niño. Three months ago, WFP had warned that about fifty million people were at risk of being affected by drought in southern Africa, with fourteen million already facing hunger in the region.

But help was on the way. The International Maize and Wheat Improvement Center (CIMMYT) is introducing drought-tolerant maize varieties. To popularize the new varieties, the project is championing seed production, field days, and demonstration plots for smallholder farmers. The project is also providing capacity building for private sector seed companies, agrodealers and government seed inspectors to improve quality and seed marketing.

The project also uses other technologies, such as CA, keeping crop residues on the soil, and diversification through rotation or intercropping maize with other crops.

Hannas Matola was excited by the performance of drought-tolerant maize varieties: "The different maize varieties showcased here are unique in the way they cope with, and withstand the drought experienced this year compared to the other maize varieties in the neighboring field."

Source: "Drought-Tolerant Maize Rescues Malawian Farmers," *The Nation Online* (blog), May 1, 2016, http://mwnation.com/drought-tolerant-maize-rescues-malawian-farmers/.

Often farmers may need to work as a community to find a sustainable solution. In particular they may need government help, for example, to build protective infrastructure or to develop specific policies that mitigate the effects of drought or flooding. Other approaches include crop insurance or the creation of safety nets. Also important is agricultural research and extension, the creation of irrigation schemes, or the dissemination of appropriate agrometeorological information. Some of these strategies will be technological, others social, economic, or political.

Mitigation

CSA tries to partner adaptation with mitigation. In the short and long term we need both. If existing agricultural technologies and processes are applied on sufficient scale, farmers could potentially face the challenges. An effective approach to increase adaptive capacity while reducing GHGs is to prioritize land use and land use change strategies (box 4.3).

Box 4.3. Rights to trees and livelihoods in Niger

With no incentive to maintain trees on their property—and with families to feed—farmers in need of agricultural land regularly removed trees and other natural vegetation across Niger. This practice led to worsening soil erosion and reduced soil fertility and yields, which pushed farmers to cultivate ever more marginal lands. By the late 1960s farmers became extremely vulnerable to droughts. After independence, international NGOs and donors began to promote simple, low-cost soil and water conservation techniques combined with agroforestry to support local livelihoods. Around the same time, Niger's government reassessed its governance of rural land and natural resources. New laws and regulations strengthened local rights to benefit from trees, whilst the Forest Service was transformed from a paramilitary institution that punished farmers for cutting trees into an extension service that helped them adopt simple tree-management processes.

As a result, farmers began nurturing underground roots and tree stumps in their barren fields. Today, more than five million hectares of land have been revitalized by smallholder farmers. The trees that grow have enriched the soil and provide food, fodder, fuelwood, and other goods. Crop yields and incomes have increased too. Moreover, the increased carbon in the trees and in the soil serves to reduce GHG emissions.

Sources: Reproduced from Montpellier Panel, "The Farms of Change: African Smallholders Responding to an Uncertain Climate Future" (London: Agriculture for Impact, 2015), https://www.mamopanel.org/media/uploads/files/THE_FARMS_ OF_CHANGE-_AFRICAN_SMALLHOLDERS_RESPONDING_TO_AN_ UNCERTAIN_CLIMATE_FUTURE_2015.pdf.

Africa's agricultural potential could be unlocked and the productivity of smallholder farmers increased on a continental scale, first by significantly increasing irrigation capacity, second with improved land management practices, and third by implementing various forms of soil carbon sequestration.

Farmers can and will undertake actions that have co-benefits for mitigation, but they need to be given payments to help them manage their land or watersheds better, conserve biodiversity, or sequester carbon. Such financing needs to be within the overall framework of CSA which helps agricultural systems be better adapted to the adverse effects of climate change, while minimizing the emissions of GHGs and restoring lost carbon into the soil.[27]

Carbon Sequestration

As we noted earlier, agriculture is one of the largest contributors to GHG emissions, in particular from soils and livestock. The principal GHGs emitted are nitrous oxide (N_2O), methane (CH_4), and carbon dioxide (CO_2).

Globally, the soil contains about fifteen hundred gigatons (Gt) of soil organic carbon (SOC), more than double the amount of carbon in the atmosphere, and three times that contained in plants, animals, and micro-organisms. In natural, undisturbed woodlands and forests the gains and losses are more or less balanced. But when the land is converted to agriculture the SOC is depleted by as much as three-quarters in tropical regions. Ploughing destroys the humus; over centuries farmers have mined humus to grow food and, in the process, released CO_2 into the atmosphere. There are wide estimates of humus thus lost, but the cumulative historic loss from agriculture is between fifty and seventy-eight Gt.[28]

The challenge is to restore SOC through the process of carbon sequestration, which occurs when more organic matter is added to the soil and then decays. Plants take up CO_2 from the atmosphere and convert it through photosynthesis to organic matter, part of which remains in the soil as humus. But this has to be protected, primarily against wind and water erosion and other processes.

A possible approach is CA (see box 6.2).[29] In practice, no-till systems result in greater sequestration than undertilled crops. Sequestration is also encouraged and protected when the soil is kept covered, using cover crops or rotations or when fallows are reduced or eliminated. Nevertheless, the amount of SOC sequestration can vary. There is no simple rule of thumb, but in general conventional CA systems tend to sequester a maximum of 0.1 to 0.4 tons per hectare of carbon per year. However, the current total amount of carbon sequestration in Africa on 1.5 million hectares of CA is over 5.6 Mt CO_2 yr^{-1}, with a potential to raise this to 533 Mt of CO_2 per year—nearly 100 times greater.[30] CA is thus more than a promising sustainable agricultural system; by offseting agricultural CO_2 emissions, it can also effectively contribute to mitigating global warming.

An alternative is to employ agroforestry systems, typically via annual crops grown under leguminous trees, such as Faidherbia.[31] They accumulate carbon above and below ground in the range of two to four tons per hectare of carbon per year, roughly an order of magnitude higher than CA. Estimates of the carbon stocks in agroforestry systems overall in Africa range from one to eighteen tons of carbon per hectare in above-ground biomass and up to two hundred tons of carbon per hectare in soils.[32] They also provide better protection from carbon loss through soil erosion.

Methane and Nitrous Oxide

Some technologies to reduce N_2O are available, but considerable research still needs to be done. For example, Urea Deep Replacement (UDP)—the microdosing of urea—can lower the amount of nitrogen that escapes from rice fields by simply using less.[33] Urea is the main nitrogen fertilizer for rice and is usually applied liberally by broadcasting across fields. This is very inefficient, resulting in the loss of 60 to 70 percent of the nitrogen applied. The answer lies in a climate-smart solution known as UDP. Tiny briquettes, one to three grams, of urea are placed at seven to ten cm of soil depth after the paddy is transplanted. By targeting the urea to the root of the rice paddy, its efficiency rises by 50 percent. Moreover, yields rise by 25 percent for every 25 percent reduction in urea use. Some studies show up to 40 percent reduced methane emissions for irrigated rice. Given the success achieved by the Bangladesh Department of Agricultural Extension, where it is used on 1.3 million hectares by 2.5 million farmers, the technique is being expanded to Africa, with good results in Burkina Faso, Niger, and Nigeria.[34]

Livestock

Livestock are a large contributor to global warming, contributing about 15 percent of global anthropogenic GHG emissions.[35] Over 30 percent of the emissions from livestock systems are CO_2 from land use and its changes, including production of feed and deforestation; about 30 percent are of N_2O from manure and slurry management, and 25 percent of CH_4 production from ruminants.

One approach to reducing emissions from livestock is by improving their diets. A study by Philip Thornton and Mario Herrero of the International Livestock Research Institute in Nairobi has shown that the productivity, say, of milk or meat, per unit of animal can be achieved by increasing the digestibility of feeds, such as stover (fibrous crop residues) or by adding supplements.[36] However, this procedure also tends to increase the methane per unit of animal. If fewer animals are needed to meet production targets, this will result in an overall reduction of methane production. This potential reduction is also true of agroforestry, where leguminous shrubs such as *Leucaena* can improve livestock diets, again producing less methane if the land required is less. For agroforestry, however, there are also the more significant benefits of carbon sequestration.

Most of the results from this study involve reductions in animal numbers while increasing their productivity. Yet there are likely to be sociocultural trade-offs involved. In many pastoralist societies in Africa wealth is measured at least partially in terms of numbers of livestock.[37] But reducing the numbers may affect and reduce their ability to manage risk. The value of livestock to livelihoods in marginal environments goes far beyond the direct impacts of their productive capacity.

What is urgently needed are systems in which the production of methane is less per unit of animal production. Improved breeds with higher milk production potential and higher body weights produce only modest reductions in methane emissions per unit of milk produced. Methane emissions can be reduced by faster growth, higher milk yields, and shorter dry periods in lactating cows. An increase in longevity and hence in the number of lactations per lifetime can also reduce methane loss per unit of milk yield.[38]

GHG emissions can be reduced if livestock are more intensively farmed.[39] Mitigation of N_2O from solid manure heaps could be achieved through the use of high-carbon additives and compaction. Anaerobic digestion of slurries can be used to directly reduce methane emissions through biogas generation (heat and energy production) and may indirectly reduce N_2O emissions when slurries are applied to land by decreasing the readily available carbon content.

Socioeconomic Threats

As noted earlier, severe socioeconomic challenges include unstable and high prices of basic commodities. These are rarely situations in which poor people and especially poor farmers have any capacity to exert influence. They often simply have to suffer and cope, but government interventions can make a difference.

One of the main instruments of government intervention in African countries is the creation of national food reserves, but their role has been very contentious. Joachim von Braun and Máximo Torero of the University of Bonn believe food markets are now closely connected to the speculative activities in financial markets and hence should be subject to the kind of regulation that is applied to the banking and financial systems.[40] They also propose that new regulatory processes should be accompanied by a three-tiered grain reserves policy:

1. The creation of a small, independent physical reserve at WFP, exclusively for emergency response and humanitarian assistance.
2. A modest physical reserve shared by nations at the regional or global level.
3. A virtual reserve to which each country would commit to supplying to a fund, if needed, for intervention in grain markets (especially maize and wheat).[41]

These recommendations, which were initially regarded as somewhat controversial, are being implemented by countries such as Kenya and Nigeria, at least at the national level; Kenya tripled its grain reserve in 2011, and Nigeria has adopted a policy of holding in reserve 15 percent of the total annual grain harvest.[42]

In recent years national governments in many countries in SSA have restructured their food reserve systems. Forward contracting with registered farmer organizations, is being tested to ensure that benefits accrue to smallholder farmers. Another approach is to diversify the commodity basket beyond cereals and across commodity value chains. For example, adding specific commodities such as cowpeas can benefit women farmers since most of the production and marketing activities in SSA are undertaken by them.[43] Procurement of processed commodities that have low volume-to-weight ratio and are easy to store, such as gari, made from cassava in West Africa, strengthens the entire value chain.

Besides national reserves, initiatives are also under way to create regional food reserve systems. If placed under the auspices of the regional community, blocs play a major role in optimizing supply chain efficiencies across national borders and enhancing national and regional food security. The West Africa Regional Food Security Reserve under the Economic Community of West African States (ECOWAS) is currently under development.

Resilient Markets

In theory, the more open, efficient, and transparent the markets, the greater the price stability. But instead there has been extreme volatility in global prices, and there is general agreement that this development cannot be dampened, at least in the short run, by leaving it to the market. The situation was made worse by panic responses, in particular by the resort to export bans. The problem requires some form of systematic, concerted action by the international community.[44]

Integrated Markets and Trade

The causes of production variability are less likely to affect an entire region than individual countries. Moreover, fluctuations in national production tend to partially offset each other, hence they are less than perfectly correlated. In most African countries national production volatility is considerably higher than regional level volatility. The only exceptions are the Democratic Republic of Congo and, to a lesser extent, Côte d'Ivoire.[45] Consequently, expanding cross-border trade and allowing greater integration of food markets would reduce supply volatility and price instability in these markets.

Therefore, as Ousmane Badiane, Sunday Odjo, and Samson Jamenah of IFPRI outline, market integration and trade raise the capacity of domestic markets to absorb local price risks by

- Enlarging the area of production and consumption, thus increasing the volume of demand and supply that can be adjusted to respond to and dampen the effects of shocks.
- Providing incentives to invest in marketing services and expand capacities and activities in the marketing sector, which raises the capacity of the private sector to respond to future shocks.
- Lowering the size of needed carryover stocks, thereby reducing the cost of supplying markets during periods of shortage and hence decreasing the likely amplitude of price variation.[46]

A country may benefit from the trade stabilization potential if its production fluctuates more than the regional average and is weakly correlated with that of the other countries in the region. The combination of high volatility and weak correlation suggests that Southern African Development Community (SADC) countries would benefit the most from increased regional trade in terms of domestic market stabilization, followed by Common Market for Eastern and Southern Africa (COMESA), then ECOWAS countries.[47]

Production levels in the ECOWAS region tend to fluctuate more in synchrony than in the other two regions, reflecting the existence of two more uniform clusters of countries, Sahelian and coastal. Nevertheless, the patterns and distribution of production fluctuations among countries in all three regions are such that increased trade could be expected to have a stabilizing effect on domestic agricultural and food markets.

The Scope for Cross-Border Trade

There is considerable scope for exploiting the less-than-perfect correlation of volatility patterns across countries. Despite the recent upward trends, the level of intra-African and intraregional trade is still very low compared with other regions. Intra-African markets accounted only for, on average, 34 percent of the total agricultural exports from African countries between 2007 and 2011. Among the three regional economic communities (RECs), SADC had the highest share of intraregional trade (42 percent), and ECOWAS the lowest (6 percent). The COMESA share of intraregional trade was 20 percent.[48]

Yet, contrary to conventional wisdom, countries in all three regions exhibit sufficiently dissimilar patterns of specialization both in production and trade that should allow higher levels of cross-border and interregional trade. A series of indicators confirms that significant scope exists to expand trade in this way, if major obstacles impeding the movement of goods and raising the cost of trading across local markets are addressed.

The improvements include three possible scenarios:

1. Across-the-board reduction in trading costs by 10 percent.
2. Elimination of informal barriers to cross-border trade.
3. Increase in crop yields, also by 10 percent.[49]

These scenarios show cumulative increases in intraregional trade in local staples of up to three to four million tons above current trends between 2008 and 2025.[50] The level of increase varies between commodities and regions and across the three scenarios, but it tends to be substantial. The same changes reduce the volatility in domestic staples markets across all three regions compared to historical levels.[51]

In summary, a more resilient approach is to integrate regional markets in ways that stabilize prices and hence reduce the impacts of volatility, especially on poor, small farm households.

Resilient Cities

There are three megacities in Africa—Cairo, Lagos, and Kinshasa—each with a population of ten million people or more.[52] There are also many smaller cities that are growing very fast, for example, Mbouda in Cameroon at nearly 8 percent per annum, while Ouagadougou, the capital of Burkina Faso, is growing at over 7 percent per annum. As a consequence, their infrastructure is rapidly becoming inadequate, and there is a lack of appropriate urban planning. In the words of Robert Muggah and Katie Hill, "the result is sprawling, fragmented and hyper-informal cities."[53]

Inevitably urban food supply and access are severely limited and liable to disruption, creating food deserts.[54] Urban agriculture and the informal food economy are weak. The food system is controlled by the supermarkets, but food of good quality is outside the reach of most poor households. Food shortages and a lack of dietary diversity are endemic. Worst off are female-headed households. Moreover, as noted, grain prices in Africa are highly volatile.

However, African cities are not standing still. Urban authorities in centers like Narok and Kisumu in Kenya and Moshi in Tanzania are investing in improved risk assessment, urban upgrading, smarter land use, and plans to strengthen environmental protection, in some instances in partnership with the 100 Resilient Cities Initiative.[55]

Resilience as a Business

African smallholders are businesspeople capable, at least potentially, of making profitable returns from their smallholdings. Farmers need cash, at the very minimum, to pay school fees, to purchase medicines, and in many cases to purchase food. If they are connected to markets in a meaningful, dynamic way, garnering cash is more likely. In effect this requires policies that help farmers move up to even more business-focused livelihoods.[56]

Examples of business opportunities include the following:[57]

- Climate finance. The level of financing currently reaching African countries is paltry. Of the US$34 billion pledged through various climate funds, SSA received just US$2.3 billion between 2003 and 2013.
- The provision of smallholder agricultural insurance linked to loans. Small and large companies are needed to provide the necessary farm inputs, and insurance companies are required to underwrite the loans, while a variety of purchasers can create a more stable market.
- Development of storage to reduce post-harvest losses requires investments in procurement and stock management, dynamic market pricing, small-farm engagement, and a diversified commodity basket.
- The creation of regional cross-border trade requires not only more government funding but also the building of both small and large private trader capacities.

Resilient business depends as well on enabling environments and policies and, in particular, on resilient rural infrastructure, for example, irrigation facilities and warehousing and processing facilities.[58] These, in turn, need to be backed by increased spending on regional and national infrastructure. Three countries, Sudan, South Africa, and Madagascar, account for two-thirds of the irrigable area developed. Yet potentially twenty million hectares of land could be brought under irrigation.[59]

In all these cases the way forward is through public–private community partnerships that bring a range of stakeholders from the private sector, government, and local rural communities together in a working relationship that recognizes each other's strengths and complementarities. In many respects, if done well the outcome can be value chains that are both highly productive and resilient.

Safety Nets

These integrated resilient approaches, nevertheless, may not work. The stresses or shocks may be too extreme or the mechanisms insufficient. In these circumstances safety net programs may be appropriate.[60] They vary widely in terms of the type of assistance provided, conditionality of assistance, and targeting method. The types of assistance may include food, cash, inputs, and assets; the assistance may be unconditional or subject to behavioral conditions; and in-kind assistance may be free, subsidized, or provided in voucher form.[61]

One approach is the guaranteed employment program, sometimes referred to as food-for-work or cash-for-work. The Ethiopian Productive Safety Net Program (PSNP) reaches more than seven million poor Ethiopians. A study of the impact of the program found variation in the size of benefits received, but those people who received at least half of the intended benefits showed significant gains in food security.

Programs that guarantee employment such as conditional cash transfer programs are an alternative. These may provide cash grants to poor households if they comply with certain requirements, such as keeping children in school, attending health clinics, or receiving pre-natal and post-natal care.

Safety net programs have been proven to provide significant benefits in terms of short-term food security and long-term investment in human capital. However, the budgetary cost is relatively high, and they require administrative capacity to identify poor households and monitor their compliance with the conditions.

The Opportunities

The application in theory and practice of the concept of resilience is the appropriate response to tackling the various threats to food security detailed. We favor highly integrated approaches since these are most likely to deliver solutions that are both effective and sustainable.

We eschew magic bullets and instead work for combinations of biological, physical, environmental, and socioeconomic levers that will deliver sustainable outcomes. These comprise integrated pest, soil, and water management as well as CSA. Examples include the control of the devastating weed Striga, application of blended fertilizers and specific micronutrients, the design of small-scale water harvesting, and practicing CSA, the use of CA to increase carbon sequestration. Integrated approaches to socioeconomic threats include programs of grain reserves, development of cross-border trade, and the institution of safety nets.

More generally, the biological, land, and water supply, climate, and socioeconomic threats described above are not just technical problems. They depend for their solution on a political economy that can be resolved only by putting in place governance systems and appropriate institutions that will create the right political and social environments.

Part 2

SUSTAINABLE INTENSIFICATION

5

SUSTAINABLE AGRICULTURE

Amadi and Tilele Elassie are Ethiopian smallholder farmers who are all too familiar with some of the challenges outlined in earlier chapters of this book. The family owns a small plot of land, just over 1.5 hectares, in the Ethiopian highlands. They and their three children and Tilele's mother have been able to live off this land, but the increasingly frequent and severe droughts in addition to the already severely degraded land have made it more and more challenging to move beyond subsistence levels and achieve a sustainable livelihood: to step up and out.

To be able to send his daughters to school, to ensure that his mother-in-law receives the health care she needs, and to purchase the much-needed fertilizer for his land, Amadi would need to earn more from increased agricultural production. Through a farmers' cooperative he joined, Amadi has acquired new farming techniques and skills and is trying to develop a more diverse livelihood for himself and his wife. He is trying to intercrop coffee and maize as well as coffee with bananas or chickpeas on parts of his field. Tilele has a job at one of the local agrodealer shops, where the dealers have convinced Amadi to plant new, improved seed varieties and to purchase some fertilizer to help regenerate the degraded soil on his farm. Because Amadi's financial resources are limited, he has applied only small doses of fertilizer directly to the root of his plants but is achieving remarkable results, up to three tons on just one hectare of land. Using the additional income he makes from selling some of the crops at local markets, he is now considering purchasing weather insurance to protect himself against crop losses should the next rains fail or another drought eradicate his harvest.

Among the main barriers marginalized smallholder farmers in Africa face when they try to move beyond subsistence farming levels are a lack of access to inputs and markets, population growth, and malnutrition. But in addition there are severe environmental constraints like the gradual decline in soil quality and, in recent years, the impacts of climate change on, for example, the frequency and intensity of rainfall or droughts. Farmers and political leaders across the continent know the challenges faced by smallholders.

As we have seen, over the past decade Africa's agriculture has made great strides, and although progress has been uneven and many challenges remain there is a sense of optimism that further progress can be made in the years to come. We believe that the way forward is to develop a prosperous, sustainable agriculture sector deeply rooted in the concept of sustainable intensification (SI). Reaching that goal will require taking the following steps:

- Producing more outputs with a more efficient and sustainable use of inputs, such as seeds, fertilizers, and pesticides.
- Adapting to climate change.
- Reducing GHG emissions.
- Improving natural capital, such as soil moisture capacity.
- Building resilience.[1]

Developing a sustainable and prosperous agriculture sector based on the concept of SI is a challenge, but it is also an opportunity for the continent and the millions of smallholder farmers seeking improved livelihoods for themselves and their families.

Unsustainability

Sustainability and its opposite, unsustainability, are concerned with the preservation or enhancement of the productive resource base, particularly for future generations. At local levels it is about whether livelihood activities maintain, enhance, or deplete and degrade the natural resource base, while at the global level the question is whether policies contribute positively or negatively to sustainable, long-term livelihoods.[2] Livelihoods can be impacted and threatened by policies, national and international, including global trade agreements, that may reduce access to global markets' livelihood products or destroy global common properties.

Some of the negative effects that arise are[3]

- Surface and groundwater depletion due to excessive irrigation.
- Salinization in poorly drained irrigated lands.
- Water pollution, adverse health effects, pest outbreaks caused by excessive agrochemical use.
- Soil erosion due to excessive tillage on steeply sloping lands.
- Soil fertility depletion due to declining fallow or inadequate application of soil nutrients.
- Deforestation and conversion of rangelands to cropping due to the encroachment of crop production.
- Overgrazing of rangeland due to continued dependence on extensive grazing, declining rangelands, rapid growth in meat demand.

In most instances these problems are caused by the policies that govern the use of natural resources or fail to incentivize farmers to farm their land more sustainably. Mark Rosegrant of IFPRI identifies some of these policies and suggests remedial counterpolicies that encourage sustainable behavior (table 5.1).[4]

One of the most ubiquitous policies that is often unsustainable in its effects is the provision of subsidies for fertilizers. A study conducted by FAO in 2012 acknowledges that large-scale agricultural input subsidies have become a de facto part of agricultural policies in many countries in SSA. The research concludes that "most of the programmes they reviewed had been successful in raising agricultural production, but that they were generally poorly designed, poorly

TABLE 5.1. Unsustainable policies and potential remedies

A. Water and irrigation policies	B. Input policies	C. Price and trade policies
• Drainage investment left out to minimize costs • Water allocation–virtually no cost, encouraging overuse, waterlogging, and salinization	• Input subsidies: keeping input prices low directly affects crop management practices • Overuse of water, energy, and fertilizers • Crowding out of public investments • Subsidized fertilizer prices favor the use of nitrogen fertilizers over other nutrients, damaging soil fertility	• Macroeconomic setting leading to unsustainable management practices—cause of degradation of intensive food systems in Asia • Trade and exchange rate policies penalize agriculture or promote it unsustainably • Crop-specific interventions—output price protection and input subsidies—often favor individual crops like rice

(Continued)

TABLE 5.1. continued

Remedies	Remedies	Remedies
• Phase out water subsidies • Secure water rights for users • Establish markets in tradable water rights • Devolve management to user or joint ownership with autonomous local institutions	• Reduction and eventual removal of input price subsidies • Investment in agricultural R&D • Non-price policies: location-specific research on soil fertility constraints and agronomic practices, improve extension, develop physical and institutional infrastructure • Design of low-subsidy, risk-reducing instruments: weather index insurance, risk-contingent credit	• Remove trade and price distortions • Adopt cropping and livestock systems approaches • Develop new resource-conserving technologies to reduce the economic and ecological cost per unit of output produced

Source: Mark W. Rosegrant, "Sustainable Intensification Is the Answer to Global Food Insecurity" (PowerPoint presentation, September 20, 2016).

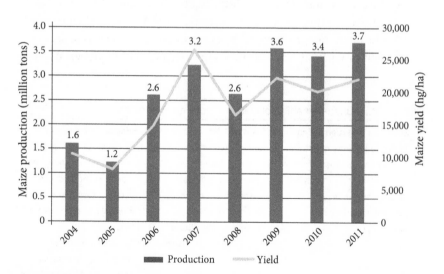

FIG. 5.1. Maize yield and production in Malawi

Source: Carolina Schiesari, Jonathan Mockshell, and Manfred Zeller, "Farm Input Subsidy Program in Malawi: The Rationale behind the Policy," *MPRA* (Stuttgart: University of Hohenheim, May 22, 2016), https://mpra.ub.uni-muenchen.de/81409/1/MPRA_paper_81409.pdf. Reproduced with data from the Food and Agriculture Organization of the United Nations, "FAOSTAT," Crops, accessed October 19, 2018, http://www.fao.org/faostat/en/#data/QC.

implemented, highly politicized, very costly, lack any strategy for phasing out, and are unsustainable in the long term."[5] One example of a partly successful subsidy program is in Malawi (box 5.1; figure 5.1).

The cost of the subsidy program grew rapidly in the first three years and then peaked in 2008–9 due to very high international fertilizer prices, totaling US$250m, or 70 percent of the budget of the Ministry of Agriculture and Food Security (MoAFS), and 15 percent of the national budget. Thereafter, the program was significantly cut back. In 2012–13 the total cost was just over US$144 million, amounting to 60 percent of the total MoAFS budget and 10 percent of the national budget.[6]

Box 5.1. Fertilizer subsidies in Malawi 2005–2009

Malawi, which is highly dependent on agriculture, has low maize productivity (the dominant staple crop, accounting for around 70 percent of cultivated area).

In 2004–5 the maize harvest was the worst in a decade, total production meeting only 57 percent of the national requirement. A major consequence was the launch of an ambitious fertilizer subsidy program in 2005–6 that used vouchers targeting approximately half of the farmers. Those who were reached were able to receive fertilizers and improved seeds for maize production. Two vouchers were issued to farmers, one for a fifty-kilogram bag of 23:21:0 +4S basal fertilizer (NPK) and the other for a fifty-kilogram bag of urea for top dressing. Improved maize seeds subsidized under the program were initially OPVs, but there has subsequently been much greater emphasis on hybrid maize varieties.

The program was highly complex, involving both state and private actors, and subject to considerable political interference. Fertilizer prices have fluctuated widely, and the distribution of vouchers has been problematic, with evidence of diversion and fraud. About a third of poor farmers did not receive the subsidy. Nevertheless, for those who were reached by the subsidy, yields and total maize production have risen significantly since 2005. The very large-scale disbursement of heavily subsidized fertilizers and maize seed to very large numbers of beneficiaries across Malawi represents a major logistical achievement and led to notable increases in national maize production and productivity, while contributing to increased food availability, higher real wages, wider economic growth, and poverty reduction. But the program was affected by high international fertilizer and maize prices, the latter undermining the program's food security, poverty reduction, and growth benefits for the majority of Malawian farmers.

Sources: Ephraim Chirwa and Andrew Dorward, *Agricultural Input Subsidies: The Recent Malawi Experience* (Oxford: Oxford University Press, 2013), https://doi.org/10.1093/acprof:oso/9780199683529.001.0001; Ephraim Chirwa and Andrew Dorward, "The Implementation of the 2012/13 Farm Input Subsidy Programme," *FISP Policy Brief* 2014, no. 2 (January 2014): 2.

Sustainability

One of the most elegant definitions of sustainable agriculture was written by a great Roman writer and landowner of the first century BC, Marcus Terentius Varro. He had recently remarried and given his wife an estate near Rome, accompanied by a book, *Rerum rusticarum*, of guidance on how to fruitfully manage the estate:

> [Agri cultura] est scientia, quae sint in quoque agro serenda ac facienda, quo terra maximos perpetuo reddat fructus.
>
> [Agriculture is a science, which teaches us what crops are to be planted in each kind of soil, and what operations are to be carried on, in order that the land may produce the highest yields in perpetuity.][7]

This is a definition that was echoed at a global level by Gro Harlem Brundtland, the former prime minister of Norway in *Our Common Future* (more commonly known as the Brundtland report) in 1987. In the words of her commission, "sustainable development is development that meets the needs of the present without compromising the ability of future generations to meet their own needs."[8] The report marked a turning point in thinking on environment, development, and governance. The UN-sponsored commission issued a bold call to review institutional mechanisms at all levels to promote economic development and transformation that would guarantee "the security, well-being, and very survival of the planet."[9]

While the report's definition of sustainable development was welcomed as a spur for political action, the debate that has followed since then has been confusing at times, as different interest groups and stakeholders have wrestled with its practical implementation. *Sustainability* as a term can at times be too abstract

TABLE 5.2.   Contested agricultural policies and practices

Food sovereignty	Irrigation
GM crops	Water harvesting
Conservation farming	Farmer association
Agroforestry	Local production
Modern hybrids	Vegetarian diet
Farmer breeding	Vegan diet
Free-range livestock	Farmer markets
Fortified crops	Supermarkets
Organic farming	Gluten-free food

for farmers, extension workers, and governments who are trying to design food systems and agricultural practices that are fit to withstand and even prosper amid the challenges they face. As a consequence, different groups of individuals argue, sometimes vehemently, for or against one or more technologies or practices (table 5.2).

One way forward is to combine and integrate the definitions recognized by diverse disciplines. Thus, agronomists and plant breeders aim to maintain or increase yields and production on a long-term basis. To environmentalists, the means are crucial: sustainable agriculture is a way of providing sufficient food without degrading the natural resource base. To economists, it represents an efficient, long-term use of resources, and to sociologists and anthropologists it embodies an agriculture that preserves traditional values, institutions, and methods.

What is appropriate at the farm level applies to the household as well. The sustainability of rural livelihoods has many aspects: a livelihood can be sustainable environmentally, in its effects on local and global natural resources. It may also be sustainable socially, able to cope with stresses and shocks. In the context of smallholder agriculture in Africa, sustainability is thus a function of how resources and capabilities are utilized, maintained, and enhanced so as to preserve, strengthen and improve livelihoods.[10]

Agroecosystems

Agricultural processes are governed by continuous economic and social decisions. Smallholder farmers in Africa cooperate or compete with one another and sell, exchange, or consume their produce. The resulting system is as much a socioeconomic system as it is an ecological one. We call this new, complex, agro-socioeconomic ecological system, bounded in several dimensions, an agroecosystem. More formally, an agroecosystem is "an ecological and socio-economic system, comprising domesticated plants and/or animals and the people who husband them, intended for the purpose of producing food, fibre or other agricultural products."[11]

Agroecosystems defined in this way fall into a hierarchy. At the bottom is the individual plant or animal in its microenvironment. At the next level is the crop within a field (figure 5.2). For example, a West African rice field is formed from the natural environment by building up a ridge of earth that defines its boundary. Inside the field, biodiversity and the original wildlife is reduced to a set of crop, pest, and weed species—while retaining some of the natural elements, such as fish and predatory birds.

The basic ecological processes—(1) competition between rice and weeds (2) herbivory of the rice by the pests, and (3) predation of the pests by their natural enemies—remain the same. Yet these ecological processes are now governed by the agricultural processes of cultivation, use of inputs (with fertilizers), control (of water, pests, and diseases), and harvesting.[12]

Such fields combine to form a farming system that is managed by a farm household. And the hierarchy continues upward in a similar fashion.

Livestock Agroecosystems

The agroecosystems containing livestock of various kinds can be difficult to define. Where animals such as cattle, sheep, and pigs are kept in fields there is a well-defined biophysical boundary, and the concept in figure 5.2 is applicable, with modifications. In Africa a large number of cattle are kept by nomadic

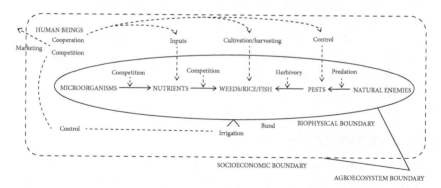

FIG. 5.2. A West African rice field as an agroecosystem

Source: Gordon Conway, *One Billion Hungry: Can We Feed the World?* (Ithaca: Comstock Publishing Associates, 2012).

people, such as the pastoralists in the Sahel, so the agroecosystem becomes more difficult to describe although there is a clear socioeconomic boundary, defining the limits to the range. At the other end of the spectrum, some animals, in particular poultry, are kept in often very confined conditions, extending from battery farms to containment in barns, and in some circumstances where there is some free-range grazing.

Properties of Agroecosystems

Agroecosystems have distinctive properties that can be measured and used as indicators of performance. These properties are productivity, stability, resilience, and equitability (figure 5.3). They are relatively easy to define but not as easy to measure:

> Productivity measures how much an agroecosystem produces over time (e.g., tons of maize per hectare).

> The stability of production can also be measured: How does production vary from year to year? Productivity and stability can be either high or low.

> Resilience measures how well the productivity tolerates or recovers from stress or shock, and equitability measures how fairly the products of an agroecosystem are shared among its beneficiaries, for example, among the members of a household.[13]

For African agriculture and smallholders to thrive, we need to find farming methods, agricultural technologies, and processes that generate high levels of all four properties, minimizing possible trade-offs between them.

We can use these characteristics to assess how different agroecosystems perform. Table 5.3 gives an example comparing the characteristics of a traditional rice field and a home garden.

In figure 5.4 we show how these different characteristics can be overlain. The small area overlapping high values in the figure represents what we commonly refer to as *sustainable agriculture*. It is a key means of obtaining SI and, more broadly, an agricultural transformation in Africa.

The complexity of the challenge lies in designing and implementing a sustainable food system in which high productivity coincides with stability and resilience to withstand climatic and socioeconomic shocks and equitability is high. And such a food system needs to work for smallholder farmers like Amadi and Tilele Elassie and their family.

PRODUCTIVITY

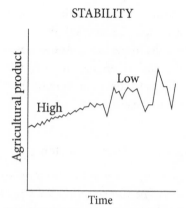

Productivity: The output of
valued product per unit of
resource input.

STABILITY

Stability: The constancy of productivity
in the surrounding environment (usually
measured from a time series by the
coefficient of variation in productivity).

RESILIENCE

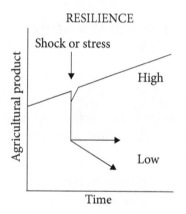

Resilience: The ability of the
agroecosystem to maintain
productivity when subject to a
stress or shock.

EQUITABILITY

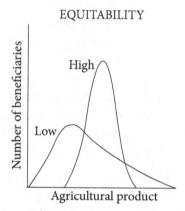

Equitability: The evenness of distribution
of the agroecosystem among the human
beneficiaries, i.e., the level of equity that
is generated (a common measure is a
Lorentz curve).

FIG. 5.3. The dynamics of agroecosystems

Source: Gordon Conway, *The Doubly Green Revolution: Food for All in the Twenty-First Century* (Ithaca: Comstock Publishing Associates, 1998).

TABLE 5.3.   Using agroecosystem characteristics to compare a home garden with a rice field

	HOME GARDEN	RICE FIELD
Productivity	Higher biomass Higher net income Variety of crops and livestock	Higher gross income
Stability	Year-round production High year-to-year stability	Seasonal production; vulnerable to climatic and disease variability
Resilience	Maintains soil fertility Protects from soil erosion	Heavy pest and disease attack
Equitability	In most households harvest may go to landowner Bartering of products	Income goes to others in the value chain

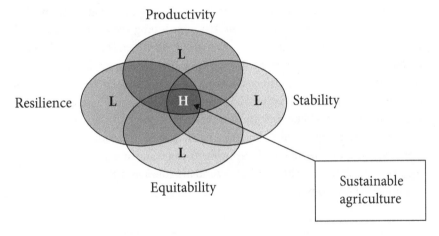

FIG. 5.4.   The trade-offs between the different characteristics of agroecosystems

Source: Gordon Conway, *One Billion Hungry: Can We Feed the World?* (Ithaca: Comstock Publishing Associates, 2012).

Sustainable Intensification

The sustainable intensification of smallholder agriculture is the only way to achieve the goal of increasing farmers' agriculture productivity and improving their resilience against external shocks, while safeguarding the environment.

Food security and malnutrition have been a major concern in Africa since the 1970s. The Green Revolution that occurred in Asia largely bypassed the continent, its millions of smallholder farmers and rural populations. However, after a period of economic stagnation between the 1970s and 2000, many African countries have recently seen rapid economic transformation and growth.[14] As a result, the proportion of the population in SSA below the poverty line declined from 54.7 percent in 1990 to 41 percent in 2015. However, largely due to population growth the absolute number of people living below the poverty line has gone up from 280.2 million in 1990 to 413 million in 2015.[15]

Crop yields have also experienced significant increases in countries such as Ghana, Uganda, and Zambia. And there are signs of similar progress in many other countries across Africa. While this progress achieved over the past decade is remarkable and a reason for optimism, governments and other stakeholders must act to build on current trends of agricultural growth and prosperity to withstand challenges to sustainable food systems. Future demand for food in Africa will have to be met under conditions of decreasing amounts of land area under protection, reduced water availability, and changing climate patterns.[16]

An increase of food production in Africa, including cereals and legumes as well as meat and dairy products, is necessary, but growth must occur on the same amount of land as before or less, using the same amount of water or less. This will require restoration of degraded lands across the continent—currently 26 percent of arable land in Africa is considered "degradation hotspots"[17]—increased supplies of inputs, and a better quality of freshwater resources.[18]

The preferred strategy must therefore be SI, defined as "producing more food from the same area of land while reducing its environmental impact."[19] According to Tara Garnett of Oxford University and her colleagues, there are four premises underlying SI (box 5.2).

Box 5.2. The core premises of SI

a. Achieving sustainable food security is not only about addressing the supply—quantity, access to, and affordability of—food. Rather, it also involves managing demand aspects, including for resource-intensive foods such as meat and dairy products, and reducing food waste. Sustainable food security also requires systems of governance that improve the efficiency and resilience of the food system.

b. In order to avoid the expansion of agricultural land which in turn carries major environmental costs, it is essential that increased production is met through higher yields. Most unused potentially arable land consists of forests, wetlands, and grasslands, whose conversion would greatly increase GHG emissions and contribute to the loss of biodiversity and important ecosystem services.

c. Hence food security is as much about environmental sustainability as it is about increasing productivity. Achieving sustainable food security requires a radical rethink of food production to achieve major reductions in environmental impact.

While SI presents a desirable outcome, the approaches by which it can be achieved—conventional high-tech, agroecological or organic—can vary, each of which must be assessed against its socio-ecological context.

Source: T. Garnett et al., "Sustainable Intensification in Agriculture: Premises and Policies," *Science* 341, no. 6141 (July 5, 2013): 33–34, https://doi.org/10.1126/science.1234485.

There is no silver bullet that will bring about this goal. Approaches need to be chosen and choices made based on local, site-specific economic, social, and biophysical conditions (box 5.3).[20]

Box 5.3. SI is an ambitious but achievable objective

Achieving SI will require a focus on being:

- Prudent in the use of inputs, particularly those which are scarce, expensive, and/or encourage natural resource degradation and environmental problems.
- Efficient in seeking returns and in reducing waste and unnecessary use of scarce inorganic and natural inputs.
- Resilient to future shocks and stresses that may threaten natural and farming systems.
- Equitable in that the inputs and outputs of intensification are accessible and affordable amongst beneficiaries at the household, village, regional, or national level to ensure that the potential to sustainably intensify is an opportunity for all.

Source: Reproduced from Montpellier Panel, "Sustainable Intensification: A New Paradigm for African Agriculture" (London: Agriculture for Impact, 2013), https://www.mamopanel.org/media/uploads/files/SUSTAINABLE_INTENSIFICATION-_A_NEW_PARADIGM_FOR_AFRICAN_AGRICULTURE_2013.pdf.

In simple terms, "*intensification* can be defined as producing more units of output per unit of inputs, and through new combinations of inputs and related innovations. It involves improving physical input–output relations and increasing the overall efficiency of production."[21] Traditionally, intensification was aimed at strengthening productivity levels, increasing yields, and raising incomes per unit of land through greater financial investments, use of inputs like pesticides and fertilizer and more farm labor. However, intensification can take many different forms dependent on climate and land, household resources, individual choice, and market demands. In this way, intensification results in greater amounts of output—of food produced and consumed and the income generated by subsistence farmers themselves or consumers of their agricultural produce. Table 5.4 provides an overview of the definitions and sources of the three outputs of agricultural intensification.

TABLE 5.4.   Definitions of three outputs of agricultural intensification

PRODUCTION	INCOME	NUTRITION
DEFINITION	**DEFINITION**	**DEFINITION**
Total amount or yields of food per unit output	*Amount of net income generated per unit output*	*Human consumption of nutrients per unit input*
Resulting from:	**Resulting from:**	**Resulting from:**
Improved high yielding, drought-, pest-, and disease-tolerant crop varieties or livestock breeds Better crop cultivation or livestock husbandry: · More effective inputs of water, nutrients, or means of control of pests, diseases, and weeds · Exploiting synergies between crops and livestock[1]	Access to fair and efficient output markets Greater market and price information Shifts from low-value to high-value crops or livestock Diversification of income-generating activities, including: · Adjustment of the farm or household enterprise · Exploiting new market opportunities[2] · Increasing nonfarm income	New varieties of staple crops or breeds of livestock with improved nutritive value Diversification of production toward higher overall nutritive value

Sources: Jules Pretty and Zareen Pervez Bharucha, "Sustainable Intensification in Agricultural Systems," *Annals of Botany* 114, no. 8 (December 2014): 1571–96, https://doi.org/10.1093/aob/mcu205; Asian Development Bank et al., "Investment in Agricultural Water for Poverty Reduction and Economic Growth in Sub-Saharan Africa: Synthesis Report" (ADB, FAO, IFAD, IWMI, and World Bank, 2007), http://siteresources.worldbank.org/RPDLPROGRAM/Resources/459596-1170984095733/synthesisreport.pdf.

[1] Jules Pretty and Zareen Pervez Bharucha, "Sustainable Intensification in Agricultural Systems," *Annals of Botany* 114, no. 8 (December 2014): 1571–96, https://doi.org/10.1093/aob/mcu205.

[2] Asian Development Bank et al., "Investment in Agricultural Water for Poverty Reduction and Economic Growth in Sub-Saharan Africa: Synthesis Report" (ADB, FAO, IFAD, IWMI, and World Bank, 2007), http://siteresources.worldbank.org/RPDLPROGRAM/Resources/459596-1170984095733/synthesisreport.pdf.

TABLE 5.5. Direct and indirect inputs to agricultural intensification

Direct inputs: Use of which can directly alter the outputs from the farm	· **Labor**, in either human or mechanized form · **Water**, either through irrigation or rainfall · **Inorganic chemicals and/or organic matter**, such as fertilisers, manure, crop residue, and pesticides · **Biodiversity**, be it a new variety of crop or breed of livestock
Indirect inputs: Use of which are often required to facilitate or modify the use of direct inputs	· **Financial capital**, for investment in inputs and other changes to the farming system · **Knowledge**, of new methods of working and of local solutions · **Infrastructure**, to enable access to input and output markets · **Technology**, which generates and supports new forms and ways of using direct inputs · **Markets**, as an outlet for increased ouputs

Like outputs, the type and amount of inputs used in any intensification process vary according to the type of farming system and the local, site-specific social, economic, and environmental conditions. Table 5.5 highlights some examples of the direct and indirect inputs of agricultural intensification.

One challenge with the term *SI* is that it can be interpreted as code for industrialization. However, intensification can refer to greater and more focused use of ecological processes and practices, greater combinations of genetic traits, or more intense socioeconomic relationships. In certain situations, some of these can be constituents of more industrial agriculture, but to achieve SI all three of these forms of intensification must be brought together to solve particular agricultural problems. This ensures that methods which are ecologically and socially appropriate to the particular environment are used. One of the consequences is the creation of a precise, more sustainable agriculture.

Making Farming Precise

Many farmers in North America and Europe are already striving to ensure their inputs, such as fertilizer and water, are used in a more targeted, efficient way, seeking to maximize returns on the inputs used while preserving the natural resource base. To do so, farmers are increasingly relying on new technologies like satellite imagery, information technology, and geospatial tools. These technologies allow farmers to analyze and plot in detail the nutrient levels in different parts of their fields and then use tractors equipped with satellite positioning systems to apply different fertilizer mixes depending on the soil types and needs in specific locations on their farms.[22] Such precision farming is technologically very advanced and expensive and mostly not appropriate for smallholder farmers in Africa. Yet the same principles apply in both locations.

Universally, "precision agriculture aims to ensure that inputs—whether nutrients, pesticides, seeds, or water—are used in a precise, sparing, effective, and strategic way to ensure that they exert minimal environmental impact."[23] It recognizes the spatial and temporal variability of crop production at field level and accounts for this variability by targeting the application of inputs to optimize and maximize returns.[24] Taking this approach, allows for a reduction in the amount of inputs used to achieve increased production levels. Precision agriculture methods were developed in response to increasing environmental degradation and the rising cost of inputs, which threatens food production around the world.

Fertilizer Use

Smallholder farmers in Africa are eager to use appropriate amounts of fertilizer in a cost-effective manner: fertilizers are increasingly costly, are often inefficiently used, and, when overused, can cause severe environmental damage.

According to the World Bank Fertilizer Index, fertilizer is thought to be responsible for 60 percent of yield increases seen globally in the past fifty years. World fertilizer prices increased steadily starting in 2002 but then peaked following the 2007–8 food price crisis at over five hundred dollars a ton. Since 2011, global fertilizer prices have been steadily falling again. However, the Fertilizer Price Index is expected to rise 2 percent in 2019, due to high energy costs and tight supplies.[25] In 2007, Africa accounted for less than 1 percent of the global fertilizer market, and the cost of fertilizer can vary greatly between and within countries.[26] The cost to move fertilizers from ports to landlocked countries and central areas is high, further limiting access for many African farmers.[27]

As a consequence, fertilizer use in SSA is very low, with farmers using on average just 7kg/ha and accounting for only 3 percent of global fertilizer consumption. Farmers in Asia, in contrast, use about 150kg/ha on average.[28] In June 2006 the African Union Assembly of Heads of State and Government adopted the twelve-resolution declaration at a special summit in Abuja, Nigeria, to increase fertilizer use to 50kg per hectare by 2015.[29] Although 50 kg/ha may be excessive under some circumstances, no region of the world has been able to increase

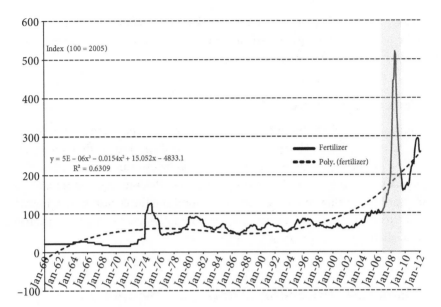

FIG. 5.5. World fertilizer price index

Source: Reproduced with permission from Hervé Ott, "Fertilizer Markets and Their Interplay with Commodity and Food Prices," JRC Scientific and Policy Reports (Seville, Spain: European Commission, Joint Research Centre, Institute for Prospective Technological Studies, 2012), ftp://ftp.jrc.es/pub/EURdoc/JRC73043.pdf.

agricultural growth and sustainably reduce hunger and malnutrition without increasing fertilizer use.

Inevitably, smallholder farmers may be unwilling to purchase fertilizers because they may not be guaranteed a return on their investment or because they have insecure land tenure and rights. Moreover, fertilizer application is often inefficient. Between 1960 and 2000 the efficiency of nitrogen use in global cereal production decreased from 80 to 30 percent.[30] Such low levels of nutrient usage in Africa are causing widespread mining of soil nutrients.

African farmers need to strike a difficult balance between managing soil organic matter, fertility, moisture content and a sustainable use of inorganic fertilizers. Farmers must complement existing, traditional farming methods— manure applications and intercropping with nitrogen-fixing legumes or crop residues—with increased but targeted use of fertilizers to return nutrients to the soil, a form of precision agriculture.

Training in relatively simple forms of digital technology, such as cell phones, will give farmers access to digital services that use satellite imagery, information technology, and geospatial tools. They can use these technologies and services to collect, analyze, and plot data on productivity levels and on environmental and soil quality in distinct parts of their fields and subsequently to apply fertilizer mixes in accordance with soil needs.

Precision Agriculture

Precision agriculture, through the prudent, targeted application of inputs, can contribute to SI by enabling farmers to increase their yields with fewer inputs compared to other application methods, such as broadcasting (scattering over a large area) fertilizers or seed, for example (box 5.4). Precision agriculture can also improve soil quality and moisture while minimizing the environmental impact that excessive input use can have, and can help farmers be more competitive through low production costs.[31]

Box 5.4. Precision farming in Rwanda

Everest and Joyce are a young couple living in Kagabiro village in Rwanda. Their home is perched on a steep hill overlooking Lake Kivu. Like most of their neighbors, they are farmers. They grow maize, beans, coffee, and bananas. A few years ago, they decided to join One Acre Fund (OAF), an agriculture organization that works with smallholder farmers in Rwanda, Burundi, and Kenya. Joyce and Everest wanted access to seed and fertilizer, financing, training, and market facilitation. OAF taught them about appropriate seed spacing for their crops and provided them with a planting kit which cost a little over US50¢. The kits include a fertilizer scoop for microdosing, a planting string, and a top-dressing stick, which farmers are taught to use properly through regular training sessions.

The planting kits have also demonstrated how to improve yields of crops such as maize by as much as 10 percent, equating to a US$30 increase in income.

In the first season using their OAF kit Joyce and Everest planted 2kg of beans, from which they harvested 100kg. This is highly significant in comparison to previous seasons when they had planted 30kg of beans and yielded only 40–50kgs.

Source: Alice Marks, "Ecological Intensification: More Food and a Healthier Environment," *One Billion Hungry: Can We Feed the World?* (blog), August 11, 2015, https://canwefeedtheworld.wordpress.com/2015/08/11/ecological-intensification-more-food-and-a-healthier-environment/.

The Practice of Microdosing

Microdosing is a technology that permits the prudent and targeted use of inputs, such as fertilizers, thus improving soil quality and moisture while minimizing the environmental impact that excessive use can cause. It also reduces costs and helps improve nutrient use efficiency and protection against drought.[32]

In practice, microdosing replaces traditional methods of seed planting, such as broadcasting, with precise seed spacing. It improves germination rates by ensuring that there is better seed-to-soil contact and that seeds are planted at the optimal depth.

Precision agriculture ensures that inputs are highly targeted and kept to a minimum. This curtails their impact on the ecosystem, such as algal blooms resulting from fertilizer overuse, pesticides killing the wrong species, or aggravated water shortages from an overuse of water for irrigation.

Microdosing of Fertilizers

Microdosing of fertilizers improves soil quality and moisture while minimizing the environmental impact that excessive use can cause (box 5.5). It also reduces costs and helps improve nutrient use efficiency and protection against drought.[33]

Box 5.5. Microdosing fertilizers

Placing small doses of fertilizer—about four to six grams for two to four plants—at the roots of a young plant or in the seed planting pit boosts the root system so that it is capable of capturing more water and coping with stresses. Through support from the International Crops Research Institute for the Semi-Arid Tropics (ICRISAT), more than three hundred thousand farmers in Mali, Burkina Faso, and Niger have learned the technique for microdosing. It involves filling a soda bottle cap with fertilizer and applying it directly to the root of the crop. The total amount of fertilizer applied per hectare is far lower than in conventional methods.

A combination of 30 percent to 100 percent higher yields for sorghum and millet, improved seeds, and access to finance, storage systems, and markets has resulted in income growth between 50 and 130 percent. After the rain-fed cropping season, leftover fertilizer can be used for vegetable production, giving farmers a source of additional nutrients and income.

Source: International Crops Research Institute for the Semi-Arid Tropics, "Fertilizer Microdosing: Boosting Production in Unproductive Lands" (Patancheru, India: ICRISAT, January 2009), http://www.icrisat.org/impacts/impact-stories/icrisat-is-fertilizer-microdosing.pdf.

To take another example, conservation farmers in Zambia rely on careful spacing of the planting holes. They use a so-called Teren rope that has bottle tops squeezed at 70cm intervals along the rope. This indicates where the planting holes are to be dug to ensure a maximum yield with minimum fertilizer.[34]

Microdosing Herbicides

Microdosing can also be applied to the use of pesticides, such as herbicides that, far too often, are sprayed indiscriminately, killing not only weeds but also other wild plants and sometimes damaging the crops themselves (box 5.6).

Box 5.6. Herbicide microdosing to control Striga

Striga, otherwise known as witchweed, is a devastating weed that causes yield losses in maize, sorghum, millet, and upland rice in SSA, ranging from 20 to 80 percent and even total crop failure in a severe infestation. Some fifty million hectares are infected with an annual damage in Africa worth US$8 billion, affecting the livelihoods of more than one hundred million people.

The weed is a parasite that siphons off water and nutrients from the crop plants, resulting in the characteristic "witch" appearance: the plants are stunted and withered. Striga seeds remain dormant and viable in the soil for up to twenty years. Striga is killed by herbicides. One such is ima-zapyr (IR), a very effective herbicide produced and marketed by BASF, a chemical company based in Germany. The problem is that it also tends to damage or kill the crop.

Recently BASF used artificial selection to produce an herbicide-resistant, mutant gene in maize by culturing seedlings in an artificial medium containing the herbicide. This has now been bred into local maize hybrids. The seed of one such mutant variety, known as StrigAway, is coated with low doses of the herbicide, giving an application rate of about 30g of IR per hectare—a minuscule amount. As the maize germinates, it absorbs some of the herbicide coating the seed and also stimulates the Striga to germinate. It is then killed as it attaches to the maize root. The maize grows unharmed, and there are minimal impacts on the surrounding environment.

Various seed companies now apply the herbicide to the StrigAway hybrid seed, selling it to farmers in Kenya and Tanzania. One company in Kenya, Freshco, now has an automated treater that can treat ten metric tons a day; they are planning to reach three hundred thousand farmers over the next two years. Smallholder farmers obtain yields about 40 to 80 percent higher than those currently obtained from traditional maize varieties. If 20 percent of severely infested land in western Kenya is cultivated with IR maize, it is possible to produce an extra sixty thousand tons of maize, or enough to feed at least one hundred thousand households.

Grace Lugongo, a farmer from Butula in western Kenya, said, "Until 2007, I had never known the meaning of harvesting a full sack of maize from my 0.5ha piece of land thanks to the 'Striga' weed. All my efforts would yield only 2 *gorogoros* (a tin measuring about 2kg) of maize. I decided to try the IR maize and over the years my yields have increased to 10 bags from the same piece of land. From the harvest I am able to cater for my subsistence needs and also afford some surplus to sell to cater for my other needs such as school fees for my children."

Sources: African Agricultural Technology Foundation, "Frequently Asked Questions on Striga and the IR Maize," Striga Control in Maize, 2012, accessed May 31, 2018, https://striga.aatf-africa.org/about-us/frequently-asked-questions-striga-and-ir-maize; J. Ndwiga et al., "Integrated Striga Management in Africa Project. Constraints and Opportunities of Maize Production in Western Kenya: A Baseline Assessment of Striga Extent, Severity, and Control Technologies," Integrated Striga Management in Africa (International Institute of Tropical Agriculture, 2013), accessed May 31, 2018, https://aatf-africa.org/files/files/publications/Constraints-and-Opportunities-of-Maize-Production.pdf.

Microdosing can be applied to a wide range of inputs. For example, drip irrigation is a method of water microdosing in which a limited amount of water is applied directly to where it is most needed, reducing wastage and evaporation.

The Three Pillars of Sustainable Intensification

Precision farming focuses on just one aspect of SI, namely, the precise and prudent use of inputs. More generally, SI is a concept that includes three mutually reinforcing pillars: ecological intensification, genetic intensification, and socioeconomic intensification (figure 5.6).

SI can derive from sustainably increasing the use of inputs, such as water, introducing a new input to the system, such as a new fertilizer, or using an existing input in a new way. Examples include using an improved rainwater harvesting technique to increase access to water or planting new high-yielding seed varieties. This requires access to technologies and information as well as the skills and knowledge to generate new inputs or novel ways of employing them.

There are two main approaches to achieving SI—one is the application of agricultural ecological processes (ecological intensification), the other is to utilize

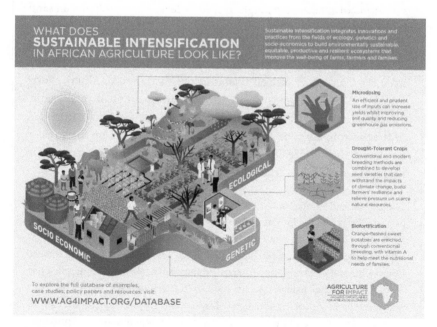

FIG. 5.6. Sustainable intensification of African agriculture

Source: Reproduced with permission from Agriculture for Impact, *What Does Sustainable Intensification in African Agriculture Look Like?*, 2013, https://ag4impact.org/database/.

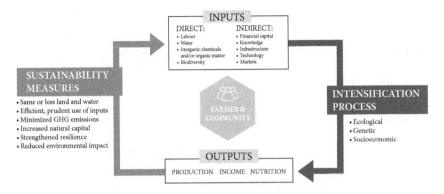

FIG. 5.7. Theoretical model of sustainable intensification

Source: Reproduced with permission from Montpellier Panel, "Sustainable Intensification: A New Paradigm for African Agriculture" (London: Agriculture for Impact, 2013), https://www.mamopanel.org/media/uploads/files/SUSTAINABLE_INTENSIFICATION-_A_NEW_PARADIGM_FOR_AFRICAN_AGRICULTURE_2013.pdf.

modern plant and livestock breeding (genetic intensification). Socioeconomic intensification provides the enabling environment that supports technology adoption and develops markets (figure 5.7).

Sustainable intensification hence integrates innovations and practices from the fields of ecology, genetics, and socioeconomics to build environmentally sustainable, equitable, productive, and resilient ecosystems that improve the well-being of farms, smallholder farmers, and rural communities. It offers a practical pathway toward the goal of producing more food while ensuring the natural resource base on which we depend is sustained, and indeed improved, for future generations.[35]

We need food systems that are fit to withstand the challenges of the twenty-first century, including climate change, urbanization, demographic changes, and a nutrition transition, while allowing the millions of smallholder farmers across Africa and other developing countries to improve their livelihoods. Substantial progress has been made over the years in achieving sustainably intensified agricultural and food systems, and there are many examples we can learn from and that can be brought to scale. Ultimately, it is the interplay and presence of all three aspects of SI that allows food systems and farmers to intensify production in a sustainable way, preserving and at times restoring the natural resource base on which a thriving agriculture sector depends.

AGRICULTURE AND ECOLOGY

Chembo and Ngosa Kumwenda own about three hectares of land in southwest Zambia. Traditionally they have practiced a long fallow system, clearing the bush and sowing several crops of maize before leaving the land to revert to bushland. They were able to harvest less than one ton of maize per hectare. Recently, a local NGO came to their village and encouraged them to practice conservation agriculture. They complied and discovered there were considerable benefits. Their yields went up to an average of 2.8 tons.

They discovered that they needed less labor and less farm power, which lowered their input costs and led to higher profits. Chembo and Ngosa previously received food aid, but via conservation agriculture they had a surplus of grain they could sell. Increased income allowed them to send their children to school, cover medical expenses, and purchase more cattle.[1]

Ecological approaches, among other innovative approaches, practices, and technologies can play a critical role in strengthening sustainable food systems to fight hunger, malnutrition, and poverty in Africa.[2]

Ecology is the study of the processes that influence the distribution, abundance, and interactions of organisms, and ecosystems. Understanding these processes has underpinned agriculture from the very early beginnings of domestication and cultivation.

Our food comes for the most part from managed agroecosystems—modified natural ecosystems created by farmers, as well as from marine and freshwater systems and forests (see figure 5.2). Within each agroecosystem the diversity of the original field biodiversity is reduced to a set of crops, livestock, pests, and weed species. However, as many of the basic ecological processes remain the same, ecological intensification seeks to create and support sustainable forms of crop and livestock production.[3]

The aim is to use land, water, and nutrients more ecologically efficiently and in ways that minimize any negative environmental impacts. The ecological principles and practices that can be used to sustainably intensify the agroecological system include the processes of competition and mutualism between crops and weeds, and the decay of organic matter.

A shorthand for this approach is *agroecology*, which is defined by Miguel Altieri of the University of California in Berkeley as a management system that can be "tailored and adapted in a site-specific way to highly variable and diverse farm conditions typical of resource-poor farmers ... using ... elements of a research agenda in natural resource management that is compatible with the needs and aspirations of peasants."[4]

Much that we describe below fits within this overall definition. However, we are aware that for some development workers agroecology goes beyond a scientific disciple to "embrace a sustainable development strategy which emphasizes food sovereignty, conservation of natural resources and agrobiodiversity and empowers rural social movements."[5] In this sense it is part of a wider advocacy strategy with a strong political agenda. The common thread, however, is a desire to achieve sustainable agricultural development, as we discussed in chapter 5.

Here, we describe sustainable ecological intensification as including the building of natural capital, conservation agriculture, the contribution of livestock, water harvesting, diversification, and organic farming.

Building Natural Capital

Natural capital is defined as the biophysical assets within the natural environment that deliver economic value through ecosystem services and upon which we rely for our survival and well-being.[6] Soil, air, water, and living organisms provide a range of ecosystem goods and services, such as the food we eat and the plant materials we use for fuel, building materials, and medicines. Other less visible ecosystem services include, for example, climate regulation and natural flood defenses provided by forests; carbon stored in soil and peatlands; and the pollination of crops by insects. According to estimates by the Millennium Ecosystem Assessment (MA), in 2005, two-thirds of ecosystem services globally have degraded or are in decline owing to the unprecedented scale of human activities in recent decades.[7]

Energy- and resource-intensive or unsustainable farming systems and activities deplete natural capital through land degradation, pollution and depletion of water resources, a reduction in species and genetic diversity, and an increase in global GHGs, the effects of which disproportionately affect poor people in developing countries.[8] Poor communities, including smallholder farmers and rural communities, are often particularly dependent on ecosystem goods and services and unable to employ substitutes when they are depleted or lost, for example, the use of irrigation when rains fail or the use of fertilizer when soils lose fertility.[9] Rural and isolated communities also often do not have sufficient financial resources or technical capacities to manage the risks associated with climate change and loss of natural capital.[10]

The loss of natural capital can and must be prevented by using resources more efficiently. Conservation agriculture (CA) and organic agriculture are two farming systems that aim to holistically conserve and utilize natural capital to improve the quality and quantity of food production. Water conservation on farms, through a variety of techniques like drip irrigation, can also be part of broader ecological farming methods or used to reduce water loss through a more efficient use.

Conserving and Enhancing Soils

Fundamental to building natural capital is the conservation and enhancement of soil quality, one of the components of ISM. The quality is not only about nutrients but also about soil structure. Organic matter and inorganic fertilizers can be combined to improve the quality of the humus and its soil organic carbon (SOC).

Improving soil quality is fundamentally an ecological process that helps build the soil humus. This increases the storage of water and nutrients available to the plant, the activity and diversity of soil biota, soil structure and tilth, its resistance to erosion, and resilience against climatic variations and changes. The quality and amount of humus and its SOC is thus a key determinant of soil quality and crop productivity (box 6.1). A high SOC makes nitrogen more readily available to plants on a sustainable basis. Thus restoring the concentration of SOC is critical for plant health and productivity and is therefore essential to addressing global food security and nutrition.

Soil organic matter (SOM) provides nutrients for the crop and is a crucial element for the stabilization of soil structure. Prolonged intensive agriculture can lead to soil erosion and a decrease in productivity levels. While the process is particularly dramatic in tropical climates it is visible across the world.

Box 6.1. The importance of soil organic carbon (SOC)

When the concentration of SOC falls below a certain threshold, key soil properties are adversely affected, inhibiting plant growth. While the threshold level varies among soil types, climate, and land use, in general it is 1.1 to 1.5 percent for soils in the tropics. For some severely eroded and degraded soils in SSA, the SOC concentration is just 0.5 percent or even as low as 0.05 percent . . . .

Increasing the amount of humus and SOC in the soil requires adding nitrogen (N) and other plant nutrients, such as phosphate (P) and sulfur (S) in order for the transformation of biomass carbon into SOC to occur. To increase the SOC pool by one ton per hectare requires 75–80kg of N, 15–20kg of P, and 12–15kg of S, in addition to the amounts directly required for growth of the crop. The nutrients may come from inorganic fertilizer, manure, or legumes. If they are not present or supplied, accumulation of humus will not occur even with general application of crop residues. . . .

Restoring the concentration of SOC to above the threshold level is therefore essential to addressing global food and nutritional security.

Source: Reproduced from Montpellier Panel, "No Ordinary Matter: Conserving, Restoring and Enhancing Africa's Soils" (London: Agriculture for Impact, 2014), https://www.mamopanel.org/media/uploads/files/NO_ORDINARY_MATTER-_CONSERVING_RESTORING_AND_ENHANCING_AFRICAS_SOILS_2014.pdf.

Conservation Agriculture

CA is an integrated approach of soil, water, and biological resource management combined with external inputs with the objective of improving agricultural production through the adoption of economically, ecologically, and socially sustainable farming methods.

CA involves abandoning plowing and soil tillage in order to improve soil quality, build up nutrients, and water. Shirley Phillips of the University of Kentucky defines no-till agriculture as "the introduction of seed into unploughed soil in narrow slots, trenches or bands of sufficient width and depth for seed coverage and soil contact."[11] Particularly in temperate climates, farmers commonly till the soil before sowing seeds to loosen and aerate the soil and to destroy any weeds. Tillage helps to break up heavy clay soils, but for many soils prone to erosion or drought, common in Africa, tilling can contrarily harm soil structure and increase water and carbon loss.[12] Although soil tillage has been associated with increased fertility—originating from the mineralization of soil nutrients as a consequence of soil tillage—it has been found that in the long term it can lead to a reduction of SOM.

No-till farming reportedly helps to conserve and enhance the quality of the soil, leading to higher yields and the protection of the local environment and ecosystem services.[13] However, on its own, no-till results in a yield penalty of 10 percent overall, particularly for cereal crops, while other crops, such as oil seeds, cotton, and legumes, showed no advantage.[14] Only when combined with techniques like mulching and rotations can significant benefits of no-till be seen.

CA is a combination of techniques characterized by three linked principles (box 6.2).[15]

Box 6.2. The three principles of conservation agriculture (CA)

Zero/minimal till: Minimal soil disturbance requires that seeds are planted directly into the soil either using hoes, ox-drawn or tractor-drawn drills. The disturbed area must be less than 15 cm wide or 25 percent of the cropped area, whichever is lower.

Mulch cover: Crop residues or cover crops are left on fields to provide permanent organic soil cover. Three categories are distinguished: 30 to 60 percent, 61 to 90 percent, and 91 percent ground cover, measured immediately after the planting operation. Ground cover of less than 30 percent does not qualify as CA.

Crop rotation: Different crops have varying root structures which reach a different depths. By rotating crops of different root depths, organic matter is placed in different soil strata, thereby making the soil more fertile. To make crop rotation even more effective, planting nitrogen-fixing legumes can help the crops that follow. These are crops that allow the conversion of atmospheric nitrogen into growth-stimulating nitrogen compounds in the soil.

Source: Agriculture for Impact, "Conservation Agriculture," Sustainable Intensification Database, 2019, accessed April 26, 2019, https://ag4impact.org/sid/ecological-intensification/building-natural-capital/conservation-agriculture/.

A team at the University of Reading calculated the global spread of CA.[16] They used three practical criteria derived from the principles enumerated in box 6.2:

1. Continuous zero or minimum mechanical soil disturbance: no periodic tillage that disturbs an area less than 15cm wide or less than 25 percent of the cropped area, whichever is lower.
2. Permanent soil mulch cover with biomass: using crop residues, stubbles, and cover crops. Areas with less than 30 percent cover are not considered as CA.
3. Crop diversification through rotations/sequences/association: should ideally involve at least three different crops.

Applying these criteria in seventeen African countries in 2015–16, showed more than 1.5 million ha were under CA, including two million small-scale farmers across the continent, and a 211 percent increase since 2008–9.[17]

Innovative participatory approaches are being used to develop supply chains enabling smallholders to access CA equipment and to explain the ecological principles underlying CA and to make it attractive for use in local farming.

Probably the biggest challenge facing CA in Africa is the burden of weeds. Herbicides may work providing they do not damage the crop, but they do; hand weeding is very laborious but intercropping as described below can reduce weed infestation. Moreover, in many instances the benefits are not immediately obvious.

Conserving Water

Conserving water is just as important as conserving soil. In many countries across Africa water is abundant, yet it is badly managed, resulting in waterlogging, salinization, non-sustainable drawdown of aquifers and pollution. In some parts of the continent there is also plenty of potential to increase the amount of irrigation up from the current 4 percent of total arable land that is irrigated. However, this has to be done in such a way that non-renewable water resources are not depleted. In some other parts of SSA water is very scarce. Some two hundred million people in SSA face serious water shortages.[18] These shortages are particularly acute in North Africa (figure 6.1).

The challenge is to design and implement affordable, efficient small-scale water harvesting systems that allow farmers to collect rainwater for later use as it runs off the land or to develop locally appropriate irrigation technologies and systems that do not deplete groundwater resources.

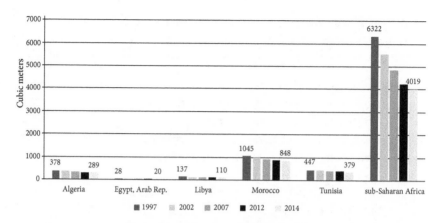

FIG. 6.1.   Renewable internal freshwater resources per capita per year (in m³)

Source: World Bank, *World Development Indicators* (Washington, DC: World Bank, 2012), http://data.worldbank.org/data-catalog/world-development-indicators.

Even in very dry conditions there is usually some water available; the challenge is to harvest this in an affordable and efficient manner. Water harvesting from short slopes is relatively straightforward and cheap and can be highly efficient because of the distances involved. An example is the *zaï* (water pockets) technique pioneered by farmers in northwest Burkina Faso decades ago as a way to create more arable land. It has now spread throughout similar climates in the Sahel, including the rest of Burkina Faso, in Mali, and Niger (box 6.3).[19]

Box 6.3. The *zaï* system

This technique, known as *zaï* in the local language of northern Burkina Faso, originated in Mali among farmers in the Djenné Circle. It was adopted and improved in northern Burkina Faso by farmers after the drought of the 1980s, when many farmers left the region.

Farmers apply the zaï technique to restore crusted, almost impermeable land. A zaï is a circular planting pit, approximately 20 to 40 cm wide and 10 to 20 cm deep, varying according to the type of soil. Between twelve thousand and twenty-five thousand pits per hectare are dug during the dry season from November to May. After the first rainfall, about 0.6kg/ha of organic matter is added to the pits and covered with a thin layer of soil.

Seeds, typically millet or sorghum, are placed in the middle of the pit. The excavated earth is ridged around the pit to improve its water-retention capacity. The zaï system

1. Captures rain and surface/runoff water.
2. Protects seeds and organic matter from being washed away.
3. Concentrates nutrient and water availability at the beginning of the rainy season.

These factors work in tandem to increase yields. In Burkina Faso grain yield has increased by 120 percent, equivalent to around eighty thousand tons of extra grain per year. At the same time, soil structure is improved, and there may also be a reduction in CO_2 emissions.

Sources: World Bank, "Burkina Faso: The Zaï Technique and Enhanced Agricultural Productivity," May 2005, https://openknowledge.worldbank.org/handle/10986/10754; Hamado Sawadogo, "Using Soil and Water Conservation Techniques to Rehabilitate Degraded Lands in Northwestern Burkina Faso," *International Journal of Agricultural Sustainability* 9, no. 1 (February 1, 2011): 120–28, https://doi.org/10.3763/ijas.2010.0552.

Water harvesting from long slopes requires semi-permeable stone bunds along the contours, which will slow water runoff and encourage infiltration. In the desert margins of North Africa such harvesting targets the periodic flash floods through systems of barriers across the wadi floors. Under the Nabataeans and Romans, the combination of engineering and local knowledge produced elaborate systems of water harvesting, producing large quantities of wheat and olives in areas that today are largely desert.[20] A modern equivalent in the Central Plateau of Burkina Faso consists of low, semi-permeable dams that concentrate and redirect water flows. Natural terraces are formed as the sediment is deposited, on which yields of sorghum increase two- to threefold.[21]

The Contribution of Livestock

In the twentieth century, alongside the Green Revolution but less well understood and celebrated, there was revolutionary growth in livestock production, distinguished by the great diversity of products it embraced: meat, milk, cheese, eggs, skins, wool, fur, and oil from, variously, cattle, sheep, goats, pigs, poultry, and other, more exotic creatures.[22] There are actually nearly four thousand species of domesticated animals, but only twelve dominate global livestock production. In Africa livestock owners rely on cattle, sheep, goats, donkeys, and camels. Most of these are ruminants: they possess a rumen in front of the stomach that provides a slow, pre-gastric fermentation of plant fiber by bacteria, protozoa, and fungi. As a result, ruminants can live on fibrous, low-protein feeds. Another advantage is that the microbes in the rumen can detoxify plant toxins.

A team at IFPRI documented the dramatic growth in livestock husbandry that occurred in the second half of the twentieth century, coining the phrase *Livestock Revolution* to highlight its importance.[23] Today, livestock systems occupy about 30 percent of the planet's ice-free terrestrial surface area and directly support the livelihoods of six hundred million smallholder farmers in developing countries.[24] Keeping livestock, if managed carefully, can contribute to soil and water conservation and can also be an important risk-reduction strategy. The popularity of livestock production and consumption is not difficult to comprehend. A list of its many benefits makes the point (box 6.4).

Box 6.4. The benefits of livestock production and consumption

- Contribute 40 percent of the global value of agricultural output.
- Support the livelihoods and food security of almost a billion people.
- Provide food and increase incomes.
- Contribute 15 percent total food energy and 25 percent dietary protein globally.
- Provide essential micronutrients (e.g., iron, calcium) that are more readily available in meat, milk, and eggs than in plant-based foods.
- Are a valuable asset, serving as a store of wealth, collateral for credit, and an essential safety net during times of crisis.
- Are central to mixed farming systems: consume agricultural waste products, help control insects and weeds, produce manure and waste for cooking, and provide draft power for plowing and transport.
- Provide employment, in some cases especially for women.
- Have cultural significance.

Source: "Livestock in the Balance," *The State of Food and Agriculture* (Rome: FAO, 2009).

Inevitably, alongside the benefits some of the consequences have been negative or threaten to be so. Free-range animals, especially cattle and goats, can have serious effects on ecosystems—on vegetation, soils, and water and on biodiversity—if not managed well. In addition to suffering from climate change, livestock are also direct and indirect producers of GHGs.

The range and diversity of livestock systems include grazing systems, mixed systems, and industrial livestock systems.

Grazing Systems

Grazing systems occupy some 26 percent of the earth's ice-free land surface.[25] The most extensive forms exist in the dry areas of the world that are marginal for crop production. They typically support ruminants grazing mainly grasses and other herbaceous plants, often on communal or open-access rangelands. Both animals and humans often move considerable distances across the grazing lands, and the owners may be nomadic.

Much of the grazed rangeland is, depending on the purpose to which it is put, degraded. For many years this was attributed to overgrazing, but recent ecological research suggests the concepts of overgrazing and degradation have been seriously oversimplified. At the heart of the problem has been the misapplication of management theories developed to maximize beef production on temperate grasslands in developed countries. In developing countries overgrazing is relative to the aims of the farmer, as is degradation. Stable conditions are rare and carrying capacities difficult, if not impossible, to estimate. Pastoral livestock populations thus tend to go through periodic cycles of boom and bust.[26] The large number of people involved in pastoralism, the diversity of products being sought, and the great unpredictability of climatic conditions dictate an approach that is flexible and opportunistic (box 6.5).

Box 6.5. Maasai pastoralism in Kenya

The Maasai are one of the best-known nomadic herders, but in recent years many have become sedentary pastoralists, partly because of the lack of protection the government has afforded their lifestyle. This has also caused declines in natural resources and wildlife. For example, the fencing of habitat for agriculture prohibits the migration of wild animals such as wildebeest and increases illegal poaching and retaliatory killings in defense of agricultural holdings and livestock.

In a study of the Kitengela plains a team from the International Livestock Research Institute (ILRI) found coexistence between wild animals and livestock to be possible and even beneficial for the wildlife, given their preferences for feeding on nutritious, short grass found in and near pastoral lands. Maps produced with the aid of Geographic Information Systems (GIS) helped community monitoring of animal distributions and were used to determine payments to farmers for leaving land unfenced, thus protecting corridors for animal migration. ILRI subsequently developed a conservancy model that enabled Maasai landowners working with tourism companies to manage settlements and livestock and to implement payment for ecosystem services. Three conservancies now manage around 350 km² of land, generating an income of US$3 million per year for around one thousand local households.

Sources: Ian Scoones, "New Challenges for Range Management in the 21st Century," *Outlook on Agriculture* 25, no. 4 (December 1996): 253–56, https://doi.org/10.1177/003072709602500407; R. H. Behnke and Ian Scoones, "Rethinking Range Ecology: Implications for Rangeland Management in Africa" (Commonwealth Secretariat Technical Meeting on Savanna Development and Pasture Production, Woburn, UK: IIED, ODI, 1992), http://pubs.iied.org/pdfs/7282IIED.pdf; Camilla Toulmin, "Tracking through Drought: Options for Destocking and Restocking," in *Living with Uncertainty: New Directions in Pastoral Development in Africa*, ed. Ian Scoones (Rugby, Warwickshire, UK: Practical Action Publishing, 1995), https://doi.org/10.3362/9781780445335; Ian Scoones, "Wetlands in Drylands: Key Resources for Agricultural and Pastoral Production in Africa," *Ambio* 20, no. 8 (1991): 366–71, http://www.jstor.org/stable/4313867.

In their review of rangeland management in Africa researchers at the International Institute for Environment (IIED) argue for explicit recognition of the inherent instability of pastoral systems and for encouraging governments to support supplementary feeding during severe droughts through the provision of feed and the establishment of feeding pens. They also recommend rapid destocking and restocking at the beginning and end of drought years through livestock markets designed for this purpose.[27]

Mixed Systems

The other major livestock system in the developing countries is the mixed system, in which cropping and livestock rearing are carried out on the same holding with some degree of integration. FAO defines these systems as occurring where either more than 10 percent of the dry matter fed to animals comes from crop by-products or stubble or more than 10 percent of the total value of production comes from non-livestock farming activities.[28] There is a great diversity of such systems, and in practice there are no hard-and-fast distinctions between mixed systems and grazing or industrial systems.

However, a fundamental principle of mixed systems is the mutual utilization of waste—crop waste to feed animals and livestock waste to provide nutrients for crops—but there are many other cross-benefits. They may vary from providing a continuity of labor demand to grazing vegetation under trees. For example, grazing with cattle and goats under oil palm can produce better oil palm harvests, and it saves on the costs of weed control as well as increasing sources of income.[29]

There has been a progressive evolution from grazing toward mixed farming systems. It is driven partly by population pressure and partly by changing markets. Arable farmers need to increase production; the presence of animals on a farm can provide wastes for fertilization and a useful form of traction, allowing for cultivation of more land. Crop residues are increasingly collected from the arable fields and transported to the homestead to feed animals that are kept in kraals or stables. Eventually, farms adopt zero grazing, with animals being fed on residues or grain, either grown on the farm or purchased. At the same time, pastoralists left with less and less land for grazing (and often it is of poor quality) migrate to the cities or adopt arable farming.[30]

Cattle and buffaloes are not the only producers of milk. Goats also produce milk, and it is highly nutritious, having a composition similar to human milk, which makes it easily digestible by infants.[31] It is an excellent source of calcium, phosphorus, and vitamin A. Goats are also efficient producers of milk in conditions where cattle do not thrive. They are "often raised at the margins of communities; goats are well adapted to the harsh conditions and poor quality feed found at the interface between deserts, mountains and cultivable land, and on 'waste' land within cropped areas where poor and landless people are also found."[32] The downside is their capacity to inflict severe environmental degradation through overgrazing, and it is partly for this reason that attempts are made to bring them into mixed farming systems with low or zero grazing. Since mixed farming systems require relatively little investment, it should be within the reach of poor farmers (box 6.6).

Industrial Livestock Systems

Just as there has been an evolutionary trend from grazing systems to mixed systems, there has been a similar trend, and for similar reasons, from mixed to

Box 6.6. Dairy goats in Ethiopia

Ethiopia is not self-sufficient in animal products and is a net importer of food. Only 7 percent of food energy is derived from animal source foods, and daily per capita protein and fat consumption is 7g and 8g, respectively, far below the recommended levels. Annual per capita milk consumption fell from about twenty liters in 1993–94 to sixteen liters in 2003, while annual meat consumption is as low as eleven to twelve kilograms per person.

The Dairy Goat Development Project was initiated in Ethiopia with the help of an international NGO, FARM-Africa, to increase both incomes and milk consumption. The focus was on women because they are the traditional keepers of goats. They were encouraged to grow fodder and were trained in goat management. The poorest women identified by the community were each given two female goats on credit, to be repaid by returning a weaned kid to the project that was to be loaned to another woman. As the project progressed, the women organized themselves into groups to handle a credit disbursement and repayment scheme. They also established joint saving schemes, which enabled them to gain access to a source of finance. Over time and with further extension support and animal health training the group members were able to use imported goat varieties to improve their existing stocks.

In eastern Hararghe, in the southern province of Oromia, 20 percent of households had no access to milk, and nearly 60 percent of households consumed no meat at the beginning of the project. Many of the households gave infants and young children water mixed with sugar and fenugreek juice as a substitute for milk. These children exhibited signs of ill health, including chronic diarrhea, itching, and skin infections.

Three years later there were clear improvements, the benefits reaching over five thousand households. The women proved to be adept at managing crossbred goats, and milk yields increased from two hundred milliliters per day to over two liters, while lactation length increased from two to three months to over twelve months in some cases. Each participating household was milking its lactating goats twice a day and providing an average of seventy-five liters of milk a year. Per capita milk consumption averaged fifteen liters a year. Goats could be sold during periods of drought, reducing communities' dependence on aid.

As Ayele and Peacock comment, "Each of the households has managed to generate steady annual income from goat sales. Through this, they have since acquired diversified assets such as cows, oxen and donkeys, have been able to start up small businesses of their own, or have invested in improved agricultural technologies, such as inorganic fertilizers, improved poultry stocks and select grain seed. Such initiatives have raised crop and animal production and enabled the households to send their children to schools as well as improve their welfare."

Sources: Zewdu Ayele and Christie Peacock, "Improving Access to and Consumption of Animal Source Foods in Rural Households: The Experiences of a Women-Focused Goat Development Program in the Highlands of Ethiopia," *Journal of Nutrition* 133, no. 11 (November 1, 2003): 3981S-3986S, https://doi.org/10.1093/jn/133.11.3981S; "The Goat Model: A Proven Approach to Reducing Poverty among Smallholder Farmers in Africa by Developing Profitable Goat Enterprises and Sustainable Support Services," Working Paper, Farm-Africa (London: FARM-Africa, 2007), https://www.farmafrica.org/downloads/resources/WP9%20The%20Goat%20Model.pdf.

industrial livestock systems. Operations have become progressively larger and more intensive, benefiting from technical advances and economies of scale.[33] There has been a strong tendency toward vertical integration, in which all parts of the supply chain are united in a common enterprise. Such integration is pronounced in poultry production. Although typical of industrial countries, such systems are becoming common in developing countries, especially in the emerging economies.

The rising demand for livestock products is increasingly being met by large-scale, intensive, technologically sophisticated producers. However, there are a number of severe downsides to this enterprise.[34] On the one hand, high-density animal production operations can

- Increase livestock disease incidence, the emergence of new, often antibiotic-resistant diseases leading to catastrophic losses.
- Increase air, groundwater, and surface water pollution associated with animal waste.
- Require feeding with subtherapeutic doses of the same antibiotics used in human medicines. These prophylactic treatments cause agriculture to use, in total, a larger proportion of global antibiotic production than human medicine.[35]

On the other hand, animal waste could be treated by composting to create a crop fertilizer that no longer harbors pathogens, via methods that minimize nutrient leaching. This closing of the nutrient cycle decreases dependence on synthetic fertilizer production and is more efficient when animal and crop production are combined locally.[36] Both pastoral and mixed grazing systems, based on ecological processes and built on diversity, are, in many respects, preferable.

Diversification

Diversity is generally considered to be a key factor in maintaining stable, resilient agroecosystems.[37] It measures the number and relative abundance of flora, fauna and microorganisms relative to other species in a defined location. Conventional agricultural systems are typically simplified from natural ecosystems to maximize the production of a certain number of crops or livestock. However, such simplification can make the system more vulnerable to external shocks and stresses. Across the world, this has led to a significant loss of genetic diversity of domesticated plants and animals.

Crop diversity in the world's food-producing systems has largely been underutilized. FAO estimates that of the 4 percent of the 250,000 to 300,000 known edible plant species, only 150 to 200 are used by humans. Only three—rice, maize, and wheat—contribute nearly 60 percent of calories and proteins obtained by humans from plants.[38] More than 90 percent of crop varieties have disappeared from farmers' fields; half of the breeds of many domestic animals have been lost. Where fisheries are concerned, all the world's seventeen main fishing grounds are now being fished at or above their sustainable limits, and many fish populations are effectively becoming extinct.[39] The intensification of agricultural production has led to a notable loss of genetic diversity of domesticated plants and animals, a diversity believed to be crucial to future food production and security particularly in the face of climatic shocks and stresses.

Diverse agroecosystems can have multiple benefits. Mixtures of crops can supply a diverse and healthier diet, deter pests, and, during times of crises like droughts or cyclones, provide a form of insurance when at least one crop survives. Diversified farming systems (DFS) intentionally include functional biodiversity to maintain ecosystem services such as soil fertility, pest and disease control, water use efficiency, and pollination.[40]

Monocultures may produce greater yields by selecting varieties based on their ability to grow well under specific weather and environmental conditions. However, this can result in crops that are unable to withstand changes to their environment. Monocultures are also more vulnerable to diseases and insects, and the effect is even greater if the crops are genetically uniform and concentrated in one area. Without genetic diversity, there is a lower likelihood that crops are resistant to pathogens or tolerant of fluctuating conditions in the population. Such crops also rely on a host of other species, such as insects, birds, and bacteria, for their survival.

Within agroecosystems different species can benefit each other. Trees and shrubs provide shade for herbs, legumes provide nitrogen essential for plant growth, and livestock provide much-needed manure.[41]

However, merely increasing the number of crops and livestock on a farm will not necessarily create the ecological heterogeneity and biotic interactions to support the full suite of ecosystem services needed for productive agriculture.[42] Studies have found that it is not the sheer number of species present that affects diversity, stability, and resilience but their nature, function in the systems, and the relationships they have with one another.[43] Diversification can be achieved with various forms of intercropping.

Intercropping

A form of ecological intensification that is potentially highly sustainable is the utilization of the mutually beneficial ecological relationships that arise when two or more crops are grown in association, either as mixtures or rotations. There are numerous examples of such intercropping across Africa (box 6.7).

Box 6.7. Types of intercropping systems

Mixed cropping: interspersion of different crops on the same piece of land, either at random or more commonly in alternate rows usually designed to minimize competition but maximize the potential for both crops to make use of the available nutrients, such as N, supplied by a legume.

Rotations: the growing of two or more crops in sequence on the same piece of land.

Agroforestry: a form of intercropping in which annual herbaceous crops are grown interspersed with perennial trees or shrubs. The deeper-rooted trees can often exploit water and nutrients not available to the crops. The trees may also provide shade and mulch, creating a microenvironment, while the ground cover of crops reduces weeds and prevents erosion.

Sylvo-pasture: similar to agroforestry, but combining trees with grassland and other fodder species on which livestock graze. The mixture of shrubs, grass and crops often supports mixed livestock.

Green manuring: the growing of legumes and other plants to fix N and then incorporating them in the soil for the following crop. Commonly used green manures are *Sesbania* and the fern *Azolla*, which contains N-fixing, blue-green algae.

Source: Reproduced from Montpellier Panel, "Sustainable Intensification: A New Paradigm for African Agriculture" (London: Agriculture for Impact, 2013), https://www.mamopanel.org/media/uploads/files/SUSTAINABLE_INTENSIFICATION-_A_NEW_PARADIGM_FOR_AFRICAN_AGRICULTURE_2013.pdf.

Intercropping balances two key ecological processes: competition, on the one hand, and commensalism (one plant gaining benefits from the other) or mutualism (both plants benefiting each other) on the other. Typically, crops will

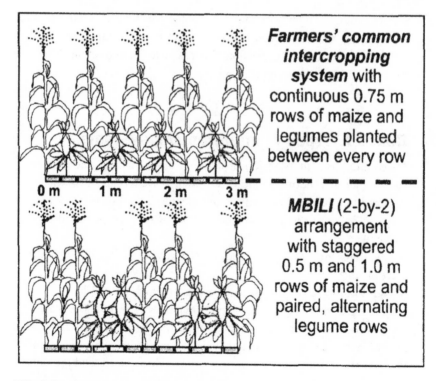

FIG. 6.2. Conventional (upper) and MBILI (lower) maize–legume cropping systems

Source: Reproduced with permission from P. L. Woomer, M. Lan'gat, and J. O. Tungani, "Innovative Maize–Legume Intercropping Results in above-and below-Ground Competitive Advantages for Understorey Legumes," *West African Journal of Applied Ecology* 6, no. 1 (January 1, 2004), https://doi.org/10.4314/wajae.v6i1.45609.

be planted as close together as possible to maximize all available land, but not so close that yields are impacted by competition. When different crop species or varieties are grown together, the competition may be fierce; trees grown in a maize field, for example, may shade out the crop. This can be compensated for: the tree may be a legume and supply nitrogen for the crop plant beneath, an example of a commensal relationship. When two or more crops are grown together, either as mixtures or rotations, nutrients mined by one crop can be replaced by another. This is especially true when one is a nitrogen-fixing legume, such as beans, peas, clover, alfalfa, or groundnuts.[44] (box 6.8; figure 6.2).

Box 6.8. The MBILI system

Farmers in Kenya, employing intercropping, have planted maize together with beans for many years. This system allows them to produce crops for both household food supply and, during better years, for sale. But the yields of maize and beans on most farms have declined due to nutrient depletion and pest and disease accumulation resulting from continuous maize–bean intercropping. Even during the best years it has been difficult to show a profit because the price of maize and beans became too low to offset the cost of inputs. Simple rotation of beans with other legumes reduces pest and disease and improves soil fertility, but the maize canopy, especially for large-statured, long-maturing varieties, does not allow sufficient light for intercropping with groundnut, green gram, or soy bean. Nonetheless, farmers remain committed to maize–bean intercropping because it meets their needs, if not their expectations.

The Sustainable Agriculture Centre for Research and Development Africa has worked closely with farmers to develop an innovative intercropping system that is designed to fulfill farmers' expectations of greater yields and rising market value. Simply by reorganizing the arrangement of the rows of maize and intercropping with different legume crops brought surprising benefits to farmers. The key was to stagger the rows of maize while maintaining the same crop population, allowing for greater light penetration to the understory legume.

MBILI stands for managing beneficial interactions in legume intercrops. It also represents a Swahili word for the number two that describes the intercropping system to a farmer: "Mbili because the maize and legume intercrops occur in two-by-two staggered rows! Mbili because the legume is now an equal partner with maize in terms of its yield potential and value! Mbili because farmers and researchers have found new ways to work together!"

Growing different legumes in intercrop rotation allows access to more and better markets and healthier crops through the disruption of pests and disease cycles. On-farm research demonstrated that the crop value of conventional maize–bean intercropping worth about US$325 could be almost doubled to approximately US$637 by adopting MBILI with groundnuts.

Sources: Kelah Kaimenyi, "Farmers at Center of Sustainable Agriculture in Kenya," International Maize and Wheat Improvement Center (CIMMYT), June 30, 2017, https://www.cimmyt.org/farmers-at-center-of-sustainable-agriculture-in-kenya/; P.L. Woomer, M. Lan'gat, and J. O. Tungani, "Innovative Maize–Legume Intercropping Results in above-and below-Ground Competitive Advantages for Understorey Legumes," *West African Journal of Applied Ecology* 6, no. 1 (January 1, 2004), https://doi.org/10.4314/wajae.v6i1.45609.

Annual herbaceous crops that discard their leaves and stems at the end of the growing season can be interspersed with perennial trees or shrubs to return nutrients to the soil. The trees may also provide shade and mulch, creating a microenvironment while the ground cover of crops reduces weeds and prevents erosion.

An example of a tree-based intercropping system uses the leguminous tree Faidherbia.[45] Faidherbia sheds its leaves in the wet season, thereby supplying nutrients to the soil and allowing for light to pass through. Consequently, it is possible to plant and grow maize under the trees, creating systems of agroforestry. Depending on the nitrogen fixed by the trees, yields can be over three tons per hectare even without fertilizers. The trees also contribute two tons or more per hectare of carbon to the soil, while mature trees can store over thirty tons of carbon per hectare.

Home Gardens

A good example of intensive intercropped cultivation is the home garden, the small area around a dwelling where a farmer, often a woman, cultivates a great diversity of plants and often keeps some small livestock. Such gardens are well known in Indonesia, where they are most developed on the island of Java.[46]

They contain an extraordinary diversity of plants arranged in layers, herbs at the base, fruit-bearing shrubs in the middle layers, and, emerging above, bananas and coconut trees.

Africa has a less rich variety of home gardens, but in several countries they play an important role in smallholder agriculture. One form of garden flourishes among the Tswana people of South Africa's North West Province, where the rainfall is only 300–700mm (rainfall in Java is about 1,750mm). Yet in this region over five hundred useful plants were recorded in home gardens, and, on average, forty species per garden in deep rural areas (figure 6.3).

The diversity of plants and their species is remarkable. Twelve percent of the species were for medicinal purposes, 21 percent were for food, and 46 percent were ornamental. Seventy species of food crop were recorded, including twenty-four vegetables, twenty-eight leafy vegetables, four tubers, three fodders, and eleven grains. Twenty to 30 percent of these species and most of the medicinal plants are indigenous.

Nutrition

According to the FAO, a well-developed home garden can supply a family with essential micronutrients: roots and tubers rich in energy and legumes, which are important sources of protein, fat, iron, and vitamins.[47] While, green, leafy vegetables and yellow- or orange-colored fruits provide minerals, particularly folate, and essential vitamins like A, E, and C. In the South African *Zulu Muzi* garden (home garden) there are mangoes, papaya, guava, avocado, cucurbits, and sweet potatoes as well as many indigenous fruits that may contain key minerals. Given these benefits, there is a strong case to be made for encouraging more investment in home gardens.

In many circumstances, growing a diverse variety of crops is critical to nutrition, particularly where households grow the majority of the food they eat. Micronutrient deficiency, or hidden hunger, occurs when the intake or absorption of vitamins and minerals—iron, folic acid, vitamin A, zinc, and iodine—is below healthy thresholds and too low to sustain good health and development in children and normal physical and mental functions in adults. These deficiencies usually affect growth and the immune system but can also cause such conditions as anemia (iron deficiency).[48] Although the direct link between agricultural biodiversity and human nutrition is generally difficult to make, the nutritional importance of a diverse diet is now widely recognized.[49] In developing countries, for example, this can mean integrating local crops with staple crops supplemented with wild-harvested species.[50]

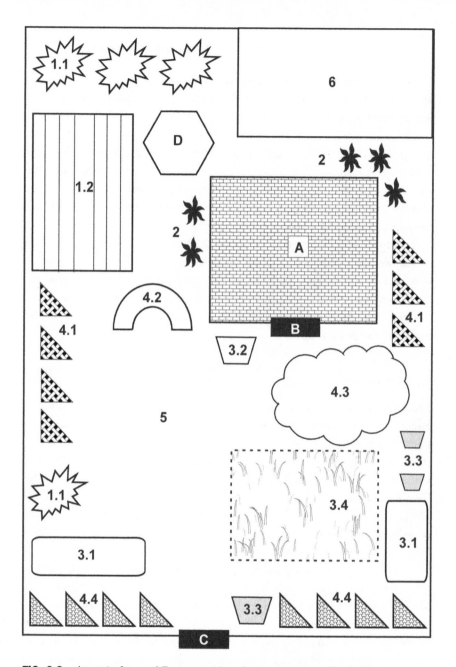

FIG. 6.3. Layout of a rural Tswana *tshimo* (home garden) in North West Province, South Africa. Key: (A) position of the house; (B) front door of house; (C) main entrance gate; (D) livestock holding pen; (1.1) orchard; (1.2) vegetable garden; (2) medicinal garden; (3.1) flower bed; (3.2) container; (3.3) succulent container; (3.4) lawn; (4.1) windbreak; (4.2) fire screen; (4.3) shade tree; (4.4) hedge; (5) open space (*lebala*); (6) natural area (*naga*). Figure not drawn to scale.

Sources: Reproduced with permission of Lerato Y. Molebatsi et al., "The Tswana Tshimo: A Homegarden System of Useful Plants with a Particular Layout and Function," *African Journal of Agricultural Research* 5, no. 1 (November 4, 2010): 2952–63, http://citeseerx.ist.psu. edu/viewdoc/similar?doi=10.1.1.899.6884&type=cc.

Organic Farming

Organic agriculture (OA) is a highly sustainable form of crop and livestock production relying on a strong intensification of ecological processes. OA is defined as a "system of farm management production that combines best environmental practices, a high level of biodiversity, the preservation of natural resources, the application of high animal welfare standards, and a production method in line with the preference of certain consumer products using natural substances and processes."[51]

Most farming systems in Africa are organic and low input by default. If yields are low, so is the quantity of leaf, stem, and other residue that can be incorporated in the soil. Likewise, the manure from malnourished livestock is less nutritive.

OA aims to mimic nature by making use of natural ecological processes and resources to provide nutrients that sustain soil fertility and control pests, diseases, and weeds. By building natural capital in this way, farms can be more resilient against shocks and stresses as well as more productive. Transforming farms to become fully organic may be valuable in drought-affected areas, improving yields where the soils have been severely degraded.[52] The potential of OA and agricultural ecology to increase yields and farmers' incomes sustainably is considerable in developing countries, especially in areas faced with degraded soils and lack of capital. In developing countries OA can be a strategy for ecological intensification. In contrast, in developed countries low yields can lead to the *extensification* of agricultural land to meet demand.

Conventional farming, by contrast, relies heavily on synthetic fertilizers and pesticides and can be extremely productive. In Asia grain yields can average three to five tons per hectare and in developed countries over ten tons, but in Africa yields for crops such as maize are often only one ton or less per hectare. Moreover, if the inputs are used imprudently there can be serious consequences: increased soil erosion through agrochemical runoff and contamination of waterways, causing adverse impacts on aquatic ecosystems. Soils often do not adequately absorb nutrients when fertilizers are haphazardly applied, for example, when broadcast on crops.[53] Excessive fertilizer use, apart from being wasteful, may result in high emissions of GHGs. If done well and according to the rules, however, OA can be a more sustainable and resilient form of agriculture. In the long term, the improvements may lead to higher yields.

As in the case of CA, probably the biggest challenge facing OA in Africa is the burden of weeds. Synthetic herbicides are banned, and hand weeding is very laborious and usually a slow process. Herbicides produce a quick result, but the alternative is to employ cultural weed management to reduce weed emergence, for example, through appropriate choice of crop sequence, tillage, smother/cover crops, and by improving crop competitive ability, relying on appropriate choice of crop genotype, sowing/planting pattern, and fertilization strategy.[54]

Certified Organic

Organic export crops from Africa, such as coffee and cocoa, are in considerable demand, but yields are typically about 20 percent lower on organic than on conventional farms. This is a challenge for farmers when production is below subsistence or prices drop dramatically.[55] Low production calls into question whether yields produced through organic agriculture can be increased at scale in order to ensure food security.

OA, at least in developed countries, has strict regulations on the amount and nature of manure that can be applied and, with the exception of various so-called natural chemicals, bans all synthetic fertilizer, herbicides, and most insecticides and pesticides. Use of genetically modified organisms (GMOs) is prohibited, and in livestock farming there is a ban on the routine use of drugs and antibiotics, as well as a regulation that requires livestock feed to be organic.

The land under certified organic production worldwide has grown steadily to about fifty-one million hectares in 2015, representing about 1.1 percent of the world's farmland.[56] However, this does not include the millions of African smallholder farmers who by default do not use inorganic fertilizers or synthetic pesticides. Such non-certified organic agriculture may be practiced on another ten to twenty million hectares in developing countries.[57] A lack of official, robust data in many African countries makes it hard to estimate the extent of certified organic production. Nevertheless, the availability and quality of information are improving in most countries.

The cost of conversion from conventional to OA is one of the biggest hurdles to the adoption of OA practices. Certified OA is often oriented toward export. The certification process is costly and bureaucratic, which makes certification inaccessible to smallholder farmers with limited resources. In South Africa certification can cost a farmer between R9000 (US$746) and R15000 (US$1244.5) per year.[58]

Financial and logistical support with the certification process and linking farmers to both internal and external markets would enhance the benefits of OA for smallholder farmers. Payment for ecosystem services (PES) schemes, for example, may be used to help farmers convert to OA. The agriculture and environmental policies of the countries in the European Union (EU) and the Organisation for Economic Co-operation and Development (OECD) support PES schemes for the development of OA, but potential problems arise when the incentives conflict with the market. For example, schemes designed to encourage conversion to OA may result in an increased supply of organic products above current demand, resulting in falling prices and leaving producers worse off.

Traditional production systems are considered as near-organic in that sometimes they do not completely fulfill the organic standards. Recently, so called participatory guarantee systems (PGS) for OA were introduced in Tanzania. PGS are defined as "locally focused quality assurance systems. They certify producers based on active participation of stakeholders and are built on a foundation of trust, social networks and knowledge exchange."[59] PGS are an alternative to third-party certification, which is increasingly being used to offer an affordable and participatory guarantee, particularly in developing countries.

Organic in East Africa

In 2015 there were almost 1.7 million hectares of certified organic agricultural land in Africa, constituting 3 percent of the world's organic agricultural land, and seven hundred thousand producers.[60] This represented a 33 percent increase since 2008. Tanzania had the largest organic area (270,000 hectares), and Ethiopia the highest number of organic producers (more than 200,000). Currently, the majority of certified organic produce in Africa, as noted, is destined for export markets. Key crops are coffee, olives, nuts, cocoa, oilseeds, and cotton. At the time of writing only Morocco and Tunisia had regulations governing OA, while seven countries were in the process of drafting one and eleven countries had national standards but not yet a national legislation.

In Kenya the compilation of organic sector data for 2015 showed an impressive growth compared to just four years before. The demand for organic food has continued to grow among the urban middle class, providing huge market opportunities. If the trend continues, the projection is that more farmers are likely to convert to OA once the rising demand for organic products cannot be met. An example of a group of organic farmers included in a PGS in Tanzania is given in box 6.9.

Box 6.9. The Maendeleo Farmer Group of organic farmers in Tanzania

The Maendeleo Farmer Group has 23 members and is located in Towelo, a village in the Uluguru Mountain range . . . southeast of Morogoro town, between altitudes from 700 to 2400 m above sea level. Rainfall is bimodal with short rains in October–December and long rains in March–May. The area is home to the matriarchal organized Luguru tribe whose members depend on subsistence agriculture.

In 2010, SAT [Sustainable Agriculture Tanzania] started to teach the group OA practices, such as: cultivation of medical plants, intercropping of vegetables (e.g., maize and beans, carrots and leeks, tomatoes and onions), production of botanical pesticides from neem tree (Azadirachta indica), terrace building, and compost making. . . .

Group members are organized in different committees (e.g., for training, marketing, inspection) with emphasis on collective responsibility and carry out different tasks according to their capabilities. Their organic produce is used for own consumption and surplus is sold in the SAT Organic Shop in Morogoro and in an Organic Shop in Dar es Salaam. The PGS system enables the group to benefit on [an] individual and community level without having the cost-intensive third-party certification and paper work. . . . Benefits from the new practices [include savings from less fertilizer use and cheaper pest management]. . . . Self-sufficiency increases, as well as farmer's income and access to finance. . . .

[However,] manure is not available close by and farmers have to walk long distances to get it, . . . [inspections are difficult because the plots are scattered over a large area, and farmers] have difficulties to allocate enough time for family activities.

Source: Reproduced from Mirjam Moser, "Essay on Development Policy: Organic Agriculture—A Powerful Approach to Enhance Household Food Security in the Highlands of Tanzania?" 2014, 12, https://www.ethz.ch/content/dam/ethz/special-interest/gess/nadel-dam/documents/mas/mas-essays/MAS_2012_Moser_Mirjam.pdf.

There is a wealth of knowledge available on OA, especially in European countries; however, such knowledge is very context-specific and cannot be transferred to regions such as Africa without caution and modification. There is also a need to build the capacity of African farmers, providing them with peer-to-peer training to ensure that information and practices are locally adapted to suit their land and needs. In Africa the absence of secure land rights means that many poor farmers are unlikely to take on additional risks and efforts to gradually build up the natural capital of their farms beyond a one- or two-year horizon. To ensure that smallholder farmers invest in the transition to sustainable agriculture on a long-term basis, major efforts to secure their land rights are needed, particularly in low-income countries.

Integrated Approaches

In general, to increase the uptake of sustainable agricultural practices in Africa, organic approaches need to be combined with a prudent use of necessary inputs. On Africa's depleted soils, production cannot be increased and maintained without bringing nutrients in from the outside, either through livestock manure, mineral fertilizer, or cultivation of legumes. Long-term experiments and detailed analysis of soil processes have shown why the addition of nutrients is so important, not only for higher yields but also for yield sustainability (box 6.10).[61]

Box 6.10. Long-term African crop trials

Twenty-one long-term arable cropping trials in different environments across SSA took place between 1948 and 1988. The trials exhibited the following shared characteristics:

1. Yield decline, often with a relatively rapid fall to a low level equilibrium.
2. A significant decline in soil organic matter when land was cultivated: between greater than 5 percent per annum loss on sandy soils to around 2 percent on better textured soils.
3. Yield declines from prolonged treatments with organic matter alone (animal manure, green manure, crop residues), although yields held up better than when treated with inorganic fertilizers alone.
4. Rotational treatments, including sequences with legumes and fallow periods, had lower declines than monocultures and lower rates of soil organic matter loss.
5. The best results invariably were those treatments that combine inorganic and organic inputs.

Source: Reproduced from Montpellier Panel, "No Ordinary Matter: Conserving, Restoring and Enhancing Africa's Soils" (London: Agriculture for Impact, 2014), https://www.mamopanel.org/media/uploads/files/NO_ORDINARY_MATTER-_CONSERVING_RESTORING_AND_ENHANCING_AFRICAS_SOILS_2014.pdf.

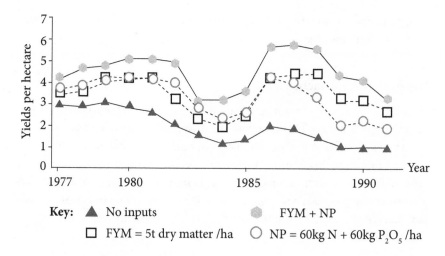

FIG. 6.4.   Long-term trials with maize, Kabete, Kenya

Source: Camilla Toulmin and Ian Scoones, "Policies for Soil Fertility Management in Africa. A Report Prepared for the Department for International Development" (London: UK Department for International Development, 1999), http://pubs.iied.org/7407IIED/.

The general lesson here is that ecological approaches to agricultural development have much to offer, especially in terms of sustainability. They can help smallholders hang in and sometimes step up, but to achieve meaningful increases in productivity requires new breeds of high-yielding crops and livestock coupled with the judicious use of synthetic inputs.

THE NEW GENETICS

At the beginning of this book we described the plight of Sylvester and Beatrice Nama-runda, who farm a hectare of eroded land in western Kenya. Shortages of almost everything—land, money, labor—and poor-yielding crops mean that they are often unable to provide their family with adequate food. But if they could sow seeds of a high-yielding crop such as maize and if they could control the weeds, pests, and diseases, they would be able to produce over two tons per hectare, even if there was a mild drought. Sylvester and Beatrice could then feed their family and even have a surplus that would enable them to sell enough grain every year to pay for a more diverse diet, medicines, school fees, and other needs.

But for this to happen they must have access to the high-yielding seeds. Traditionally they have sown seed kept from the previous year's harvest, often not only low yielding but decreasing in yield from year to year. The alternative is to sow a new hybrid seed variety that has been bred by plant breeders working at the Kenya Agricultural Research Institute (KARI). KARI has produced better yielding, drought tolerant seeds suitable for western Kenya. However, these have to be available for purchase from a local agrodealer and at a cost Sylvester and Beatrice can afford. They most likely will need a loan.

Sustainable genetic intensification consists of developing crop varieties and livestock breeds that contain multiple genes capable of producing improved yields on a sustainable basis.

Plant and animal breeding is both an art and a science, nearly as old as agriculture itself. The early farmers selected seed from vigorous, high-yielding plants and used them for sowing in the following season. By degrees wild grasses were transformed into domestic cereals—wheat, barley, maize, rice, sorghum, millet—the process of selection creating distinctive varieties adapted to local conditions and needs. The initial genetic changes often involved only one or two genes. For example, selection of certain wheat plants made them easier to harvest. Instead of the individual grains falling to the ground when they matured, they were retained on the plant and hence could be easily harvested with a sickle. Livestock changed morphologically and became tamer as well as less wary and thus increased their productivity.

Farmers soon came to look for promising natural mutants and crosses. Bread wheat, a natural cross between emmer wheat and a wild goat grass that arose about seven thousand years ago somewhere to the southwest of the Caspian Sea, was recognized and cultivated by early farmers. It became a cornerstone of European and, eventually, world agriculture.

For thousands of years plant and animal breeding were family affairs, conducted in and around the farm dwelling by men and women using simple ground rules and relying on intuition, personal experience, and wisdom passed on from generation to generation. The science of plant breeding owes its origins to Charles Darwin, who in his discussions of pigeon and dog breeds explained the basis of selection, and to Gregor Mendel, who in his study of the garden sweet pea identified the particulate nature of the basis of heredity.

One consequence of these scientific discoveries has been the emergence of professionals and breeders in institutes and research stations who can identify and explain the underlying mechanisms and hence make breeding more predictable and efficient. Nevertheless, although plant and animal breeding are now considerably more sophisticated than they were a hundred years ago, in its essentials it has little changed. Mendel, if he were alive today, would recognize the processes that led to the creation of the Green Revolution.[1]

Farmers' Varieties

It has been estimated that smallholder farmers in developing countries acquire up to 90 percent of their seed through informal mechanisms, mostly their own stock or through local markets. The estimate is the result of an intensive survey of six countries, including four in Africa: Malawi, Kenya, South Sudan, and Zimbabwe.[2]

Since farming began, farmers have exerted selection pressures on crop varieties they recognize as valuable.[3] One consequence is that farmers have domesticated wild species—and they continue to do so. Overall, farmers are largely responsible for the extraordinary genetic diversity within crop species that exists today. There are several beneficial consequences of farmer selection: the genetic diversity of farmers' varieties (1) contributes to production system resilience in response to stresses, especially those created by climate change; (2) helps reduce the incidence and impact of crop pests and diseases; and in some situations farmers' varieties (3) outperforms formally improved varieties, especially when deployed in difficult environments and in systems where farmers cannot afford inputs that are recommended in the formal sector; (4) is an important source of nutrition in diversified food systems; and (5) often plays an important role in reinforcing cultural identity and continuity.[4]

In practice, farmers may access seeds from both the formal and informal sector, including their own seed, and manage them on their own farms.[5] Participatory plant breeding with mixed teams of farmers and formal sector researchers can result in the development of new and useful crop diversity to be deployed in farmers' fields. Community-led seed enterprises and community seed banks are gaining increased attention.[6]

Open Pollinated Varieties (OPVs)

Crops that are self-pollinating, like rice, wheat, and barley, change relatively slowly. But new characteristics are reasonably easy to select for, and new varieties are relatively easy to create. Open pollinators, including maize, pearl millet, and the brassicas, cross-pollinate and hence change rapidly. New and distinctive traits are common but will be difficult to maintain and preserve in the face of exchange of genes from other varieties of the same and closely related species.

The most important of the OPVs in Africa is maize, or corn, as it is referred to in the United States.[7] A maize plant is characterized by a tassel, an inflorescence of male flowers that releases pollen carried by the wind to fertilize nearby ears and the female flowers, producing the cobs that contain the grain. The result is a fairly random mixture of genotypes, but farmers have learned that distinctive varieties can be created by saving the grain for replanting, if it is isolated from other maize varieties or harvested from the middle of the field. Farmers, with skill, can produce varieties in this way that essentially breed true. By contrast, a hybrid results from the deliberate crossing of two or more lines of inbred maize lines.

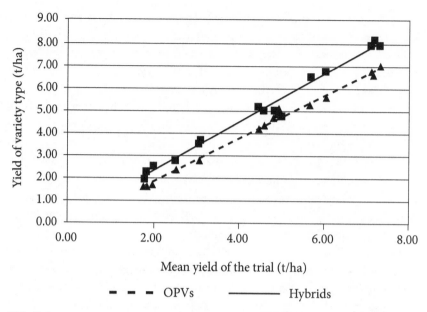

FIG. 7.1. Average grain yields of elite OPVs and hybrids at sixteen locations in Zimbabwe

Source: From Kevin Pixley and Marianne Bänziger, "Open-Pollinated Maize Varieties: A Backward Step or Valuable Option for Farmers?," in *Integrated Approaches to Higher Maize Productivity in the New Millennium* (Seventh Eastern and Southern Africa Regional Maize Conference, Nairobi, Kenya: CIMMYT, 2001), 22–28.

Improved OPVs, produced in the formal sector by crop breeders, are effectively synthetics of multiple lines that can be replanted (recycled) for up to three years without a significant loss in yield, but they yield approximately 20 to 25 percent less than hybrids.[8] In optimal environments. OPV usually produce less uniform and lower yields than hybrids, however OPVs are more stable than hybrids in stress environments (box 7.1; figure 7.1).

Box 7.1. Open pollinated varieties versus hybrids

A number of experiments in Africa have looked at the pros and cons of maize OPVs and hybrids. In one experiment conducted in Zimbabwe by the International Maize and Wheat Improvement Center (CIMMYT), the average yields of hybrids varied between about two and about eight tons per hectare over sixteen locations, exceeding the OPV yields by an average of 16 percent.

In a second experiment, the consequence of saving grain from hybrid or OPV crops for use as seed in subsequent crops in trials at five sites in Zimbabwe was examined. The first-generation seed from the hybrids produced about 30 percent more grain than the OPVs and 20 percent more than the topcross hybrids (where one of the parents is a male of an open pollinated variety). However, the effect of planting recycled, or second-generation, seed had a negligible effect on yield of the OPV, but a 30 percent reduction for hybrids and a 15 percent reduction for topcross hybrids.

The authors' conclusions were that if yield is below 1.5 t/ ha and hybrid seed and fertilizer prices are high relative to the price of grain, the highest return on investment may result from use of improved OPV seed, which is cheaper than hybrid seed and can be recycled with little or no yield loss. The improved OPVs are especially advantageous if the money saved by using OPV instead of hybrid seed is used to purchase additional inputs, such as fertilizer and herbicide or hiring more labor.

Source: Kevin Pixley and Marianne Bänziger, "Open-Pollinated Maize Varieties: A Backward Step or Valuable Option for Farmers?" in *Integrated Approaches to Higher Maize Productivity in the New Millennium* (Seventh Eastern and Southern Africa Regional Maize Conference, Nairobi, Kenya: CIMMYT, 2001), 22–28.

Given these and similar findings, it is not surprising that less than 30 percent of the maize in SSA is planted to hybrids. Hybrid seeds are generally available only where there is an established commercial seed sector since their production requires a lot of capital and expertise. As a result, selling hybrid seed has been unprofitable in many African countries, above all in remote rural areas where farmers are poor. However, maize yields in Africa are very low, not much above one ton per hectare compared with the European average of four to six tons per hectare and the average of the state of Iowa in the United States of over eleven tons. In the two latter locations maize hybrids are grown. Higher yields are attainable in Africa with hybrids and blended fertilizers, but this requires purchase of inputs such as seed and fertilizers, and farmers are reluctant to risk the investments, especially in the face of climate change. One answer to risk lies in the provision of insurance.

Hybridization

A hybrid in everyday language refers simply to the result of a cross between two plants or animals that are distinctive in some way. It can result from crossing two species or two geographical races or subspecies or two *cultivars*—cultivated varieties—or simply two genetically different plants or animals.[9] Sometimes it refers to a cross between two separate species. The term is also used to describe the first generation cross between two distinct selections of a plant. Such hybrids often show increased vigor. That is, they tend to outperform both of their parents, although for reasons that are not fully clear. Here, we largely confine the term *hybrid* to this latter meaning, using the term *cross* elsewhere.

Modern Wheat

Wheat and rice were first crossed at scale as part of the Green Revolution. Norman Borlaug, working for the Rockefeller Foundation in conjunction with the Mexican government in the 1940s, soon recognized that the way to get higher wheat yields was to apply more fertilizer. The plants became more vigorous, but because of their increased weight they tended to fall over—to lodge—as they approached maturity, and much of the harvest was lost. The answer, he decided, was to try to breed shorter-strawed varieties. Dwarfing genes in wheat were discovered in Japan, and in 1935 Japanese breeders crossed a local semi-dwarf variety containing a dwarfing gene with Mediterranean and Russian varieties to produce a new cultivar, Norin10. This, in turn, was crossed with other U.S. varieties, and one of these crosses was sent to Borlaug for crossing with the Mexican tropical and subtropical varieties. He was very successful, soon producing superior wheat varieties that were grown in South Asia and Mexico. Average yields in Pakistan and India took off in 1967, more than doubling by the mid-1980s. The threat of widespread famine was averted.[10]

Modern Rice Varieties

Rice consumption is increasing at about 8 percent a year in many SSA countries. This contrasts with an increase in yield per year that is less than 6 percent, and in some cases yield is decreasing.[11] About thirty million tons more rice will be required in Africa by 2035, Nigeria requiring almost one-third of this additional intake.[12]

Capturing the Dwarfing Gene

In many respects the capture of the dwarfing gene in rice was very similar to the wheat story. The genes, originally from the Chinese variety *Dee-geo-woo-gen*, are alleles (forms) of the genes that also act on the same growth hormone as in wheat, reducing stem elongation. These were first used in the 1950s by Taiwanese breeders to develop a semi-dwarf variety known as Taichung Native 1 (TN1) and later at IRRI in crosses with the *indica* rice variety Peta to produce the "miracle rice" IR8 that was rapidly adopted in Asia. Yields in Indonesia quadrupled between 1967 and the 1980s.[13]

In both wheat and rice, the hybridization process was relatively straightforward and the semi-dwarf genes are now present in short-strawed, fertilizer-responsive varieties throughout the world. It has been a simple and powerful process, reliant for its success on the existence of naturally occurring genes capable of being easily transferred from one plant to another by the traditional methods of plant breeding.

Hybrid Rice

By contrast, modern hybrid rices have been developed in China more recently, with a dramatic effect on rice production both there and elsewhere. The system is complex and difficult because rice is self-pollinated and because the tiny florets—with male and female organs in the same floret—flower for only a short time.

The solution was to develop a rice with sterile male flowers. Under the leadership of Longping Yuan, the director general of China's National Hybrid Rice Research & Development Center, the Chinese developed a cytoplasmic male sterility system that consisted of crossing three lines: a parent male sterile line, a maintainer line used as a pollinator, and a pollen parent that restores fertility.[14] The maintainer lines are repeatedly crossed with the male sterile line until a stable sterile plant is achieved. This is then crossed with the restorer line, producing fertile seed for farmers to plant.

In 1974 the first new rice hybrid, Nan-You 2, was bred, and in the winter of 1975, "the largest group of hybrid rice researchers and technicians in China's agricultural history went to Hainan to produce hybrid rice seeds in more than 4,000 ha of land."[15] Since then average yields have grown to over seven tons per hectare (figure 7.2). They account for about 50 percent of the rice area in China and are now widespread around the world.

Trials have been conducted with Chinese rice hybrids in various West African sites.[16] They show promise; the grain yield of the most promising hybrids was

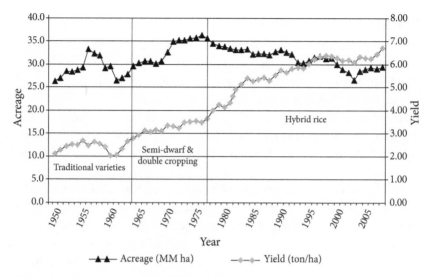

FIG. 7.2. The growth of Chinese rice yields

Source: Jiming Li, Yeyun Xin, and Longping Yuan, "Hybrid Rice Technology Development: Ensuring China's Food Security," IFPRI Discussion Paper (Washington, DC: IFPRI, 2009), http://ebrary.ifpri.org/cdm/ref/collection/p15738coll2/id/23379.

higher than that of the best local inbred cultivars. However, the hybrids exhibited a wide-ranging grain yield, affected by the testing location and growing season; their performances were different across sites from country to country. They were also very susceptible to gall midge, rice yellow mottle virus, and rice blast.

The NERICA

Another process of rice crossing has been specifically focused on Africa. While the Asian rice hybrids have considerable potential in Africa, their performance is highly variable, and they are prone to severe pest and disease attack. To address this challenge, crosses have been made between the Asian rice species (*Oryza sativa*) and the African species (*O. glaberrima*), thus capturing the yield benefits of the former and the adaptive benefits of the latter (box 7.2).

Box 7.2. New rice for Africa (NERICA)

Making crosses between Asian and African rice species is possible and has been recorded in farmers' fields, but the process is easier if the resulting embryo is grown in a culture medium. Early efforts to apply this embryo-rescue technique did not work well. Collaboration with Chinese scientists, however, provided a new tissue culture method involving the use of coconut oil that proved to be highly successful in producing the new hybrids.

Like the African species, these new rice crosses grow well in drought-prone and upland conditions and are both resistant to local pests and diseases and tolerant of poor nutrient conditions and mineral toxicity. They also show early vigorous growth and crowd out weeds. Later in their development, characteristics of the Asian rice species appear: they produce more erect leaves and full panicles of grain and are ready to harvest thirty to fifty days earlier than current varieties.

Today there are eighteen NERICA varieties suitable for upland rice cultivation in SSA. Most recent varieties are products of three series of crosses, using the same *O. glaberrima* parent but different *O. sativa* parents. Some of the NERICA varieties have a yield advantage over their two parents arising from superior weed competitiveness, early maturity (seventy-five to one hundred days), drought tolerance, pest or disease resistance, tolerance of soil acidity and iron toxicity, and their higher yielding potential.

In addition, the grain quality of some of the NERICAs is often better than that of their parents. For instance, the protein content of some of the NERICAs is 25 percent higher than that of the Asian rice on the market.

Farmers were exposed to NERICA varieties through the use of participatory varietal selection and community-based seed systems. The NERICA varieties appear frequently among the top varieties most preferred by farmers, and the potential adoption rate is up to 68 percent. Furthermore, given their shorter growth cycle and higher weed competitiveness, the labor burden put on children is reduced.

Sources: Gordon Conway, *One Billion Hungry: Can We Feed the World?* (Ithaca: Comstock Publishing Associates, 2012); "NERICA : The New Rice for Africa—a Compendium (2008 Edition)" (Cotonou, Benin: Africa Rice Center [WARDA]), 2008, http://www.africarice.org/publications/nerica-comp/Nerica%20Compedium.pdf.; Edwin Nuijten et al., "Evidence for the Emergence of New Rice Types of Interspecific Hybrid Origin in West African Farmers' Fields," ed. Hany A. El-Shemy, *PLOS ONE* 4, no. 10 (October 6, 2009): e7335, https://doi.org/10.1371/journal.pone.0007335; Savitri Mohapatra, "The Rice Man of Africa," *Rice Today* 6, no. 2 (June 2007): 28–29, http://www.africarice.org/publications/ricetoday/riceman.pdf; Ernest Harsch, "Africa: Rice for the Future," *Africa Recovery*, January 2004, http://www.africafocus.org/docs04/rice0401.php.

In 2000 the Africa Rice Center (AfricaRice) received the prestigious Consultative Group on International Agricultural Research (CGIAR) King Baudouin Award for the NERICA breakthrough, and in 2004 Monty Jones, formerly of AfricaRice, was awarded the World Food Prize in recognition of his leading role in the development of NERICAs.

Hybrid Maize

The Native Americans who first domesticated maize recognized that it was, at least in practice, a cross-pollinating crop. As a result when farmers collect seed from his or her crop at the end of the season, to be used for planting in the next season, it is a naturally occurring hybrid seed—and is usually highly variable with poor yield outcomes. But the early maize farmers learned that if the seed was kept distinct it would breed true, that is, they could get offspring that were essentially the same as the parents. In effect, they were producing OPVs. By the time of Columbus they had developed all the major types of corn—flint, flour, pop, dent, and sweet—that are consumed today.[17]

By the nineteenth century U.S. plant breeders and farmers had been experimenting with deliberately hybridizing maize (corn). But real progress was not made until the beginning of the twentieth century with the invention of detasseling, that is, the removal of the tassels and their pollen and male flowers from the maize plant. Detasseling prevents the plants from fertilizing themselves, making controlled and predictable crosses possible.

Then, in 1909, George Shull at the Carnegie Institute's Cold Spring Harbor Research station showed that by inbreeding via self-pollination for several generations to produce pure lines and then crossing the lines, new hybrids could be achieved; these combined the best features of the lines, indeed, they performed better than either parent, giving much-increased yields—an expression of hybrid vigor.[18] So successful were the early hybrids that by the 1950s most of the maize in the United States was hybrid.[19] Yet another reason for the rapid spread, possibly the most important one, was the 1934–36 drought that produced the Dust Bowl, when the hybrid strains were strikingly more resistant than the OPVs then in use.[20]

Subsequently, the process of hybridization has become increasingly sophisticated and costly. Today, African farmers have a choice between hybrids and OPVs, each with its own distinct advantages and disadvantages. Yields of hybrids are often higher than those of OPVs, but their seed needs to be purchased each year, and the costs may be unaffordable. Yet the costs of OPVs are very low, and modern certified OPVs are produced by breeders for specific environments.[21]

Modern maize varieties have had consequential impacts in the developing countries. Mexican production, for example, stands at twenty-four million tons in 2015 compared with six million tons in the 1960s.[22] Nevertheless, the overall uptake has been poor. Less than 50 percent of the tropical maize area is sown to hybrids or OPVs (the rest is in low-yielding local varieties), and the yield gap is often very high.[23]

Several other crop species, for example, sorghum, sunflowers, onions, tomatoes, and other horticultural crops, have been successfully subject to hybrid breeding through techniques similar to those above.

Livestock Crosses

Since the first domestication of animals, farmers have been selecting for useful traits in their flocks and herds. Cattle have been selected for such obvious characteristics as size, color, and the shape of their horns; sheep have been selected for better quality and chickens for the number and quality of eggs they produce. Livestock of all kinds have been selected for the taste and quality of their meat.

Animals have also been selected for resistance to disease. This process, like conventional crop selection, can be very effective but tends to be slower than for plants because the time to reproductive maturity in animals is longer. One way to speed up the process has been through artificial insemination (AI), the mechanical insertion of fresh or stored semen into the female reproductive tract. So far AI has been little used in developing countries. The technology, although apparently simple, requires relatively high levels of skill and experience. For example, success depends on accurate heat detection and timely insemination. AI is particularly useful in cross-breeding.

Cross-Breeding Livestock

Crossing very different parents has been as important in animal as in plant breeding. In Africa, the main focus has been on improving the milk production of dairy cattle. There are two dominant species of cattle in the world: the taurine cattle (*Bos taurus*) of the temperate climates of Europe, North Asia, and West Africa and the humped zebu cattle (*Bos indicus*) of the hot arid and semi-arid regions of Africa and Asia. Although these two species can naturally cross, they are very different today because of the selection pressure for milk production in taurine cows, which has led to the dominance of such very high producers as the Holstein-Friesian types.[24] In contrast, natural selection has produced zebu cattle, which have a high degree of heat tolerance, resistance to many tropical diseases, and the ability to survive long periods of feed and water shortage. Their dairy potential is poor; they have low milk yield, are late maturing, and usually do not let down milk unless stimulated by the suckling of the calf.[25]

Kenya has been very successful success in integrating dairy into smallholder farming systems, particularly in the highland areas. Friesian and Ayrshire breeds have been introduced; this has enabled farmers to keep smaller herds with fewer heifers but more cows, increasing stocking rates through stall feeding, growing fodder, purchasing feeds, and becoming more dependent on external inputs and services. As a result of this intensification smallholders are selling more milk.

A number of sophisticated cross-breeding schemes have been introduced in Kenya.[26] In the Kilifi plantation near Mombasa in Kenya, a rotational crossing scheme alternating with bulls from the two breeds has resulted in Sahiwal x British Ayrshire crosses producing three thousand kilograms of milk per year, mainly from pasture.[27]

Breeding-Improved Forage

If the growing demand for livestock products is to be met without increased pressure on both land and environmental resources, breeding is also needed to develop a higher quality of fodder and feed to improve livestock breeds.[28]

So far, most forage breeding has taken place in the temperate climates of the developed countries, but there have been notable efforts at breeding tropical forages in Australia and in Latin America.[29] In the humid and semi-humid tropics of Latin America and elsewhere, most pastures consist of native species of inferior nutritional quality, which limits the intensification of livestock production. However, in recent decades a number of tropical grasses and legumes have been identified that are highly productive, of superior nutritional quality, and are well suited to marginal lands characterized by low soil fertility and drought.[30]

For the past thirty years Centro Internacional de Agricultura Tropical (CIAT), based in Colombia, has been developing improved forages for three Latin American agroecosystems: the savannas, the forest margins, and the hillsides. In each case they are seeking forages that not only improve livestock production but also reduce erosion, help to control weeds, and reverse land degradation.[31]

One such grass is Brachiaria, a predominantly African genus (although not much utilized in Africa) with about a hundred species, some perennial and well suited as forage grasses. Several species were introduced into tropical America some decades ago and are now grown extensively in over seventy million hectares in the region, comprising more than a third of the total savannas. Provided that phosphorus, lime, and various trace elements are added to the soil, Brachiaria can be established and will be very productive (live weight gains of 100 to 300 kg/ha/year for several years). But Brachiaria breeding faces a number of challenges (box 7.3).

Box 7.3. Breeding Brachiaria forage grasses

Brachiaria breeders have to cope with several serious problems. For example, some cultivars are prone to attack by a spittle bug, and others lack tolerance to the acid soils common in the savannas.

The commercial Brachiaria species, *B.brizantha, B. decumbens*, and *B. ruziziensis*, are all native to East Africa and were introduced to tropical Latin America in the mid-twentieth century. Brazilian breeders have released a cultivar of *B. brizantha* that is resistant to the spittle bug but is not tolerant of acid soils. In contrast, CIAT breeders have found a cultivar of *B. decumbens* that is tolerant of the soils and results in high weight gains. The challenge has been to combine the two.

Unfortunately, *B. brizantha* and *B. decumbens* normally reproduce asexually, by apomixis; that is, an embryo is produced without fusion of male and female gametes, so the offspring are true clones. The apomixis is associated with tetraploidy (four sets of chromosomes), but at least one species, *B. ruziziensis*, is diploid and reproduces sexually. A clever solution developed by scientists at the University of Louvain is to treat this species with a natural chemical, colchicine, to produce a sexual tetraploid *B.ruziziensis* that can then be crossed with two apomictic tetraploids, *B. decumbens* and *B. brizantha*, thus building a bridge between them. The progeny of these original crosses has been used to form fully sexual, synthetic, recurrent selection populations that form the basis of breeding programs in Colombia and Brazil. The many crosses produced are now being evaluated.

Sources: John W. Miles et al., eds., *Brachiaria: Biology, Agronomy, and Improvement* (Campo Grande, Brazil: Centro Internacional de Agricultura Tropical (CIAT); Empresa Brasileira de Pesquisa Agropecuária (EMBRAPA), 1996), 259 https://cgspace.cgiar.org/bitstream/handle/10568/54362/Brachiaria.pdf?sequence= 1&isAllowed=y; Narda Jimena Triviño et al., "Genetic Diversity and Population Structure of Species and Breeding Populations," *Crop Science* 57, no. 5 (2017): 2633, https://doi.org/10.2135/cropsci2017.01.0045; J. W. Miles, C. Cardona, and G. Sotelo, "Recurrent Selection in a Synthetic Brachiariagrass Population Improves Resistance to Three Spittlebug Species," *Crop Science* 46, no. 3 (2006): 1088, https://doi.org/10.2135/cropsci2005.06-0101.

The quality of tropical forages can also be improved either by increasing desirable compounds, such as lysine, or by reducing the concentration of undesirable compounds, such as lignin.[32] These improvements are likely to result in greater intake and digestibility of fodder.

Thus pigs and chickens need lysine in their diets. Although legumes, such as peas and lupins, have more lysine than cereals, they are poor in the sulfur amino acids methionine and cysteine, which are needed to increase the production of meat, milk, and wool in cattle and sheep. High levels of these amino acids are present in sunflower seeds and the chicken egg protein, ovalbumin. So far it has been possible to insert the encoding genes into peas. The next step is to insert the same or similar genes in forage legumes, such as alfalfa and clover, with suitable promoters so that they are expressed in the foliage.

In tropical forages the carbohydrates are often protected from the rumen fungi and bacteria by the presence of lignin and so are not available to the ruminant animal eating them. There has been some success in reducing lignification through conventional breeding and selection, but attention is now turning to biotechnology. So-called brown midrib mutants that block the pathway that produces lignin sometimes occur in maize, sorghum, and millet. When this happens, 50 percent less lignin is produced, and the digestibility is 10 to 30 percent higher. Research is now aimed at cloning these genes and inserting them into forage legumes.[33]

Modern Biotechnology

Conventional plant and animal breeding techniques have contributed a great deal to food security over the past 150 years. They still have much to offer and will remain a mainstay of breeding for the foreseeable future. They are powerful techniques in the hands of plant breeders in national research institutes, in the centers of the CGIAR, and in the hands of small and multinational seed companies.

Nevertheless, as has been long recognized, conventional techniques have practical limitations. Conventional breeding in the hands of the multinational seed companies tends to focus on key commercial crops to the detriment both of crops grown and consumed by poorer individuals and of the stability of agricultural systems overall. Furthermore, it is not as efficient or speedy a process as it might be. The crossing of two parent plants, each with desirable characteristics, is essentially a random process. While some desirable characteristics may emerge, others may be lost. Potential yield may increase, but often any such growth comes at the expense of pest or disease resistance or some other characteristic that is already present, such as superior grain quality. There are also natural limitations to conventional plant breeding. Traits that a breeder wishes to incorporate in a plant or an animal may not be present in any variety, breed, or species with which a cross can be made, although they may occur in quite unrelated species.[34]

The Power of Biotechnology

The revolutionary achievements of cellular and molecular biology that began in the 1940s are crucial in the context of the limitations of conventional breeding.[35] Modern cellular and molecular techniques allow breeders to speed up the design and engineering of new plant and animal types, with much less reliance on random processes. Under the general heading of biotechnology, these techniques are already having a significant impact on plant and animal breeding, benefiting poor people as well as those who are better off.

The application of this knowledge to crop breeding is pursued through four practical techniques:

- marker-assisted selection
- cell and tissue culture
- recombinant DNA (also known as genetic engineering [GE] or genetic modification [GM])
- gene editing

Each of these is beginning to bring benefits to developing country farmers, both large and small.[36]

Marker-Assisted Selection (MAS)

The idea of selecting for valuable traits through the identification of genetic markers began to gain traction only with the development of new techniques for identifying sequences of DNA. For the breeder, the trick is to find a region on the plant genome that can be readily identified and is closely inherited along with a gene or genes that code for a trait of interest or value.[37] Once a number of markers are identified, they can be assembled into a marker map of a genome; the genes are then located by statistical association with the markers.

Sometimes only one or two genes determine a trait, but most important agronomic traits are governed by quantitative trait loci (QTL); that is, they are controlled by many genes, each tending to have a relatively small effect. Yield is a typical quantitative trait in plants, and milk production in livestock is another. The use of marker-assisted selection (MAS) focused on QTLs for disease resistance is increasingly being used in crop improvement.[38]

A major benefit of MAS is the possibility of determining the presence of a trait at the seedling or even the seed stage. A small piece of the seed or seedling is cut out and subjected to DNA analysis. In the past, breeding for, say, insect resistance meant the seeds from a cross with a resistant parent would have to be sown in a nursery and, when the plant was mature, infested with insects to see which crosses had the resistance gene. The MAS process greatly speeds up the breeding process and makes it cheaper, as there is no longer any need for the construction of large insect-rearing facilities. New varieties can be brought to near commercialization in four to six generations instead of ten.

An example is breeding for maize streak virus (MSV), which is transmitted by leafhoppers. This is the most serious disease of maize in Africa, causing serious epidemics with yield losses of up to 100 percent.[39] Although genetic resistance to MSV has been known for over twenty years, it has not been bred into local maize varieties because few national breeding programs can afford to maintain the insect colonies and other infrastructure. Now, using DNA markers that flank the gene, it is possible to identify the precise location of the resistance gene and hence to backcross it into local varieties.

Cell and Tissue Culture

Because all the cells of a plant contain the full complement of genes, it is often possible to grow individual cells and pieces of tissue under sterile conditions in a suitable medium into full healthy plants.[40] The medium contains a range of macro and micro nutrients together with growth regulators that induce rooting and shoot formation. Tissue culturing is a technique that has long been practiced, under the title of micropropagation, to produce large numbers of clones of a plant. Because they are isolated and raised in contained, sterile media, tissue culturing is a highly effective way of producing pest- and disease-free planting material.

Although commonly used for high-priced ornamental and horticultural crops, tissue culture has been very successful in East Africa in producing staple bananas free of diseases (box 7.4) Bananas are a major source of food and income throughout East Africa. Ugandans, for example, are the largest consumers of bananas in the world, eating on average nearly 1 kg/person/day.

Box 7.4. Breeding healthy bananas through tissue culture

Bananas are often a staple crop in East Africa. But the plants are susceptible to disease because new plants are grown directly from cuttings from a "mother plant," thus transferring any disease present, even if it is not visible.

The Black Sigatoka fungus, a leaf spot disease, has been particularly devastating to banana crops worldwide since its first outbreak in Fiji in 1963. It arrived in East Africa in the late 1970s, decreasing yield by over 30 percent. The fungus can be controlled with fungicides, but it has developed increasing resistance over the years, making this option both expensive and damaging to the environment.

After the end of apartheid in South Africa, the Kenyan agricultural scientist Florence Wambugu visited there to observe the previously closely guarded work on tissue culture bananas. She applied the technique in Kenya and found she could quickly generate healthy new plants that could be planted in the field. KARI undertook trials on local varieties in the mid-1990s, and a training program was initiated.

After they are generated and grown in a laboratory under sterile conditions, the banana plantlets are hardened in a greenhouse for six weeks. Tissue culture (TC) speeds up the multiplication process drastically; up to two thousand healthy bananas can be produced from a single shoot, compared to only a few suckers for conventional bananas. Furthermore, TC bananas produce fruits in 340 days as compared to 420 for conventional, and the average yield is thirty to forty tons per hectare, more than twice the yield for conventional breeds.

Sources: Neena Bhandari, "Going Bananas: Fighting Hunger with Africa Harvest," People and the Planet, November 20, 2008, http://www.peopleandtheplanet.com/index.html@lid=28950&section=34&topic=27.html; Patrick K. Mobambo et al., "Factors Influencing the Development of Black Streak Disease and the Resulting Yield Loss in Plantain in the Humid Forests of West and Central Africa," Tree and Forestry Science and Biotechnology 4, no. Special Issue 1 (2010): 47–51, http://www.globalsciencebooks.info/Online/GSBOnline/images/2010/TFSB_4(SI1)/TFSB_4(SI1)47-51o.pdf; "Tissue Culture Banana Farming in Kenya" (Kirinyaga, Kenya: Aberdare Technologies Limited), accessed May 3, 2018, http://atl.farm/wp-content/uploads/2016/05/Tissue-Culture-Banana-Farming-in-Kenya.edited.pdf; Agriculture for Impact, "Tissue Culture," Sustainable Intensification Database, accessed April 26, 2019, https://ag4impact.org/sid/genetic-intensification/biotechnology/tissue-culture/.

Recombinant DNA

Recombinant DNA technology is a very sophisticated process of plant microsurgery that enables genes to be taken from one DNA helix and spliced into another and hence transferred between chromosomes.[41] Although an artificial act, it is, in essence, the same process as occurs when the plant or animal breeder crosses one plant with another or one animal with another. During the crossing process, chromosomes transfer pieces from one to another, but the new combinations are usually randomly determined. The great advantage of recombinant DNA technology (also known as Genetic Engineering [GE] or Genetic Modification [GM]) is that the new combinations are determined beforehand and, with skill and care, are precisely achieved. As a result, the plant breeder is no longer restricted to the genetic variation that arises in traditional breeding programs.

The process of transferring a gene to a new plant or animal can follow one of several routes.[42] One of the earliest and most successful techniques employs *Agrobacterium tumefaciens*. This bacterium, which naturally invades potatoes, tomatoes, and alfalfa, among other plants, serves as a carrier of new genes to plants. The technique is surprisingly easy and now works effectively on cereals as well as broadleaf plants.

Alternatively, the new genes can be injected more forcefully. One approach is to apply a coat of gold particles to the DNA, which are then fired into the plant cell with a microparticle gene gun. It is customary for millions of cells to be treated, and those in which the new gene has lodged are identified by means of a marker and cultured.

Every year the International Service for the Acquisition of Agri-biotech Applications (ISAAA), under the leadership of Clive James, an agricultural scientist who was previously the deputy director general at CIMMYT, produces an independent estimate of global progress on the adoption of recombinant DNA crops (referred to in their reports as "biotech crops").[43] In 2017 ISAAA reported that the area of biotech crops had reached 190 million ha in a total of twenty-four countries, over 50 percent in developing countries (figure 7.3). Notably, fourteen of the eighteen countries growing more than 50,000 hectares were developing countries in Latin America, Asia, and Africa. James asserts that biotech crops are the "fastest adopted crop technology in the history of modern agriculture."[44]

While it is relatively easy to calculate economic gains for a specified crop in a particular place, obtaining a global figure for the benefits of growing biotech crops is difficult. James, however, has come up with a figure of economic gains at the farm level of about $65 billion since 1996. Of this amount, just less than half, 44 percent, resulted from reduced production costs (less plowing, fewer pesticide sprays, and less labor) and just over half, 56 percent, from substantial yield gains of 229 million tons.[45]

Recombinant DNA can create new plant varieties and animal breeds that not only deliver higher yields but also solve biotic and abiotic challenges, thereby

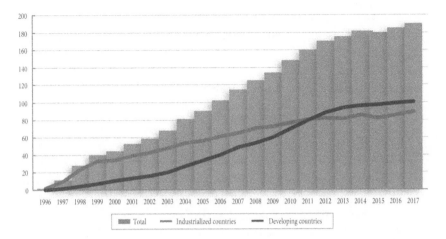

FIG. 7.3. Global, industrial, and developing country areas of biotech crops (million ha)

Source: ISAAA Global Status of Commercialized Biotech/GM Crops in 2017: Biotech Crop Adoption Surges as Economic Benefits Accumulate in 22 Years, ISAAA Briefs no. 53 (Ithaca: ISAAA, 2017), http://www.isaaa.org/resources/publications/briefs/53/download/isaaa-brief-53-2017.pdf.

reducing the need for chemical inputs such as fungicides and pesticides and increasing tolerance to drought, salinity, chemical toxicity, and other adverse circumstances. A meta-analysis by Wilhelm Klümper and Matin Qaim of the University of Göttingen in Germany has concluded that "on average, GM technology adoption has reduced chemical pesticide use by 37%, increased crop yields by 22%, and increased farmer profits by 68%."[46]

In developed countries some of the most successful applications have resulted from engineering herbicide tolerance in crop plants, making it safe for herbicides to be applied to growing crops so that the weeds are killed but the crops are left unharmed. This has been achieved in maize and soybeans treated with the herbicide glyphosate. It is less relevant to developing countries, in part because hand weeding is a cheaper form of control. Brazil and other South American countries have employed such crops on a large scale, although maize double-stacked with insect resistance and herbicide tolerance has begun to be grown in the Philippines.

Gene Editing

Gene editing is a revolutionary new technique that, unlike recombinant DNA, does not primarily move DNA from one plant or animal to another. Instead, it focuses on changing, inserting, or deleting one or a few base pairs (permutations of the four amino acids of the DNA helix) at a specific targeted location in the plant's or animal's genome. In this way genes can be edited far more precisely than ever before.

One of a number of techniques that have been developed is the so-called CRISPR-Cas9 system. Cas9 is the name given to the protein that acts like a pair of scissors cutting the DNA and allowing replacement DNA involving a new gene or a repaired gene to be inserted.

As Jennifer Doudna and Samuel Sternberg of the University of California at Berkeley have written in their book *A Crack in Creation: The New Power to Control Evolution,* an organism's entire DNA content, including all its genes, has become "almost as editable as a simple piece of text. . . . Practically overnight, we have found ourselves on the cusp of a new age in genetic engineering and biological mastery—a revolutionary era in which the possibilities are only limited by our collective imagination."[47] In the early days of recombinant DNA efforts were focused on editing animal genes, but attention has turned to crop plants—producing, for example, disease-resistant rice, tomatoes that ripen more slowly, and soybeans with healthier polyunsaturated fat content.[48]

Concerns and Hazards

The potential of biotechnology is almost infinite, and while it's exciting for scientists many laypeople find this interfering with the "natural world" deeply troubling. Some are opposed even to hybridization even though bread wheat is the result of a complicated, although natural, hybridization that occurred seven thousand years ago. Cell and tissue culture, akin in many ways to the propagation carried out by gardeners throughout the world, seems to be readily acceptable. The most vociferous and fairly widespread opposition is to the production and cultivation of recombinant DNA crops.[49] The reasons vary, from perceptions of serious health hazards to environmental concerns to opposition to the power of multinational seed companies.

In 1992 an article in the *New York Times* opposing GM tomatoes referred to them as "Frankenstein foods," a description that continues to be used by the tabloid press.[50] People have been consuming GM foods for decades or more without any obvious signs of ill health, but concerns over health hazards persist. Many studies purporting to show deleterious health risks in laboratory animals or humans are quoted, but few survive the peer review process and appear in the scientific literature.

In a two-part review of GE crops, Penny Lemaux of the University of California at Berkeley examined, in an exhaustive review, the evidence relating to health risks and to environmental protection and concluded that "although no human activity can be guaranteed 100% safe, the commercial GE crops and products available today are at least as safe as those produced by conventional methods. Particularly with regard to environmental safety, we must stay vigilant in our evaluation of GE crops and their impacts to ensure long-term utility, just as with those created using classical methods. Although we should exercise caution, we should not hold GE crops and products to standards not required for food and feed products produced by other technologies."[51]

Strong arguments hold that gene editing, because of its precision and confinement to the editing of DNA base pairs, should not be subject to the same precautionary legislation as recombinant DNA is. The environmental organization Greenpeace argues that the process "can still display unexpected and unpredictable effects, which can have implications for . . . food, feed or environmental safety" and that therefore these new techniques should not be exempted from the regulations applied to GM organisms.[52] Yet it is not clear that the hazards arising from gene editing of DNA base pairs are any different from those in conventional plant and animal breeding.

Sustainable Breeding Interventions

The breeding of hybrids and the use of modern biotechnology techniques certainly intensify the bringing together of potentially beneficial genes in crop and livestock genomes. The question is, To what extent do these interventions contribute to SI?[53]

Improving Nutrition

For various reasons, the diets of poor African households tend to be dominated by basic staple foods like maize, rice, wheat, cassava, millet, and sorghum; these are usually deficient in micronutrients like vitamin A, iron, and zinc that are necessary to combat malnutrition. Home gardens, as described earlier, can provide more nutritious foods rich in micronutrients. Another promising approach is biofortification, the breeding of crops with enhanced nutritional value.

An early example is the breeding of quality protein maize. The poor nutritional value of maize grain is well known. In particular maize lacks two essential proteins, the amino acids lysine and tryptophan.[54] Most of the protein in a mature maize kernel is contained in the endosperm and the germ. The endosperm protein is low in quality, in contrast to the germ protein, which is of superior quality. However, because the endosperm constitutes the bulk of the grain, contributing as much as 80 percent of the total kernel protein, any major improvements for quality protein have to target the endosperm (box 7.5). Another success story is the development of orange-fleshed sweet potatoes, also via the use of conventional hybridization (box 7.6).

Box 7.5. The breeding of quality protein maize (QPM)

In the early 1960s researchers at Purdue University discovered two mutant maize alleles, opaque-2 (*o2*) and floury-2 (*fl2*), that alter the amino acid profile and composition of maize endosperm protein, resulting in a two-fold increase in the levels of lysine and tryptophan. Unfortunately, the mutations adversely affect agronomic performance, including yield, and consumer aspects, particularly kernel characteristics.

A decade later Surinder Vasal and Evangelina Villegas began their collaborative research in Mexico while they were working at CIMMYT. Villegas managed the lab investigating protein quality, and, as a plant breeder, Vasal was assigned to work on developing QPM varieties that would ultimately gain widespread acceptance.

Vasal and Villegas collaborated to combine existing opaque-2 maize with genetic modifiers by integrating cereal chemistry and plant-breeding techniques. Using these techniques through the 1970s they produced and analyzed germplasms extremely quickly, sometimes processing up to twenty-five thousand samples a year. By the mid-1980s they had produced a QPM germplasm with hard kernel characteristics and good taste similar to the traditional grain and with much higher quality levels of lysine and tryptophan.

Nevertheless, many nutritionists felt that it would be possible to add protein to the diets of the poorest in other ways. As a result, the discovery by Vasal and Villegas remained until the early 1990s, when CIMMYT gained funding to begin promoting QPM in Ghana and several other African countries.

Babies and adults consuming QPM are healthier and at lower risk for malnutrition disorders. QPM offers 90 percent the nutritional value of skimmed milk. The varieties are grown on roughly nine million acres (36,000 km²) worldwide; in total, QPM germplasm has contributed over US$1 billion annually to the economies of developing countries.

Source: S. K. Vasal, "Quality Protein Maize Story," Improving Human Nutrition through Agriculture: The Role of International Agricultural Research (Washington, DC: IFPRI, 1999), http://ebrary.ifpri.org/cdm/ref/collection/p15738coll2/id/125920.

Box 7.6. Orange-fleshed sweet potatoes in Mozambique

A classic food security crop, the roots of sweet potatoes can be left in the soil and lifted when other crops are not available. Sweet potatoes grow well on marginal land but are white-fleshed in Mozambique, meaning they are rich in carbohydrates but lacking in beta-carotene, which our bodies convert into much needed vitamin A.

To overcome this deficiency, beta-carotene rich, orange-fleshed varieties of sweet potato were introduced for breeding by the National Institute for Agronomic Investigation (INIA) in 1997. Three years later nine new orange-fleshed varieties were released just in time to help within the recovery from devastating floods in southern Mozambique. By 2005 half a million households had received improved planting material.

The same year a severe drought in the country brought home the need to breed for drought tolerance as well. Using an accelerated conventional breeding programme, Maria Andrade and her team at INIA halved the time needed to produce new varieties from eight to four years. By 2011 15 new drought-resistant varieties were released, capable of producing up to 15 tons/ha.

Adoption rates are high, including amongst women and children, with nearly a doubling of daily intake of beta-carotene and significant increases in serum retinol, the form in which vitamin A circulates in the blood.

Source: Reproduced from Montpellier Panel, "Sustainable Intensification: A New Paradigm for African Agriculture" (London: Agriculture for Impact, 2013), https://www.mamopanel.org/media/uploads/files/SUSTAINABLE_INTENSIFICATION-_A_NEW_PARADIGM_FOR_AFRICAN_AGRICULTURE_2013.pdf.

But in some instances conventional breeding will not suffice. In rice, for example, beta-carotene is not present in the grain endosperm, so scientists are introducing genes with the appropriate coding (box 7.7).

Box 7.7. Golden rice

Beta-carotene is present in rice leaves and stalks as well as in brown unmilled rice in minute amounts, but it is not in the grain endosperm. In many parts of SSA poor families consume rice as the basic staple of their diet, and babies are often weaned on rice gruel. Boiled rice often has a layer of milky liquid on the surface: it looks like milk, and mothers like to use it to wean their babies, but it isn't milk and has no beta-carotene content.

The approach has been to find suitable genes elsewhere and to use recombinant DNA to insert them into a new variety of rice. The outcome was golden rice, so named because of its distinctive color. In the early 1980s Ingo Potrykus of the Swiss Federal Institute of Technology and his colleague Peter Beyer of the University of Freiburg first transferred two daffodil and one bacterial gene into rice. The biochemical pathway leading to beta-carotene is largely present in the rice grain but lacks two crucial enzymes: phytoene synthase (psy), provided by a daffodil gene, and carotenedesaturase (crtlI), provided by a bacterium gene. In the greenhouse this transfer gave beta-carotene levels of about 1.6 µg/g, significant but not large.

Subsequently, scientists at Syngenta found new versions of the psy gene in maize, which, when introduced to rice, increased the beta-carotene levels to 31 µg/g. Given a conversion ratio of beta-carotene to vitamin A of 4:1, the new golden rice (Golden Rice 2) will be able to provide the necessary boost to daily diets, even after being stored for six months. This second rice has already been developed into locally appropriate varieties in the Philippines, India, and Bangladesh. In 2017 a submission was made to the Philippine Department of Agriculture–Bureau of Plant Industry for a biosafety permit for direct use of the latest version of golden rice in food, feed, or processing. In Bangladesh breeders at the Bangladesh Rice Research Institute, after two successive years of confined field trials, are seeking approval of unconfined field trials prior to seeking variety release.

Sources: "Golden Rice," Wikipedia, March 17, 2018, https://en.wikipedia.org/w/index.php?title=Golden_rice&oldid=830900455; X. Ye et al., "Engineering the Provitamin A (Beta-Carotene) Biosynthetic Pathway into (Carotenoid-Free) Rice Endosperm," Science (New York, NY) 287, no. 5451 (January 14, 2000): 303–5; Reaz Ahmad, "Wait Nearly Over for Golden Rice Release in Bangladesh," United News of Bangladesh, November 5, 2018, http://www.unb.com.bd/special-news/Wait-nearly-over-for-Golden-Rice-release-in-Bangladesh/62266.

All three of these examples have strong sustainability components:

First, they all demonstrably improve the intake of critical dietary components, including micronutrients and essential amino acids, among children and, in the case of golden rice, in infants. They improve health and prolong lives, and they have the capacity to do this for generation after generation.

Second, these essential nutrient-rich varieties are already or potentially easily accessible and at affordable prices.

Third, their sustainability is reinforced by the time it has taken to go from the early beginnings to products that work in farmers' field. Each process has been one of considerable care and attention, correcting mishaps, trying alternative pathways, and, most important, learning in the process.

Finally, in the future their sustainability will be improved by including them in integrated nutrition programs, for example, providing ingredients for baby foods or in school feeding programs.

Resilience to Pests and Diseases

Many serious and often devastating pests, diseases, and weeds attack African crops. While plants and livestock tend to be naturally resistant to pests, diseases, and weeds in the regions of the world where they originate, they encounter new pests and pathogens that can be devastating when they are moved to other regions.

In at least the short term, both breeding and the use of utilizing biotechnology can greatly strengthen resistance to attack. Nevertheless, pests, diseases, and weeds will overcome the resistance unless very careful precautions are taken.

In 1950 a new race of wheat stem rust exploded in the United States and southern Canada and was carried by high winds into Mexico. This was the first in what became a series of epidemics, including an outbreak of another highly virulent race named Ug99 that appeared in Uganda in 1999 (box 7.8).

Box 7.8. A new rust, Ug99, on wheat

Rusts are extremely serious fungal pathogens that attack wheat worldwide. In 1999 a new strain, Ug99, of stem rust was first detected in Uganda. It initially spread through the highlands of East Africa, causing wheat losses in Kenya as high as 80 percent. Seven races belonging to the Ug99 lineage have since spread, by wind or humans, to various wheat-growing countries in the East Africa highlands as well as to Zimbabwe, South Africa, Sudan, Yemen, and Iran.

In 2005 Norman Borlaug raised the alarm and warned the world about the serious threat Ug99 could pose to food security, and a response under the umbrella of the Borlaug Global Rust Initiative (http://www.globalrust. org) was initiated.

In the past, massive epidemics of stem rust have been overcome by the selection of certain Sr genes. Ug99 and its variants differ because of the virulence of its gene Sr31. However, screening has identified a low frequency of resistant wheat varieties, and these are being used to breed for enhanced, more diverse resistance. The new hybrids contain a number of genes, each of which has a low level of resistance but when combined are very effective and yield more than current popular varieties. But the ability of the fungus to mutate and evolve means protracted resistance is unlikely.

That the rice is resistant to the entire taxon of rust fungi is a promising discovery. If the mechanism of resistance can be identified and the genetic information translocated to wheat, a range of durable, resistant varieties could be created, varieties less restricted by geographic and biological boundaries.

Sources: Ravi P. Singh et al., "The Emergence of Ug99 Races of the Stem Rust Fungus Is a Threat to World Wheat Production," *Annual Review of Phytopathology* 49, no. 1 (September 8, 2011): 465–81, https://doi.org/10.1146/annurev-phyto-072910-095423; Ravi P. Singh et al., "Current Status, Likely Migration and Strategies to Mitigate the Threat to Wheat Production from Race Ug99 (TTKS) of Stem Rust Pathogen," *CAB Reviews: Perspectives in Agriculture, Veterinary Science, Nutrition and Natural Resources* 1, no. 054 (March 1, 2006), https://doi.org/10.1079/PAVSNNR20061054; Javed Ahmad, "Incorporation of Rust Resistance (Especially Stem Rust Race Ug99) from Rice to Wheat through Wheat? Rice Crossing," GlobalRust.org, accessed February 13, 2018, https://www.globalrust.org/content/incorporation-rust-resistance-especially-stem-rust-race-ug99-rice-wheat-through-wheat-rice.

Breeding for resistance to insect pest attacks has benefited from engineering based on the genes that code for toxins (crystalline cry proteins) produced by *Bacillus thuringiensis* (Bt), a naturally occurring bacterium widespread in the soil. The bacterium or extracts of the cry protein can be sprayed on crop leaves to kill insects feeding on the plants, especially caterpillars of moths, such as corn earworms. Once ingested, the protein kills the insect. Useful insects like honey bees and natural parasites and predators do not feed on the sprayed plants and are not affected. Moreover, the toxins do not harm humans. For these reasons Bt has been used by organic farmers for over fifty years.[55]

The genes encoding for cry proteins were first isolated in the early 1980s and have now been transferred to crops ranging from cotton to maize to rice to cowpea. Inevitably, though, the use of cry proteins will lead to selection for resistance, as does the use of chemical insecticides, synthetic or natural. By 2006 Bt cotton and Bt maize were being grown on more than 162 million hectares worldwide, "generating one of the largest selections for insect resistance ever known."[56] Bruce Tabashnik, an entomologist, and colleagues at the University of Arizona found a number of insect species showing resistance to Bt in the laboratory, and the first cases of resistance in the field were in Arkansas and Mississippi in 2003–4.[57]

Fortunately, a number of different cry proteins are produced by different Bt genes. Combining at least two different Bt genes means that it is more difficult for insects to develop resistance to both toxins simultaneously. Alternatively combining multiple toxic genes can work. A promising companion to the Bt gene is a gene that encodes for a proteinase inhibitor contained in the tropical giant taro plant. This confers high resistance to insect attack.

Selection for resistance can be slowed by setting up refuges of host plants that do not contain Bt genes.[58] The rare resistant insects surviving on Bt crops will mate with abundant susceptible pests from the refuges, and the hybrid offspring will be killed by Bt crops, markedly slowing the evolution of resistance.

In Africa only two countries, Sudan and South Africa, are growing recombinant DNA crops, although others have grown them, and several countries are undertaking research. At the National Agricultural Research Organisation (NARO) in Uganda a dozen such crops are undergoing field trials. One example is the development of bananas resistant to devastating banana wilt in Uganda, a program entirely funded from public sources. The resistance genes have been obtained from sweet peppers and donated by the Academia Sinica.

South Africa has had a twenty-year history of planting recombinant DNA crops, and, based on hectarage, it is currently ranked eighth in the world in planting such crops (box 7.9).

Box 7.9. Bt maize in South Africa

In 2016 South Africa planted 2.66 million hectares of recombinant DNA crops, of which maize constituted 2.16 million ha. The yield of Bt maize has doubled in the past twenty years, with economic gains of about US$2,000 million for the period 1998 to 2015.

Farmers who have adopted Bt maize have gained from increased yield when the Bt-targeted pests have been prevalent and have also benefited from a reduction of the time required to manage pests as well as the reduced costs associated with labor for pesticide applications. A drought hit the region during the 2015–16 production season, setting back production; a record crop in 2017 allowed South Africa to return to being a net exporter of corn with no import demand.

However, Bt resistance in stemborers was first reported in the field in 2006. A survey of commercial farmers in the main maize production region on the Highveld of South Africa found that compliance with refugia requirements was low, especially during the initial five to seven years after release. An alarmingly high number of farmers applied insecticides as preventative sprays on Bt maize and refugia, irrespective of stemborer infestation levels. Many farmers also reported significant borer infestation levels on Bt maize, and between 5 percent and 93 percent of farmers in all districts applied insecticides to Bt maize.

The survey revealed irresponsible management of Bt crop technology by farmers and chemical and seed companies. However, farmers perceived little, if any, negative impact on non-target organisms and remained positive about the technology in spite of resistance development. Nevertheless, they were concerned about consumers' acceptance of Bt maize and its marketability on the export market.

Sources: Global Status of Commercialized Biotech/GM Crops: 2016, ISAAA Briefs no. 52 (Ithaca: ISAAA, 2016), https://www.isaaa.org/resources/publications/briefs/52/download/isaaa-brief-52-2016.pdf; Graham Brookes and Peter Barfoot, "GM Crops: Global Socio-Economic and Environmental Impacts 1996–2015" (Dorchester, UK: PG Economics, June 2017), https://www.pgeconomics.co.uk/pdf/2017globalimpactstudy.pdf; Justina Torry and Dirk Esterhuizen, "Agricultural Biotechnology: Annual Biotechnology in South Africa" (South Africa: Agricultural Biotechnology Annual, South Africa: Global Agricultural Information Network, USDA Foreign Agricultural Service, 2016), 30, https://gain.fas.usda.gov/Recent%20GAIN%20Publications/Agricultural%20Biotechnology%20Annual_Pretoria_South%20Africa%20-%20Republic%20of_11-21-2016.pdf; J. B. J. van Rensburg, "First Report of Field Resistance by the Stem Borer, Busseola Fusca (Fuller) to Bt-Transgenic Maize," *South African Journal of Plant and Soil* 24, no. 3 (January 2007): 147–51, https://doi.org/10.1080/02571862.2007.10634798; M. Kruger, J. B. J. Van Rensburg, and J. Van den Berg, "Transgenic Bt Maize: Farmers' Perceptions, Refuge Compliance and Reports of Stem Borer Resistance in South Africa: Stem Borer Resistance to Bt Maize," *Journal of Applied Entomology* 136, no. 1–2 (February 2012): 38–50, https://doi.org/10.1111/j.1439-0418.2011.01616.x.

These two interventions emphasize that the major challenge is preventing or overcoming resistance. Achieving sustainable crop production, especially with the use of Bt genes, is unlikely unless the biotech component is integrated in a IPM program incorporating elements of sound and tested ecological approaches.

Resilience to Climate Change

Climate change threatens crop and livestock production in Africa. The stresses and shocks caused by higher temperatures and lack of rainfall mean that growing seasons are becoming shorter, and there are more frequent and severe extreme events, such as flooding and heat waves. Nearly 40 percent of Africa's maize-growing area faces occasional drought stress, resulting in yield losses of 10 to 25 percent; nearly 25 percent suffers frequent drought, with losses of up to half the harvest.[59]

Breeding has been approached in three ways. First, new crop varieties are subjected to a range of stresses in the field, including drought, and assessed by using farmer participation. Breeding in a greenhouse or on an experimental farm tends to focus on only one stress at a time. An advantage of carrying out the breeding trials on farmers' fields and with farmers' involvement is to assess the tolerance of the varieties under a range of simultaneous stresses, including drought, and to harness farmers' knowledge and responses. The technique involves a network of "stress breeding sites" with two main components:[60] "mother trials," involving up to twelve varieties, located close to the community, and managed by schools, colleges, or extension agents; and "baby trials," involving four to six varieties and located in the fields of farmers who used their own inputs and equipment.

For the past decade there has been a major collaborative program of breeding for drought tolerance relevant to African crops. The program involves private breeding companies large and small, institutes of the CGIAR, and national agricultural research institutes. In developed countries, especially in the United States, a wide variety of drought-tolerant crops are now commercially available. In Africa considerable progress has been made under the Drought Tolerant Maize for Africa Project, implemented among the National Agricultural Research systems by CIMMYT and the International Institute of Tropical Agriculture (IITA).[61] Over nine years (2007–15) the project developed drought-tolerant (DT), well-adapted maize hybrids and OPVs for farmers across thirteen countries in eastern, west, and southern Africa. In 2014 alone the project supported production of nearly fifty-four thousand tons of certified DT maize seed, benefiting an estimated 5.4 million households—or forty-three million people.

The yields of the new drought-tolerant varieties are superior to those of currently available commercial maize varieties, under both stress and optimum growing conditions. Nevertheless, the uptake has been variable. Surveys of nearly four thousand farm households in six countries have revealed considerable variation in farmer uptake, ranging from 9 percent of maize plots in Zimbabwe to 61 percent in Malawi.[62] The major barriers to adoption include unavailability of improved seed, inadequate information, lack of resources, high seed price, and perceived attributes of different varieties. Part of the answer to overcoming these barriers is to ensure that seed companies and agrodealers ensure adequate supply of DT maize seed in local markets and sell the seed in affordable micropacks of one or two kilograms.

Another collaboration, the Water Efficient Maize for Africa (WEMA) partnership, was delivering as of 2015 conventional seeds under the brand Drought-TEGO™, with forty new hybrids approved for commercial release and more in the development pipeline.[63] Seed licenses are available, royalty-free, to all seed companies, and more than twenty seed companies have made the seeds commercially available to African farmers. Farmers growing these hybrids are expected to harvest 20 to 35 percent more grain under moderate drought conditions compared to the seed they have historically planted.

A third approach has been to focus on recombinant DNA drought tolerance. In the past decade a suite of genes that regulate drought adaptation and/or tolerance have been identified and used in breeding.[64] One such gene is a so-called chaperone gene that can confer tolerance to stress of various kinds, including cold, heat, and lack of moisture.[65] The gene helps to repair misfolded proteins caused by stress so that the plant recovers more quickly. One chaperone gene, found in bacterial RNA, has been transferred to maize with excellent results in field trials. Plants with the gene show a 12 to 24 percent increase in growth in high-drought situations, in comparison with plants without the gene. The first transgenic trial was initiated in 2009 in South Africa. Maize varieties with stacked drought tolerance and insect resistance were approved in 2015, but seeds were available only in late 2017 to a limited number of smallholders. The official wide-scale release to commercial farms was planned to take place in 2018.

Nitrogen Fixation

What progress has been made in the quest for nitrogen-fixing cereals and other crops? The problem is that many crops are not efficient at absorbing and making use of nitrogen in the soil. This is true whether the nitrogen comes from inorganic fertilizer or from crop residue or manure. Nitrogen use efficiency is a complex trait with many components. Efficiency levels have been declining, with less than half of N applied to crops ending up in the harvested product. One way nitrogen utilization can be improved is through the planting of nitrogen-fixing crops such as many legume species, for example, soybeans.[66] Such fixation is an important part of the nitrogen cycle, as it replenishes the overall nitrogen content of the biosphere and compensates for the losses that are incurred owing to denitrification.[67]

Genetic intensification is aimed at taking up and utilizing nitrogen in crops that are already nitrogen fixers and also crops, such as the cereals, in which nitrogen-fixation is currently absent. The most promising approach is to target N-fixing bacteria that convert atmospheric ammonia to N using an enzyme, nitrogenase. The resulting fixed nitrogen is less prone to leaching and volatilization compared with synthetic fertilizer N since it is utilized in situ.[68]

One of the most evolved nitrogen-fixing systems is root nodule symbiosis (RNS). This is produced when certain bacteria colonize host plants, providing fixed nitrogen in exchange for carbohydrates. Such symbiotic bacteria, known as rhizobia, live in nodules on the roots, mostly of legumes such as peas, lupines, clover, and alfalfa. The crop plants furnish some of the products of their photosynthesis, and the bacteria reciprocate by supplying N.

Rhizobia already colonize the root zone (rhizosphere) of cereals, producing improvements in plant growth. This may have been the origin of root nodule symbiosis in legumes. Fundamentally, the process depends on "signaling pathways," one molecule sending a signal to the next and so on down the chain. An understanding of how this pathway evolved to function in RNS will help in engineering the same pathway for cereals, thereby enabling them to recognize nitrogen-fixing bacteria. Attempts are being made to produce nitrogen fixation in a similar fashion by reconstructing the evolutionary process in legumes and then to duplicate this in wheat, rice, and other cereals. It will, however, take some time to identify the relevant genes and engineer them into cereal varieties.

VALUE CHAINS

Mohammed and Fatima Adul Habid live in the Tamale region of northern Ghana. There are few all-weather roads in the region. Cell phone connections are good. The soils are generally adequate, but they lack organic matter as well as a range of micronutrients and may suffer from salinity and aluminum toxicity. In recent years the rainfall has become more erratic. Made up of six people in the household, the family farms a couple of hectares of land, growing rice, maize, soybean, and various other crops, earning about US$700–800 per year. They harvest about 2½ tons of rice per hectare and 1½ tons of maize. Less than 50 percent of their neighbors use fertilizers, and only 5 to 10 percent sow improved seeds.

Their circumstances are about to improve. A program of the Alliance for a Green Revolution in Africa (AGRA) is strengthening a number of key local institutions, among whom are the following:

- The Savannah Agricultural Research Institute (SARI) is providing foundation seed for the Savannah Seed Company.
- Some four hundred agrodealers have been helped with their start-ups and with ongoing training in business and management skills, fertilizers, agrochemicals; in many respects they are becoming a form of private extension service.
- The Evangelical Presbyterian Development and Relief Agency works with some forty communities, both Christian and Muslim, helping to develop and grow a range of farmer-based organizations, on average two per community.

> *They assisted in management, in negotiating supply of inputs from the prin-*
> *cipal agrodealers, in obtaining extension advice, and in bargaining with the*
> *purchaser of their products, the Savannah Farmers Market Company.*
>
> *There is already clear evidence of improvements in key crop yields, achieved by*
> *following advice from SARI. Large soybean yields, of 3 tons per hectare, resulted from*
> *using certified seed, coupled with phosphate fertilizer, use of rhizobium inoculum,*
> *and application of a proprietary compost.*[1]

The AGRA grant making program is essentially enabling in nature. It is neither top-down nor dependent on the interventions of outside bodies and experts. However, it does rely on supportive government policies and, in some circumstances, on advice from outside experts. It is this approach that makes it likely to be sustainable.

The third pillar of SI focuses on the development of sustainable socioeconomic intensification.[2] It encompasses the relationships between farmers and each other and between farmers and agricultural value chains, and how these may be sustainably intensified. The result is the development of innovative, sustainable institutions on the farm, in the community, and across regions and nations as a whole. Value chains also encompass improvements to the enabling environment and to social and human capital, resulting in more sustainable livelihoods.

Farmer Associations

Many African smallholder farmers suffer from isolation. They often live far from cities and towns and are poorly served by roads, especially all-season rural roads. Markets that provide inputs may be many kilometers away and essentially inaccessible. The same is true of the output markets where they may wish to sell their produce. If farm households are to step up and step out, in Andrew Dorward's phrase, they require equitable access to input and output markets and help with joining remunerative value chains.

Part of the response of rural people to the isolation they experience is to create associations of one kind or another, partly to exchange views and experiences and partly to improve their financial circumstances.[3] Consciously or unconsciously, these people and especially the farmers among them aim to build social cohesion with one another, with buyers and sellers of goods and services, with people from other walks of life, and with government officials. In the process, they build social capital, including relationships based on trust and solidarity that enable them to achieve collective action and cooperation for the common good.

Farmer associations also enable smallholders to exert their bargaining power in purchasing inputs and selling their produce. They can exploit production and managerial economies of scale, overcome market entry barriers, reduce transaction costs, and build value chain relationships.

As farmers establish linkages to markets they become more aware of the existence of value chains and of the need to shift more of the value of produce to the hands of the farmers themselves who produce the value. Far too often smallholders participating in the chain may find the rewards are low and the risks are high. The situation is made worse by middlemen in market chains who transfer the risks to those with the least power, namely, the smallholder farmers.

There are numerous types of farmer associations, ranging from savings and loan associations to formal cooperatives and contract farming, each with its own benefits and drawbacks.

Savings and Loan Associations

There is a long tradition of cooperation, mutuality, reciprocity, and solidarity in African societies. These relationships are expressed in a variety of community associations encouraging both savings and some form of loan arrangement. These are often locally rooted, defined by the community and by social class boundaries. Usually they are small in membership, and they can take a variety of forms.[4]

Only about 40 percent of adults in developing economies have an account at a financial institution, and in SSA it is less than a third.[5] In some countries there is a tradition of small banks serving a local population, sometimes with specialist bankers in agricultural credits. In South Africa some forty rural banks have been created by the Financial Services Association. Local people can open savings accounts and are encouraged to be shareholders. They are proving to be very popular.[6]

For very poor farmers and other rural dwellers, who generally have neither the knowledge nor the skills to interact with formal financial institutions, CARE and other NGOs have been promoting a savings-led microfinance model called Village Savings and Loan Associations (VSLAs). VSLAs are based on the belief that for the extremely poor, particularly women, the best approach is to begin by building their financial assets and skills through savings rather than debt.[7] A major objective is to enable households to save and borrow in ways that allow them to smooth out cyclical consumption patterns.

VSLAs essentially provide a simple, community-based commitment savings product with an option to borrow attached. Members are able to save as little as the equivalent of US10¢ per week in some cases and can borrow as little as US$5. Although they may start out saving very little they tend to increase their savings amount annually; a woman saving US10¢ per week in her first year of joining a VSLA will save US$1–2 per week within a year or two. If aggregated with the rest of her group, the members can save $30–40 per week. At that level, it starts to make financial sense to begin making loans or to deposit excess savings with a financial institution.

Alissa Abdoulkarim of Dan Gado village near Maradi City in Niger is a VSLA village agent who trains groups in the mechanics of savings and loan groups. She says she is proud to do the training because VSLAs show women and girls how to make money for themselves, and that brings them independence: "It's a symbol of happiness, because when it's open, people take loans and start businesses. There's freedom in that. It's a way for women to fight for themselves, to get out of poverty."[8]

Cooperatives

Formal cooperatives have a long history in both the developed and developing countries. The Rochdale Equitable Pioneers, the first true cooperative, was formed in 1844 in the northern UK town of Rochdale.[9] A group of poor cotton weavers pooled their resources and set up a shop selling staple foods. Soon the cooperative membership was opened to all customers, who became shareholders with democratic decision-making rights. The principles set out by the Rochdale Society have influenced the way in which cooperatives have been managed throughout the world ever since.

Dairy cooperatives have been successful in many parts of the world. In the Netherlands over 75 percent of the dairy market is provided by cooperatives.[10] In India the dairy cooperative Amul spurred the country's so-called White Revolution and is now the world's largest producer of milk and milk products.[11] A limited study shows a significant growth in the numbers of active cooperatives and their membership (table 8.1).[12]

It is estimated that 7 percent of the African population belongs to a cooperative, and some countries, including Egypt, Senegal, Ghana, Kenya, and Rwanda, report a rate of over 10 percent. Teams from Maseno University in Kenya and Katholieke University of Leuven, Belgium, have carried out an empirical study of cooperatives in these five countries using a livelihood perspective. They found there was a significant contribution to poverty reduction by mobilizing and distributing financial capital; creating employment and income-generating opportunities; providing a forum for education and training; and creating solidarity schemes that cater to

TABLE 8.1.   Growth in numbers of active cooperatives and their members in selected African countries

	NUMBER OF ACTIVE COOPERATIVES		COOPERATIVE MEMBERS (IN MILLIONS)	
	1992	2005	1992	2005
Ghana	1,000	2,850	n/a	2.4
Kenya	4,000	7,000	2.5	3.3
Nigeria	29,000	50,000	2.6	4.3
Senegal	2,000	6,000	n/a	3.0

Source: Frederick O. Wanyama, Patrick Develtere, and Ignace Pollet, "Encountering the Evidence: Cooperatives and Poverty Reduction in Africa," SSRN Electronic Journal, 2008, https://doi.org/10.2139/ssrn.1330387.

unexpected expenses related to illness, social welfare, death, and other socioeconomic problems.[13] Yet very few cooperatives have been able to successfully integrate vertically to enable smallholders to participate in emerging value chains.

Contract Farming

Another, sometimes complementary approach is through contract farming, developed in SSA as a response to imperfect markets and poor service provision.[14] Usually it entails a formal or informal agreement between a central processing or exporting agency and a number of independent farmers.[15] Such arrangements exploit economies of scale in both purchases and sales. Farmers benefit from services provided by the processing firms, such as credit, seeds, fertilizer, and technical assistance, and have easy access to a relatively guaranteed market for their products. However, they tend to be geared toward better-off farmers; the poorest households lack the assets and resources to overcome the entry barriers.

The structure of the system, how it works, and the overall objectives can vary. Researchers at IFPRI argue that, at least for Uganda, there are several different, but often overlapping, models of contract farming.[16] None are ideal. In more formal, centralized forms, the farmers are often exploited if they are not well organized, and disputes may arise when extracontractual sales occur, as happens in the sugarcane and organic cotton growing industries. More informal models tend to be simple but lack access to finances and extension services; farmers may experience a high risk of default. The IFPRI-led study concludes that the only system which has safeguards against farmer exploitation is a multipartite model involving many stakeholders in the management, although overheads may eat into the benefits.

The Challenges for Farmer Associations

A persistent challenge, as characterized by Nigel Poole and Annabel de Frece, is that farmer associations tend to

- Lack capital to grow in scale and complexity, particularly investment in physical assets for value addition through processing and
  manufacturing.
- Lack management capacity and good organizational governance.
- Compete in markets against economic forces that confound
  their traditionally bureaucratic and unresponsive structures and
  strategies.[17]

There are other shortcomings: farmer associations can be exclusive, leaving out marginal groups such as widows, AIDS-affected households, or ethnic minorities. State support or interventions by development agencies may be necessary for their implementation and regulation. Nevertheless, although collective decision making may be cumbersome, it can, in the appropriate circumstances with a fair, far-sighted governance, provide sustainable solutions to these challenges.

Smallholder Producer Organizations

The various forms of farmer organization referred to above are rarely geared toward participation in modern value chains. They tend to lack the organizational, commercial, and technical capacities to operate effectively at national or regional scale.[18] African smallholders today need to contend with far more complex and competitive markets and cope with growing market specialization, rapidly changing consumer preferences, and increasingly intricate technical specifications.

With the exception of producers of major traditional and some high-value export commodities, the large majority of African smallholders are isolated from the rest of the agricultural value chain for a variety of reasons, most of which center on their small scale, their geographic isolation, and their lack of capital.[19] Because they are small, they cannot realize economies of scale for input procurement and output commercialization. The firms dealing with the farmers tend to be measurably larger and better capitalized. When it comes to selling their output, farmers find themselves in a poor negotiating position. Competition between them lowers prices further, relegating many household farmers to subsistence production or migration out of farming.

The quality of what smallholders produce is inconsistent and of unreliable quality, and there may be high costs associated with of assembly, storage, and transport. Small transaction sizes and the dispersion of holdings raise the cost of providing financial services, which in turn raises the cost of capital to those who wish to borrow.[20] Smallholders operating individually are unlikely to generate the demand for financial services necessary to stimulate significant investment by the banking sector. In turn, the banking sector offers a limited range of services, few of which meet smallholders' needs.

The successful transformation of African agriculture and the effective integration of smallholder farmers into modernizing value chains will require the creation of smallholder producer organizations (SPOs) that have the technical, commercial, and financial resources necessary to position their members as credible business partners.[21] Modern value chains require integrated solutions that link numbers of farmers with all major interfaces between smallholders and other value chain actors. Today's SPO has to be more than an advocate or marketing body; it needs to offer a comprehensive set of services to its members and that requires improved skills as well as institutional and technical innovations that help to serve and empower smallholder farmers.

One practical option that integrates smallholders at scale, cost effectively, and within a reasonable time frame is to deploy modern information and communications technologies (ICT).[22] This can help them overcome the physical, infrastructural, and institutional obstacles they face. It can also build the commercial and technical capacities of SPOs enabling them provide effective business credibility for their members.

The Value of Value Chains

A food value chain describes the complicated process of transformation involving a sequence of events from the molecular product of one or more genes in crops or livestock, through intermediate stages of husbandry, harvesting, processing, marketing, and consumption, to the final molecular changes in the human who consumes the food product. The chain runs from molecule to molecule, creating value for the participants at each stage.

A good example is the value chain involving orange-fleshed sweet potatoes in Mozambique (box 8.1).

Box 8.1. The orange-fleshed sweet potato value chain in Mozambique

Maria Andrade of the International Potato Centre, who is based at the Agricultural Research Institute of Mozambique (IIAM), is both a pioneer

---

plant breeder and a creator of a highly successful value chain (in 2016 she, along with three other scientists, was awarded the World Food Prize for her work). Andrade breeds new varieties by crossing local white-fleshed sweet potatoes with imported orange-fleshed ones, producing new, locally adapted, high-yielding orange-fleshed potatoes. In effect, through intensive breeding she changes the molecular structure of the potatoes, thus adding value. The new varieties contain beta-carotene, a source of pro-vitamin A. The potatoes are tested and selected for those with improved performance, creating further value. These are then multiplied in local nurseries, which add value by distributing and selling them to farmers. Use of appropriate fertilizer can further add value by increasing yields to fifty tons per hectare. Innovative seed storage in the dry season can also add value. The farmers, in turn, harvest the potatoes and either consume them or place them on the market, adding direct monetary value. Consumer preferences are also being investigated to discover where the added value lies. Men typically prefer dryer varieties, while babies like wetter ones; some people eat the leaves, some enjoy the potatoes raw, and others cook them. Finally, when the orange-fleshed potatoes are consumed, the consumers had higher levels of Vitamin A in their livers.

Sources: International Potato Center, "Orange Fleshed Sweetpotato," *International Potato Center* (blog), accessed May 22, 2018, https://cipotato.org/impact/photostories/orange-fleshed-sweetpotato/; The World Bank, "A Sweet (Potato) Solution to Malnutrition," World Bank, December 16, 2015, http://www.worldbank.org/en/news/feature/2015/12/16/a-sweet-potato-solution-to-malnutrition; Jan W. Low et al., "A Food-Based Approach Introducing Orange-Fleshed Sweet Potatoes Increased Vitamin A Intake and Serum Retinol Concentrations in Young Children in Rural Mozambique," *Journal of Nutrition* 137, no. 5 (May 1, 2007): 1320–27, https://doi.org/10.1093/jn/137.5.1320.

Along this and other, similar value chains many actors can be involved: breeders, chemical analysts, graders, nurserymen, and smallholder farmers to storers, processors, sellers, and buyers in local and regional markets. Plant- or animal-based goods flow up the chain until they reach consumption, in exchange for financial flows that flow down the chain from the final consumer back to the original producer. At each stage value is added, and the actors along the chain retain a share of the additional value, usually in financial units, making each actor a beneficiary who makes a profit. Ideally the farmers should capture a sizable

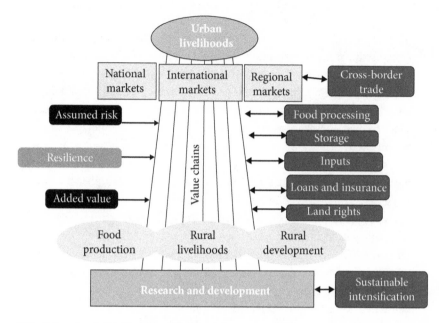

FIG. 8.1. A schematic value chain

Source: Gordon Conway et al., "Creating Resilient Value Chains for Smallholder Farmers," *Africa Agriculture Status Report 2017: The Business of Smallholder Agriculture in Sub-Saharan Africa* (Kigali, Rwanda: AGRA, 2017), https://agra.org/aasr2017/chapter-5/.

amount of the value, but usually those at the top of the chain, who produce and sell a final product on the market, capture most of the value (figure 8.1).

For smallholder farmers, a successful agricultural and livelihood transformation depends on the effective and inclusive integration of smallholder farmers in value chains. Such integration, up and down the value chain, can lead to

- greater productivity and value; and
- a more diverse chain.

It can also contribute to reduced risks, greater value chain resilience, and improved sustainability. In practice, only segments of value chains are considered. Thus supply chains, usually operating from farm to fork, focus on the agrobusiness component of value chains.

During the Green Revolution in Asia in the 1960s and 1970s value was pushed up from the base of the cereal value chain, deploying the new short-strawed wheat varieties. Now it is pulled from the top by urban demand that encompasses not only more staple food but also a greater variety of foods, especially more nutritious foods (see chapter 2).

The Components of the Value Chain

Each component of the value chain, each structure or process has its distinctive characteristics, especially its own capacity to generate value. At the base are two strong components: research and development and land rights.

Research and Development

At the bottom of the value chain is the research and development (R&D) conducted in public or private research laboratories and field stations, producing new crop and livestock breeds and improved husbandry practices that add initial value.

As we noted earlier, for the value chain to be sustainable it has to be based on the technologies and processes of SI. Much can be achieved by utilizing existing knowledge, but because of the nature and scale of the challenges posed, innovation is also required.[23] Innovating may involve new ideas, new technologies; or novel applications of existing technologies, new processes, or institutions; or, more generally, new ways of doing things in a place where they have not been practiced before or by people new to such processes. Modern innovation is usually stimulated by innovation systems and pathways.

Science and innovation have long informed agriculture. From the application of ecological knowledge to increase the resilience of agricultural systems to the revolution in biotechnology made possible by the discovery of DNA, science, both fundamental and applied, can bring about transformations in the way food is produced and accessed.[24] R&D in Africa produces a notable impact, with an average rate of return on investments in agricultural R&D between 1975 and 2014 of over 40 percent per year.[25] Agricultural R&D increases agricultural productivity, and this in turn reduces poverty.[26]

Innovation at the time of the Green Revolution was relatively straightforward: breeding of new, short-strawed varieties of wheat and rice able to take up more nitrogen and other nutrients, resulting in higher harvest index. R&D could be largely conducted in a single research institution. Today the challenges are considerably more complex. Development planners and practitioners need to go beyond sector silos in academia, business, and government and think more strategically and holistically about how they can cope with interconnected issues that require integrated approaches and solutions. Planners and practitioners have to rethink their research and innovation systems in multiple dimensions, as outlined by Calestous Juma et al.:

- Focussing on multiple benefits—not only higher yields and production and more nutritious foods, but also more selective use of inputs, reduced environmental impact, greater resilience, minimized emissions of greenhouse gases and improvements in natural capital.

- Engaging with multiple partners—to ensure all benefits are considered and to utilize different approaches. Partners will include both the public and the private sectors, Civil Society Organisations (CSOs) and NGOs. Gender equity and balance is also crucial.
- Utilising multiple approaches—[the three pillars of SI, agriculture, and ecology, the new genetics and value chains, often concurrently in an integrated fashion and ensuring that there is an] . . . enabling environment for technological and institutional innovation and technology adoption.
- Working on multiple scales—from the individual field, to the farm, to the community, to the watershed and to whole landscapes, to ensure multiple benefits are fully realised.[27]

Innovation is becoming increasingly global. At the same time, African countries are developing their own innovation systems. Thus CGIAR (formerly the Consultative Group on International Agricultural Research) has been able to conduct and coordinate research at scale and to partner with National Agricultural Research Systems (NARS). They are often innovative in their own right, but they also help to adapt international research, so creating national strategies, and building domestic capacity and competences.

NGOs can also be highly innovative. They often work at a village or community level, but some operate on a larger scale, playing an important role in bridging between international and national organizations. Farmers on the ground can complement the efforts of the national extension services in promoting innovations for use by smallholder farmers.[28] Universities, too can be major sources of innovation as well as training innovators for work in a laboratory or the field. The private sector in developed countries provides the largest share of agricultural R&D focusing on the translational and applied components of the R&D portfolio as well as on the more commercially viable crops.[29] There is increasing interest in the private sector (both large and small) in providing innovations for smallholder agriculture in Africa.

It is relatively straightforward to develop innovations that achieve two or more benefits, for example in yield, nutrition, income, or the environment, in addition to those intended or targeted (table 8.2). The difficulty lies in achieving the combination of benefits that meet all the requirements of SI. Inevitably there are trade-offs. Fewer inputs often mean lower yields. Higher yields may increase GHG emissions and come at the expense of resilience. Natural capital may suffer whatever the other benefits are. The challenge is to try to find innovations that

TABLE 8.2. The added values generated by research and development in Africa

TECHNOLOGY	RESULTS	OTHER BENEFITS
Microdosing	2,000 paired-plot trials in Zimbabwe showed a 30–50% increase in grain yields 25,000 smallholder farmers in West Africa increased millet and sorghum yields by 44–120%	• Household incomes in West Africa increased by 50–130% when microdosing was combined with a "warrantage" system • Lower, more selective, precise, and targeted use of fertilizer: approximately thirty kilograms of fertilizer for every hectare which equates to one-tenth of the amount typically used on wheat; increased nutrient use efficiency and drought tolerance
Orange-fleshed sweet potato (OFSP)	The Tainung variety in Kenya yields three times more than traditional varieties, is drought tolerant, and quicker to mature	• 125g of OFSP provides primary school children with over twice the recommended daily allowance of vitamin A • For over 24,000 households in Uganda and Mozambique, between 2007 and 2009, vitamin A intake by women and children doubled
Water Efficient Maize for Africa (WEMA)	Yields increase 20–35% under moderate drought compared to conventional varieties New drought-tolerant genes will increase yields 12–24% in high drought conditions	• Building in resistance to pests such as stem borers
Faidherbia	Maize under Faidherbia albida yielded an average of five tons per hectare (t/ha) compared to two t/ha outside the canopy	• Source of fodder and firewood • Helps retain soil cover for enhanced fertility and protection from erosion; nutrient levels were 42%, 25%, and 31% higher with Faidherbia canopies than without for total nitrogen, potassium, and organic carbon, respectively

Source: Calestous Juma et al., "Innovation for Sustainable Intensification in Africa," Briefing Paper (London: Montpellier Panel, Agriculture for Impact, 2013), https://www.mamopanel.org/media/uploads/files/INNOVATION_FOR_SUSTAINABLE_INTENSIFICATION_IN_AFRICA_2013.pdf.

satisfy multiple benefits from the outset and that place the farmer at the center of these intersecting circles, where the trade-offs are minimal.

Land Rights

Also at the bottom of the food chain, and in many respects as crucial to value chain performance as R&D, is secure ownership of or access to land. Lacking such rights, farmers will not invest in improving the soil, water, and other resources on which agriculture depends. In the past, changes to the systems of land rights in Africa were not thought essential to increasing agricultural productivity because land was abundant and farmers' rights to work as tenants on the basis of customary systems of ownership were deemed sufficient. Neither belief is valid any longer.

Since the rise of world food prices in 2008 there have been concerted efforts to transfer land out of customary tenure (under the control of traditional authorities) to the state or to private individuals who, it is argued, can exploit the productive potential of the land more effectively and thus meet national food security objectives.[30] Customary tenure is designed to afford free "birthright access" to land by smallholder farmers in the community and generally does so where the traditional authorities still have land left to allocate.[31]

But much of SSA is experiencing new farmland ownership patterns. The number of medium-scale farms, that is, between five and one hundred hectares, resulting from land acquisition is growing. For example, the quantity of recorded new land titles in Zambia over ten hectares since 1995 amounts to 12 percent of the land cultivated nationally, with the mean title deed size being roughly fifty-two hectares.[32] Nevertheless, the distributional effects of converting land from customary to state-titled land continue to be contested.[33] Such conversion generally reflects the ceding of power and authority from traditional authorities to the functioning of land markets and ultimately to the state.[34] Land transferred from customary to state tenure provides so-called bonanza discount purchases to the first buyer, generally privileged people, and then afterward is bought and sold based on willingness and ability to pay. Land under subject to this process almost never goes to poor smallholder farmers.

Land Titling

A crucial factor in ensuring fair and equitable land access and ownership is the process of conferring or purchase of land titles. This can benefit small farm households that are hanging in and also can enable land sales and the creation of rental markets.[35] An example is the system of land titling developed in Rwanda (box 8.2).

Box 8.2. The Rwanda land tenure registration program

The Rwanda land tenure registration program is a pioneering process. The speed and efficiency with which it was carried out has shown that it is possible to implement national land registration processes quickly and cheaply. In many respects it has been a game changer. The government sought for the first time to systematically issue leases under the 2008 Organic Land Law. The new mass land registration process was designed to be bottom-up, including the landholding community itself to conduct and officiate the demarcation and adjudication of property. It was an elegant process, employing professional surveyors and legal officers, as well as the latest technology in global positioning systems (GPS), mobile computing, low-cost satellite, and aerial imagery.

The program set out to survey, compile, rectify, and issue lease certificates to the rightful claimants for an estimated 7.9 million plots. The plots were mapped by parasurveyors drawn from the village. They walked the perimeter of the land with the claimant, their neighbors, and the Umudugudu leader to ensure that they had all agreed on the boundaries. Although this meant that the processes was democratic and largely local, it also turned out that millions more plots needed to be processed.

The program was completed in less than five years and delivered at a cost per title of around US$7, a historic benchmark in land registration. Moreover, the government's Gender Monitoring Office reported in 2012 that "the land registration process is a positive mechanism to improve gender equality."

Similar registration projects in Lesotho, Mozambique, and Namibia have subsequently confirmed that large-scale, low-cost land registration is possible in a variety of contexts.

Source: John Leckie, "Ethiopia Land Registration Ready for Lift Off: Now What?," in *Developing Alternatives*, accessed May 23, 2018, http://dai-global-developments.com/articles/ethiopia-land-registration-ready-for-lift-off-now-what/; Owen Edwards, "Delivering Large-Scale Land Certification Programmes: Lessons from Rwanda," in *Developing Alternatives*, an online publication of Development Alternatives, Inc. (DAI), accessed May 23, 2018, http://dai-global-developments.com/articles/delivering-large-scale-land-certification-programmes-lessons-from-rwanda/.

In Rwanda and Ethiopia a new experimental program known as its4land project is adapting land tenure recording based on small, fixed-wing, unmanned aerial vehicles (UAVs or drones), smart sketch maps, automated feature extraction, and "geocloud" services.[36] The aim is to help map land rights even more quickly, cheaply, and transparently for all stakeholders, women explicitly included.

Land Markets

Land rental markets are developing rapidly in the more densely populated areas of Africa.[37] However, there are dangers in this process. While there is some evidence that they advance equity, this is not inevitable. Converting titles from customary to more formal renting may be a front for relatively affluent domestic and international investors to obtain land relatively cheaply, thus increasing land pressures in high-density areas. The rise of land rental markets may help the growing rural labor force to access land, but because renting land generally involves providing the equivalent of one-third or more of the crop proceeds to the landlord, tenants must be extremely productive to make a reasonable livelihood by renting land. Thomas Jayne of Michigan State University and his colleagues argue that potentially the greatest threat to broad-based agricultural growth in Africa is the rapidly spreading process of customary lands being sold or leased to a small but growing class of African elites.[38]

More generally, governments can improve access to land for rural households through a coordinated strategy of public goods and services that raises the economic value of customary land, which is currently remote and underutilized.[39] Investments in infrastructure and service provisions will link currently isolated areas with existing road and rail infrastructure, coupled with investment in schools, health care facilities, electrification, water supply, and other public goods.

Loans and Insurance

A potential benefit of land titling is the acquisition of loans, but African banks are notoriously poor at writing loans for agriculture, let alone for smallholder farmers.[40] Banks often require up-front collateral of 20 to 50 percent. To excuse these high rates, banks usually claim that farmers are poor at paying back loans. The evidence shows otherwise. Akinwumi Adesina, currently the president of the African Development Bank, tells a story of his time with the Rockefeller Foundation when highly productive, disease resistant bananas had been developed in Uganda with foundation funds:

The challenge was to get the disease resistant bananas into the hands of millions of farmers. With huge potential to yield over 40 tons per hectare, compared to about 15 tons farmers were getting, it was stuck, as one single plantlet cost $1.50, way above the daily earnings of many farmers. A solution had to be found. With support of the Foundation, I was allowed to use a $500,000 grant from the Foundation to support a rural bank in Uganda to agree to lend to these farmers, as an experiment. The deal was simple: they would lend the Foundation's funds on condition that if farmers repaid, the Bank would commit one million of its own monies the following year. It worked! Over a 4-year period, the total loss was just $4,500! A point was demonstrated: the main reason banks don't lend to farmers was perceived risks of loss, and not real risks. I got to know several years later the bank had lent some $20 million of its own monies. Tissue culture bananas spread rapidly across Kenya and other East African countries.[41]

One solution is that a bank receives a guarantee against loan default repayment risk in exchange for a fee.[42] Nigeria was the first country in SSA to develop a Credit Guarantee Fund for the agriculture sector. The scheme, set up in 1977, is funded jointly by the central government and the Central Bank of Nigeria. It allows banks to recover up to 75 percent of the principal in case of default as well as the equivalent of the interest lost from defaulted loans. From 1997 to 2015 the proportion of Nigerian bank loans made to the agriculture increased from 0.7 percent to over 5 percent.[43] But in many countries obtaining a loan remains a near insurmountable challenge for a smallholder.

African farmers face a variety of risks: they can lose their collateral if there is a calamity and they lose their land and they can lose their crop growth because of adverse weather events like droughts or hail. A farmer can reduce the risk by deciding not to grow a susceptible crop in a given high-risk area, but the choices may be limited. One solution may be to invest in irrigation. Alternatively, risk can be transferred through a financial instrument such as insurance, which diminishes and smooths out the risk exposure of both the smallholder farmers and their supply chain partners.

Types of Insurance

Purchasing insurance entails a small cost to prevent the effects of a large, disruptive loss. A risk is characterized as insurable if the premium paid is sufficiently small in comparison to the value of the asset insured. While a variety of agricultural risk transfer solutions are available across the supply chain, here we focus on the risk of crop production loss that farmers incur and is the first cause of supply chain disruption.

Agricultural insurance worldwide has grown to surpass US$20 billion in premiums. However, whereas developed markets in North America, Europe, and Asia jointly represent more than 95 percent of global agricultural insurance volume, the African market represents less than 1 percent.[44]

Traditional agricultural insurance for smallholders may be unsuitable. But over ten years ago a new type of insurance known as "parametric insurance" was developed for smallholder farmers. It is based on the estimation of crop loss derived from a parameter or index that acts as proxy for yield loss and can be computed without the need to visit the farm.[45] For instance, the rainfall data recorded by a weather station is used to build an index that acts as proxy for crop yield loss in the vicinity of the station. Such insurance has been developed using satellite data, and several pilots have been implemented in SSA. Although this type of insurance offers the advantage of shielding the insurance company against moral hazard, the potential of mismatch of index-estimated losses compared to real losses can limit its usability.

There are many examples of insurance schemes in Africa, but most are at a relatively small scale.[46] In 2008–9 Malawi was the first low-income country to adopt a weather-derivative instrument. A national "maize index" was designed to act as a proxy of national maize production driven by precipitation, based on twenty-three weather stations managed by the national meteorological agency. This allowed the country to receive an immediate payout of up to US$4.4 million as soon as the index fell below 10 percent of its historical average. The World Bank acted as intermediary between the country and the international reinsurance market, while the premium paid by the Malawi government was financed by the UK Department for International Development.

Livestock Insurance

Livestock in Africa are highly susceptible to adverse weather conditions. Thus approximately 75 percent of livestock deaths in the Horn of Africa are caused by severe drought, repeatedly leaving herders, their families, and entire communities destitute. In October 2015 the first government livestock insurance scheme in Africa, the Kenya Livestock Insurance Program (KLIP), was successfully piloted in two counties in the north of Kenya.[47]

The program uses a satellite-based index insurance, enabling protection of pastoralists in remote areas. Satellites assess the state of the grazing conditions in a certain region by measuring the color of the ground. Green is good, yellow is very dry. Once a certain threshold is reached, the pastoralists automatically receive a lump sum payment, allowing them to supply their cows, goats, and camels with feed and water. The system allows the pastoralists to hold on to their way of life and means of survival.

The KLIP pilot was launched in October 2015 with Kenyan government funding, and is being extended across the whole country. The premiums are free to herders registered under the Hunger Safety Net Program and cover five animals per household. Herders can choose to insure additional animals at their own expense. In the 2016–17 season an epic drought desiccated fields and forages in the Horn of Africa, and the Kenyan government, in partnership with Kenyan insurers, announced payments to over twelve thousand pastoral households under the livestock insurance plan.[48]

Insurance Linked to Loans

A potentially better approach than KLIP is to link insurance to loans.[49] An example is a pilot study in Tanzania under the Farmer to Market Alliance of the WFP whereby insurance is coupled with loans for inputs given to farmer associations.[50]

The project, supported by the EU's ClimateKIC program, has developed a new technology based on big data, supercomputing, and satellite data. The aim is to build new financial instruments that de-risk both the participation of smallholder farmers in local to global supply chains and the supply chains of banks, food buyers, and retailers to weather risk.

This approach is based on a mathematical construct that computes information on yields for 5 km^2 pixels using weather data from satellite imagery combined with information on technologies and management practices. Among the various stakeholders, in addition to WFP, are Yara, Cargill, and SAB Miller, with insurance provided by a local company and through Munich Re. All stakeholders have an incentive to increase resilience and productivity and this directly translates into higher profitability for all. Such insurance permits farmers to invest in new inputs based on technologies and farming processes that are genuinely transformative.

Inputs

Seeds

In the past it was common in Africa for farmers to grow crops from seed they retained, often of very poor quality, or to obtain hybrid seed from a few large seed companies. With the development of local seed companies relying on local entrepreneurs these practices began to change. A classic case is that of Victoria Seeds in Uganda and Josephine Okot. She is a remarkable young Ugandan woman born in the north at Gulu and educated at Makerere University. To set up a seed company she tried to obtain a loan from a bank, but no one would support her. Finally, in 2004, USAID came to the rescue. Her business is now thriving.[51] She is a one-stop agricultural services provider, marketing cereal, legume, oil, vegetable, and pasture seeds as well as herbicides. So popular is her store on the outskirts of Kampala that at the height of the sowing season lines of farmers stretch around the block. She has other processing facilities and retail shops elsewhere in Uganda and is expanding into Rwanda.

Okot is passionate about empowering farmers through training, capacity building, and promoting innovative technologies. In particular, she focuses on the risks of rain-fed agriculture, dealing with uncertain weather, disease, pests, and the ever-increasing price of fuel. Her seed is drought tolerant, early maturing, disease resistant, and gives better yields. Furthermore, she offers technical information and extension support.

Fertilizer Blenders

Although occurring at a slow pace, the development of local fertilizer-blending companies, is equally a sign of progress. Fertilizer recommendations for crops in Africa are often outdated. Farmers are given blanket recommendations based not on soil nutrient status but on the availability of a limited choice of fertilizers, mostly diammonium phosphate (DAP), urea, or nitrogen, phosphorus, and potassium mixes (NPKs). They do not take account of the local conditions, in particular, specific absences of key soil micronutrients. Inevitably yields are lower than need be. For example, fields in southern Ethiopia can produce maize yields of four to six tons per hectare with a high-performing variety plus a blended fertilizer plus boron, which is lacking in the soil.[52]

Nevertheless, there are countries in Africa where the fertilizer industry is investing in blended fertilizer production. Since 2003 the ARM Mavuno Company in Kenya has been producing a range of crop and soil-specific fertilizers that are scientifically blended.[53] They contain eleven essential plant nutrients: nitrogen, phosphorus, potassium, calcium, magnesium, sulfur, zinc, boron, copper, manganese, and molybdenum. When combined, the company claims, these fertilizers improve soil fertility and yield, and over time their blends also reduce soil acidity and improve nutrient uptake. This process is aided by the development of digital mapping techniques that greatly accelerate the production of soil maps, leading to specific local fertilizer formulations.

Herbicides

One of the biggest threats to production on farms is weed infestations, which has led to a growing sale of herbicides. This growth has been particularly pronounced in Ethiopia, where herbicides that are predominantly imported have grown from about US$10 million in value in 2010 to US$25 million in 2014, shifting from almost exclusive use of 2–4-D to glyphosate. Other, more expensive herbicides are also becoming increasingly important. Herbicide use is resulting in less weeding by women (figure 8.2).

Besides the increase in overall labor productivity of 9–18 percent from herbicide use, there is added social value: liberating women from weeding tasks reduces their workload and increases the welfare of rural households in general, since it affects the time allocated for housekeeping, cooking, childcare, and other activities.[54]

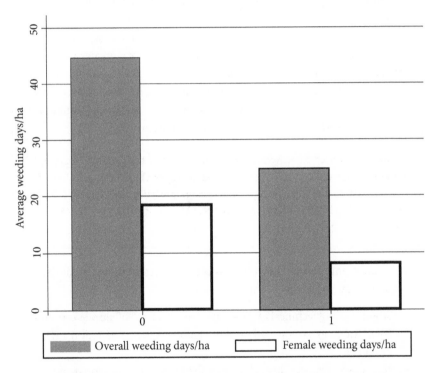

FIG. 8.2.   Effect of use of herbicides (right-hand bars) versus non-use (left-hand bars) in Ethiopia

Source: Seneshaw Tamru et al., "The Rapid Expansion of Herbicide Use in Smallholder Agriculture in Ethiopia: Patterns, Drivers, and Implications," ESSP II (Washington DC: IFPRI and Addis Ababa, Ethiopia: Ethiopian Development Research Institute, 2016), http://ebrary. ifpri.org/cdm/ref/collection/p15738coll2/id/130716.

Agrodealers

Local shops that sell seeds, fertilizers, and other products for rural households are not new, but their numbers have mushroomed in recent years. So-called mom and pop stores, often run by women, have become key elements in value chains (box 8.3). No two stores are the same, but the best are locally run and managed, often at a village level.

Box 8.3. Portrait of an agrodealer

Odette, an agrodealer from Rubengera, Western Rwanda, sells OAF-supplied seed and fertiliser that she buys on credit alongside other inputs such as seeds for vegetables, her own bean varieties, inputs for livestock, and basic farm tools. . . . She also uses the land [near the store] for a maize demonstration plot to highlight the benefits of applying fertiliser to her local clients. The additional income that Odette has made [in recent years] . . . allows her to send her younger children to secondary school. However, she [would like to] . . . expand the business, to stock a greater variety of products and to increase her customer base. Eventually, she would like her shop to operate as a local distribution centre, selling to middlemen who can then sell on her products to more remote areas. She also has ambitions to open a second shop, staffed by her adult children.

Source: Reproduced from Agriculture for Impact, "Off the Ground: Investing in Rwanda's Agriculture Value Chains," Briefing Paper (London: Agriculture for Impact, May 2016), https://www.mamopanel.org/media/uploads/files/OFF_THE_GROUND-_INVESTING_IN_RWANDAS_AGRICULTURE_VALUE_CHAINS_2016.pdf.

A recent report shows that it is possible to professionalize agrodealers and increase their sales through a combination of

- Strengthening technical and commercial capacities of agrodealers and government extension staff, so they can offer farmers technical advice on input use.
- Technology transfer through farmer field days, visits to crop demonstrations, and other good agricultural practices.
- Agrodealer study tours and exchange visits to successful agrodealers in other regions or countries.
- Training in how to establish business linkages between agrodealers and banks, fertilizer distributors and seed producers, producer groups, and business associations.[55]

There have been some remarkable successes in which entrepreneurial agrode-alers have become agents of change. They have grown into professional service providers who have partly taken over the role of government extension services.

Storage

Even if farmers' crops or livestock have developed well and survived exposure to the risks of climate change, soil degradation, and pests, diseases, and weeds, and been successfully harvested, they are still at risk. Most immediate are the risks of post-harvest loss.

In SSA most post-harvest loss occurs toward the farm end of the supply chain, that is, during harvesting and subsequent handling.[56] In particular, over 80 percent of the losses occur during storage. The losses can be caused by shrinkage of the volume of food or its deterioration owing to insects, disease, or contamination (for example, with aflatoxin) or, in the case of roots and tubers, by the damage caused by mechanical farming implements.

Establishing how much is lost is difficult, and there is considerable variation in the estimates. A recent meta-analysis of six countries found that losses of cereals and pulses amount to about 25 percent,[57] while those that are largest occur in fruits, 56 percent, and vegetables, 44 percent. In the case of the national maize harvest, however, annual household surveys of self-reported losses on farms in three SSA countries puts them at only 1.4 percent to 5.9 percent.[58]

Smallholder farmers often store their harvest in their dwelling or in a nearby small family store, with little protection. There, the grains are attacked by a wide variety of insects, fungi, and bacteria as well as rates and other vermin. Needless to say, the losses can be huge. In response, farmers often try to sell their harvest straightaway to middlemen who visit the farm, usually getting a low price. To them, a better, easily accessed, and inexpensive way of storing the harvest is highly desirable.

Local Storage

A variety of secure storage systems have been devised for use by smallholder farmers. One of these is described in box 8.4.

Box 8.4. Small scale storage system

Fifty percent of cowpeas in Africa, an important, nutrient-rich food source in parts of West and Central Africa, are lost each year to pest damage once stored after harvest.

Larry Murdock, a professor of entomology, at Purdue University . . . recently developed a technology . . . that uses ordinary materials manufactured in Africa to . . . almost completely control the insects in stored grain without the use of chemicals. . . . Under the system, farmers place their cowpeas in a polyethylene bag and seal it. That bag is surrounded by another, identical bag and sealed, and the double-bagged crop is held within a third, woven polypropylene bag. The woven bag gives strength to the unit and allows the bag to be handled without bursting the inner polyethylene bags. The inner bags deprive the insects of oxygen and . . . water. . . . The insects eventually die due to desiccation.

The [Purdue Improved Cowpea Storage] project, which began in 2007, found that hermetic storage of the cowpea . . . was practical and profitable for African farmers and ensured a supply of the nutritious legume for many months after harvest. Without the storage, farmers have to sell their cowpeas immediately after harvest when the price is at its lowest or treat them with sometimes dangerous and costly insecticides. . . . The plans are to disseminate the triple-layer sack technology in 28,000 villages in West and Central Africa.

Source: Reproduced from Calestous Juma et al., "Innovation for Sustainable Intensification in Africa," Briefing Paper (London: Montpellier Panel, Agriculture for Impact, 2013), https://www.mamopanel.org/media/uploads/files/INNOVATION_FOR_SUSTAINABLE_INTENSIFICATION_IN_AFRICA_2013.pdf.

Neighborhood Stores

Large, neighborhood storage facilities have been built in various African countries, for example, in Uganda (box 8.5). Unfortunately, they are few and far between, and the country could benefit from at least a dozen more.

Box 8.5. The AgroWays (U) grain warehouse near Jinja

The AgroWays (U) grain warehouse in Jinja offers services to small farmers, including transport, cleaning, drying, grading, and storage at affordable prices. Farmers' associations supply their maize grain to Village

Aggregation Centers in amounts of at least five metric tons per consignment. The company commits to picking the grain up and delivering it to the AgroWays (U) warehouse in Jinja within two days. This tight time frame ensures that the maize is spared from mold and aflatoxin, fungi that immediately render the grain unfit for sale. At the warehouse the grain is cleaned, dried, and graded into either grade 1 or 2 maize and stored in a fumigated store.

Farmers gain mainly from reducing post-harvest loss, but also through direct price negotiation with buyers. When buyers appear, the representatives of the farmer associations meet with them and agree on a price. Once the deal is done the farmer associations are paid for the amounts of grade 1 or 2 maize they have deposited and wish to sell, less the warehouse charges.

The key element of this system is that the farmers retain ownership of their grain. If they find they can get a better deal elsewhere, farmer associations can take the equivalent number of bags back, pay the warehouse charges, and sell them privately. The charges are clearly laid out prior to the farmers depositing their grain.

Source: Gordon Conway, personal communication with Herbert Kyeyamwa, managing director of AgroWays (U) Ltd, April 18, 2014.

Home Grown School Feeding (HGSF)

Home Grown School Feeding (HGSF) is a way of countering child malnutrition as well as a form of decentralized food reserve that can play the role of a reliable market intermediary from both the demand and supply sides.[59] At the center of HGSF is local food procurement, smallholder engagement, nutrient-rich and diverse foods, and high regularity in meal provision. In effect these are an important set of principles that enable the creation of shorter, localized value chains and supply chains. They are an instructive example of a government-led effort to develop alternate food networks that are more resilient to demand and supply risks while promoting food and nutrition security.

HGSF procurement presents a unique example of mediated markets as it is explicitly shaped by the geographic localization and a diversified commodity basket based on menus. Such menus are designed according to accepted nutrition requirements and based on local availability and/or agro-ecological suitability. Through these menus-based demand, HGSF also addresses the market bias toward staples which in turn makes food networks more resilient and improves the participation of small farm and women in the production and through the supply chain. Thus localized market interventions like HGSF strengthen commodity-specific value chains and promote sustainable food networks.

Food Processing

Agribusinesses in value chains can create new opportunities for entrepreneurship and employment in both rural and urban areas, and they can potentially generate high levels of value. Food processing, in particular, is proliferating throughout Africa, one example being the rapid diffusion of such firms in Tanzania (box 8.6).[60] The emergence of such small and medium enterprises (SMEs) in Africa has been called the Quiet Revolution in agrifood systems.

Box 8.6. Food processing in Tanzania

Jason Snyder and colleagues at Michigan State University looked at five hundred processed food products across five product categories—milled grains, packaged rice, dairy, fruit juices, and poultry—identified in retail outlets in Dar Es Salaam.

They found that local and regional processing rather than imports from outside the continent dominated the market. The companies producing maize meal and blended flours were primarily small or micro in size. Branding had also become more prominent with branded maize meal overtaking sales in all retail outlet types. More than fifty branded blended flour products and twenty brands of packaged rice were now available. However it was uncertain as to whether such local companies can be competitive in such a rapidly changing market. Therefore there is a need to identify policies and programs to sustainably enhance their competitiveness.

Source: Jason Snyder et al., "Local Response to the Rapid Rise in Demand for Processed and Perishable Foods: Results of an Inventory of Processed Food Products in Dar Es Salaam," Feed the Future Innovation Lab for Food Security Policy, Policy Research Brief 6 (East Lansing: Michigan State University, May 1, 2015), https://www.canr.msu.edu/resources/local-response-to-the-rapid-rise-in-demand-for-processed-and-perishable-foods-results-of.

As an element of the Quiet Revolution, processed foods like these will account for the bulk of future urban food demand. A vibrant, competitive, domestic processing sector can help smallholders to capture a share of this demand and realize the related potential income. Currently, the processing and distribution of staple foods, despite the presence of a few modern, medium-scale operators, is dominated by a large number of informal, small-scale enterprises, a majority of which are owned and operated by women entrepreneurs.[61]

Because many of these systems are not mechanized and do not show economies of scale, smallholders can create improved livelihoods through intensive use of labor. At the same time, they can compete on costs and quality if they invest in production and can market their crop quickly. But for this to happen, smallholder farmers need to deliver new products and attain a more sophisticated market orientation. This requires a "threshold" of knowledge of how to grow what is essentially a non-traditional product. The farmers may also need a vehicle to get the produce to market and also an all-season road and some bridges. A packing shed would be useful to sort the product so they can get better prices and they might need to have an aggregation facility or even a cooperative. In effect, they are creating "pre-processing informal SMEs."

In many places food processing is becoming more sophisticated and profitable through the adoption of mechanization techniques (box 8.7).

Box 8.7. Introduction of mechanization to food processing

Cereal processing

La Vivrière is a local microprocessing company, created in 1992 by a female farmer in Senegal. All products, which are marketed under the brand name WIIW ("Bravo" in Wolof), are based on millet, maize, and cowpea, the most widely grown and consumed crops in Senegal and across West Africa. . . .

[Previously,] small-scale artisanal milling . . . used domestic cooking utensils and family labor and . . . all millet processing operations were done manually. In 1996, due to the growing demand for its products, La Vivrière started mechanizing the processing [of millet, maize and cowpea] to increase its daily production capacity. . . . The most strenuous tasks were gradually mechanized through the use of dryers and mills. . . . The packaging and labeling of [the products have progressed] . . . significantly, moving from unprinted polyethylene bags to printed, and then multi-layered, packaging and product-specific cardboard cases using barcodes and other commercial information to comply with international trade standards.

Initially, products were sold door to door, but now they can be found in supermarkets and at wholesalers and retailers across the country. Some products are also exported to Europe, the United States, and Asia.

Mango processing

Mangoes are grown widely across the eastern province of Kenya. During peak mango season, which lasts from December through March, the supply of mangoes greatly exceeds the demand, leading to high losses for farmers.

The Arid Lands Resource Management (ALRMP) project has worked with women mango farmers to maximize profits and reduce losses by facilitating access to fruit processors to process and transform surplus mangoes. Training and an advance of US$4,200 allowed the 40 members of the women's group to invest in a fruit processor, which can produce up to 100 liters of mango juice and pawpaw jam in less than an hour. The juice is then blended with preservatives, hot water, and citric acid to produce a higher quality juice that can compete with other products on the market. The introduction of mechanization in the processing segment has greatly improved the women's income since mango juice sells for US$1 per liter, compared to a mere US$0.01 for four mangoes.

Sources: Reproduced from "Mechanized: Transforming Africa's Agriculture Value Chains" (Dakar, Senegal: Malabo Montpellier Panel, 2018), https://www.mamo panel.org/media/uploads/files/MaMo2018_Mechanized_Transforming_Africas_ Agriculture_Value_Chains.pdf; "La Vivriere," accessed October 29, 2018, http:// www.lavivriere.com/; High Level Panel of Experts on Food Security and Nutrition, "Food Losses and Waste in the Context of Sustainable Food Systems," HLPE Report (Rome: Committee on World Food Security, FAO, June 2014), http://www. fao.org/3/a-i3901e.pdf.

The fundamental challenge for the processing SMEs is to raise the necessary finances, which depends on the reliability of supply. A reason for some optimism is that the rise in demand for processed foods and quality-branded foods creates more "focused points of demand."[62] A more sustainable and resilient approach is likely to arise from clustering similar firms and thus creating a critical mass of demand.

Markets

Only through sustainable access to markets can poor farmers increase the income from their labor and lift themselves and their families out of poverty. Yet most poor farmers are not linked to markets and hence a poor understanding of and ability to react to market forces.

Markets in Africa, national, regional, and international, are changing under the influence of a myriad of factors (see chapter 4) including urbanization, population growth, increasing per capita incomes, changes in consumer preferences, the modernization of food processing and retailing, as well as improvements in transport and communications infrastructure. In addition, farmers in developing country increasingly have become sources of commodities for large, multinational agrifood companies. As a consequence, produce markets have become highly differentiated. On the one hand village markets sell locally produced, locally consumed staple crops; on the other, global markets sell packaged, off-season vegetables. This offers new opportunities for smallholder farmers, yet it also poses heightened risks as well as new and difficult barriers to surmount.

Contrary to conventional wisdom, as noted earlier, countries in all three regions of Africa exhibit sufficiently dissimilar patterns of specialization both in production and trade that should allow higher levels of transboundary and interregional trade. A more efficient and resilient approach to trade is to integrate regional markets in ways that stabilize prices and hence reduce the impacts of volatility, especially on poor, small farm households.

Consumers

The final elements in agricultural value chains are the people who ultimately purchase and consume food products. Income growth and urbanization are leading to rapid changes in diets, as consumers turn to higher-value foods as well as quicker, more convenient ones. Like other developing regions, Africa is undergoing a nutrition transition, as diets diversify and show decreased shares of staples and growing shares of animal-based foods and processed, perishable foods. Overall calorie availability and the availability of protein and fat have increased. The effects of these changes on nutrition are complex. The increase in dietary diversity can be expected to improve nutrition, and many forms of undernutrition have improved markedly in Africa in the past two decades. However, undernourishment, child malnutrition, and micronutrient deficiencies remain widespread. In addition, African countries now face a double burden of malnutrition, in which, as noted above, undernutrition coexists with over-nutrition, and this carries severe health risks. The WHO estimates that adult overweight is increasing in every African country; SSA's rate of overweight, 28 percent in 2016, is growing more quickly than the world average. Diets too rich in calories, fat, and sugar are leading to increasing rates of diabetes and other chronic health conditions.[63]

The nature of new, processed food products is complex as well. In some cases, time-pressed urban consumers are turning to unhealthy processed products rich in oils and fats. In many other cases, they seek healthy traditional staples in forms which are faster and easier to prepare, for example, the expansion of processed millet value chains to urban areas in Dakar. The potential for local producers and processors to reach urban consumers with more convenient forms of traditional foods depends on their ability to meet consumers' preferences for food safety and quality as well as marketing. Consumers participating in focus group discussions in Accra, Ghana, and Lagos, Nigeria, revealed that they prefer traditional foods but turn to imported products because their desire for convenience and lack of confidence in the quality of local processed staples.[64] The development of and adherence to quality and safety standards will accelerate the expansion of opportunities in the food processing sector.

The Resilience of Whole Value Chains

How are whole value chains made more resilient? In general, it seems likely that the resilience of whole value chains depends on the sustainability of each of the components in the chain and the nature of the links between them. But there is an urgent need for more research on this topic.

Another question is whether short or long value chains are more resilient. On the face of it, long, complex chains should be more resilient because of the multiple alternative pathways they may contain. But there is one telling example of highly resilient short value chains. This is the HGSFs (see above). Short systems like these ought to be highly vulnerable and prone to collapse, but the evidence shows otherwise. In areas where there have been conflicts, for example, in Mali and Côte d'Ivoire, HGSFs have flourished.[65] The reason appears to be the high number of stakeholders engaged in the value chains: farmers who produce the food crops, groups of women who purchase the food crops and make the meals, the school-children, the teachers, parents, and local officials. They all benefit despite the surrounding conflict in the environment. Everyone has a stake in success.

If value chains are to be sustainable and resilient they clearly need a range of stakeholders providing positive and complementary benefits. What smallholders need is not only to become more productive but also to step out from poverty. They need inexpensive loans backed by insurance, followed by efficient warehousing and access to stable markets where they can get a fair and reliable return for their agricultural produce. Integrating farmers in value chains is a key route to a better future; it is essential if farmers and their families are to achieve greater labor productivity and move beyond subsistence, in other words to step up and step out.[66]

The more difficult challenge is to put such integration into practice and at scale. The various components of a value chain need to each be efficient and sustainable and link with each other in a resilient fashion. This will require not only technical knowledge and sound micro and macro-economic policies but also leadership from government that recognizes the capabilities and understanding of African smallholders.

Part 3

AGRICULTURAL TRANSFORMATION

DIGITAL FARMERS

There are more than 500 million smallholder farms worldwide feeding billions of people. One such farm belongs to Mama Churi, who lives in the community of Mangula B, in the Southern Agricultural Growth Corridor of Tanzania. She has lived there, together with her family, for fifteen years. She says the area is good for her family. Her husband works as a teacher, which is a good job, but he only earns half of what the family needs to subsist each year. The rest of their income comes from Mama Churi's farming: maize and rice production, beekeeping, and a small fish farm. . . . But she is concerned that she doesn't have access to the right information to ensure that her farm and the surrounding land remain productive in the face of climate change and other uncertainties. . . . Maize and rice farming together account for 42 percent of Mama Churi's farm income, but this year the maize yield was very low, and it is becoming increasingly difficult for her to figure out when to plant. And if the rain comes before she can plow, then she won't get any yield at all. "If someone could help us forecast when the rains are coming, we would be very grateful, because then we would know when to plant so the harvest will be good," she says.[1]

"What if Mama Churi could access both short- and long-term weather forecasts through her cell phone and take some of the guesswork out of deciding when and what to plant? What if her phone could also give her access to information about which crops will thrive in the unique soils in each of her different farm plots and in this season's weather? She also wants to find out not only which crops to plant but also which varieties and which distributers have them available, so she knows where to go and what the seeds will cost."[2]

Using her cell phone, Mama Churi can connect to other farmers in Africa who are trying to cope with similar soil and climate issues. This will break down her isolation, extending her social network and her community beyond her village to become part of a global knowledge network.

For Mama Churi and the millions of other smallholders like her in Africa, achieving food security is not going to be easy. Numerous technologies and practices can increase agricultural production and food security in a sustainable fashion; there is increasing demand from the African middle class for diverse, nutritious foods, and the presence of many financial instruments and institutions can facilitate these diverse processes. But the challenge is to bring all these components together in a manner that makes the transformation happen, at a scale, efficiently, sustainably, and inclusively.

Both research stations and farmers have experiences and tools that can be drawn upon to capitalize on these opportunities. Foremost among the tools are digital technologies, both hardware (cell phones, satellites, supercomputers) and software (applications to facilitate decision making, digital soil maps, and faster breeding cycles for traditional African crops).[3]

The Digital Revolution

The explosion in the number of cell phones in Africa is astonishing. When Strive Masiyiwa, the CEO of Econet, founded the company in the mid-1990s, he observed that nearly three in four Africans had never heard a telephone ring. Today, thanks to the growth in the telecom industry, more than three in four Africans have a cell phone.[4] There are forecast to be nearly one billion cell phone accounts on the continent by 2022, more than in Europe and North America combined (figure 9.1).[5]

Africa is going digital. Millions of Africans can connect for the first time. This is the result of investment in infrastructure—increased access to mobile broadband, fiber-optic cable connections to households, and power supply expansion—combined with the rapid spread of low-cost smartphones and tablets. The effect has been to revolutionize the lives of African farmers in at least three major ways:

- *By overcoming isolation.* Many African smallholder farmers live far from cities and towns and are often poorly served by roads. Markets that provide inputs or purchase outputs may be many kilometers away and essentially inaccessible. Digital technology has the potential to effectively shorten the distance between previously isolated smallholders and the other components of the food value chain. . . .

- *By speeding up change.* Traditional extension is a ponderous process relying on poorly paid extension workers to travel from farm to farm or village to village. Digital Green uses technology-enabled dissemination based on projectors and web portals in local languages that greatly speeds up the transfer of information while improving its quality and relevance. Local access to credit can also be made more timely and efficient through digital technology, as can access to micro-insurance. The marketing of farmer products can be made more accessible. . . . Farmers no longer have to wait for buyers to come to them, as they can actively seek out better deals.

- *By taking success to scale.* Throughout Africa there are numerous successful projects and programs delivering greater yields, more nutritious foods, higher incomes, accessible fairer markets, and benefiting more women. Many are intrinsically sustainable. The challenge many organizations have taken on is determining how to scale them up. . . . A key component of going to scale is the generation, analysis, and accessibility of mega-data.[6]

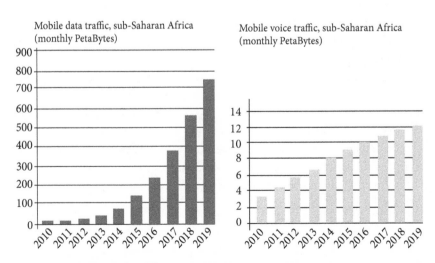

FIG. 9.1. Mobile phone use in sub-Saharan Africa (data traffic on left and voice traffic on right)

Source: Reproduced with permission from Ericsson, "Ericsson Mobility Report June 2017" (Stockholm: Ericsson, June 2017).

The Impact on Agriculture

Digital connectivity has enormous implications for agriculture and nutrition. Information can be sent on nutrition and health, providing timely information on weather predictions, crop selection, and pest control to management and finance. Even in areas where internet coverage is poor or non-existent, short message service (SMS) messages can remind families of child welfare visits and child health days, deliver simple nutrition information, inform parents about child feeding, provide updates on market prices and fertilizer pick-up locations, and offer a wealth of other health and agriculture messages to previously isolated rural households.[7]

SMS messaging in local languages is powerful. For example it can give advice on household meal practices, including suggestions for healthier alternatives. Social marketing can also promote specific crops, hopefully increasing market demand and producer incentives.

In Ethiopia traditional agriculture extension advice emerging from agricultural research centers can take many years to filter down to smallholder farmers. In 2014 an interactive voice response (IVR) and short message system (SMS) platform was developed to deliver information directly to farmers through cell phones.[8] Ethiopia's first agricultural, automated hotline was 8028. The system functions in three local languages, Amharic, Oromiffa, and Tigrigna, providing information on all major cereal, pulses, and high-value crops. Keypad menu options allow farmers and development agents to select their special areas of interest and receive automated information whenever they call in.

The hotline administrator can also "push" tailored information, for example, on drought or pest and disease outbreaks based on crop or geography. The demographic data is captured when farmers first registered to use the system. Over seven million phone calls had been logged by 2015, the majority from smallholder farmers. As Andualem Admassie, the CEO of Ethio Telecom, has reported, "Over 100,000 SMS messages have already been sent out, informing smallholders on using improved seeds and farming techniques to increase their yields. . . . Additionally, 400,000 IVR messages have been sent, explaining how to identify and protect crops against wheat rust and maize necrosis lethal diseases."[9]

Identifiers for Farmers

To see the promise of the benefits of digital technology for African farmers fulfilled, every smallholder farmer needs to be assigned a unique identifier, so that whoever is communicating with her or him knows who they are communicating with.

The needs of the African smallholders are still not well understood. Policies are too often based on anecdotal evidence. As a consequence, policy makers make trade-offs with inadequate information. Should they prioritize investments in, say, post-harvest storage or in input subsidies? To make this decision, it would help policy makers to know how much the farmers are producing and how much of the harvest is being lost to spoilage.

As Sam Dryden, formerly of the Bill and Melinda Gates Foundation, points out "Right now, agricultural data is based on samples and extrapolations. As a result, it is not accurate or complete."[10] Unique identifiers, together with better and more precise information derived from satellite imaging technology, can take agricultural information to scale. In the process, scientists, extension workers, and policy makers will understand better where farmers live, how much land they cultivate, what they grow, what inputs they use, how much they yield, what they eat and what they sell, and what price their crops fetch.[11] An information revolution of this kind could transform the agricultural and food sector at every level, from individual farmers to global institutions.

Dryden asks whether it is really possible to reach every single African farmer given that they are spread out across a vast and often remote continent.[12] He thinks they can and cites the example of the successful polio eradication campaign in Africa that used high-resolution satellite imagery coupled with global positioning systems employing vaccinators who were able to reach virtually every child on the continent. In a similar fashion the eWallet program (see below) has reached over seventeen million farmers.

African leaders are thinking in bold ways about the future of their food systems. To realize their vision, they will need to build digital infrastructure that can deliver on the promise of the information age. If the potential of the fifty million smallholder farms on the continent is to be exploited, the first building block will be unique identifiers for every single farmer.[13]

The Financial Services Revolution

The ubiquity of the cell phone has been a revolution in financial services. Telecom companies have begun with mobile payments and diversified into credit, savings, merchant payments, and insurance.[14] There are now five times more mobile money agents than commercial banks in the developing world. In effect, the telecom sector has disrupted centuries-old practices in financial services, changing the architecture of financial service delivery. SSA has led the way with over two-thirds of the world's one hundred million active mobile money users.

As Bill Gates argues, cell phones have recreated the economics of providing financial services to the poor.[15] Formal banking requires buildings, piles of paperwork, security guards, and tellers. The costs per transaction were so high that there was no profit in serving poor people, who transacted in tiny amounts. As a result, the poor led their financial lives informally, paying exorbitant amounts in fees and interest to borrow, save, and send money.

Phones do away with all of this. There is now competition to serve the poor. And in the process of competing for poor people's business these companies will develop new financial products that meet the unique needs of poor people. One example is a company called M-KOPA, which markets small solar-powered lighting systems.[16] M-KOPA enables six hundred thousand customers in three African countries to pay for solar electricity—instead of kerosene—in small daily installments through their cell phones.

As noted above, Strive Masiyiwa, is one of the great pioneers of digital technology in Africa. "How," he said, "can we ensure that our farmers find it as easy to get better farm inputs or new farm equipment as they do SIM cards or mobile financial services? How can we catalyze a sustainable and inclusive African green revolution using these digital platforms?"[17] Econet's products are examples of success.

EcoCash and EcoFarmer

Econet has pioneered two platforms: EcoCash (a mobile wallet) and EcoFarmer (a suite of mobile agricultural services). EcoCash was launched in Zimbabwe at the start of 2011, just after the height of the country's period of hyperinflation. As the private sector shrank and employment dwindled, the informal sector came to dominate economic activity, providing an opportunity to help service the informal economy, where mobile penetration was high but payments infrastructure was lacking.[18]

By 2016 EcoCash had five million customers, over 70 percent of the adult population in Zimbabwe.[19] This compares with just over nine hundred thousand bank account holders before the launch. Among other services, EcoCash can

- Transfer (send) money across all networks
- Pay for goods and services locally and internationally
- Pay bills such as school fees, Council utility bills (water, rates), DSTV [satellite television], etc.
- Withdraw money (Cash-Out)
- Buy Econet prepaid airtime, text, data bundles or pay a direct connect account for yourself and other Econet subscribers
- Make secure online payments

- Receive money from diaspora
- Deposit money (Cash-In)
- Save money
- Access loans
- Link your EcoCash wallet to a bank account[20]

In 2015 EcoCash processed over $6 billion in transactions, representing nearly 40 percent of Zimbabwe's GDP. However, Masiyiwa realized there was more Econet could do with and for Zimbabwe. He decided to develop a mobile services platform helping the nearly two-thirds of Zimbabwe's population that live in rural areas and is mostly dependent on farming for their livelihoods.

When he launched EcoFarmer in 2013 Masiyiwa deliberately avoided the conventional payments-first approach; instead, he offered two initial offerings: an information service that sends advisory extension services through SMS to farmers and a weather-indexed insurance product.[21] Farmers receive daily updates on three topics: farming tips, market prices, and weather data, all customized to the farmer's district, ward, and frequently grown crops. Farmers then use the information to improve their crop planting and farm management practices, such as the best time to plant and the best place to sell their harvest.

Masiyiwa also began to pilot a weather insurance product tied to the purchase of quality seeds. EcoFarmer insures 10kg bags of certified maize seed, produced by Seed Co., a local seed company. A registered EcoFarmer can purchase the insurance using an Econet-enabled cell phone. He or she dials an Unstructured Supplementary Service Data (USSD) code entering a voucher number contained in a plastic capsule within the seed pack. The farmer then uses EcoCash to pay a premium of US8¢ a day, or roughly $10 for a season of 125 day. Any excess rain or drought is monitored through weather stations covering the location of the farm, Farmers then receive a payout of ten times the premium paid, $100, through EcoCash. By 2016 EcoFarmer had over 550,000 farmers using the agricultural information service.

Masiyiwa's experience in developing and scaling EcoCash and EcoFarmer taught him three main lessons, which he believes are broadly applicable to how digital technologies can improve the livelihoods of smallholder farmers in Africa (box 9.1).[22]

Digital Green

Traditional agricultural extension is typically top-down. This approach worked well in the Green Revolution, where the aim was to pass along simple messages to

Box 9.1. Strive Masiyiwa's lessons

- *Lesson 1: Designing systems for scale starts with simplicity and understanding the needs of your clients.*

Although we had big ambitions for EcoCash and knew there were a lot of other products that we could deliver, at launch we deliberately focused only on person-to-person money transfer. We chose a simple payment mechanism, whereby customers could send and receive money using the most basic phones. We wanted customers to easily understand and use the product first, before we added complexity. We kept our tariff structures simple and were transparent about what we charged people for the service. We also made the tariffs progressive, to increase the volume of low value transactions.

The same lesson held for EcoFarmer. . . .

- *Lesson 2: Adoption at scale, even for digital technologies, requires an extensive field presence and trusted intermediaries.*

When we moved into mobile financial services, we recognized that distribution and marketing would make or break EcoCash's success. Mass adoption would come not from new product features, but from whether people saw the need for EcoCash or EcoFarmer in their lives.

We worked hard to educate consumers on the value of EcoCash. . . .

- *Lesson 3: Without regulatory support you cannot achieve transformation at scale.*

When we started experimenting with EcoCash, we anticipated that the banking sector would fight our entry into the financial services market and resist any disruption to their industry. In addition, the idea of being able to send and receive money via phone was foreign to many of our regulators.

Well in advance of our launch, therefore, we made sure that policymakers understood the product and how it worked. . . .

Source: Reproduced from Strive Masiyiwa, "Mobile Revolution 2.0: Lessons for a Sustainable Green Revolution in Africa," in "African Farmers in the Digital Age: Overcoming Isolation, Speeding up Change and Taking Success to Scale," ed. Kofi Annan, Gordon Conway, and Sam Dryden, special issue, *Foreign Affairs* (2016): 93–99, https://files.foreignaffairs.com/pdf/sponsored-anthology/2016/african_farmers_in_the_digital_age_final.pdf.

farmers: plant new, short-strawed wheat or rice in rows, with an application of a general fertilizer, and liberal use of insecticides. Today, the challenge is different, especially in Africa, where farmers in a diversity of environments plant a diversity of crops on diverse soils. Ideally an African farmer needs his or her personal extension agent! In practice, digital tools can effectively do this.

One example is an NGO called Digital Green, created by Rikin Gandhi, that trains development agencies and people in the communities with which they work to produce and distribute locally relevant knowledge, mainly in the form of videos (box 9.2).[23]

Box 9.2. The Digital Green approach

Digital Green describes their approach as follows: "Together with our grassroots partners, we create digital solutions for rural communities around the world. How do we know what is appropriate? Simple. We listen closely—to people, and to data. Then we build technology that is of the community and for the community.

We understand that there are both informal and formal networks already in place—and that the people and organizations working in that community are best positioned to understand what will, and won't work. So, we listen to those people and assess those systems to identify gaps and opportunities for improvement, using technology as an entry point to transform systems from the inside out.

The technology is the production and showing of communal videos, each one targeted to an individual district. The videos, which feature information about farming techniques and nutrition practices, are then screened by frontline workers among farmer groups, using battery-operated mobile projectors. Most of the videos that a farmer views are produced in the same district in which he or she resides. The audience assesses the relevance and trustworthiness of what they see, considering not just the featured farmer's language but also factors like the clothes she is wearing and the type of dwelling she lives in to determine whether she is someone they can identify with. Seeing is often believing for rural farmers—often women with a low level of literacy—and visual cues pertaining to a person or a crop can be crucial in their decision to adopt a practice.

Traditional agricultural extension primarily targets men, but the bulk of agricultural labor on small farms is done by women. One reason for

Digital Green's success is that they reach out to women and other margin-alized farmers, who form the major part of their audience. They have also found that women tend to be more receptive to videos featuring fellow women, just as men tend to identify with fellow men."

Source: Digital Green, "Digital Green," accessed May 25, 2018, https://www.digital green.org/solutions/.

Using the Digital Green approach a practice can be demonstrated on a video by a frontline worker. This boosts farmers' recall. The frontline workers, who typically live in the same village as the farmers viewing the video, can vouch for the local applicability of the practices taught. Farmers ensure that viewers under-stand the videos, farmers are connected to necessary inputs (such as seeds and fertilizers), and their produce is aggregated for sale at market. The whole process builds farmer confidence.

Digital Green's network of partners and community members has produced over four thousand videos in twenty-eight languages. They have reached more than eight hundred thousand smallholder farmers, more than 60 percent of whom subsequently apply at least one new practice. Moreover, a facilitated video viewing can spur farmers to adopt new agricultural practices for about one-tenth the cost of traditional extension systems. They estimate that the adoption of these practices has increased crop yield by at least 20 percent.

Most of the Digital Green work is with smallholder food crop producers, but in one example they partnered with the World Cocoa Foundation in Ghana to implement a pilot project promoting better cocoa-farming practices.[24] They pro-vided training and supervision to WCF and the Cocoa Board of Ghana (on video production and dissemination). The pilot revealed a high demand among the farmer community for video-based information services; of the eighteen hun-dred farmers who watched the videos, about 85 percent adopted at least one new practice. As Gates has said "Digital Green isn't cool because of the technology. It's cool because of the impact."[25]

E-Wallets

For forty years the Nigerian federal government had been procuring seed and fertilizers and filtering them down through layers and layers of state and local governments until, in theory, they got to the smallholder farmers who needed them.[26] Except the theory rarely played out in practice. Only 11 percent of the fertilizer procured by the government went to farmers. The system existed to serve profiteers, not the smallholders who were supposed to benefit.

According to Akinwumi Adesina, then the new minister of agriculture and rural development appointed in 2010, "With corruption and inefficiency like this, it wasn't hard to explain why a country with 84 million hectares imported almost all of its food."[27] He decided to replace government-run agriculture with a set of small and medium enterprises that provided inputs to smallholder farmers at one end to transporting, processing, and selling food at the other. The aim was to bypass government bureaucracies, build supply chains directly into rural communities, stimulating further positive effects.

In less than a hundred days, the public procurement system was dismantled. By 2013 the number of seed companies operating in Nigeria had increased from just eleven to more than one hundred and the new fertilizer market mobilized five billion naira (about US$31 million) from private investors. Major players like Syngenta, that had stopped doing business in Nigeria because of the corruption, reentered the market. Five thousand mom and pop shops (agrodealers) were enabled to sell various products and provide agricultural training to farmers.

The key was to make fertilizer and seeds affordable enough for smallholders to try. So Minister Adesina instituted a 50 percent subsidy, not a new idea but a radical one because it was partnered with a new digital delivery mechanism: the eWallet program. There were already 130 or 140 million cell phones in Nigeria, holding the potential to reach millions of farmers (figure 9.2).

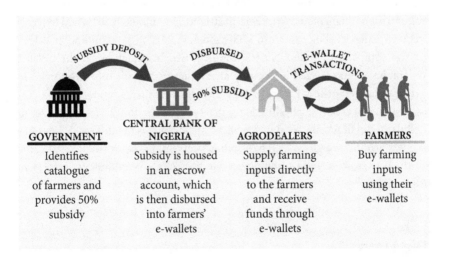

GOVERNMENT	CENTRAL BANK OF NIGERIA	AGRODEALERS	FARMERS
Identifies catalogue of farmers and provides 50% subsidy	Subsidy is housed in an escrow account, which is then disbursed into farmers' e-wallets	Supply farming inputs directly to the farmers and receive funds through e-wallets	Buy farming inputs using their e-wallets

FIG. 9.2. The flows in the e-wallet system

Source: "August 2017," *Cellulant* (blog), August 2017, https://cellulant.blog/2017/08/.

The farmers received four text messages:

- a GES ID number
- which farming inputs they are entitled to, e.g., two bags of 50kg fertilizer and one 40kg bag of maize
- location of the agro-dealer and the amount of cash they should go with to collect their inputs
- transaction confirmation once they successfully purchase the inputs.[28]

The eWallet program also helped the ministry make contact with farmers, so stimulating a reciprocal program of providing information about the farmers and giving them opportunities to communicate back. Millions of once-inaccessible smallholders could become part of the dialogue. Later, the eWallet platform began to deliver other benefits, including vouchers for nutritional supplements. By 2017 the system was benefiting seventeen million farmers, twenty-five thousand agribusinesses, eight hundred e-extension workers, and over twenty-five hundred service points in Nigeria.[29] Minister Adesina was especially proud of the fact that several million of the subscribers were women farmers, people who had historically been neglected by agricultural programs.

The eWallet program stimulated demand, but there was a lack of capital for agricultural start-ups. Minister Adesina decided to create easier credit by stimulating the Central Bank of Nigeria to share risk with banks and encourage them to make more loans to agricultural businesses. The banks rapidly increased their lending to the agriculture sector: bank lending to seed companies and small agricultural input retailers rose from zero in 2011 to $53 million in 2013; and to fertilizer companies lending rose from $100 million in 2012 to $500 million in 2013.[30]

The company Cellulant Nigeria Limited, which implemented the eWallet system, has been engaged in creating an eWallet system for other countries in Africa and also for the Ministry of Agriculture Irrigation & Livestock in Afghanistan, aimed at creating self-sufficiency in wheat production.[31] The cofounder of Cellulant, Bolaji Akinboro, stated that the technology is the gift of Cellulant to farmers around the globe: "Afghanistan is beautiful to us, we are glad to come all the way from Nigeria to empower the lives of the smallholder farmers in Afghanistan."[32]

Big Data

All around us is big data.[33] In the soil, billions of microorganisms abound. Our crops and livestock contain countless genetic permutations of DNA. The weather derives from combinations of rain, wind, temperature unique from one location to another. People too are just as diverse in their characteristic natures and their activities. Until recently the scale and complexity of the data in the world have seemed to defy understanding. But that is changing and changing fast.

Digital technology is enabling people to record, identify, and characterize the innumerable data points in soils, crops, and weather patterns, and indeed the unique data points belonging to ourselves. Their nature can be identified and stored in unique digital formats that can be related to the unique digital formats of other points. These digital interactions can then be analyzed, enabling people to understand how the world is behaving. For example, one can take a country's long-term rainfall records and use them to predict the likely rainfall patterns in the future, and from them estimate the probability of crop failure. Similarly, one can examine the different genes and their alleles in crops and determine how specific genetic changes will affect agricultural outcomes.

Soils and Fertilizers

An obvious example of big data relevant to Africa is the mapping of soils and their nutrients. Traditionally this has been done by collecting soil samples over a wide area and carrying them back to a laboratory, where they are subject to thorough chemical analysis. Now, via access to digital mapping techniques, mapping can be done far more speedily.

In Ethiopia, as in other parts of Africa, the use of the fertilizers DAP and urea is ubiquitous; they are recommended irrespective of the nature of the soils. For the past thirty years and more Ethiopian farmers have followed a blanket recommendation of one hundred kilograms of DAP and one hundred kilograms of urea. Now the Agricultural Transformation Agency of Ethiopia has created a Soil Information System (EthioSIS) project that has gathered and analyzed soil samples from each of the country's eighteen thousand agricultural *kebeles*, or neighborhoods, utilizing remote sensing and satellite technology to create a digital map of the country's soil and fertilizer recommendations for each region (box 9.3).[34]

Since its launch in 2012 EthioSIS has completed soil sampling and fertilizer recommendations for the Amhara, SNNP, Tigray, and Harari regions as well as Dire Dawa City Administration.[35] Regional atlases have been published for Tigray, SNNP, and Amhara that include recommendations aimed at improving the production and productivity landscape of the country. In these regions, 614 agricultural woredas (districts) and 59 confluence points have been mapped. Soil fertility surveying is complete in Benishangul-Gumuz and Gambella, while work in Afar and Somali is underway.

Box 9.3. Modern soil analysis in Ethiopia

EthioSIS deploys remote-sensing satellite technology and other state-of-the art techniques for soil surveying. This pioneering initiative uses wet-chemistry analysis using instruments with high-detection limits, rapid, non-destructive infrared spectroscopy, and laser diffraction particle size distribution analysis techniques to develop national soil property maps.

Using its extensive soil sampling work, the project is then able to recommend plans to improve nutrient deficiencies of soils around the country, including through the use of at least twelve different fertilizers, which can be applied with or without potash depending on the status of each soil.

A fertilizer-blending project runs parallel with EthioSIS to produce tailored fertilizers for different types of soil. The government of Ethiopia is supporting five farmers' cooperative unions (FCU) to produce blended fertilizers in four of the largest states in the country. Each blending factory has an annual blending capacity of fifty thousand metric tons of fertilizers.

Source: Ethiopian Agricultural Transformation Agency, "EthioSIS," *ATA* (blog), accessed May 25, 2018, https://www.ata.gov.et/highlighted-deliverables/ethiosis/.

Thus by combining powerful, context-specific data with the connectivity of cell phones, valuable, real-time information is delivered to farmers, information that allows them to optimize their agricultural practices.

Weather Insurance

The increase in the availability of data as well as of high-performance computing offers an unprecedented opportunity to increase the understanding and management of complex agro-ecological systems. For instance, recent estimates indicate that by 2030 over 150 petabytes of satellite data could be available—by comparison, the US Library of Congress uses 10 terabytes (1 petabyte equals 1,000 terabytes).[36]

The role of weather insurance in facilitating productive and resilient value chains is critical. Sophisticated models of weather insurance have been developed by Erik Chavez and colleagues at Imperial College London.[37] These involve the acquisition, analysis, and manipulation of a wide variety of big data, especially weather data. Since the first meteorological satellite experiment in 1959, the dramatic increases in spatial, spectral, and temporal resolutions of satellite observations data have dwarfed ground-based observations, in terms of both size and quality.[38]

Polar orbital satellites typically capture two daily global measurements and allow tracking of global-scale climate and weather dynamics. In contrast, geostationary satellites gather continuous measurements over specific regions of the globe. The use of both types of satellites together with the improvement of space-borne sensors technology delivers unprecedented volumes of information on both global and regional weather and climate dynamics.

The rapidly increasing volume of data creates new challenges of data storage and global accessibility as well as data selection and analysis. This is why machine-learning techniques will increasingly play a fundamental role in approaches to weather risk management and adaptation driven by satellite data. An example of the use of machine learning and supercomputing to analyze various sources of data is the development of financial de-risking mechanisms to provide insurance to smallholder farmers in Tanzania. A project led by Imperial College London developed a machine-learning-based model in which remote sensing data (5 km^2), digital soil data, crop genetic traits datasets as well as pixel-level management practices are used to generate optimum insurance instruments that de-risk input loans. The parametric insurance thus generated allows farmers and banks alike to be shielded against the risk of crop loss driven by rainfall or temperature variability.

In effect, new computing technologies are being used to de-risk the weather risk for both the participation of smallholder farmers in local to global supply chains and the supply chains of banks, food buyers, and retailers. Thus the loan/insurance construct, in turn, is embedded within a multi-stakeholder value chain that brings together a range of public and private actors, providing the insurance and reinsurance, the inputs such as fertilizers, and buying the harvest. The model output is communicated in terms of economic losses and gains to the farmer associations. For the thirty thousand smallholder farmers in the successful pilot conducted in 2017, about a third received a payout.

Genomics

A genome is all of a living organism's genetic material—the hereditary instructions for building, running, and maintaining an organism. This is "enormous data" in the form of DNA, packaged in chromosomes. The relationships between the individual pieces of data can be envisaged "as a set of Chinese boxes nested one inside another—the largest box is the genome, inside is box representing the chromosomes, inside that a box representing the genes and finally inside the smallest box the DNA."[39] Making up the DNA are four nucleotides: C (cytosine), G (guanine), A (adenine), and T (thymine), existing in many combinations.

Organisms can contain many thousands of genes, and the science of genomics involves the sequencing and analysis of genomes to reveal where the genes are and how they interact with each other. Analysis of the crop plant pearl millet is an example. It has recently been decoded and sequenced by a global team of sixty-five scientists from thirty research institutions, revealing a genome of 1.79 Gb containing over thirty-five thousand genes.[40]

Pearl millet, grown on about twenty-seven million hectares, is a staple food for more than ninety million farmers in arid and semi-arid regions of SSA, India, and South Asia. It is a cereal for drylands that is rich in protein, fiber, and essential micronutrients like iron, zinc, and folate. It is also an important source of fodder for millions of farms. But there is a drawback. Pearl millet is mainly grown in poor soil conditions, without irrigation and the use of minimal or no fertilizer or other agricultural inputs. As a result, yields have remained low over the past six decades.

The genomic sequencing was co-led by the International Crops Research Institute for Semi-Arid Tropics (ICRISAT), based in Hyderabad, India. The latest innovations in DNA sequencing and analysis employed genetic tools such as molecular markers to identify drought and heat tolerance and resistance to downy mildew. Pearl millet has an extraordinary capacity to resist heat up to 42°C; by comparison, rice or maize can withstand temperatures only up to 35°C. Most important, the analysis of the genome has identified a diversity of genes for natural wax proteins, which act as thermal protection for the plant. This information can be used in the future as an ingredient of gene editing, identifying, and improving the performance of those genes conferring heat tolerance.

Machine Learning

Big data, as its name implies, requires the handling and analysis of vast quantities of information. The COSMIC-2 sensor captures weather data over a 200 × 200 km field and can accumulate over 8,000 observations per day.[41] Another sensor, STORM-1, captures weather data over a 2 × 2 km spatial field and performs over 135 million observations over the duration of a storm.[42]

Analyzing such data is a major challenge. Machine learning is a field of computer science that uses statistical techniques to give computer systems the ability to "learn" through data, without being explicitly programed.[43] Conventional computer algorithms rely on programmers to enter rules and facts to guide the system's output. Machine-learning systems—and a subset, deep-learning systems, which simulate complex neural networks in the human brain—derive their own rules after combing through large amounts of data.[44]

Weather is well suited to analysis by deep-learning approaches.[45] In 2016 researchers reported the first use of a deep-learning system to identify tropical cyclones, atmospheric rivers, and weather fronts: loosely defined features whose identification depends on expert judgment.[46] The ultimate goal is to improve scientists' ability to assess and predict how these events are shifting in the face of climate change.

Blockchains

A blockchain is a highly sophisticated form of ledger based on computer science. Each "block" is a record of various activities stored in a highly secure manner. Blocks can be added but not taken away from the chain. A blockchain uses a global peer-to-peer network to provide an open platform that can deliver neutrality, reliability, and security. The basic mechanism was originally proposed in 2008 as part of a solution for securing transactions in cryptocurrencies like bitcoin through a shared accounting ledger. In essence, a blockchain can be used to implement an arbitrary set of rules that no one, neither the users nor the operators of the system, can break.[47]

As Jessi Baker of Provenance has argued, the key differences between blockchain and other computer solutions are

> Non-localization—No single machine . . . governs the business logic or the data on which a blockchain operates. . . . Users can then *unambiguously* discover the state of the system (e.g., the current level of stock . . .), not from a single particular authority but rather by independently applying common rules and publishing data openly.
>
> Security— . . . It does not matter who or where the user is, because all information provided to the blockchain is accepted only if it is *authenticated*. This authentication is provided in the form of an unforgeable digital signature. . . .
>
> [Auditability]—A blockchain is different, as by design is perfectly auditable. Each individual operation or interaction, such as the provision of a new employee or the recording of outgoing stock, is perfectly recorded and archived. . . . Combined with the absolute guarantees of authenticity for every interaction . . . [blockchains are] at their core resilient to coercion and human factors.[48]

One use of blockchain is to add another security layer to the physical-world practices of virus banks, gene banks, and seed vaults.[49] The blockchain could be the digital instantiation of physical-world storage centers like WHO—designated repositories for pathogen storage of, for example, the smallpox virus. In the case of disease outbreaks, response time can be hastened as worldwide researchers are private key-permissioned into the genetic sequencing files of pathogens of interest.

It would be possible to create blockchains on the basis of the value chains described in chapter 7. For example, a pearl millet blockchain could begin with genetic analysis, pass to breeding trials, seed production, and distribution, planting, disease occurrence, harvesting, storage, and marketing, with individual records (blocks) providing details of certification and value at each stage.

More Intelligent Farming

Farming is becoming a more intelligent process throughout the world. In the developed countries this more intelligent farming is linked to increasing use of satellite navigation equipment that permits sophisticated tractors to track, down to a few meters or even centimeters, where they are on a field, and undertake highly targeted application of inputs like fertilizers or herbicides.

An example of intelligent farming is the private consulting company IPF, which can provide a coordinated set of components of intelligent precision farming, including creation of separate soil management zones on the farm, accurate and reliable nutrition maps, satellite scanning, optimal fertilizer and crop protection management, advanced weather models and yield predictions, together with other components and a toolbox at the center that manages the data.

This system of IPF is clearly one designed for relatively large commercial farms in the United Kingdom. However, the company now has over four thousand hectares being managed in Zimbabwe, Zambia, and Botswana.[50] In some respects, these are very different from the average African smallholder with less than two hectares, often operating at a subsistence level, but it is possible to take the principles of precision farming and apply them on a small-scale efficiently and effectively.

TRANSFORMING AGRICULTURE

Sylvester and Beatrice Namarunda, whose story we recounted earlier, are subsistence farmers living on the poverty line. At the end of each season they ordinarily harvest less than one ton of maize, an amount insufficient to feed their family. There is an alternative scenario, however (figure 10.1; cf. figure 1.1). They can apply fertilizer or manure or both to their land and obtain a modern, drought tolerant, hybrid maize seed. They can use a variety of methods to control the weeds, pests, and diseases that attack their crops. In that scenario they can obtain, even in a moderate drought year, over two tons of maize per hectare. With this expected yield they are able to plant half the hectare in maize, obtaining enough harvest to adequately feed the family, and put the other half hectare into a crop like bananas that they can sell to their neighbors or on the market. This will bring them much-needed cash to pay for their children to go to school and to cover the costs of medical treatment if the children fall ill.

The Nature of Transformation

For the Namarundas to achieve their dream of food security and a modest income they need access to inputs—from agrodealers, local fertilizer blending companies and sources of high-quality seed. They also need loans and some form of insurance. Once their crop is harvested they need to be linked into value

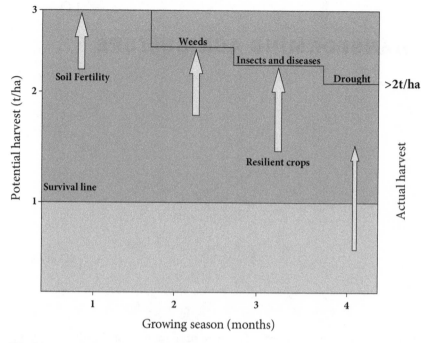

FIG. 10.1. A secure farm in Africa

Source: Gordon Conway and Gary Toenniessen, "Science for African Food Security," *Science* 299, no. 5610 (February 21, 2003): 1187–88, https://doi.org/10.1126/science.1081978. Reprinted with permission from AAAS.

chains providing warehousing, sources of information on markets and prices, and access to local food processors.

Increasing Productivity

Creating a system that realizes these various forms of access is at the core of agricultural transformation. And its success is measured in terms of productivity since one of the most effective ways to reduce rural poverty is to raise the productivity of the resources that the poor and vulnerable depend on. As smallholder farmers produce more and become more competitive, poverty is reduced and food and nutrition become more secure. This, coupled with the effects of improved nutrition, better health care, and education, leads to lives that are more secure and livelihoods that are more resilient and sustainable.

In Africa farmers' resources are primarily their land and their agricultural labor, and this is reflected in different measures of productivity (box 10.1).

Box 10.1. Measures of productivity

Agriculturalists frequently measure total production of agricultural goods and services per household or region or nation. They are interested in how production changes.

Productivity is the net increment in valued product per unit of resource—land, labor, energy, or capital.

Land productivity is measured by most smallholder farmers in terms of yield, expressed as kilograms of grain or tubers, or meat per hectare, or per kilogram of nitrogen or manure they have applied.

Labor productivity is measured in terms of output per hour, day, or year of human effort, that is, per worker, whether a farmer or a farm laborer.

Net income or profit is a measure of the monetary value of the agricultural production at the market, usually expressed as income less expenditure; that is, as net income or profit.

We also measure the total factor productivity (TFP). Change in TFP is the ratio of total output growth to total input growth. It compares the increase in total output with the increase in total inputs (such as land, labor, and fertilizers) and measures the difference. In effect, it estimates the importance of other factors in the enabling environment, such as investments in research, extension, human capital, and infrastructure.

Because African populations are rising fast, it is not going to be enough to simply raise land productivity; its growth must exceed that of the population engaged in agricultural production. This is why the key measure to have in mind is labor productivity. It is the most crucial factor because it determines whether poor people, especially poor rural farmers and their families, escape poverty. The economist Steve Wiggins of the Overseas Development Institute has estimated that labor productivity needs to reach approximately $800 per worker per year to get agricultural workers and their dependents out of poverty.[1] However, many African countries have not yet reached this level (figure 10.2).

Agricultural labor productivity varies widely across countries. South Africa has undergone transformation of its agricultural sector and has shifted to large, mechanized commercial farms with high labor productivity. Several West African countries have experienced rapid growth in labor productivity, and the region has reached around $2,700 in agricultural value added per worker on average. The regional average for eastern Africa remains just above the $800 level, while

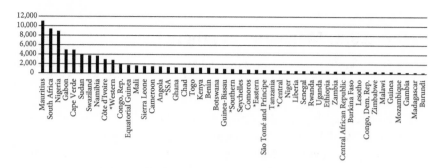

FIG. 10.2. Labor productivity (value added per worker) in African agriculture (2017). 2010 US$ per worker

Source: IFPRI, "ReSAKSS (Regional Strategic Analysis and Knowledge Support System)," ReSAKSS Database, accessed October 22, 2018.

for central Africa it is well below that figure. Over 40 percent of SSA countries having data available have not surpassed the $800 level.[2]

In many respects the challenge of raising labor productivity lies at the heart of agricultural transformation. Yet globalizing markets have created a context for African agricultural transformation different from that of Asia in the 1960s, when the Green Revolution occurred. On the one hand, given rising competition from producers across the globe, the challenge faced by African countries is not only to produce more but also to compete better. On the other hand, rapid urbanization and a rising middle class have created new and different opportunities for African agriculture. In particular, modernization of staples value chains and expanding urban staple food markets create considerable potential for future income growth for smallholder farmers. But realizing this income potential requires the successful integration of millions of geographically dispersed smallholder farmers into these new value chains, turning them into credible business partners for other value chain actors.

Charting a course for a successful agricultural transformation leading to broad-based employment and income growth starts with a good understanding of the history of agricultural dynamics and their underlying factors. A review of trends and patterns in the agricultural sector and economy-wide growth is instructive, as are the patterns and quality of the transformation process and strategies for the successful, smallholder-friendly modernization of staple food and other agribusiness value chains.

Growth and Productivity

The first decade of independent Africa, the 1960s, was marked by strong overall economic growth performance. But this started to deteriorate rather rapidly in the decade after. By the 1980s GDP growth had dropped to 1.5 percent per year and GDP per capita was showing absolute declines, representing a low point in Africa's post-independence performance (table 10.1). Agricultural growth also slowed, averaging only 0.5 percent per year during the first half of the 1980s, far below the population growth rate of around 3 percent.

In the late 1980s, however, there was a turnaround in agricultural growth, followed in the late 1990s by an acceleration in overall economic growth. By the first decade of the twenty-first century the agricultural growth rate at 5 percent was nearly twice the rate of population growth of 2.7 percent. Since the turn of the millennium, African countries have experienced the longest period of sustained economic and agricultural growth since independence. Incredibly, not only has growth accelerated, it has also spread broadly across all the major subregions.[3]

Yet these are aggregated GDP and agricultural growth trends which mask significant sub-regional and national differences. Several countries are still facing considerable growth challenges. Apart from West Africa, agricultural sectors in most other countries in Africa are growing at rates that are far below the 6 percent target set under the African Union's Comprehensive Africa Agriculture Development Programme (CAADP).[4]

Trends in productivity also exhibit patterns of decline and recovery similar to those of the overall growth trends. Economists may disagree about the exact periods of growth or decline and the relative rates of productivity growth in later periods compared with earlier stagnating or falling productivity levels, but they all agree that the pace of productivity growth has picked up in the past decade or two.[5]

Land and labor productivity grew at around 5 percent and 3 percent per year in 2001–11, respectively, having accelerated considerably from the preceding two decades (table 10.1). Slow or even negative growth in labor productivity from 1980 to 2000 in most sub-regions gave way to healthier growth rates in the

TABLE 10.1.   Economic and agricultural growth and productivity rates, sub-Saharan Africa (per annum)

PERIOD	GDP	GDP/CAPITA	AGRICULTURE VALUE ADDED	LABOR PRODUCTIVITY	LAND PRODUCTIVITY
1980s	1.4%	–1.4%	3.1%	0.2%	1.7%
1990s	2.7%	0%	3.6%	–0.4%	1.5%
2000s	6.3%	3.5%	5.0%	3.0%	5.2%
2010s	3.5%	0.7%	3.8%	2.4%	5.2%

Source: For data on GDP, GDP per capita, and agriculture value added: World Bank, "World Development Indicators (WDI)," May 3, 2018, https://datacatalog.worldbank.org/dataset/world-development-indicators. For labor and land productivity: ReSAKSS, "Tracking Indicators," Regional Strategic Analysis and Knowledge Support System, accessed April 5, 2018, http://www.resakss.org/node/11.

FIG. 10.3. Agricultural output per worker, sub-Saharan Africa (constant 2004–6 US$)

Source: Based on data from Alejandro Nin-Pratt, "Agricultural Intensification in Africa: A Regional Analysis," IFPRI Discussion Paper (Washington, DC: IFPRI, 2015), http://ebrary.ifpri.org/cdm/ref/collection/p15738coll2/id/129096.

next decade in all sub-regions. But it was West Africa's rapid labor productivity growth of nearly 6 percent per year that drove the notable improvement in SSA as a whole (figure 10.3).[6]

The growth in agricultural output continues to be driven by the expansion of agricultural land.[7] During 1980–2000 growth in arable land generally exceeded growth in labor productivity, again with the exception of West Africa. However this was reversed in the following decade, when labor productivity grew more than twice as fast as the expansion of arable land in all subregions except East Africa, which had the fastest arable land growth but the lowest labor and land productivity growth of all subregions.

Agricultural Imports

The difficulty in raising the pace of agricultural growth above that of population growth has led to a rapid increase in agricultural import expenditures by African countries. The total value of agricultural imports rose *tenfold* between 2001 and 2011 to nearly US$80 billion annually. Although the value of agricultural exports during this time has quadrupled to above

US$40 billion, the agricultural trade deficit has widened significantly and is about to reach the same value as overall agricultural exports.[8]

Several structural factors have made the surge in imports inevitable. Three major forces—continued population growth, faster income growth, and rapid urbanization—have contributed to an increase in food demand in general and food imports in particular. As demonstrated by the strong growth in Africa's exports, the agricultural trade deficit does not reflect a failure of African agriculture. Rather, these three forces, coming after a long period of economic stagnation and depressed demand, have accelerated demand growth to a pace more rapid than that which agriculture, as a biological process, can achieve. The agricultural trade deficit thus is a symptom of the resurgence in demand. However, the deficit also underlines the opportunities available to African agriculture if it remains sufficiently dynamic to seize them. Given the limited scope in other major world regions to raise agricultural output, African countries will face two major consequences if they fail to accelerate and sustain the growth of their own agricultural sectors: On the one hand, they stand to miss the opportunity of capturing a larger share of the steadily expanding demand of African and global agricultural markets and, hence, the opportunity to create wealth in Africa and earn foreign exchange. On the other hand, faced with otherwise slower-growing global food supplies, they would have to pay higher prices for rising food imports, in the context of possibly greater volatility in food prices.

The Impact on Poverty

Africa's overall economic and agricultural growth performance over the past five decades is mirrored by changes in poverty levels. Although poverty in Africa was lower in the 1980s than in East Asia and Pacific and South Asia, poverty rates began to rise in the following decade as they declined in the other two regions.[9] But as Africa's economic growth began improving in the mid-1990s, poverty rates started declining along with rates in East Asia and Pacific and South Asia.[10] Although in SSA the poverty rate has fallen to 41 percent of the population as of 2015, the total number of very poor is still very high is at 431 million people.[11] These 431 million tend to be smallholder farmers in rural areas who live on less than $1.90 per day, the World Bank's new definition of poverty.[12]

The MDGs set a target of halving poverty by 2015. All developing regions had achieved this target by 2011, with the exception of SSA.[13] In 2006 Ghana was the first country in SSA to achieve the target, but while poverty levels have fallen across the board, in the 2000s none of Africa's subregions, with the exception of central Africa, have been able to meet the poverty goal (figure 10.4). This suggests

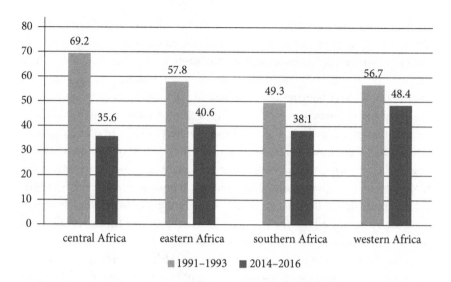

FIG. 10.4. Changes in poverty rates in major African regions

Source: IFPRI, "ReSAKSS (Regional Strategic Analysis and Knowledge Support System)," ReSAKSS Database, accessed October 22, 2018.

that considerably more effort is needed if the goal is to be achieved any time soon. The slow progress in eliminating poverty has a great deal to do with agricultural growth trends.[14]

A Stunted Agriculture

Unchanging or even rising poverty levels in Africa coincided with a period of externally driven government policies that shifted widely from one focus to the next and failed to establish conditions the agricultural sector needed to thrive. In particular, the first generation of African leaders pursued policies that emphasized industrial development and treated agriculture as a source of rents to finance and protect nascent industries. The government attempted to manage the development process alone, leaving little freedom for the private sector. Smallholder farmers like the Namarundas were suffocated between expensive consumer goods, government-dictated agricultural prices and marketing constraints, and a deterioration in living conditions owing to a lack of investment in rural areas.

As a result, many small farmers left agriculture to seek employment in the cities. However, the economy outside agriculture was not growing fast enough to absorb the influx of labor. These dynamics produced something that is unique to the pace and patterns of transformation of African economies: the stunting of agriculture, meaning a faster-than-usual decline of the agricultural sector combined with a larger-than-usual non-agricultural sector dominated by an oversized services sector.

Compared to other regions at a similar stage of economic development, agriculture today plays a much smaller role in African economies, while the opposite is true in the predominantly informal services sector; in SSA up to 90 percent of jobs outside agriculture are in the informal sector.[15]

Moreover, slow growth in productivity and incomes continues to make it hard for the Namarundas to significantly change their living conditions, while their neighbors and relatives who decided to migrate to the city struggle to find well-paying jobs to vastly improve theirs. The countries with the highest degrees of agricultural sector stunting or underperformance tend to have the highest levels of poverty (figure 10.5).

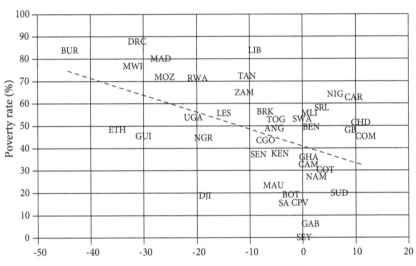

Gap between actual and expected AgGDP shares

FIG. 10.5. Agricultural sector underperformance and poverty. The horizontal axis measures the extent to which the actual size of the agricultural sector differs from what would be expected based on the level of economic development of a given country. A negative number means that agriculture represents a smaller share of the country's economy than one would expect, and the larger the absolute value, the higher the level of stunting.

Source: Ousmane Badiane and Margaret S. McMillan, "Economic Transformation in Africa: Patterns, Drivers, and Implications for Future Growth Strategies," in Ousmane Badiane and Tsitsi Makombe, *Beyond a Middle Income Africa: Transforming African Economies for Sustained Growth with Rising Employment and Incomes. ReSAKSS Annual Trends and Outlook Report 2014* (Washington, DC: IFPRI, 2015), http://ebrary.ifpri.org/cdm/ref/collection/p15738coll2/id/130007.

A Turnaround

African leaders entered a new era in the early 2000s with the launch of the New Partnership for Africa's Development (NEPAD) and its framework for agriculture-led development, CAADP. The policy renewal represented by NEPAD and the focus on enhanced agricultural performance as key to growth and poverty reduction have coincided with the remarkable agricultural and economic recovery and improvements in poverty levels.

Compared to the 1990s, in the 2000s African governments have nearly doubled annual public expenditures going to agriculture. The size of the agricultural sector has grown by about two-thirds. During the same time, the share of the population living under the poverty line dropped by more than a third, and the improvement in nutrition indicators ranges between 20 and 43 percent.[16]

Attempts to explain the recent recovery have focused on rising commodity prices and other changes in global markets or even on changing rainfall conditions. Given that the same changes have taken place in the past but have not resulted in growth of this magnitude, have not encompassed this many countries, and have not been sustained over such a long period, they cannot explain the whole story. The fundamental question is why African economies have, this time around, responded so strongly and positively to changes in the global economy.

Internal factors must have been at the root of the improved performance. These include improvement in sector governance, both in terms of policies and institutions, which in turn have structurally changed the way the economies operate and respond to opportunities, domestic as well as global. The heavy bias in national policies against agriculture has been significantly reduced. Space has been created for the private sector to play a vastly greater role compared to the period prior to the 1990s. Private sector firms are not only leading investments in traditional (e.g., coffee, tea, etc.) and emerging (fruits and vegetables, flowers) export sectors; they are also investing in new processing enterprises and distribution networks to transform traditional staples such as cassava and millet into new value chains dominated progressively by new products catering to urban consumers. Farmers are getting higher shares of the prices paid by consumers in domestic and foreign export markets. The changed economic environment has also stimulated growth in the non-agricultural sector, led by infrastructure, construction, telecommunications, financial services, and transport but also light manufacturing. This has led to a rapidly growing middle class, which fuels demand for processed traditional staples and creates new markets for smallholder farmers.

Taken together, the above changes indicate that African economies have undergone a real structural change. They are better positioned for growth and transformation than they have ever been. They find themselves, however, only at the start of the journey to higher growth and improved livelihoods. The improved policy and strategy environment is just a beginning. More needs to happen to transform African economies and make a real difference in the lives of the Namarundas, their fellow dwellers of the rural areas, and those who have moved to the city.

A New Way Forward

The fundamental changes in the quality of sector governance and increased public sector investment which began in the early 2000s have to be sustained to bring about real transformation to African economies. Real transformation has to lead to employment creation and income growth that are broad based and rapid enough to markedly reduce poverty and raise standards of living in the context of a still-growing population.

Sectoral Changes

The nature and patterns of the recent economic transformation can be discerned by looking at changes in sectoral employment shares in Africa. Using the patterns seen in other regions historically as a reference allows one to assess the extent to which the process of economic transformation in Africa diverges, or not, from what would be expected on the basis of countries' income levels.

In Africa, as incomes rise and countries climb to higher levels of development, the share of employment in agriculture decreases, and that in services and manufacturing increases, as would be expected from a successful process of economic transformation (figure 10.6). The recent patterns of structural transformation in Africa, therefore, mirror the historical trends observed in other regions. A more in-depth analysis of employment dynamics results in a better appreciation of the quality of economic transformation in Africa, that is, its contribution to creating employment with higher labor productivity and incomes.

Emerging Dynamics

How has employment changed by category of occupation, age, and gender? The occupations analyzed here include agriculture, professional services, other services, unskilled manual labor, skilled manual labor, not working, and, for the young, in school. Agriculture includes subsistence farmers as well as commercial

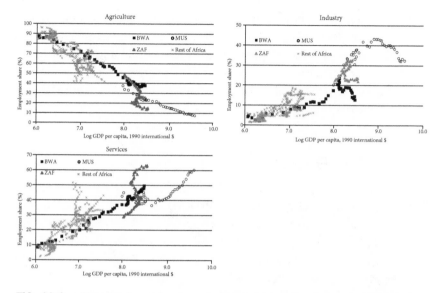

FIG. 10.6. Changes in sectoral employment shares. Employment shares in agriculture, industry, and services, respectively, are plotted on the vertical axis and the log of GDP per capita on the horizontal axis for Botswana (BWA), South Africa (ZAF), Mauritius (MUS), and other African countries with available data for the years 1960–2010.

Source: Xinshen Diao, Kenneth Harttgen, and Margaret McMillan, "The Changing Structure of Africa's Economies," IFPRI Discussion Paper (Washington, DC: IFPRI, 2017), http://ebrary. ifpri.org/utils/getfile/collection/p15738coll2/id/131048/filename/131259.pdf.

farmers, as the data does not distinguish the two. Like agriculture, all other occupations include both formal and informal sector workers.

The decadal changes in the share of population working in each occupation by gender and geographic location are revealing. The share of population engaged in agriculture declined sharply overall while rising slightly in urban areas, and this is equally true for men and women (figure 10.7). The rise in agriculture-based employment in urban areas reflects the growth in peri-urban and non-traditional segments of the sector. In other words, as the group including the Namarundas is slowly declining in size, others, including some migrating from the latter group into small and larger towns, are taking up farming around urban areas to cater to the rising urban demand.

Employment in clerical and sales services has risen in rural areas but has declined in urban areas (figure 10.7). This is a reflection of the fact that families like the Namarundas are diversifying into other, off-farm occupations as the changes in the

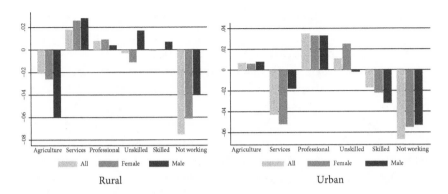

FIG. 10.7. Average change in working population by occupation, 2000–2012

Source: Ousmane Badiane and Margaret S. McMillan, "Economic Transformation in Africa: Patterns, Drivers, and Implications for Future Growth Strategies," in Ousmane Badiane and Tsitsi Makombe, *Beyond a Middle Income Africa: Transforming African Economies for Sustained Growth with Rising Employment and Incomes. ReSAKSS Annual Trends and Outlook Report 2014* (Washington, DC: IFPRI, 2015), http://ebrary.ifpri.org/cdm/ref/collection/p15738coll2/id/130007.

structure of the economy reach into the rural areas. In urban areas fewer people are engaged in skilled manual labor across all groups, unlike in rural areas where there are more men, young and old, engaged in skilled manual labor. Unskilled manual labor for women has seen growth only in urban areas, whereas in rural areas the share of the population working in unskilled manual labor increases only for men. The most significant change is the drop in the population who report that they are not working. In other words, labor force participation by men, women, the young and the old alike appears to have risen over the past decade.

Taken together, these findings show that, although structural change might have been delayed in much of Africa during earlier decades, the continent may have made a turn and is now on the same trajectory as observed historically in other regions.

Policy and Institutional Reforms

The quality of sector governance and changes in agricultural policies and strategies have played a determining role in the rise, decline, and later recovery of growth performance among African countries. The perception that somehow what farmers produce is a collective property is still far too common and interferes with the realization of farming as a business and the farmer as an entrepreneur.

It is that perception that makes a government want to set the price, control the marketing, or ban the export of a given crop. Such policies and associated institutional arrangements are not only essentially questionable because they are impossible to manage properly but also unfailingly counterproductive, as they end up against the interests of farmers. Governments will sustain and deepen the current recovery and ultimately accelerate the process of economic transformation only by adopting adequate policies, creating operational institutions, and making the necessary investments that enhance the capacities of farmers to compete in domestic and foreign markets, thus seizing the growing opportunities of a globalizing world and a rapidly urbanizing continent.

The efforts to promote mutual accountability and evidence-based policy planning and implementation under CAADP are an important step in that direction. Policies, institutions, and investments that will accelerate agricultural sector and economy-wide transformation have to facilitate better utilization and harnessing of new and emerging technologies that will support intensification of agricultural production processes. The yield gaps observed across Africa and between Africa and other regions, including within countries, are an indicator of the potential to boost productivity through the use of existing technologies.

However, given the pressure to achieve faster progress and the size and variety of changes that need to take place, African countries have few other options than to invest heavily in mastering new, emerging technologies. Biotechnologies (BT) and information and communications technologies (ICT) would help countries leapfrog by cutting the cost and time required to overcome technical, physical, and organizational obstacles hampering faster agricultural transformation. These technologies will determine the future competitiveness of domestic agricultural sectors, including not only the big producers but also smallholder farmers, in a globalizing agricultural sector.

Industrialization Strategies

The most dramatic change facing African smallholders is the rapid transformation of value chains of traditional staples fueled by fast-paced urbanization and rising incomes. At nearly 4 percent, the rate of urbanization in Africa has matched and surpassed that in other parts of the world.[17] According to projections by the UN Population Fund, the level of urbanization in Africa will reach 50 percent by 2020 and 65 percent by 2050.[18] While there were only two cities in Africa with more than a million inhabitants in 1950, there were fifty of these large cities by 2010, and this number is expected to nearly double by 2025. As the number of cities increases, they are becoming less concentrated. Instead of large metropolitan areas growing larger, growth in urbanization is also being driven by the emergence of many small cities.[19] In West Africa only 40 percent of the urban population live in large metropolitan areas while the remaining 60 percent live in secondary and tertiary cities in the rural areas and around or along highways to large cities.[20]

A growing urban population, bolstered by the fastest economic recovery in the history of the continent, is boosting urban food demand, which in turn is driving an explosion of demand for traditional—albeit processed—food staples. African food markets are projected to grow sixfold by 2025.[21] Already, urban centers account for half to two-thirds of total food demand.[22]

While the share of urban population was rising, so was the share and number of people with higher disposable incomes. For instance, the number of people earning between $2 and $20 per day rose from a little more than one hundred million in the 1990s to around three hundred million currently, most of whom, in particular those at the higher end of the income bracket, reside in urban areas.[23]

Processed Foods

Rising incomes are driving rapid transformation in diets and thus value chains for staple foods, with a sharp increase in processed foods. The share of processed foods is projected to increase five to tenfold between 2010 and 2040. By that time processed foods will account for nearly 75 percent of staple food demand (table 10.2). Africa's total urban food market is estimated to reach $150 billion by 2030, and smallholder farmers could capture as much as $30 billion of that.[24]

The rise of the processing sector is accompanied by a lengthening of the staples value chains. From traditionally short chains limited to home-based processing and confined predominantly to rural areas, the transforming value chains now primarily supply small towns and large urban centers with a range of branded ready-to-cook and ready-to-eat products. The urban-based value chains are fueled by the introduction of new processes, sometimes mechanized, of producing and distributing traditional foods outside of the household setting through specialized enterprises.

TABLE 10.2.   The transformation of staples value chains and the rise of processed foods

		UNPROCESSED	PROCESSED LOW VALUE ADDED	PROCESSED HIGH VALUE ADDED
Non-perishable	Increase in share, 2010–40	4x	5.5x	7x
	Share of diets, 2040	(8%)	(17%)	(23%)
Perishable	Increase in share, 2010–40	6.5x	8x	10x
	Share of diets, 2040	(20%)	(18%)	(15%)

Source: David Tschirley et al., "Towards a Middle Income Africa: Long Term Growth Outlook and Strategies," December 2012, http://africa.isp.msu.edu/africa/news/?id=2115.

Modern Staple Value Chains

An example of the transformation of staples value chains is that of millet in Senegal (box 10.2). The transformation of the staples value chains, from cassava and maize to millet, is driven by thousands of small- and medium-sized, often women-led enterprises employing a handful of workers.

Box 10.2. A millet value chain in Senegal

Until [very] recently the [millet value] chain in Senegal hardly went beyond [home-based milling] . . ., where millet grown on the farm was milled in a neighborhood mill and the flour processed in the household into various products for home consumption or sales in the same neighborhood. The chain was so short that most of these products were hardly ever found outside of the main millet production areas, leading to a continuous decline in millet consumption not just in the capital city, Dakar, but also in other large cities, including some near or inside the main production areas.

Several projects and efforts at the National Institute of Food Technologies in the 1980s and 1990s developed and extended new processing and conservation technologies, laying the foundation for the emergence of a millet processing industry. The second stage of the chain, consisting of bringing branded flour and other ready to cook derivatives to the urban markets, started in the early 2000s. The third stage, a range of ready to eat meals, is in the middle of a rapid expansion.

This transformation is not only responding to strong increases in urban demand in Dakar and other major cities, but also rapidly changing the eating habits of urbanites. Middle-class households now regularly consume millet-based meals on weekends. Lower-income households too are major consumers of these products, in particular the "ready-to-cook" brands. The "ready-to-eat" products are becoming popular meals on the go for travelers. A recent new trend is to eat millet-based meals on the day after major Muslim religious holidays.

Source: Reproduced from Ousmane Badiane and John Ulimwengu, "Business Pathways to the Future of Smallholder Farming in the Context of Transforming Value Chains," in *Africa Agriculture Status Report 2017*, issue 5 (Nairobi: AGRA, 2017), http://ebrary.ifpri.org/cdm/ref/collection/p15738coll5/id/5981.

Local Enterprises

The extent to which smallholder farmers will benefit from the rapidly expanding demand for urban food will depend on the capacity of the domestic processing sector to compete in urban and regional food markets. This in turn depends on the capacity of countries to deepen the transformation of the off-farm segments of agricultural value chains. The strategic challenge here is how to ensure that the emerging processing sector successfully transitions from a situation with a large and increasing number of small enterprises producing low-quality goods with low and declining profits to a situation in which enterprises can improve product quality, expand operations, raise profitability, and become more competitive in and capture a larger share of urban markets.

There are several phases of the transformation process through which the emerging local enterprise sector passes.[25] The initiation phase is driven by the introduction of simple new processes to produce traditional meals for the domestic urban markets (table 10.3).

Once a new product or business makes a successful appearance in local markets, it is copied by a large number of imitators and new entrants who apply the same technology and produce the same low-quality goods for the same local

TABLE 10.3. Phases of development of staples processing sector and policy priorities

PHASE	INNOVATION, IMITATION, AND PRODUCTIVITY GROWTH	POLICY PRIORITIES AND ACTIONS
Initiation	Imitation of foreign technology to manufacture traditional food for domestic urban markets	1) Markets to lower transactions costs
Quantity expansion	Entry of a growing number of followers, imitation of imitated technologies, and stagnant productivity	2) Vocational training to improve management practices 3) Infrastructure: roads, communication, electricity to lower operating costs
Quality improvement	Multifaceted innovations, exit of noninnovative enterprises, and increasing productivity and export	4) Knowledge transfer from abroad, industrial zones, access to credit, intellectual property

Sources: T. Sonobe and K. Otsuka, *Cluster-Based Industrial Development—A Comparative Study of Asia and Africa*, 1st ed. (London: Palgrave Macmillan UK, 2011), //www.palgrave.com/gb/book/9780230280182; Ousmane Badiane and Margaret S. McMillan, "Economic Transformation in Africa: Patterns, Drivers, and Implications for Future Growth Strategies," in *Beyond a Middle Income Africa: Transforming African Economies for Sustained Growth with Rising Employment and Incomes. ReSAKSS Annual Trends and Outlook Report 2014*, by Ousmane Badiane and Tsitsi Makombe (Washington, DC: International Food Policy Research Institute, 2015), http://ebrary.ifpri.org/cdm/ref/collection/p15738coll2/id/130007.

markets. During this phase of quantity expansion, there is a rapid increase in the number of firms and supply of products, leading to a progressive decline in profitability. In the absence of innovation in production technology and business practices, the number of enterprises continues to rise and profits to decline. The result is a growing concentration of low productivity and persistently small enterprises not equipped to compete with foreign suppliers of imported products in local urban markets.

Strategies to turn the situation around, sustain the expansion of the processing sector, and foster the industrialization of agribusiness value chains would have to enable a critical mass of enterprises to eventually succeed in improving product quality, raising profitability, and growing in size through innovation in production technology and management practices. The sector enters a phase of maturation during which many enterprises that are not capable of innovating will be forced to exit. The result is a decrease in the number of firms, an increase in average firm size, and a rise in profitability and competitiveness in urban food markets.

Key policy priorities to help transforming value chains successfully transition through these phases include (i) the facilitation of access to markets to

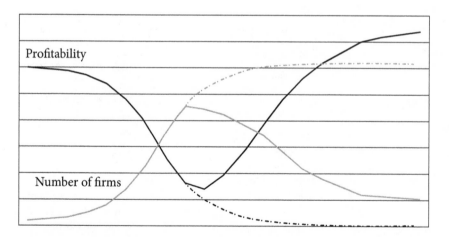

FIG. 10.8. The emerging processing sector. Solid (dotted) lines denote progression of number of firms and profitability with (without) multifaceted innovation and enterprise maturation.

Source: Ousmane Badiane and Margaret S. McMillan, "Economic Transformation in Africa: Patterns, Drivers, and Implications for Future Growth Strategies," in Ousmane Badiane and Tsitsi Makombe, *Beyond a Middle Income Africa: Transforming African Economies for Sustained Growth with Rising Employment and Incomes. ReSAKSS Annual Trends and Outlook Report 2014* (Washington, DC: IFPRI, 2015), http://ebrary.ifpri.org/cdm/ref/collection/p15738coll2/id/130007.

lower transactions costs; (ii) vocational training to develop and upgrade skills to improve management practices and capacities for product and process innovation; (iii) improvements in infrastructure, including roads, communication, and electricity to lower operating costs; (iv) technology transfer from abroad, access to credit, intellectual property, and industrial zones to foster quality improvement, raise competitiveness in domestic markets, and enter foreign export markets (see table 10.3).

Realizing the Potential

African economies have experienced a remarkable economic and agricultural growth recovery since the early 2000s. They have enjoyed rates of growth unprecedented in the continent's post-independence history. Yet the progress has not been strong or sustained enough to compensate for the effects of the lost decades, and poverty levels across Africa are still unacceptably high.

At the same time, the rapidly modernizing agribusiness value chains, in particular the staple foods processing sector, present a major opportunity for labor-intensive industrial development. The sector has the potential to become a large source of employment offering higher incomes, particularly for youth and women. The rapidly growing demand of the middle class for more sophisticated food products creates a favorable environment for product innovation and upgrading across major segments of the sector.

Successful industrial development policy targeted at staple foods and other agribusiness value chains should allow African countries not only to sustain and even accelerate the recent pace of economic growth but also to broaden the impact of future growth in terms of employment and wealth creation. Across Africa thousands of small enterprises are processing, packaging, and distributing traditional staples to cater to the growing number of middle-class households.

Strategic priorities need to focus on raising the stock of technology capabilities and managerial skills and promoting their applications to produce goods with better quality and higher value. The goal, in the short to medium run, is to increase the number of successful entrepreneurs by effectively improving production methods as well as marketing and management skills. In the medium to long run, attention needs to turn to infrastructure and support services as well as regulatory and macroeconomic policies.

LEADERSHIP AND PERFORMANCE

During their growth process economies go through a series of changes that reflect the collective outcome of a complex web of decisions by generations of actors, private and public. Their actions over time and across space affect the way resources are combined and turned into goods and services to meet the needs of the various segments of the population. Leaders' main challenge is determining how to create and maintain a policy and institutional environment that ensures that actions by private actors in pursuit of private goals and aspirations are collectively in harmony with long-term national goals and lead to outcomes that are desirable for a society as a whole.

This challenge is considerably greater for countries in the early stages of economic development that are struggling with limited institutional, financial, and technical resources. During the first decades that followed independence around 1960, generations of leaders have faced this challenge. Their success or lack thereof has, over the years, affected the pace of overall economic performance and in particular growth in the agricultural sector. If policy makers are to sustain the current pace of strong growth well into the future they need a good understanding of the role of leadership in the shaping of past progress in terms of enhancing livelihoods and improving food security among the most vulnerable segments of the population.

Generations of farmers lived through the dramatic changes in Africa's economies during the first fifty years since independence. They saw their livelihoods improve gradually throughout the 1960s and halfway through the 1970s, when

African countries played a significant role as net exporters in global agricultural markets. African smallholder producers dominated major export markets ranging from oilseeds to cotton and to tropical beverages. Then, as now, the decisions and actions by farmers and their communities determined the pace of agricultural and economic growth in African countries. Their work and lives are affected by many events that are entirely out of their control: weather, pests, diseases, and the availability or lack thereof of fertilizers, improved seeds, and funds or credit to purchase them. A less obvious, but critically important influence on their ability to farm their land and manage their livelihood is the set of agricultural and economic policies pursued by their national government.

In every sector of the economy the quality, coherence, and continuity of government policies, rules, and regulations have a considerable effect on the decisions of economic agents. That reality is valid for agriculture and the farming communities where most of the poor people live and work. In the decades since the independence era, agricultural policies in the continent have undergone perpetual changes with far-reaching consequences for the ability of farmers to make production and marketing decisions, access the resources they need, and earn a living from their farms. At the center of these developments were difficulties in finding the right balance between agriculture and industry as the main driver of growth and between government and the private sector as key actors in regulating economic activity.

Africa, unlike any other developing region, has struggled for decades to find the proper strategic approach and direction for economic policy design and sector governance. At the time when most countries gained independence, the economic development profession itself had an incomplete understanding of how countries transitioned from predominantly agrarian to primarily industry-based economies and hence of how to successfully manage that transition. Consequently, agricultural and development policies during the early post-independence decades in many African countries were based on a still-forming theory of economic development and implemented by newly constituted state bureaucracies with serious capacity limitations. The lack of local expertise and lingering ties with colonial powers resulted in another major complication in the governance of the agricultural sector in these countries: the strong influence of external agencies in determining policy and strategy priorities and choices.

The lack of leadership by African governments and constituencies in policy and strategy formulation in the agricultural sector has, over many decades, led to widely shifting rules and regulations that made it extremely difficult for farmers to work productively. Hence efforts to sustain and accelerate the current growth recovery to meaningfully improve livelihood conditions, end hunger, and sharply reduce poverty in farmers' communities require a good understanding of the evolution of national policies in order to draw lessons for the future.

How African governments have historically managed the tensions between agriculture and industry and between public and private sector operators in national development strategies is a complex story, one that encompasses strategies for governments and other stakeholders to build on recent progress in evidence-based policymaking and ensure that future policies avoid the mistakes of the past.

Failing Policies and Strategies

New, post-independence African governments, struggling to forge new nations and faced with a serious lack of expertise, experimented with alternative options to spur growth, raise living standards among impoverished masses, and modernize their young economies. The policy and strategy choices facing the newly independent African states have been conceptualized by Badiane and Makombe (2015) (figure 11.1). Limited government capacity and an overbearing global

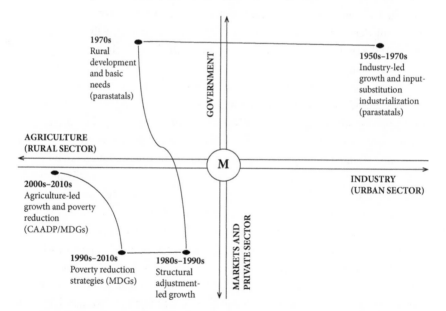

FIG. 11.1. Sixty years of evolution of agricultural sector policies and strategies in Africa. The x-axis represents the relative sector emphasis of country strategies between agriculture and industry, and the y-axis the emphasis on government versus private sector roles. The point labeled "M" describes a strategy exhibiting no bias either between the public and private sectors or between industry and agriculture.

Source: Ousmane Badiane and Tsitsi Makombe, "Agriculture, Growth, and Development in Africa: Theory and Practice," in *The Oxford Handbook of Africa and Economics*, ed. Célestin Monga and Justin Yifu Lin (Oxford: Oxford University Press, 2015), https://doi.org/10.1093/oxfordhb/9780199687107.013.016.

development community produced externally driven development agendas plagued with constant changes in policy and strategy priorities and directions.[1]

The frequent shifts from one end to the other of the policy space described by the four quadrants in figure 11.1 illustrate the lack of coherence, consistency, and continuity that made life for farmers extremely difficult.

Industry or Agriculture?

For each decade the position of the main strategic thrust in the four quadrants of figure 11.1 describes the relative biases of strategy choices along the agriculture versus industry and government versus private sector axes. The first two decades of economic development policy post-independence were characterized by strong biases in favor of industry as a source of growth and of government as the main economic player. National development policies were located near the top right-hand corner of the diagram in figure 11.1. Many governments pursued strategies that saw industry as the main engine of growth to transform the predominantly agriculture-based economies and improve the lives of a population still mainly concentrated in the rural areas.

Agriculture was seen as a source of resources to support industrialization. Policies in the agricultural sector were designed primarily to generate tax revenues to finance the nascent industrial sector. Through state-owned enterprises and organizations, governments controlled the trade of crops, including to foreign export markets, and the procurement and distribution of modern inputs: seeds, fertilizers, and pesticides. Governments also determined and enforced the prices of individual crops, by controlling trade or transportation of agricultural commodities by private sector operators. Consequently, agriculture was subjected to heavy taxation, implicitly and explicitly, and considerable regulatory disruption, all of which played a significant part in the poor performance of the agricultural sector and in the broader economic decline and stagnation long after the demise of the pro-industry policy era.[2]

The potential rates of growth were substantially higher in industry than agriculture, but not well understood was the fact that industrial growth was possible only when fueled by faster agricultural growth.[3] As the source of employment and income for the vast majority of the population, a growing agricultural sector was needed to sustain the necessary purchasing power to pay for goods being produced in the manufacturing sector. The heavy burden put on farmers by these policies and their impact in preventing productivity and income growth among farming communities ended up hurting the very industries they were supposed to help. By the early 1970s it had become clear that national development strategies were not working as African economies entered a long period of decline, and income inequality rose sharply between rural and urban areas. The industrialization policies of the time had a distinct bias towards urbanization which resulted in considerable rural-urban migration. Despite rapidly growing cities, the industrial sector was unable to rapidly absorb the influx of workers.

Rural Development and Basic Needs

To address growth and equity issues, donors and international development agencies directed the first in a series of major shifts in their support strategies to emphasize integrated rural development (IRD) and basic human needs (BHN). The new strategies sought to increase agricultural productivity together with access to social services such as health and education in rural areas.[4] The World Bank, for instance, substantially increased its investment in projects in this area and broadened its lending to include small farmers. To support the rural poor, the World Bank also included within its portfolio projects to finance agricultural research, extension services, marketing, provision of credit, and small-scale irrigation as well as services beyond agriculture such as clean water, rural roads, education, and health services.[5]

The call to directly address poverty and inequality through IRD and BHN now placed the focus primarily on agriculture and farming communities. Increased agricultural production, particularly food production, became a top priority for achieving food self-sufficiency and alleviating poverty. Within a decade development strategies moved from a heavy industry focus to a strong emphasis on agriculture and the rural sector. Governments remained firmly in control, however, and much of the bias against the private sector was still in place. In the context of figure 11.1, strategies merely moved horizontally from the top right-hand quadrant to the top left-hand quadrant. Agricultural policies related to BHN and IRD projects were largely unsuccessful owing to high costs of design, administration, and implementation. Economic conditions continued to worsen, and by the end of the 1970s most countries had reached a crisis point that saw falling incomes, large budget deficits, rising inflation, depleted foreign exchange reserves, stagnating official development assistance, and a serious debt crisis.[6]

Structural Adjustment Programs

In 1981 the World Bank introduced its own action plan for Africa, commonly known as the Berg Report.[7] The recommendations of the Berg Report were to be implemented through structural adjustment programs (SAPs) supported by the International Monetary Fund, the World Bank, and several leading bilateral development agencies. Agricultural policies included the privatization or restructuring of state-owned enterprises, marketing boards, and government entities competing with the private sector, the liberalization of input and output markets, the removal of fertilizer subsidies, the reduction of budget deficits, and the correction of overvalued exchange rates.[8]

The economic crisis of the 1980s helped to reveal the inefficiencies and costliness of the marketing boards, and their removal or reduced role was seen as a means of opening up participation by the private sector and bringing about market-determined prices. Development strategies made another move, this time from the top to the bottom left-hand side of figure 11.1.

The depth of the changes promoted by SAPs resulted in limited cooperation or outright resistance by governments, which undermined consensus and impeded adequate design and implementation. The focus on cutting expenditures to reduce budget deficits, beat inflation, and make economies more competitive made it difficult to undertake investments in improving technologies, infrastructure, and market institutions that were essential to boost productivity and growth in the agricultural sector.[9] Meanwhile, the removal or reduction of input and output subsidies and pricing regulations resulted in reduced fertilizer use for key staple crops and in higher food prices, outcomes that were detrimental to the food security of low-income households, particularly net food buyers.

Poverty Reduction Strategies

After a decade into SAPs, there was little progress in social and economic measures across Africa. Concerns over the lack of meaningful progress in the developing world, especially in Africa, resulted in international summits at which various targets for promoting sustainable human development were set and later compiled in 2000 as the Millennium Development Goals (MDGs). The World Bank was exploring other avenues to enhance the development impact of its work.[10] Thus, in 1999 the World Bank and the IMF introduced the Poverty Reduction Strategy Papers (PRSP) which defined economic and social-sector policies to promote growth and reduce poverty in line with the MDGs over a three- to five-year period. The PRSPs would focus on low-income countries, which would be given greater room to lead strategy and priority setting and program preparation through a participatory process.

While countries acknowledge the important role of agriculture in accelerating pro-poor growth, evaluations of PRSPs suggest that agricultural policies of the SAP era have largely been maintained. Moreover, there had been little change in investments made to the agriculture sector by governments or donors, despite PRSP rhetoric on the importance of sector. Countries continued to espouse the need to liberalize agricultural input and output markets and trade as well as foster privatization of parastatals. PRSPs have therefore primarily moved strategies further toward agriculture while maintaining the core tenets of SAPs as far as the role of the private sector is concerned.

Good Leadership and Policy Renewal

Common to all the above strategy thrusts is the fact that they were primarily conceived and led externally. Constant changes in direction and lack of continuity and consistency made it difficult for African countries to design and execute coherent strategies at scale and long enough to turn the tide and restore growth. This contributed to a long period of economic decline and steep deterioration in living conditions.

The increasingly difficult economic situation left African leaders disillusioned by global development strategies they felt had failed to deliver on their promises. With a sense that early development strategies had been largely determined by foreign actors, African leaders and technocrats under the aegis of the Organisation of African Unity (OAU) made an attempt in the 1980s to take matters into their own hands. The goal was to come up with a strategy to reverse the growth malaise and place Africa on a trajectory toward sustained economic growth and self-sufficiency. Several consultations among Africa's leadership resulted in the "Lagos Plan of Action for the Economic Development of Africa, 1980–2000" (LPA) and the "Final Act of Lagos" (FAL) in 1980. This was unprecedented, as for the first time African leaders had come up with an Africa-wide effort at transforming the continent's economic development.

The Lagos Plan of Action

The LPA was more of a political than a programmatic document. It clearly expressed the frustration of African leaders in the face of continued deterioration of economic and living conditions in the continent after twenty years of experimenting with a host of strategies to promote growth and economic development. They viewed "with distress, that our continent remains the least developed of all the continents" with "20 of the 31 least developed countries of the world." They pointed out that "Africa was directly exploited during the colonial period and for the past two decades; this exploitation has been carried out through neocolonialist external forces which seek to influence the economic policies and directions of African States."[11]

With respect to the agricultural sector, the main structural weaknesses were "low production and productivity, and rudimentary agricultural techniques" and "insufficient agricultural growth, especially of food production, in the face of the rapid population growth [which] has resulted in serious food shortages and malnutrition in the continent." The LPA was far from an agenda for action, however. At least for the agricultural sector, there were broad and non-actionable priorities with a lack of specific targets, except perhaps with respect to reduction of food losses. It is therefore not surprising that the LPA and FAL were not implemented as planned. African countries were still finding it difficult to take leadership of the development agenda, and the LPA and FAL faded away in front of competition from the SAPs and PRSPs.

A New African Leadership

Not until another twenty years later did a series of new developments on the continent create the conditions for the establishment of real African leadership. The considerable controversy that accompanied the SAPs took a significant toll on the readiness of the global community to continue down the path of externally driven agendas. On the political front, the end of apartheid created a lot of optimism and brought a new generation of leadership around President Thabo Mbeki of South Africa, who succeeded President Nelson Mandela. This succession coincided with the return to power in Nigeria of President Olusegun Obasanjo, who would be a strong partner of President Mbeki. The third major change was the election of President Abdoulaye Wade, a historic pan-Africanist opposition politician, in Senegal.

A new African leadership had now emerged at the beginning of the new millennium with a strong sense of confidence and desire to take ownership of the development agenda. President Mbeki had launched the African Renaissance, which included the following key elements:[12]

- The recovery of the African continent.
- The establishment of political democracy on the continent.
- The need to break neocolonial relations between Africa and the world's economic powers.
- The mobilization of the people of Africa to take their destiny into their own hands and thus prevent the continent from being a place for the attainment of geopolitical and strategic interests of the world's most powerful countries.
- Rapid development of people-driven and people-centered economic growth and development aimed at meeting the basic needs of people.

Presidents Obasanjo and Abdelaziz Bouteflika of Algeria would later join President Mbeki to develop the Millennium Partnership for African Recovery Program (MAP), inspired by the African Renaissance. Following his election, President Wade later launched the OMEGA Plan for Africa, the third piece in the construct that would pave the way for a new leadership of the development agenda in Africa.[13] While the African Renaissance provided a broader framework, the MAP set the parameters for global partnership, and the OMEGA Plan offered implementation modalities. Together, the strategy documents addressed priority sectors including infrastructure, health, education, and agriculture in addition to peace, security, and governance. The MAP and OMEGA Plan were merged into a single document, the "Compact for African Recovery," which would later lead to the New Partnership for Africa's Development (NEPAD), adopted in 2001 by the OAU and in 2002 by the African Union, the successor to the OAU.[14]

The New Partnership for Africa's Development

NEPAD, as a rejection of the narrative of an Africa at the mercy of international initiatives, is an effort to put Africa in the leading role in directing development efforts on the continent. It first and foremost challenges African governments to improve the quality of political and economic governance and manage for better results and development outcomes. It defines an Africa-wide development agenda with clear priority areas and implementation modalities, including a Heads of State–level committee to oversee its execution and a technical secretariat to coordinate action on the ground. NEPAD also advocates a new form of partnership between Africa and the international community, a partnership in which African countries define the agenda, based on their priorities, to which global agencies align their technical and financial assistance.

NEPAD's core values go beyond African ownership and leadership and the alignment of development efforts to Africa's priorities. They also emphasize inclusivity and the participation of a range of stakeholder groups in the definition and implementation of policies and programs, including the private sector, farmers' organizations, and civil society organizations. Participation is encouraged through open and inclusive dialogue among stakeholders based on shared accountability for actions and results. The NEPAD principles of accountability and review are exemplified by the African Peer Review Mechanism (APRM), founded in 2003 as an instrument for self-assessment and peer review at the Heads of State level (box 11.1).

The overarching goal of NEPAD urges countries to work toward achieving and sustaining an average economic growth rate of 7 percent over a twenty-year period. Its agenda is built around two main components: (i) political governance, including peace and security, and (ii) economic and corporate governance. Sectoral priorities emphasize health, human resources, agriculture, science and technology, and markets.

Box 11.1. The African Peer Review Mechanism

The African Peer Review Mechanism (APRM), established under NEPAD in 2003, introduced the concept of governments' responsibility to account at the level of Heads of State for the quality of political and economic governance. The purpose of the APRM is to facilitate the adoption of laws and practices that increase stability, growth, sustainable development, and regional integration.

Countries participate in the APRM on a voluntary basis. As of 2016, thirty-five countries had joined the APRM, of which twenty had undergone a review. During a review, countries first perform a self-assessment in the areas of democracy and political governance, economic governance and management, corporate governance, and socioeconomic development and produce a preliminary national Programme of Action. Following the self-assessment, a panel of experts visits the country to interview representatives of the government, private sector, civil society, media, and other groups to assess the Programme of Action and develop a country report. The government then responds to the country report and finalizes the Programme of Action, taking the panel's recommendations into account. The country report, government response, and national Programme of Action are approved by APRM member states and made public six months afterward.

The APRM's reviews have enabled many countries to undertake recommended actions to improve governance. In other cases, reviews warned of tensions and risks that were not addressed by governments and later escalated into conflict. However, the APRM faced challenges in securing sufficient funding and political support to operate. In 2016 APRM member states launched a strategy to revitalize the review instrument, calling for progress on resource mobilization and better integration of the APRM into the African Union structure; the assessment and improvement of the APRM review process and its instruments; and the participation of the APRM in monitoring progress toward achieving the goals of the African Union's long-term development strategy, Agenda 2063, as well as the global Sustainable Development Goals.

Source: APRM, "APRM Strategic Plan 2016–2020: Advancing Transformative Leadership for Africa for Effective Implementation of Agenda 2063" (Midrand, South Africa, 2016), https://www.aprm-au.org/wp-content/uploads/2014/11/APRM-Strategic-Plan-2016-2020.pdf; NEPAD and African Union, "Guidelines for

Countries to Prepare For and To Participate in the African Peer Review Mechanism (APRM)" (African Union and NEPAD, 2003), https://aprm-au.org/wp-content/uploads/2014/11/APRM-Guidelines.pdf; David Omozuafoh, "Timely Rejuvenation of the African Peer Review Mechanism?," *APRM* (blog), March 16, 2016, https://www.aprm-au.org/timely-rejuvenation-of-the-african-peer-review-mechanism/.

The Comprehensive Africa Agriculture Development Program

NEPAD's agenda for the agricultural sector is articulated in the Comprehensive Africa Agriculture Development Programme (CAADP). CAADP is the continent-wide framework for agriculture-led growth and development. Launched in 2003, CAADP has since become NEPAD's flagship program in the economic development area.[15] Under CAADP, African leaders commit to two key targets: achieving a 6 percent yearly growth rate of agricultural production and, in pursuit of that goal, allocating 10 percent of annual public expenditures to agriculture. CAADP also embraced the NEPAD values and principles of African ownership and leadership; inclusivity and dialogue; and review and accountability. When launched in 2003 CAADP focused on four pillars: (i) sustainable land and water management, (ii) agribusiness development and market access, (iii) hunger and social safety nets, and (iv) science and technology.

CAADP is implemented at the country level through a four-step process followed by all countries which includes (i) the organization of a multi-stakeholder roundtable meeting to discuss agricultural sector priorities, (ii) the signing of a CAADP Compact, which lays out policy and investment priorities, (iii) the development of a National Agriculture Investment Plan (NAIP), and (iv) the holding of a business meeting, including an independent technical review to assess the quality of the NAIP and discuss funding as well as partnership modalities. Putting CAADP into practice involves building a broad constituency by engaging with the private sector, civil service, and government branches beyond Ministries of Agriculture; consulting with all stakeholders; creating a base of knowledge and evidence to inform setting investment priorities; and mobilizing resources for agricultural investments. Implementation is guided by the African Union Commission and NEPAD Planning and Coordinating Agency at the continental level and regional economic communities (RECs) at the regional level.

Rwanda was the first country to officially launch its CAADP process in 2007. Afterward, the rollout of CAADP across the continent accelerated. As of August

2018, forty-two countries had held a CAADP Roundtable and signed a CAADP Compact; thirty-four countries had drafted, reviewed, and validated a NAIP; and twenty-nine countries had held a business meeting.[16]

After ten years of implementation, African Heads of State adopted the Malabo Declaration on Accelerated Agricultural Growth and Transformation for Shared Prosperity and Improved Livelihoods. The declaration reaffirmed CAADP's core values and principles of inclusivity and mutual accountability to actions and results as well as its original goals of 6 percent annual agricultural growth and a 10 percent agricultural expenditure share. The declaration also broadened the CAADP agenda, adding goals and targets in a number of new areas. New goals to be achieved by 2025 under the Malabo Declaration include halving poverty and ending hunger, tripling intra-African agricultural trade, and ensuring resilience of livelihoods and production systems to climate risks.

The Impact of CAADP

NEPAD and CAADP mark a dramatic departure from the approach to development and international cooperation during the first four decades after independence. After more than ten years of implementation, it is a good time to ask what the impact of CAADP has been on farmers and their fellow citizens at large. As with any major policy initiative, it is hard to isolate the effects of CAADP from other factors and developments. To add to the complexity, the period of implementation of CAADP has coincided with the longest recovery period in Africa's history. But a mere look at recent trends among African countries suggests that countries implementing CAADP have experienced better sector investment and growth outcomes (figure 11.2). Indeed, this is confirmed by research evidence showing that engaging in CAADP did have positive effects on decisions to increase agricultural funding as well as on agricultural productivity and that countries that were more advanced in implementing CAADP also showed stronger effects. More specifically, countries that had engaged with CAADP saw sizable increases in both government agricultural expenditures and agricultural overseas development aid as shares of agricultural GDP compared to other countries. Furthermore, a farm family in a typical country that had completed all the implementation steps listed earlier up to the investment plan, moved to execution, and attracted external funding could see its labor productivity increase by as much as 20 percent compared to those in a country that had not engaged with CAADP.[17] In addition to these quantifiable effects, CAADP has made profound qualitative contributions by promoting a culture of review, dialogue, and accountability to improve policy and program design and implementation for better development outcomes.

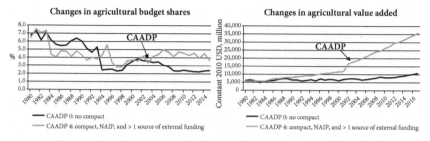

FIG. 11.2.   Sector expenditure and growth outcomes among CAADP versus non-CAADP countries

Source: From ReSAKSS, "Tracking Indicators," accessed April 5, 2018, http://www.resakss. org/node/11.

NEPAD and CAADP have also markedly affected the way the global community engages with Africa. They enhanced the embrace of the principles of country ownership and leadership at the G7 level and among major global development organizations. The success of CAADP is also illustrated by the fact that it is seen as a model and good practice. For instance, the importance of CAADP in ensuring high-quality policies was recognized by the Global Agriculture and Food Security Program (GAFSP), which not only requires African countries applying for funding to have completed a CAADP investment plan, but also asks non-African countries to have engaged in a CAADP-like process as a criterion for funding eligibility.[18] CAADP's mutual accountability work through inclusive review and dialogue platforms, informed by high-quality evidence, has also been recognized as a best practice applicable beyond Africa. The International Food Policy Research Institute now facilitates work in Asia and Latin America inspired by CAADP to help meet knowledge and evidence needs in these regions.

The Risk of Policy Reversal

The transition to stronger leadership and ownership of the development agenda through continent-wide initiatives like NEPAD and CAADP and the recent improvement in economic performance and human development indicators mean that African countries may have finally found more conducive policy and strategy choices. But even after a robust and extended recovery, African countries still face severe development challenges. Africa has the highest poverty rate by far of all world regions. Agricultural productivity has caught up to its levels following independence but must still make huge gains to catch up with the rest of the world and to meet its own potential. The food security of individuals and

countries is vulnerable. Consequently, it is still critical to broaden and accelerate the ongoing growth recovery. There may be risks that the policy, investment,
and sector-governance changes that have paved the way for the recovery may be
reversed or weakened.

Several factors suggest that the risk of reversal is more than hypothetical. Much
of the traditional distrust of the private sector and lack of confidence in markets
still lingers. Farming is still not recognized fully as a private business activity generating private goods belonging to free entrepreneurs. Rather, the notion that farm
products, be they traditional staples or industrial crops, are somehow collective
goods is still far too prevalent, giving the broader community a say as to how much
farmers can sell them for and to whom they may and may not sell them.

A new generation of African leaders is in power with no institutional memory
of the working and effects of failed policies that caused two decades of negative
growth and eroding living conditions for smallholder farmers and their communities, leading to swelling poverty levels across Africa. The same holds with
respect to the impact of reforms that have taken place, why they worked, and how
they led to the longest-lasting and geographically most broadly shared growth
spell in the continent's history (see chapter 10).

The current recovery not only masks the mistakes of the past, but also has
provided national governments with a much larger fiscal space to initiate and
pay for programs at scale. At the same time, improvements in governance and
openness of political systems, while highly positive developments, raise the pressure on governments to cede to populist pressures to favor action for short-term
political gain at the expense of future growth and stability.

In recent years Africa has witnessed an increasing propensity of governments
to intervene in the agricultural sector. Warning signs of a shift in the degree of
government interference include the growing popularity of poorly designed,
badly executed fertilizer and equipment subsidy programs and the growing use
of export bans and sporadic price controls to manage production and price fluctuations. In all the above cases, learning from the failed policies of the past would
have suggested approaches that would work with the private sector and enhance
the operation of local markets, including cross-border ones, to benefit smallholder farmers, not urban consumers, large farmers, and other well-connected,
rent-seeking intermediaries.

Similarly, the launching of new Agricultural Transformation Agencies and the
talk of a developmental state that would extend government oversight and management to many aspects of agricultural production and marketing constitute
a slippery slope that can lead back to the era of state enterprises and marketing
boards, with the associated fiscal burden, implicit taxation of farmers, and dis-
torted input and output distribution systems.

Good Policies

Like those before them, today's governments justify their action through the need to ensure strong agricultural production that contributes to national food security. The problem arises when there is not enough focus on carefully evaluating policies to determine their actual effectiveness and ensure that they meet a minimum level of quality or "goodness." Good policies may not be the solution to everything, but bad policies are a problem for everything else. A good policy must be based on credible evidence. It must include measurable targets and milestones. It should be subjected to rigorous technical, social, and environmental reviews. It has to be adequately tracked and evaluated and be open to inclusive consultation and dialogue to account for the viewpoints of all stakeholders. Alternative policies should be compared on the basis of their effectiveness and cost, and adjustments made in order to maximize positive impacts and minimize negative outcomes. These are critical steps to help ensure that past policy mistakes are not repeated. Creating the conditions that facilitate good policies in turn requires a number of key elements, including adequate data systems, engaged technical expertise, good knowledge management infrastructure, and systematic review and dialogue practices.

Data Systems

The practices of benchmarking, tracking, and evaluating policies are at the heart of good policy systems. They require a continuous flow of a large number of high-quality data, and the systems have to be in place to ensure that the data are readily available when needed. A good data infrastructure includes clearly defined clusters of data, say, production, trade, price, income, and expenditure at household, district, and national levels. It will be unlikely to find a single institution that will deal with all these categories of data with the detail, coverage, and frequency needed. An alternative option would be to operate through dedicated working groups or task forces involving specialized institutions, such as the bureaus of statistics or statistics departments in key ministries, agricultural research systems, professional organizations, and local administrations. The whole system would be supported by a common data platform, exchange protocol, and shared standards and norms.

Local Expertise

There is a real disconnect between policy making and knowledge communities that has significant implications for the quality of agricultural sector policies in most African countries. While ministries and other government institutions look to external centers of expertise for technical support, local centers of expertise focus primarily on teaching and academic publications. Policy making is a daily business that cannot be built on external expertise. A serious policy maker needs constant access to high-quality expertise. In addition to proximity, local expertise adds a layer of legitimacy. A good way to ensure access to such expertise is to build and maintain a network of leading centers of excellence, with appropriate coordination mechanisms and contractual instruments. The latter include agreements for long-term strategic research as well as vehicles for ad hoc, short-term technical support. A network-based strategy to mobilize local expertise is an effective way to leverage the considerable budget resources that are spent annually on these various institutions.

Knowledge Management

Policies deal with complex processes in a constantly changing environment. Therefore they have to be anchored in a culture of knowledge production, storage, and retrieval to guide the appropriate course of action in every situation. The data system and analytical expertise need to be supported by a knowledge-management infrastructure to facilitate building, maintaining, and expanding the body of relevant knowledge. A good infrastructure is one that eliminates barriers to information access and thus facilitates interaction between technical actors as well as connects knowledge generators with knowledge users. Furthermore, adequate knowledge management makes it possible to build a memory of policy actions, processes, and outcomes and allows lesson learning so as to avoid the repetition of past mistakes. Modern communications technologies offer a range of possibilities for decentralized management of disaggregated data and knowledge products, as illustrated by the Regional Strategic Analysis and Knowledge Support System (ReSAKSS) discussed below.

Mutual Review and Dialogue

Good policies need to recognize two important principles: the right of relevant stakeholders to know and be kept informed of major policy decisions affecting their lives; and the fact that collective wisdom is best. They are nurtured by an institutional culture that values the practice of open and inclusive review, evaluation and tracking of policy and program implementation progress and outcomes. For this purpose, it is important to set up dialogue platforms that help institute broad, informed debate among major constituencies around key strategic issues and policy choices.

Efforts to promote evidence-based policy planning and implementation under CAADP are built on all of the above principles and core elements of mutual accountability.

Mutual Accountability

CAADP processes of mutual accountability are an integral part of the search for good policies. Mutual accountability is a process by which multiple stakeholders hold each other accountable for respective commitments they make to each other. Its key elements include the availability of adequate data and analysis to monitor actions and outcomes; knowledge that is freely accessible; and consultations among stakeholders. As practiced under CAADP, mutual accountability processes usually include a jointly agreed, country-owned plan with goals for the sector; voluntary commitments by different groups to help achieve the plan's goals; implementation of commitments and reporting on progress; and shared responsibility to verify that the commitments made are contributing to meeting agreed-upon goals. Mutual accountability processes are key to increasing cooperation and coordinating action among multiple stakeholders, for example, governments, farmers, input suppliers, processors, and donors, to solve issues that no single group can address alone.[19]

Mutual accountability is enacted in CAADP through the continental-level CAADP Partnership Platform (PP), the regional- and country-level agricultural Joint Sector Reviews (JSRs), and, most recently, the CAADP Biennial Review at the Heads of State level. The CAADP PP is an annual meeting bringing together actors involved in the agricultural sector across the continent and from global development organizations to discuss CAADP implementation progress and performance. The 14th CAADP PP was held in May 2018 in Libreville, Gabon. Agricultural JSRs are a key opportunity for different groups to influence public agricultural policies and investments. As of 2018, 40 percent of African countries have undergone assessment processes to help them move toward enhanced JSRs that are comprehensive, more inclusive, and technically robust. At least 60 percent of African countries will have made that transition by 2019.

The CAADP Biennial Review (BR)

The BR is an important innovation in mutual accountability. Mandated by Heads of State under the Malabo Declaration, the goal of the BR is to regularly assess implementation progress and outcomes. As such, it provides a strong incentive for learning and adoption of best practices. The first BR report, reviewing the progress of African countries and regions at meeting the Malabo goals and targets, was successfully launched at the January 2018 African Union Summit. Out of fifty-five African Union member states, forty-seven submitted BR reports, which were incorporated into a continental report and scorecard summarizing agricultural sector progress.

The BR report and the Africa Agriculture Transformation Scorecard demonstrated the impressive progress made by many African countries as well as the remaining challenges to meet the ambitious Malabo goals. Of the forty-seven reporting countries, twenty were rated as on track to achieving the Malabo commitments by 2025. Five countries, Rwanda, Mali, Morocco, Botswana, and Lesotho, were recognized as having made the most progress in achieving agricultural development. At the regional level, eastern and southern Africa are on track, while northern, western, and central Africa will need to accelerate progress to meet commitments. Africa as a whole is also short of being considered on track to meet the Malabo commitments. The public unveiling of the scorecard gave countries an opportunity to challenge themselves to match their neighbors' progress.

The BR both served as an important milestone in advancing mutual accountability and provided an assessment of the progress of African countries in ensuring accountability in their agricultural policy planning and implementation. A majority of countries (thirty out of forty-seven) were rated as on track to meeting the Malabo goal of enhancing mutual accountability to actions and results (figure 11.3). Countries' progress was assessed on the basis of their capacity for evidence-based planning, implementation, and monitoring and evaluation; their success in fostering peer review and mutual accountability, including the strength of their agricultural monitoring and evaluation systems and agriculture JSRs; and the quality of their national BR processes.

Regional Strategic Analysis and Knowledge Support System (ReSAKSS)

These mutual accountability efforts are supported by the Regional Strategic Analysis and Knowledge Support System (ReSAKSS), launched in 2006 by the African Union Commission (AUC), leading regional economic communities, and Africa-based CGIAR centers. ReSAKSS, facilitated by the International Food Policy Research Institute, supports mutual accountability efforts at the country, regional, and continental levels by helping to meet knowledge, analysis, and monitoring and evaluation needs related to CAADP. ReSAKSS tracks and disseminates data on CAADP and Malabo targets through its website (www.resakss. org). Among the tools ReSAKSS has developed to aid in tracking agricultural

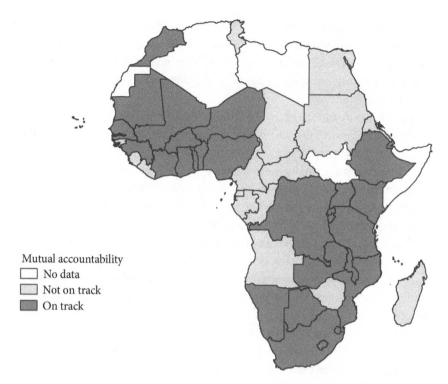

FIG. 11.3. Existence of inclusive mechanisms for mutual accountability and peer review

Source: Recreated from Her Excellency Josefa Sacko, "Report of the Commission on the Implementation of the Malabo Declaration on Accelerated Agricultural Growth and Transformation for Shared Prosperity and Improved Livelihoods: Assembly Decision (Assembly/AU/2(XXIII)) of June 2014" (PowerPoint, January 2018).

sector progress are the ReSAKSS Country eAtlases, located on the ReSAKSS website, which provide online GIS platforms that make publicly available detailed data at the subnational level on agriculture, population and health, climate, and other categories. The eAtlases have been developed for twenty-three countries as of fall 2018.

African Growth and Development Policy (AGRODEP) Modeling Consortium

Also supporting knowledge and evidence needs of CAADP as well as efforts to improve policy design and outcomes in general is the African Growth and Development Policy (AGRODEP) Modeling Consortium. Launched in 2010, AGRODEP is a network of African economic modeling experts with over two hundred members. AGRODEP was formed to build a critical mass of leading African experts to address development issues in the continent and to help early-career African economic modelers maintain and upgrade their skills, network with other experts in and outside their regions, and access opportunities to put their skills to work. AGRODEP assists its members with access to data and economic modeling tools, training opportunities, grants for research and travel to conferences, and opportunities to collaborate with international researchers. Currently the consortium is strengthening efforts to connect AGRODEP members with opportunities to provide advisory services to policy makers and other decision makers in African development policy. Strong capacities for locally based research are critical to the legitimacy and relevance of the evidence supporting national policy formulation and implementation. This is important not only for the quality of policies and programs but also for establishing credible local leadership.

Malabo Montpellier (MaMo) Panel and Forum

A third initiative supporting efforts to improve policies under CAADP is the Malabo Montpellier (MaMo) Panel and the related Forum. The core mission of the panel is to support evidence-based dialogue at the highest level and guide policy choices to accelerate progress toward the ambitious goals under the Malabo Declaration and the global development agenda. The MaMo Panel and Forum offer a space for leading decision makers to access the latest technical evidence in key strategic development areas and to reflect on the implications for the design and implementation of country policies and programs. What sets the panel apart is that its work focuses on identifying countries making the most progress in a given area of strategic importance to the Malabo agenda. It then examines what they are doing right, how they are doing it, and why they are succeeding. The lessons are synthesized in a short, accessible report and presented at a ministerial-level meeting hosted by the MaMo Forum. Through access to solid technical evidence and a platform for exchange among leading decision makers, the MaMo Panel and Forum are helping to facilitate policy innovation to support effective policy and program leadership at the country level.

Evidence-Based Policy Making

The past six decades have been a bumpy ride for Africa's farmers. Early promise at the time of independence gave way to disappointment, as expected development gains failed to materialize. The great potential of Africa's agriculture was suffocated, and the continent became progressively less able to feed itself. While other developing regions successfully translated rapid agricultural growth into overall economic development, Africa stagnated, becoming poorer as the world grew richer. Frequently shifting priorities over four decades under externally led policies and strategy agendas have been a major factor in the poor performance of African economies. The associated lack of coherence, continuity, and consistency prevented effective program design and implementation.

After four decades of decline and stagnation, Africa is now in the midst of an extraordinary recovery that is affecting all regions of the continent. Underpinning Africa's overall economic growth recovery has been the recovery in the agricultural sector, which regained the productivity it lost during the past decades. However, African agriculture has not yet caught up with that in the rest of the world. Cereal yields and labor productivity are still lower in Africa than in any other region. It is imperative that African agriculture continue its recovery in order to meet its potential and fuel continued improvements in food security and living standards. Today, African agriculture faces more opportunities than ever before. Rising incomes, the growing middle class, rapid urbanization, and a burgeoning food-processing industry are rapidly increasing the demand for agricultural products. African farmers have much to gain if they can sustain productivity growth in order to meet this expanding demand.

The recovery has also coincided with fundamental changes in the way African countries have interacted with the rest of the world. The domination of agenda-setting global development organizations has given way to leadership by African governments encouraged by the end of apartheid in South Africa and the election of new leaders joining others with similar pan-Africanist leanings. Under the auspices of the African Union, these leaders have initiated a bold agenda and challenged African countries to improve political and economic governance and the global community to align with the African agenda, all for increased policy effectiveness and better development outcomes.

Further improvements in the quality of sector policy and strategies as well as enhanced leadership by African countries are critical for the long-term sustainability of the recovery. Countries may have reversed the decline of past decades, but it will take many more years of exceptionally strong growth to make up for the lost decades of the 1970s and 1980s and catch up to the income and productivity levels they would have achieved had the growth of the 1960s been sustained. Africa cannot afford and should not accept another period of stagnation that would threaten progress in reducing poverty and hunger.

The combination of a new generation of leaders, greater fiscal position in the aftermath of strong economic growth, the absence of institutional memory regarding past policy mistakes, more open, pluralistic political systems, and the pressure for populist interventions creates a real risk for the reversal of the policy gains that have paved the way for the recovery. Governments will never be immune to making policy mistakes, which is why a process for analyzing impacts to create usable evidence and knowledge and making this knowledge widely available is so essential. It is therefore important for the African Union and its member states to sustain the advancement of mutual accountability efforts under CAADP more broadly in order to insure against policy reversal and sustain broad-based agricultural development.

The best defense against repeating past mistakes is careful attention to evidence on the impacts of policies and broad dissemination of knowledge. The NEPAD and CAADP values of evidence-based policy making, inclusive review and dialogue, and mutual accountability for actions and results will help African governments, farmers' organizations, private sector firms, civil society organizations, and research organizations resist calls for a return to heavy-handed attempts to direct agricultural development. Adherence to these values means that policies are not made on the basis of preferences but on evidence of what works. There is a place for policy experimentation, but experiments that are not successful should end, while policies that have positive impacts should be scaled up and emulated. The principle of inclusivity of actors outside of government, including farmers and the private sector, will also help to guard against temptations for the public sector to try to manage everything. The newly mandated Biennial Review, the country and regional Joint Sector Reviews, and the various review and dialogue platforms that are part of the CAADP agenda are all important building blocks for greater African leadership and improved policy processes and outcomes in the future.

Notes

INTRODUCTION

1. Gordon Conway, *The Doubly Green Revolution: Food for All in the Twenty-First Century* (Ithaca: Comstock Publishing Associates, 1998).
2. Andrew Dorward et al., "Hanging in, Stepping up and Stepping out: Livelihood Aspirations and Strategies of the Poor," *Development in Practice* 19, no. 2 (April 2009): 240–47, https://doi.org/10.1080/09614520802689535.

1. AFRICAN FARMS AND FARMERS

1. "The State of Food Insecurity in the World. Meeting the 2015 International Hunger Targets: Taking Stock of Uneven Progress" (Rome: FAO, IFAD, and WFP, 2015).
2. T. S. Jayne et al., "Africa's Changing Farm Size Distribution Patterns: The Rise of Medium-Scale Farms," *Agricultural Economics* 47, no. S1 (November 2016): 197–214, https://doi.org/10.1111/agec.12308.
3. Data on area owned or controlled by small-scale and medium-scale farms come from Ghana Statistical Survey (GSS), "Ghana—Ghana Living Standard Survey 5: 2005, With Non-Farm Household Enterprise Module," Ghana Living Standard Survey (Ghana: Office of the President, Government of Ghana; World Bank; European Union, December 15, 2008), http://www.statsghana.gov.gh/nada/index.php/catalog/5/related_materials; Ghana Statistical Survey (GSS), "Ghana—Ghana Living Standards Survey 6 (With a Labour Force Module) 2012–2013, Round Six," Ghana Living Standard Survey (Ghana: Government of Ghana; UK Department for International Development; International Labour Organisation; UN Development Programme; UN International Children's Emergency Fund, December 9, 2014), http://www.statsghana.gov.gh/nada/index.php/catalog/72/study-description; Kenya National Bureau of Statistics, "Kenya—Welfare Monitoring Survey 1994, Second Round," Welfare Monitoring Survey 1994 (Kenya: Kenya National Bureau of Statistics; World Bank, December 22, 2014), http://catalog.ihsn.org/index.php/catalog/5394; Kenya National Bureau of Statistics, "Kenya—Integrated Household Budget Survey 2005–2006," Integrated Household Budget Survey (Kenya: Ministry of Planning and National Development, Government of Kenya; Department for International Development; USAID, November 18, 2011), http://catalog.ihsn.org/index.php/catalog/1472/study-description; National Bureau of Statistics, "Tanzania—National Panel Survey 2008–2009, Wave 1," National Panel Survey (Tanzania: Tanzania National Bureau of Statistics, March 23, 2011), http://microdata.worldbank.org/index.php/catalog/76; National Bureau of Statistics, "Tanzania—National Panel Survey 2012–2013, Wave 3," National Panel Survey (Tanzania: Ministry of Finance, Tanzania; European Commission; World Bank, April 28, 2015), http://microdata.worldbank.org/index.php/catalog/2252; Ministry of Agriculture and Cooperatives and Central Statistical Office, "Zambia—Crop Forecast Survey 2007–2008," Crop Forecast Survey (Zambia: Ministry of Finance and National Planning, Government of the Republic of Zambia, December 23, 2014), http://catalog.ihsn.org/index.php/catalog/5563; Central Statistical Office of Zambia, "Crop Forecast Survey Data of Zambia, 2015—Zambia," Zambia Data Portal, January 29, 2016, http://zambia.opendataforafrica.org//ZMCRFCSD2016/crop-forecast-survey-data-of-zambia-2015?location=1000000-zambia.

4. Antony Chapoto, Arthur Mabiso, and Adwinmea Bonsu, "Agricultural Commercialization, Land Expansion, and Homegrown Land-Scale Farmers: Insights from Ghana," IFPRI Discussion Paper (Washington, DC: IFPRI, 2013), http://ebrary.ifpri.org/cdm/ref/collection/p15738coll2/id/127775.

5. "World Population Prospects: The 2017 Revision, Key Findings and Advance Tables," Working Paper, World Population Prospects (New York: United Nations Department of Economic and Social Affairs, Population Division, 2017), https://population.un.org/wpp/Publications/Files/WPP2017_KeyFindings.pdf.

6. Population Division, "World Population 2012," Wallchart (New York: United Nations Department of Economic and Social Affairs, August 2013), http://www.un.org/en/development/desa/population/publications/pdf/trends/WPP2012_Wallchart.pdf.

7. David Canning, Sangeeta Raja, and Abdo Yazbeck, eds., *Africa's Demographic Transition: Dividend or Disaster?* (Washington, DC: World Bank, 2015).

8. Elina Pradhan, "The Relationship between Women's Education and Fertility," *World Economic Forum* (blog), November 27, 2015, https://www.weforum.org/agenda/2015/11/the-relationship-between-womens-education-and-fertility/.

9. T. S. Jayne, Jordan Chamberlin, and Derek D. Headey, "Land Pressures, the Evolution of Farming Systems, and Development Strategies in Africa: A Synthesis," in "Boserup and Beyond: Mounting Land Pressures and Development Strategies in Africa," special issue, *Food Policy* 48 (October 1, 2014): 1–17, https://doi.org/10.1016/j.foodpol.2014.05.014.

10. Jayne, Chamberlin, and Headey, "Land Pressures, the Evolution of Farming Systems, and Development Strategies in Africa."

11. T. S. Jayne et al., "Smallholder Income and Land Distribution in Africa: Implications for Poverty Reduction Strategies," *Food Policy* 28, no. 3 (June 1, 2003): 253–75, https://doi.org/10.1016/S0306-9192(03)00046-0.

12. Derek D. Headey and T. S. Jayne, "Adaptation to Land Constraints: Is Africa Different?," in "Boserup and Beyond: Mounting Land Pressures and Development Strategies in Africa," special issue, *Food Policy* 48 (October 1, 2014): 18–33, https://doi.org/10.1016/j.foodpol.2014.05.005.

13. Klaus W. Deininger and Derek Byerlee, *Rising Global Interest in Farmland: Can It Yield Sustainable and Equitable Benefits?*, Agriculture and Rural Development (Washington, DC: World Bank, 2011).

14. Tony Allan et al., eds., *Handbook of Land and Water Grabs in Africa: Foreign Direct Investment and Food and Water Security*, Routledge International Handbooks (New York: Routledge, 2013).

15. George Christoffel Schoneveld, "The Geographic and Sectoral Patterns of Large-Scale Farmland Investments in Sub-Saharan Africa," in "Boserup and Beyond: Mounting Land Pressures and Development Strategies in Africa," special issue, *Food Policy* 48 (October 1, 2014): 34–50, https://doi.org/10.1016/j.foodpol.2014.03.007.

16. Lorenzo Cotula et al., *Land Grab or Development Opportunity?* (London/Rome: IIED/FAO/IFAD, 2009), http://www.fao.org/3/a-ak241e.pdf.

17. Fred Pearce, *The Land Grabbers: The New Fight over Who Owns the Earth* (Boston: Beacon Press, 2012); Carlos Oya, "The Land Rush and Classic Agrarian Questions of Capital and Labour: A Systematic Scoping Review of the Socioeconomic Impact of Land Grabs in Africa," *Third World Quarterly* 34, no. 9 (October 2013): 1532–57, https://doi.org/10.1080/01436597.2013.843855.

18. Joachim von Braun and Ruth Suseela Meinzen-Dick, "'Land Grabbing' by Foreign Investors in Developing Countries: Risks and Opporunities," *IFPRI Policy Brief 13* (2009), http://ebrary.ifpri.org/cdm/ref/collection/p15738coll2/id/14853.

19. Steve Wiggins, "Can the Smallholder Model Deliver Poverty Reduction and Food Security for a Rapidly Growing Population in Africa?," FAC Working Paper No. 08 (How to Feed the World in 2050 (Rome: Institute of Development Studies, 2009), 25.

20. Paul Collier and Stefan Dercon, "African Agriculture in 50 Years: Smallholders in a Rapidly Changing World?," *World Development* 63 (November 2014): 92–101, https://doi.org/10.1016/j.worlddev.2013.10.001.

21. Gordon Conway, *One Billion Hungry: Can We Feed the World?* (Ithaca: Comstock Publishing Associates, 2012).

22. Catherine Bertini, "Invisible Women," *Daedalus* 144, no. 4 (September 1, 2015): 24–30, https://doi.org/10.1162/DAED_a_00351.

23. FAO, "The State of Food and Agriculture 2010–2011: Women in Agriculture: Closing the Gender Gap for Development" (Rome: FAO, 2011).

24. D. E. Tempelman, "Africa," in *Rural Women and Food Security: Current Situation and Perspectives* (Rome: FAO, 1998), http://www.fao.org/docrep/003/W8376E/w8376e00.htm#Contents.

25. Montpellier Panel, "Women in African Agriculture: Farmers, Mothers, Innovators and Educators," Briefing Paper (London: Agriculture for Impact, 2012), https://www.mamopanel.org/media/uploads/files/WOMEN_IN_AFRICAN_AGRICULTURE_2012.pdf.

26. Bertini, "Invisible Women."

27. FAO, "The State of Food and Agriculture 2010–2011."

28. Agnes R. Quisumbing et al., "Women: The Key to Food Security," *Food Policy Report* (Washington, DC: IFPRI, 1995), http://ebrary.ifpri.org/cdm/ref/collection/p15738coll2/id/125877.

29. Ibid.

30. Joachim von Braun, Hartwig de Haen, and Juergen Blanken, *Commercialization of Agriculture under Population Pressure: Effects on Production, Consumption, and Nutrition in Rwanda*, Research Report 85 (Washington, DC: IFPRI, 1991).

31. Rekha Mehra and Mary Hill Rojas, "Women, Food Security and Agriculture in a Global Marketplace: A Significant Shift" (Washington, DC/New Delhi: International Centre for Research on Women, 2008).

32. Lisa C. Smith et al., "The Importance of Women's Status for Child Nutrition in Developing Countries," *International Food Policy Research Institute (IFPRI) Research Report Abstract 131*, Research Report 24, no. 3 (September 2003): 287–88, https://doi.org/10.1177/156482650302400308.

33. FAO, "The State of Food and Agriculture 2010–2011."

34. Mara van den Bold, Agnes R. Quisumbing, and Stuart Gillespie, "Women's Empowerment and Nutrition: An Evidence Review," *IFPRI Discussion Paper* 1294 (2013), http://ebrary.ifpri.org/cdm/ref/collection/p15738coll2/id/127840.

35. Bertini, "Invisible Women."

36. Ibid.

37. Lori Ashford, Donna Clifton, and Toshiko Kaneda, "The World's Youth 2006 Data Sheet" (Washington, DC: Population Reference Bureau, 2006), https://assets.prb.org//pdf06/WorldsYouth2006DataSheet.pdf.

38. John Cleland and Kazuyo Machiyama, "The Challenges Posed by Demographic Change in Sub-Saharan Africa: A Concise Overview" *Population and Development Review* 43, no. S1 (May 2017): 264–86, https://doi.org/10.1111/padr.170.

39. Agriculture for Impact, "Small and Growing: Entrepreneurship in African Agriculture" (London: Montpellier Panel, 2014), https://www.mamopanel.org/media/uploads/files/SMALL_AND_GROWING-_ENTREPRENEURSHIP_IN_AFRICAN_AGRICULTURE_2014.pdf.

40. Ibid.

41. Collier and Dercon, "African Agriculture in 50 Years."

42. Kofi Annan, Gordon Conway, and Sam Dryden, eds., "African Farmers in the Digital Age: Overcoming Isolation, Speeding Up Change, and Taking Success to Scale," special issue, *Foreign Affairs* (2016), https://files.foreignaffairs.com/pdf/sponsored-anthology/2016/african_farmers_in_the_digital_age_final.pdf.

43. Gordon Conway, "Recipe for a New Revolution: Africa's Twenty-First Century Food System Transformation," in "African Farmers in the Digital Age: Overcoming Isolation, Speeding Up Change, and Taking Success to Scale," ed. Kofi Annan, Gordon Conway, and Sam Dryden, special issue, *Foreign Affairs* (2016): 9–16, https://files.foreignaffairs.com/pdf/sponsored-anthology/2016/african_farmers_in_the_digital_age_final.pdf.

44. Ibid.

45. Andrew Dorward, "Integrating Contested Aspirations, Processes and Policy: Development as Hanging In, Stepping Up and Stepping Out," *Development Policy Review* 27, no. 2 (March 2009): 131–46, https://doi.org/10.1111/j.1467-7679.2009.00439.x.

2. HUNGER AND MALNUTRITION

1. Reprinted from Kun Li, "Hunger a Daily Reality for South Sudan's Children," May 2, 2012, https://www.unicef.org/health/southsudan_62343.html.

2. "Hunger," accessed April 18, 2018, http://www.dictionary.com/browse/hunger.

3. FAO, "Regional Overview of Food Insecurity Africa: African Food Security Prospects Brighter than Ever" (Accra: FAO, 2015), http://www.fao.org/3/a-i4635e.pdf.

4. FAO, International Fund for Agricultural Development, and WFP, "Meeting the 2015 International Hunger Targets: Taking Stock of Uneven Progress," The State of Food Insecurity in the World (Rome: FAO, IFAD, and WFP, 2015).

5. United Nations in Ghana, "MDG 1: Eradicate Extreme Poverty & Hunger," accessed April 18, 2018, http://gh.one.un.org/content/unct/ghana/en/home/global-agenda-in-ghana/millennium-development-goals/mdg-1-eradicate-extreme-poverty-and-hunger.html.

6. "MDG Report 2014: Assessing Progress in Africa toward the Millenium Development Goals" (Addis Ababa, Ethiopia: United Nations Economic Commission for Africa, African Union, African Development Bank, and United Nations Development Programme, 2014), http://www.undp.org/content/dam/rba/docs/Reports/MDG_Africa_Report_2014_ENG.pdf.

7. FAO, ed., *How Does International Price Volatility Affect Domestic Economies and Food Security?*, The State of Food Insecurity in the World (Rome: FAO, 2011).

8. FAO, International Fund for Agricultural Development, and WFP, "Meeting the 2015 International Hunger Targets."

9. FAO, ed., *Leveraging Food Systems for Inclusive Rural Transformation*, The State of Food and Agriculture (Rome: FAO, 2017).

10. Li, "Hunger a Daily Reality for South Sudan's Children."

11. WFP, "Zero Hunger," 2018, http://www1.wfp.org/zero-hunger.

12. FAO, ed., "The State of Food and Agriculture 2006: Food Aid for Food Security?," The State of Food and Agriculture (Rome: FAO, 2006), http://www.fao.org/docrep/009/a0800e/a0800e00.htm.

13. S. Hawkesworth et al., "Feeding the World Healthily: The Challenge of Measuring the Effects of Agriculture on Health," *Philosophical Transactions of the Royal Society B: Biological Sciences* 365, no. 1554 (September 27, 2010): 3083–97, https://doi.org/10.1098/rstb.2010.0122.

14. Jean-Michel Lecerf, "Fatty Acids and Cardiovascular Disease," *Nutrition Reviews* 67, no. 5 (May 2009): 273–83, https://doi.org/10.1111/j.1753-4887.2009.00194.x.

15. WHO, FAO, and United Nations University, "Protein and Amino Acid Requirements in Human Nutrition. Report of a Joint FAO/WHO/UNU Expert Consultation," WHO Technical Report Series (Geneva: WHO, 2007).

16. D. Joe Millward et al., "Protein Quality Assessment: Impact of Expanding Understanding of Protein and Amino Acid Needs for Optimal Health," *American Journal of Clinical Nutrition* 87, no. 5 (May 1, 2008): 1576S–1581S, https://doi.org/10.1093/ajcn/87.5.1576S.

17. FAO, United Nations University, and WHO, eds., "Human Energy Requirements: Report of a Joint FAO/WHO/UNU Expert Consultation: Rome, 17–24 October 2001," FAO Food and Nutrition Technical Report Series (Rome: FAO, 2004).

18. FAO, "FAO Methodology for the Measurement of Food Deprivation: Updating the Minimum Dietary Requirements" (Rome: FAO, 2008), http://www.fao.org/filead min/templates/ess/documents/food_security_statistics/metadata/undernourishment_ methodology.pdf.

19. Sangita Sharma et al., eds., *Nutrition at a Glance*, 2nd ed., At a Glance Series (Chichester, West Sussex: John Wiley, 2015).

20. Max Roser and Hannah Ritchie, "Food per Person," Our World in Data, 2017, https://ourworldindata.org/food-per-person.

21. WFP, "Rwanda: Comprehensive Food Security and Vulnerability Analysis and Nutrition Survey, July 2009," VAM Food Security Analysis (Rome: WFP, July 2009), http://documents.wfp.org/stellent/groups/public/documents/ena/wfp210888.pdf.

22. WFP, "Comprehensive Food Security and Vulnerability Analysis and Nutrition Survey 2012: Rwanda (Data Collected in March—April 2012)," VAM Food Security Analysis (Rome: WFP, 2012), http://documents.wfp.org/stellent/groups/public/documents/ena/ wfp255144.pdf?_ga=2.187122856.1062231754.1523981558-1272296001.1523981558.

23. Ibid.

24. Ibid.

25. Ibid.

26. "The State of the World's Children 2015. Reimagine the Future: Innovation for Every Child," The State of the World's Children (New York: UNICEF, 2014).

27. Micronutrient Initiative, "Vitamin & Mineral Deficiency: A Global Progress Report" (Ottawa: Micronutrient Initiative), accessed April 18, 2018, https://www.unicef. org/media/files/vmd.pdf.

28. Roger Thurow, "The First 1,000 Days: A Crucial Time for Mothers and Children—And the World," *Breastfeeding Medicine* 11, no. 8 (October 2016): 416–18, https://doi. org/10.1089/bfm.2016.0114.

29. "Malnutrition," UNICEF data, 2018, https://data.unicef.org/topic/nutrition/ malnutrition/.

30. WHO, "Breastfeeding," Nutrition, accessed May 31, 2018, http://www.who.int/ nutrition/topics/exclusive_breastfeeding/en/.

31. "Tackling Stunting: Rwanda's Unfinished Business," World Bank, accessed October 29, 2018, http://www.worldbank.org/en/country/rwanda/publication/tackling-stunting-rwandas-unfinished-business.

32. Dan Ngabonziza, "Rwanda Contracts Dutch Firm to Combat Malnutrition," *KT Press* (blog), October 1, 2015, http://ktpress.rw/2015/10/rwanda-contracts-dutch-firm-to-combat-malnutrition/.

33. Malabo Montpellier Panel, "Nourished: How Africa Can Build a Future Free from Hunger and Malnutrition" (Dakar: Malabo Montpellier Panel, 2017), https://www. mamopanel.org/media/uploads/files/RPT_2017_MaMo_web_v01.pdf.

34. Ibid.

35. Agnes Le Port et al., "Delivery of Iron-Fortified Yoghurt, through a Dairy Value Chain Program, Increases Hemoglobin Concentration among Children 24 to 59 Months

Old in Northern Senegal: A Cluster-Randomized Control Trial," ed. Jacobus P. van Wouwe, *PLOS ONE* 12, no. 2 (February 28, 2017): e0172198, https://doi.org/10.1371/journal.pone.0172198.

36. Chemonics International, "Yaajeende Agricultural Development: Mid-Term Performance Evaluation of Project," (Dakar, Senegal: United States Agency for International Development, June 9, 2014), https://www.climatelinks.org/sites/default/files/asset/document/Senegal%20-%20Mid-term%20Performance%20Evaluation%20of%20Yaajeende%20Agricultural%20Development%20Project%202014.pdf.

37. T. F. Randolph et al., "Invited Review: Role of Livestock in Human Nutrition and Health for Poverty Reduction in Developing Countries1,2,3," *Journal of Animal Science* 85, no. 11 (November 1, 2007): 2788–2800, https://doi.org/10.2527/jas.2007-0467.

38. Shannon E. Whaley et al., "The Impact of Dietary Intervention on the Cognitive Development of Kenyan School Children," *Journal of Nutrition* 133, no. 11 (November 1, 2003): 3965S–3971S, https://doi.org/10.1093/jn/133.11.3965S.

39. Partnership for Child Development, "Annual Report 2013–2014" (London: Partnership for Child Development, School of Public Health, Imperial College London, 2015), http://www.schoolsandhealth.org/Shared%20Documents/PCD%20Annual%20Report%202013%20-%202014.pdf.

40. "Obesity Update 2017" (Paris: OECD, May 2018), https://www.oecd.org/els/health-systems/Obesity-Update-2017.pdf.

41. "WHO | Obesity and Overweight," WHO, 2018, http://www.who.int/mediacentre/factsheets/fs311/en/.

42. J. Wilding, "Are the Causes of Obesity Primarily Environmental? Yes," *BMJ* 345 (September 11, 2012): e5843–e5843, https://doi.org/10.1136/bmj.e5843; T. M. Frayling, "Are the Causes of Obesity Primarily Environmental? No," *BMJ* 345 (September 11, 2012): e5844–e5844, https://doi.org/10.1136/bmj.e5844.

43. "Thrifty Gene Hypothesis," *Wikipedia*, May 10, 2018, https://en.wikipedia.org/w/index.php?title=Thrifty_gene_hypothesis&oldid=840537968.

44. W. Su et al., "Modeling the Clinical and Economic Implications of Obesity Using Microsimulation," *Journal of Medical Economics* 18, no. 11 (November 2, 2015): 886–97, https://doi.org/10.3111/13696998.2015.1058805.

45. UNICEF, WHO, and World Bank Group, "Levels and Trends in Child Malnutrition: UNICEF/WHO/World Bank Group Joint Child Malnutrition Estimates. Key Findings of the 2016 Edition," (New York: UNICEF, Geneva: WHO, Washington, DC: World Bank, 2016), http://www.who.int/nutgrowthdb/jme_brochure2016.pdf?ua=1.

46. Taru Manyanga et al., "The Prevalence of Underweight, Overweight, Obesity and Associated Risk Factors among School-Going Adolescents in Seven African Countries," *BMC Public Health* 14, no. 1 (December 2014), https://doi.org/10.1186/1471-2458-14-887.

47. Kathrin M. Demmler, Olivier Ecker, and Matin Qaim, "Supermarket Shopping and Nutritional Outcomes: A Panel Data Analysis for Urban Kenya," *World Development* 102 (February 2018): 292–303, https://doi.org/10.1016/j.worlddev.2017.07.018.

48. Malabo Montpellier Panel, "Nourished."

49. IFPRI, "Global Nutrition Report 2016: From Promise to Impact Ending Malnutrition by 2030" (Washington, DC: IFPRI, 2016), https://doi.org/10.2499/9780896295841.

50. IFPRI, "Global Nutrition Report 2015: Actions and Accountability to Advance Nutrition and Sustainable Development" (Washington, DC: IFPRI, 2015), https://doi.org/10.2499/9780896298835; Standing Committee on Nutrition, "Nutrition and the Post-2015 Sustainable Development Goals: A Technical Note" (New York: United Nations System, 2014), https://www.unscn.org/files/Publications/Briefs_on_Nutrition/Final_Nutrition%20and_the_SDGs.pdf; Zulfiqar A Bhutta et al., "Evidence-Based Interventions for Improvement of Maternal and Child Nutrition: What Can Be Done and at What Cost?," *The Lancet* 382, no. 9890 (August 2013): 452–77, https://doi.org/10.1016/S0140-6736(13)60996-4.

51. IFPRI, "Global Nutrition Report 2015."

52. Amartya Sen, *Poverty and Famines: An Essay on Entitlement and Deprivation* (Oxford: Oxford University Press, 2010).

53. Manitra A. Rakotoarisoa, Massimo Iafrate, and Marianna Paschali, *Why Has Africa Become a Net Food Importer? Explaining Africa Agricultural and Food Trade Deficits* (Rome: Trade and Markets Division, FAO, 2011).

54. IFPRI, "Food Security | IFPRI," accessed April 20, 2018, http://www.ifpri.org/ topic/food-security; Committee on World Food Security, "Thirty-Ninth Session: Coming to Terms with Terminology: Food Security, Nutrition Security, Food Security and Nutrition, Food and Nutrition Security" (Rome: FAO, 2012), http://www.fao.org/docrep/ meeting/026/MD776E.pdf.

55. Amartya Sen, *Development as Freedom* (Oxford: Oxford University Press, 2001).

56. Ibid.

57. José Graziano Da Silva and Shenggen Fan, "Smallholders and Urbanization: Strengthening Rural–Urban Linkages to End Hunger and Malnutrition," Global Food Policy Report 2017 (Washington, DC: IFPRI, 2017), https://doi.org/10.2499/9780896292529_02.

58. Thomas Anthony Reardon et al., "Transformation of African Agrifood Systems in the New Era of Rapid Urbanization and the Emergence of a Middle Class," in *Beyond a Middle Income Africa: Transforming African Economies for Sustained Growth with Rising Employment and Incomes*, ed. Ousmane Badiane and Tsitsi Makombe (Washington, DC: IFPRI, 2015), 62–74, http://ebrary.ifpri.org/cdm/ref/collection/p15738coll2/id/130005.

59. Steven Haggblade, "Modernizing African Agribusiness: Reflections for the Future," *Journal of Agribusiness in Developing and Emerging Economies* 1, no. 1 (June 3, 2011): 10–30, https://doi.org/10.1108/20440831111131532.

60. Reardon et al., "Transformation of African Agrifood Systems in the New Era."

61. David Tschirley, Steven Haggblade, and Thomas Reardon, eds., *Africa's Emerging Food System Transformation—Eastern and Southern Africa* (East Lansing: Global Center for Food Systems Innovation, Michigan State University, 2014), http://gcfsi.isp.msu.edu/ files/7214/6229/3434/w1.pdf.

62. Mthuli Ncube, Charles Leyeka Lufumpa, and Steve Kayizzi-Mugerwa, "The Middle of the Pyramid: Dynamics of the Middle Class in Africa," *Market Brief*, April 20, 2011, https://www.afdb.org/fileadmin/uploads/afdb/Documents/Publications/The%20 Middle%20of%20the%20Pyramid_The%20Middle%20of%20the%20Pyramid. pdf.

63. David Tschirley et al., "The Rise of a Middle Class in East and Southern Africa: Implications for Food System Transformation: The Middle Class and Food System Transformation in ESA," *Journal of International Development* 27, no. 5 (July 2015): 628–46, https://doi.org/10.1002/jid.3107.

64. Gordon Conway et al., "Creating Resilient Value Chains for Smallholder Farmers," in *Africa Agriculture Status Report 2017: The Business of Smallholder Agriculture in Sub-Saharan Africa* (Kigali, Rwanda: AGRA, 2017), https://agra.org/aasr2017/chapter-5/.

65. FAO, International Fund for Agricultural Development, UNICEF, WFP, and WHO, "The State of Food Security and Nutrition in the World 2018: Building Climate Resilience for Food Security and Nutrition," The State of the World (Rome: FAO, 2018), http://www.fao.org/3/I9553EN/i9553en.pdf.

3. THE THREATS TO FOOD SECURITY

1. Exodus 10:14–15 (AV), accessed April 20, 2018, https://www.biblegateway.com/ passage/?search=Exodus+10%3A14-15&version=AKJV.

2. Pietro Ceccato et al., "The Desert Locust Upsurge in West Africa (2003–2005): Information on the Desert Locust Early Warning System and the Prospects for Seasonal

Climate Forecasting," *International Journal of Pest Management* 53, no. 1 (January 2007): 7–13, https://doi.org/10.1080/09670870600968826.

3. African Agricultural Technology Foundation, "Frequently Asked Questions on Striga and the IR Maize," Striga: Control in Maize, 2012, accessed May 31, 2018, https://striga.aatf-africa.org/about-us/frequently-asked-questions-striga-and-ir-maize.

4. Peter L. Roeder, "Rinderpest: The End of Cattle Plague," *Preventive Veterinary Medicine* 102, no. 2 (November 2011): 98–106, https://doi.org/10.1016/j.pre vetmed.2011.04.004.

5. Chantal J. Snoeck et al., "Newcastle Disease Virus in West Africa: New Virulent Strains Identified in Non-Commercial Farms," *Archives of Virology* 154, no. 1 (January 2009): 47–54, https://doi.org/10.1007/s00705-008-0269-5.

6. Ibid.

7. Roger Day et al., "Fall Armyworm: Impacts and Implications for Africa," *Outlooks on Pest Management* 28, no. 5 (October 1, 2017): 196–201, https://doi.org/10.1564/v28_oct_02; Kenneth Wilson, "Armyworms Are Wreaking Havoc in Southern Africa: Why It's a Big Deal," The Conversation, February 12, 2017, http://theconversation.com/armyworms-are-wreaking-havoc-in-southern-africa-why-its-a-big-deal-72822; Kerstin Kruger, "Why It's Hard to Control the Fall Armyworm in Southern Africa," The Conversation, February 14, 2017, http://theconversation.com/why-its-hard-to-control-the-fall-armyworm-in-southern-africa-72890.

8. Ibid.

9. Ibid.

10. Montpellier Panel, "No Ordinary Matter: Conserving, Restoring and Enhancing Africa's Soils" (London: Agriculture for Impact, 2014), https://www.mamopanel.org/media/uploads/files/NO_ORDINARY_MATTER-_CONSERVING_RESTORING_AND_ENHANCING_AFRICAS_SOILS_2014.pdf.

11. Ibid.

12. Quang Bao Le, Ephraim Nkonya, and Alisher Mirzabaev, "Biomass Productivity-Based Mapping of Global Land Degradation Hotspots," in *Economics of Land Degradation and Improvement—A Global Assessment for Sustainable Development*, ed. Ephraim Nkonya, Alisher Mirzabaev, and Joachim von Braun (Cham, Switzerland: Springer International, 2016), 55–84, https://doi.org/10.1007/978-3-319-19168-3_4.

13. Oliver Kirui and Alisher Mirzabev, "Economics of Land Degradation in Eastern Africa," ZEF Working Paper Series, No. 128 (Centre for Development Research (ZEF), University of Bonn, 2014), https://www.econstor.eu/bitstream/10419/99988/1/785225005.pdf.

14. R. Lal, "Soil Carbon Sequestration Impacts on Global Climate Change and Food Security," *Science* 304, no. 5677 (June 11, 2004): 1623–27, https://doi.org/10.1126/science.1097396.

15. Ephraim Nkonya et al., "Global Cost of Land Degradation," in *Economics of Land Degradation and Improvement—A Global Assessment for Sustainable Development* (Cham, Switzerland: Springer International, 2016), 117–65, https://doi.org/10.1007/978-3-319-19168-3_6.

16. H. Eswaran, R. Lal, and P. F. Reich, "Land Degradation: An Overview," in *Responses to Land Degradation. Proc. 2nd. International Conference on Land Degradation and Desertification, Khon Kaen, Thailand* (New Delhi: Oxford Press, 2001), https://www.nrcs.usda.gov/wps/portal/nrcs/detail/soils/use/?cid=nrcs142p2_054028; Z. G. Bai et al., "Proxy Global Assessment of Land Degradation," *Soil Use and Management* 24, no. 3 (September 2008): 223–34, https://doi.org/10.1111/j.1475-2743.2008.00169.x.

17. Colin R. W. Spedding, *Agriculture and the Citizen*, 1st ed. (London: Chapman and Hall, 1996).

18. S. M. K. Donkor and Yilma E. Wolde, "Integrated Water Resources Management in Africa" (Addis Ababa, Ethiopia: United Nations Economic Commission for Africa, 2011).

19. FAO, "AQUASTAT Database," 2016, http://www.fao.org/nr/water/aquastat/data/query/index.html?lang=en.

20. Gordon Conway, *One Billion Hungry: Can We Feed the World?* (Ithaca: Comstock Publishing Associates, 2012).

21. Ibid.

22. International Bank for Reconstruction and Development/World Bank, *World Development Report 2008: Agriculture for Development* (Washington, DC: World Bank, 2007).

23. Ibid.

24. "Integrated Water Resources Management (IWRM)," International Decade for Action "Water for Life" 2005–2015, 2014, http://www.un.org/waterforlifedecade/iwrm.shtml.

25. FAO, "The State of Food and Agriculture 2016: Climate Change, Agriculture and Food Security," The State of Food and Agriculture (Rome: FAO, 2016).

26. Goddard Institute for Space Studies and NASA, "NASA, NOAA Analyses Reveal Record-Shattering Global Warm Temperatures in 2015," National Aeronautics and Space Administration, Goddard Institute for Space Studies, January 20, 2016, https://www.giss.nasa.gov/research/news/20160120/.

27. IPCC, "Long-Term Climate Change: Projections, Commitments and Irreversibility," *Climate Change 2013: The Physical Science Basis*, 2013, 108.

28. Nick Brooks, "Drought in the African Sahel: Long-Term Perspectives and Future Prospects" (Norwich: Tyndall Centre for Climate Change Research, School of Environmental Sciences, University of East Anglia, 2004), http://dcms2.lwec.ulcc.ac.uk/sites/default/files/wp61.pdf.

29. A. Giannini, R. Saravanan, and P. Chang, "Oceanic Forcing of Sahel Rainfall on Interannual to Interdecadal Time Scales," *Science* 302, no. 5647 (November 7, 2003): 1027–30, https://doi.org/10.1126/science.1089357.

30. Buwen Dong and Rowan Sutton, "Dominant Role of Greenhouse-Gas Forcing in the Recovery of Sahel Rainfall," *Nature Climate Change* 5, no. 8 (August 2015): 757–60, https://doi.org/10.1038/nclimate2664.

31. Kevin E Trenberth et al., "Observations: Surface and Atmospheric Climate Change," in *Climate Change 2007: The Physical Science Basis. Contribution of Working Group I to the Fourth Assessment Report of the Intergovernmental Panel on Climate Change*, ed. S. Solomon et al. (Cambridge: Cambridge University Press, 2007), 102, https://www.ipcc.ch/pdf/assessment-report/ar4/wg1/ar4-wg1-chapter3.pdf.

32. Gordon Conway, "The Science of Climate Change in Africa: Impacts and Adaptation," *Grantham Institute for Climate Change Discussion Paper 1*, Grantham Institute for Climate Change Discussion Paper, October 2009, 24, https://ag4impact.org/wp-content/uploads/2010/05/Grantham_Institute_-_The_science_of_climate_change_in_ Africa.pdf.

33. Trenberth et al., "Observations: Surface and Atmospheric Climate Change."

34. I Niang et al., "Africa," in *Climate Change 2014: Impacts, Adaptation, and Vulnerability. Part B: Regional Aspects. Contribution of Working Group II to the Fifth Assessment Report of the Intergovernmental Panel on Climate Change*, ed. V. R. Barros et al. (Cambridge: Cambridge University Press, 2014), 67.

35. Conway, "Science of Climate Change in Africa."

36. Gordon Conway, personal communication.

37. David B. Lobell et al., "Nonlinear Heat Effects on African Maize as Evidenced by Historical Yield Trials," *Nature Climate Change* 1, no. 1 (March 13, 2011): 42–45, https://doi.org/10.1038/nclimate1043.

38. Philip K. Thornton, "Impacts of Climate Change on the Agricultural and Aquatic Systems and Natural Resources within the CGIAR's Mandate," CCAFS Working Paper (Copenhagen: CCAFS, 2012), https://cgspace.cgiar.org/bitstream/handle/10568/21226/ccafs-wp-23-cc_impacts_CGIAR.pdf?sequence=7&isAllowed=y.

39. *Africa's Climate Challenge*, Climate 2020: Facing the Future (London: United Nations Association—UK, 2015), http://e59114bec18f33b2ba6d-67d853478b97815e7ad b8b9373d7dc7d.r53.cf2.rackcdn.com/CLIMATE2020.pdf.

40. Samuel S. Myers et al., "Increasing CO2 Threatens Human Nutrition," *Nature* 510, no. 7503 (June 2014): 139–42, https://doi.org/10.1038/nature13179; Samuel S. Myers et al., "Effect of Increased Concentrations of Atmospheric Carbon Dioxide on the Global Threat of Zinc Deficiency: A Modelling Study," *The Lancet Global Health* 3, no. 10 (October 2015): e639–45, https://doi.org/10.1016/S2214-109X(15)00093-5.

41. FAO, "State of Food and Agriculture 2016."

42. FAO, "Climate Change in Africa: The Threat to Agriculture" (Accra, Ghana: FAO Regional Office for Africa, December 2009), http://www.fao.org/tempref/docrep/fao/012/ak915e/ak915e00.pdf.

43. WFP, "Climate Change and Hunger: Responding to the Challenge" (Rome: WFP, IFPRI, New York University Center on International Cooperation, Grantham Institute at Imperial College London, and Walker Institute, University of Reading, UK, 2009).

44. "Greenhouse Gas Concentrations Surge to New Record," *World Meteorological Organization*, October 30, 2017, https://public.wmo.int/en/media/press-release/greenhouse-gas-concentrations-surge-new-record.

45. D. L. Albritton and L. G. Meira Filho, "Technical Summary," in *Climate Change 2001: The Scientific Basis. Contribution of Working Group I to the Third Assessment Report of the Intergovernmental Panel on Climate Change*, J. T. Houghton et al. (Cambridge: Cambridge University Press, 2001), 881, https://www.ipcc.ch/ipccreports/tar/wg1/030.htm.

46. Royal Society, "Climate Change Controversies: A Simple Guide" (London: Royal Society, 2008), 12.

47. Nicholas Stern, *The Economics of Climate Change: The Stern Review* (Cambridge: Cambridge University Press, 2007), https://doi.org/10.1017/CBO9780511817434.

48. P. Smith et al., "Agriculture, Forestry and Other Land Use (AFOLU)," in *Climate Change 2014: Mitigation of Climate Change: Working Group III Contribution to the Fifth Assessment Report of the Intergovernmental Panel on Climate Change*, ed. O. Edenhofer et al. (Cambridge: Intergovernmental Panel on Climate Change, Cambridge University Press, 2014), https://doi.org/10.1017/CBO9781107415416.

49. Ronald Trostle, "Global Agricultural Supply and Demand: Factors Contributing to the Recent Increase in Food Commodity Prices" (Washington, DC: United States Department of Agriculture, May 1, 2008), https://doi.org/10.2172/1218372.

50. "FAO Food Price Index," World Food Situation, accessed October 29, 2018, http://www.fao.org/worldfoodsituation/foodpricesindex/en/.

51. World Bank, "Food Price Watch (English)," 2010, sec. February 2010, http://documents.worldbank.org/curated/en/776591468181476052/pdf/531600NEWS0FIN1ne w0series101PUBLIC1.pdf.

52. P. Scott-Villiers et al., "Precarious Lives: Food, Work and Care After the Global Food Crisis" (Brighton, UK: Institute for Development Studies), September 8, 2016, http://www.ids.ac.uk/publication/precarious-lives-food-work-and-care-after-the-global-food-crisis.

53. Dennis Hamro-Drotz et al., eds., *Livelihood Security: Climate Change, Migration and Conflict in the Sahel* (Châtelaine, Geneva: United Nations Environment Programme, 2011).

54. Robert Strauss Centre for International Security and Law, "Armed Conflict and Social Conflict," Strauss Center, accessed May 1, 2018, https://www.strausscenter.org/strauss-articles/armed-conflict-acled-conflict-data.html.

55. Hamro-Drotz et al., *Livelihood Security.*

4. RESILIENT FARMERS

1. Reproduced from Gordon Conway, *One Billion Hungry: Can We Feed the World?* (Ithaca: Comstock Publishing Associates, 2012).

2. Montpellier Panel, "Growth with Resilience: Opportunities in African Agriculture" (London: Agriculture for Impact, 2012), https://www.mamopanel.org/media/uploads/files/GROWTH_WITH_RESILIENCE-_OPPORTUNITIES_IN_AFRICAN_AGRICULTURE_2012.pdf.

3. Gordon Conway et al., "Creating Resilient Value Chains for Smallholder Farmers," in *Africa Agriculture Status Report 2017: The Business of Smallholder Agriculture in Sub-Saharan Africa* (Kigali, Rwanda: AGRA, 2017), https://agra.org/aasr2017/chapter-5/.

4. Montpellier Panel, "Growth with Resilience."

5. Conway et al., "Creating Resilient Value Chains for Smallholder Farmers."

6. Conway, *One Billion Hungry.*

7. F. Voss and U. Dreiser, "Mapping of Desert Locust Habitats Using Remote Sensing Techniques," in *New Strategies in Locust Control*, ed. S. Krall, R. Peveling, and D. Ba Diallo (Basel: Birkhäuser Basel, 1997), 37–45, https://doi.org/10.1007/978-3-0348-9202-5_5.

8. Michel Lecoq, "Recent Progress in Desert and Migratory Locust Management in Africa: Are Preventative Actions Possible?," *Journal of Orthoptera Research* 10, no. 2 (2001): 277–91, http://www.jstor.org/stable/3503745.

9. Rothamsted Research, "Push-Pull Cropping: Fool the Pests to Feed the People," Rothamsted Research, May 2017, https://www.rothamsted.ac.uk/push-pull-cropping; "Push–Pull Agricultural Pest Management," *Wikipedia*, May 8, 2018, https://en.wikipedia.org/w/index.php?title=Push%E2%80%93pull_agricultural_pest_management&oldid=840210999.

10. Rothamsted Research, "Push-Pull Cropping."

11. Chantal J. Snoeck et al., "Newcastle Disease Virus in West Africa: New Virulent Strains Identified in Non-Commercial Farms," *Archives of Virology* 154, no. 1 (January 2009): 47–54, https://doi.org/10.1007/s00705-008-0269-5.

12. A. H. Jibril et al., "Application of Participatory Epidemiology Techniques to Investigate Newcastle Disease among Rural Farmers in Zamfara State, Nigeria," *Journal of Applied Poultry Research* 24, no. 2 (June 1, 2015): 233–39, https://doi.org/10.3382/japr/pfv012.

13. FAO, "FAO Launches Guide to Tackle Fall Armyworm in Africa Head-On," February 16, 2018, http://www.fao.org/news/story/en/item/1100355/icode/.

14. Nico van Burick, "Bt-Maize Provides Protection against Fall Armyworm," African Farming, February 14, 2017, https://www.africanfarming.com/bt-maize-protection-fall-armyworm/.

15. B. Vanlauwe et al., "Integrated Soil Fertility Management: Operational Definition and Consequences for Implementation and Dissemination," *Outlook on Agriculture* 39, no. 1 (March 2010): 17–24, https://doi.org/10.5367/000000010791169998.

16. Montpellier Panel, "No Ordinary Matter: Conserving, Restoring and Enhancing Africa's Soils" (London: Agriculture for Impact, 2014), https://www.mamopanel.org/media/uploads/files/NO_ORDINARY_MATTER-_CONSERVING_RESTORING_AND_ENHANCING_AFRICAS_SOILS_2014.pdf.

17. Lucie Andeltova et al., "The Rewards of Investing in Sustainable Land Management. Interim Report for the Economics of Land Degradation Initiative: A Global Strategy for Sustainable Land Management," ed. ELD Initiative, 2013, http://collections.unu.edu/view/UNU:2662#viewMetadata.

18. "Integrated Water Resources Management (IWRM)," International Decade for Action "Water for Life" 2005–2015, 2014, http://www.un.org/waterforlifedecade/iwrm.shtml.

19. S. M. K. Donkor and Yilma E. Wolde, "Integrated Water Resources Management in Africa: Issues and Options," in *Integrated Wetlands and Water Resources Management*, ed. Ger Bergkamp, Jean-Yves Pirot, and Silvia Hostettler (2nd International Conference on Wetlands and Development, Dakar, Sengal: IUCN—The World Conservation Union, Wetlands International, World Wide Fund for Nature, 1998), https://www.researchgate.net/profile/Silvia_Hostettler/publication/299540856_Integrated_Wetlands_and_Water_Resources_Management/links/56fe7b6308aea6b77468c8a9/Integrated-Wetlands-and-Water-Resources-Management.pdf#page=13.

20. Central and Eastern Europe Global Water Partnership, "What Is IWRM?," Global Water Partnership, 2011, https://www.gwp.org/en/GWP-CEE/about/why/what-is-iwrm/.

21. Donkor and Wolde, "Integrated Water Resources Management in Africa."

22. U.S. Agency for International Development Water Team, "Integrated Water Resources Management: A Framework for Action in Freshwater and Coastal Systems" (Washington, DC: USAID Water Team, 2012), http://waterwiki.net/images/8/80/IWRM_Framework_Freshwaterandcoastal.pdf.

23. Liangzhi You et al., "What Is the Irrigation Potential for Africa? A Combined Biophysical and Socioeconomic Approach," *Food Policy* 36, no. 6 (December 2011): 770–82, https://doi.org/10.1016/j.foodpol.2011.09.001; Mark Svendsen, Mandy Ewing, and Siwa Msangi, "Measuring Irrigation Performance in Africa," IFPRI Discussion Paper (Washington DC: IFPRI, 2009), http://ebrary.ifpri.org/cdm/ref/collection/p15738coll2/id/26252.

24. FAO, "Crops and Drops: Making the Best Use of Water for Agriculture" (Rome: FAO, 2002), http://www.fao.org/docrep/005/Y3918E/Y3918E00.htm; Robert Winterbottom et al., "Improving Land and Water Management," Working Paper, Creating a Sustainable Food Future (Washington, DC: World Resources Institute, 2013).

25. Climate Change, Agriculture and Food Security, "What Is Climate-Smart Agriculture?," Climate-Smart Agriculture Guide, accessed May 24, 2018, https://csa.guide/csa/what-is-climate-smart-agriculture.

26. Pradeep Kurukulasuriya and Robert Mendelsohn, *Crop Selection: Adapting to Climage Change in Africa*, Policy Research Working Papers (World Bank, 2007), https://doi.org/10.1596/1813-9450-4307.

27. Montpellier Panel, "No Ordinary Matter."

28. R. Lal, "Soil Carbon Sequestration Impacts on Global Climate Change and Food Security," *Science* 304, no. 5677 (June 11, 2004): 1623–27, https://doi.org/10.1126/science.1097396.

29. Montpellier Panel, "No Ordinary Matter."

30. Emilio J. González Sánchez et al., "Making Climate Change Mitigation and Adaptability Real in Africa with Conservation Agriculture" (Córdoba, Spain: Universidad de Córdoba, October 2018).

31. Montpellier Panel, "No Ordinary Matter."

32. P. K. Ramachandran Nair, B. Mohan Kumar, and Vimala D. Nair, "Agroforestry as a Strategy for Carbon Sequestration," *Journal of Plant Nutrition and Soil Science* 172, no. 1 (February 2009): 10–23, https://doi.org/10.1002/jpln.200800030.

33. International Fertilizer Development Center (IFDC), "Fertilizer Deep Placement," January 13, 2015, https://ifdc.org/fertilizer-deep-placement/.

34. Ibid.

35. Pierre J. Gerber et al., "Tackling Climate Change through Livestock: A Global Assessment of Emissions and Mitigation Opportunities" (Rome: FAO, 2013); Henning Steinfeld et al., *Livestock's Long Shadow: Environmental Issues and Options* (Rome: FAO, 2006).

36. P. K. Thornton and M. Herrero, "Potential for Reduced Methane and Carbon Dioxide Emissions from Livestock and Pasture Management in the Tropics," *Proceedings of the National Academy of Sciences* 107, no. 46 (November 16, 2010): 19667–72, https://doi.org/10.1073/pnas.0912890107.

37. Steinfeld et al., *Livestock's Long Shadow.*

38. Gert-Jan Monteny, Andre Bannink, and David Chadwick, "Greenhouse Gas Abatement Strategies for Animal Husbandry," *Agriculture, Ecosystems and Environment* 112, no. 2–3 (February 2006): 163–70, https://doi.org/10.1016/j.agee.2005.08.015.

39. Ibid.

40. Joachim von Braun and Máximo Torero, "Physical and Virtual Global Food Reserves to Protect the Poor and Prevent Market Failure," IFPRI Policy Brief 4 (Washington, DC: IFPRI, 2008), http://ebrary.ifpri.org/cdm/ref/collection/p15738coll2/id/11545.

41. Ibid.

42. David McKee, "Strategic Grain Reserves: Sub-Saharan Africa," *David McKee: The Grain Industry Consultant* (blog), June 3, 2011, http://www.davidmckee.org/2011/06/03/strategic-grain-reserves/.

43. Carlos Gómez, "Cowpea: Post-Harvest Operations," INPhO—Post-Harvest Compendium (Rome: FAO, June 15, 2004), http://www.fao.org/3/a-au994e.pdf.

44. McKee, "Strategic Grain Reserves."

45. Ousmane Badiane, Sunday P. Odjo, and Samson Jemaneh, "More Resilient Domestic Food Markets through Regional Trade," in *Promoting Agricultural Trade to Enhance Resilience in Africa: ReSAKSS Annual Trends and Outlook Report 2013*, ed. Ousmane Badiane, Tsitsi Makombe, and Godfrey Bahiigwa (Washington, DC: IFPRI, 2014), http://ebrary.ifpri.org/cdm/ref/collection/p15738coll2/id/128851.

46. Ibid.

47. Ibid.

48. Ibid.

49. Ibid.

50. Ibid.

51. Ousmane Badiane and Sunday Odjo, "Regional Trade and Volatility in Staple Food Markets in Africa," in *Food Price Volatility and Its Implications for Food Security and Policy*, ed. Matthias Kalkuhl, Joachim von Braun, and Máximo Torero (Cham, Switzerland: Springer International, 2016), 385–412, https://doi.org/10.1007/978-3-319-28201-5_16.

52. Robert Muggah and David Kilcullen, "These Are Africa's Fastest-Growing Cities—and They'll Make or Break the Continent," World Economic Forum, April 5, 2016, https://www.weforum.org/agenda/2016/05/africa-biggest-cities-fragility/.

53. Robert Muggah and Katie Hill, "African Cities Will Double in Population by 2050: Here Are 4 Ways to Make Sure They Thrive," World Economic Forum, June 27, 2018, https://www.weforum.org/agenda/2018/06/Africa-urbanization-cities-double-population-2050-4%20ways-thrive/.

54. Jane Battersby and Jonathan Crush, "Africa's Urban Food Deserts," *Urban Forum* 25, no. 2 (June 2014): 143–51, https://doi.org/10.1007/s12132-014-9225-5.

55. Joe Myers, "These Are Africa's Fastest-Growing Cities," World Economic Forum, June 5, 2016, https://www.weforum.org/agenda/2016/05/these-are-africa-s-fastest-growing-cities/; "100 Resilient Cities," 100 Resilient Cities, accessed October 11, 2018, https://www.100resilientcities.org/.

56. Shenggen Fan, Joanna Brzeska, and Tolulope Olofinbiyi, "The Business Imperative: Helping Small Family Farmers to Move Up or Move Out," in *2014–2015 Global Food Policy Report* (Washington, DC: IFPRI, 2015), 25–31, http://ebrary.ifpri.org/cdm/ref/collection/p15738coll2/id/129075.

57. Conway et al., "Creating Resilient Value Chains for Smallholder Farmers."

58. Ibid.

59. Montpellier Panel, "Sustainable Intensification: A New Paradigm for African Agriculture" (London: Agriculture for Impact, 2013), https://www.mamopanel.org/media/uploads/files/SUSTAINABLE_INTENSIFICATION-_A_NEW_PARADIGM_FOR_AFRICAN_AGRICULTURE_2013.pdf.

60. Fan, Brzeska, and Olofinbiyi, "The Business Imperative."

61. Franck Galtier, *Managing Food Price Instability in Developing Countries—A Critical Analysis of Strategies and Instruments* (Paris: Agence Française de Développement, 2013).

5. SUSTAINABLE AGRICULTURE

1. Jules Pretty, Camilla Toulmin, and Stella Williams, "Sustainable Intensification in African Agriculture," *International Journal of Agricultural Sustainability* 9, no. 1 (February 2011): 5–24, https://doi.org/10.3763/ijas.2010.0583; The Royal Society, "Reaping the Benefits: Science and the Sustainable Intensification of Global Agriculture" (The Royal Society, October 2009), https://royalsociety.org/~/media/royal_society_content/policy/publications/2009/4294967719.pdf.

2. Robert Chambers and Gordon Conway, *Sustainable Rural Livelihoods: Practical Concepts for the 21st Century*, DP 296 (Brighton, UK: Institute of Development Studies, 1992).

3. Mark W. Rosegrant, "Sustainable Intensification Is the Answer to Global Food Insecurity" (PowerPoint, September 20, 2016).

4. Ibid.

5. Zoé Druilhe and Jesús Barreiro-Hurlé, "Fertilizer Subsidies in Sub-Saharan Africa" (Rome: FAO, 2012), http://www.fao.org/3/a-ap077e.pdf.

6. Ephraim Chirwa and Andrew Dorward, *Agricultural Input Subsidies: The Recent Malawi Experience* (Oxford: Oxford University Press, 2013), https://doi.org/10.1093/acprof:oso/9780199683529.001.0001; Ephraim Chirwa and Andrew Dorward, "The Implementation of the 2012/13 Farm Input Subsidy Programme," *FISP Policy Brief* 2014, no. 2 (January 2014): 2.

7. Marcus Porcius Cato and Marcus Terentius Varro, *Marcus Porcius Cato on Agriculture : Marcus Terentius Varro on Agriculture ; with an English Translation by William Davis Hooper*, ed. Ash Harrison Boyd, trans. William Davis Hooper, revised and reprinted by Harrison Boyd Ash (Cambridge: Harvard University Press, 1935), https://trove.nla.gov.au/version/26317087.

8. World Commission on Environment and Development, ed., *Our Common Future*. (Oxford: Oxford University Press, 1987).

9. Ibid.

10. Chambers and Conway, *Sustainable Rural Livelihoods*.

11. Gordon Conway, *The Doubly Green Revolution: Food for All in the Twenty-First Century* (Ithaca: Comstock Publishing Associates, 1998).

12. Gordon Conway, *One Billion Hungry: Can We Feed the World?* (Ithaca: Comstock Publishing Associates, 2012).

13. Ibid.

14. Ousmane Badiane and Julia Collins, "Agricultural Growth and Productivity in Africa: Recent Trends and Future Outlook," in *Agricultural Research in Africa: Investing*

in Future Harvests, by John Lynam et al. (Washington, DC: IFPRI, 2016), 3–30, http://ebrary.ifpri.org/cdm/ref/collection/p15738coll2/id/130570.

15. World Bank Poverty & Equity Data Portal and ProvcalNet, "Poverty Headcount Ratio at $1.90 a Day (2011 PPP) (% of Population): Sub-Saharan Africa," database, People Living On Less Than International Poverty Line, 2019, https://databank.worldbank.org/embed/POV_REG_1_2017/id/505a3250?tb=y&dd=n&pr=n&export=y&xlbl=y&ylbl=y&legend=y&isportal=y&inf=n&exptypes=Excel&country=SSF&series=SI.POV.NOP1,SI.POV.DDAY&zm=n.

16. Rattan Lal, "Sustainable Intensification for Adaptation and Mitigation of Climate Change and Advancement of Food Security in Africa," in *Sustainable Intensification to Advance Food Security and Enhance Climate Resilience in Africa* (Cham, Switzerland: Springer International, 2015), 3–17, https://doi.org/10.1007/978-3-319-09360-4_1.

17. Oliver Kirui and Alisher Mirzabev, "Economics of Land Degradation in Eastern Africa, ZEF Working Paper Series, No. 128," ZEF Working Paper Series (Centre for Development Research [ZEF], University of Bonn, 2014), https://www.econstor.eu/bitstream/10419/99988/1/785225005.pdf.

18. Bruno Lanz, Simon Dietz, and Tim Swanson, "The Expansion of Modern Agriculture and Global Biodiversity Decline: An Integrated Assessment," *Ecological Economics* 144 (February 2018): 260–77, https://doi.org/10.1016/j.ecolecon.2017.07.018.

19. Conway, *One Billion Hungry*; Jules Pretty and Zareen Pervez Bharucha, "Sustainable Intensification in Agricultural Systems," *Annals of Botany* 114, no. 8 (December 2014): 1571–96, https://doi.org/10.1093/aob/mcu205.

20. Conway, *One Billion Hungry*; Pretty and Bharucha, "Sustainable Intensification in Agricultural Systems."

21. Montpellier Panel, "Sustainable Intensification: A New Paradigm for African Agriculture" (London: Agriculture for Impact, 2013), https://www.mamopanel.org/media/uploads/files/SUSTAINABLE_INTENSIFICATION-_A_NEW_PARADIGM_FOR_AFRICAN_AGRICULTURE_2013.pdf.

22. Ibid.

23. Alex McBratney et al., "Future Directions of Precision Agriculture," *Precision Agriculture* 6, no. 1 (February 2005): 7–23, https://doi.org/10.1007/s11119-005-0681-8.

24. Kenneth L. Wells and James E. Dollarhide, "Precision Agriculture: A Field Study of Soil Test Variability and Its Effect on Accuracy of Fertilizer Recommendations," *Soil Science News and Views* 8 (1998): 7; V. I. Adamchuk et al., "Guided Soil Sampling for Enhanced Analysis of Georeferenced Sensor-Based Data" (Ninth International Conference on Geocomputation, National Centre for Geocomputation, National University of Ireland, Maynooth, September 3–5, 2007), 4.

25. World Bank Fertilizer Price Index, accessed April 12, 2019, http://www.worldbank.org/en/research/commodity-markets.

26. Michael Morris et al., *Fertilizer Use in African Agriculture: Lessons Learned and Good Practice Guidelines* (Washington, DC: World Bank, 2007), https://doi.org/10.1596/978-0-8213-6880-0.

27. Montpellier Panel, "Sustainable Intensification"; Hervé Ott, "Fertilizer Markets and Their Interplay with Commodity and Food Prices," JRC Scientific and Policy Reports (Seville: European Commission, Joint Research Centre, Institute for Prospective Technological Studies, 2012), ftp://ftp.jrc.es/pub/EURdoc/JRC73043.pdf.

28. Druilhe and Barreiro-Hurlé, "Fertilizer Subsidies in Sub-Saharan Africa"; OCSPP US EPA, "Integrated Pest Management (IPM) Principles," Overviews and Factsheets, US EPA, September 28, 2015, https://www.epa.gov/safepestcontrol/integrated-pest-management-ipm-principles.

29. "Abuja Declaration: Abuja Declaration on Fertilizer for the African Green Revolution," African Development Bank, accessed October 26, 2018, https://www.afdb.org/en/topics-and-sectors/initiatives-partnerships/african-fertilizer-financing-mechanism/abuja-declaration/.

30. Jan Willem Erisman et al., "How a Century of Ammonia Synthesis Changed the World," Special Features, *Nature Geoscience*, September 28, 2008, https://doi.org/10.1038/ngeo325.

31. Montpellier Panel, "Sustainable Intensification."

32. J. Henao and C. Baanante, "Agricultural Production and Soil Nutrient Mining in Africa: Implications for Resource Conservation and Policy Development" (Muscle Shoals, Alabama, 3: International Fertilizer Development Center [IFDC], 2006), http://www.eldis.org/document/A21749.

33. Ibid.

34. Zambia National Farmers Union, ed., *Conservation Farming and Conservation Agriculture Handbook for Hoe Farmers in Agro-Ecological Regions I & IIa, Flat Culture* (Lusaka, Zambia: Conservation Farming Unit, 2009).

35. Montpellier Panel, "Sustainable Intensification."

6. AGRICULTURE AND ECOLOGY

1. M. Harty et al., "Conservation Agriculture: Measuring the Impact on Livelihoods in Zimbabwe," *Agriculture for Development*, no. 11 (2010): 20–23, https://www.cabdirect.org/cabdirect/abstract/20103354559.

2. Committee on World Food Security High Level Panel of Experts, "HLPE Report on Agroecological Approaches and Other Innovations for Sustainable Agriculture and Food Systems that Enhance Food Security and Nutrition," in *HLPE E-Consultation on the Report's Scope, Proposed by the HLPE Steering Committee* (44th Plenary Session of the Committee on World Food Security, Rome: FAO, 2017), http://www.fao.org/fsnfo rum/cfs-hlpe/sites/cfs-hlpe/files/files/Agroecology/Agroecology%20Scope%20Topic.pdf.

3. Agriculture for Impact, "Ecological Intensification: Technical Brief," Briefing Paper (Agriculture for Impact, 2015), https://ag4impact.org/wp-content/uploads/2015/07/Technical-Brief-Ecological-30-July2.pdf.

4. Miguel A. Altieri, "Agroecology: The Science of Natural Resource Management for Poor Farmers in Marginal Environments," *Agriculture, Ecosystems and Environment* 93, nos. 1–3 (December 2002): 1–24, https://doi.org/10.1016/S0167-8809(02)00085-3.

5. A. Wezel et al., "Agroecology as a Science, a Movement and a Practice. A Review," *Agronomy for Sustainable Development* 29, no. 4 (December 2009): 503–15, https://doi.org/10.1051/agro/2009004.

6. Vivek Anand Voora and Henry David Venema, "The Natural Capital Approach: A Concept Paper" (Winnipeg, Canada: International Institute for Sustainable Development, 2008), https://doi.org/10.4135/9781412963893.n343.

7. Millennium Ecosystem Assessment (Program), ed., *Ecosystems and Human Well-Being: Synthesis* (Washington, DC: Island Press, 2005).

8. UNEP, "Towards a Green Economy: Pathways to Sustainable Development and Poverty Eradication: A Synthesis for Policy Makers" (Nairobi, Kenya: United Nations Environmental Programme, 2011), https://sustainabledevelopment.un.org/content/documents/126GER_synthesis_en.pdf; Melissa C. Lott, "10 Calories in, 1 Calorie Out—The Energy We Spend on Food," *Scientific American Blog Network*, November 8, 2011, https://blogs.scientificamerican.com/plugged-in/10-calories-out-the-energy-we-spend-on-food/; WWF, "Environmental Impacts of Farming," accessed May 25, 2018, http://wwf.panda.org/our_work/food/agriculture/impacts/.

9. Wu Yang et al., "Going Beyond the Millennium Ecosystem Assessment: An Index System of Human Dependence on Ecosystem Services," ed. Just Cebrian, *PLOS ONE* 8, no. 5 (May 22, 2013): e64581, https://doi.org/10.1371/journal.pone.0064581.

10. Emmanuel Skoufias, ed., *The Poverty and Welfare Impacts of Climate Change: Quantifying the Effects, Identifying the Adaptation Strategies*, Directions in Development (Washington, DC: World Bank, 2012).

11. Shirley H. Phillips, "Introduction," in *No-Tillage Agriculture: Principles and Practices*, by Ronald E. Phillips and Shirley H. Phillips (Boston: Springer, 1984), 1–10, https://doi.org/10.1007/978-1-4684-1467-7_1.

12. Montpellier Panel, "Sustainable Intensification: A New Paradigm for African Agriculture" (London: Agriculture for Impact, 2013), https://www.mamopanel.org/media/uploads/files/SUSTAINABLE_INTENSIFICATION-_A_NEW_PARADIGM_FOR_AFRICAN_AGRICULTURE_2013.pdf.; Mutiu Abolanle Busari et al., "Conservation Tillage Impacts on Soil, Crop and the Environment," *International Soil and Water Conservation Research* 3, no. 2 (June 2015): 119–29, https://doi.org/10.1016/j.iswcr.2015.05.002.

13. Theodor Friedrich, Amir Kassam, and Francis Shaxson, "Annex 2. Case Study: Conservation Agriculture. Final Report," Agriculture Technologies for Developing Countries (Rome: European Technology Assessment Group, April 2009), https://www.itas.kit.edu/downloads/projekt/projekt_meye08_atdc_annex2.pdf.

14. Cameron M. Pittelkow et al., "When Does No-till Yield More? A Global Meta-Analysis," *Field Crops Research* 183 (November 2015): 156–68, https://doi.org/10.1016/j.fcr.2015.07.020; Ken E. Giller et al., "Beyond Conservation Agriculture," *Frontiers in Plant Science* 6 (October 28, 2015), https://doi.org/10.3389/fpls.2015.00870.

15. Phillips, "Introduction."

16. A. Kassam, T. Friedrich, and R. Derpsch, "Global Spread of Conservation Agriculture," *International Journal of Environmental Studies* (August 6, 2018): 1–23, https://doi.org/10.1080/00207233.2018.1494927.

17. Ibid.

18. "The State of Food Insecurity in the World 2015. Meeting the 2015 International Hunger Targets: Taking Stock of Uneven Progress.," The State of Food Insecurity in the World (Rome: FAO, IFAD, and WFP, 2015), http://www.fao.org/3/a-i4646e.pdf.

19. Chris Reij, Gray Tappan, and Melinda Smale, "Re-Greening the Sahel: Farmer-Led Innovation in Burkina Faso and Niger," in *Millions Fed: Proven Successes in Agricultural Development.*, ed. David J. Spielman and Rajul Pandya-Lorch (Washington, DC: IFPRI, 2009), 53–58, http://ebrary.ifpri.org/cdm/ref/collection/p15738coll2/id/130817.

20. John W. Eadie and John Peter Oleson, "The Water-Supply Systems of Nabataean and Roman Humayma," *Bulletin of the American Schools of Oriental Research*, no. 262 (May 1986): 49, https://doi.org/10.2307/1356979.

21. Ian Scoones, "Wetlands in Drylands: Key Resources for Agricultural and Pastoral Production in Africa," *Ambio* 20, no. 8 (1991): 366–71, http://www.jstor.org/stable/4313867; Reij, Tappan, and Smale, "Re-Greening the Sahel."

22. Gordon Conway, *One Billion Hungry: Can We Feed the World?* (Ithaca: Comstock Publishing Associates, 2012).

23. Christopher Linn Delgado et al., "Livestock to 2020: The Next Food Revolution," Discussion Paper, Food, Agriculture, and the Environment (Washington, DC: IFPRI, FAO, International Livestock Research Institute, 1999).

24. P. K. Thornton, "Livestock Production: Recent Trends, Future Prospects," *Philosophical Transactions of the Royal Society B: Biological Sciences* 365, no. 1554 (September 27, 2010): 2853–67, https://doi.org/10.1098/rstb.2010.0134.

25. H. Steinfeld, T. Wassenaar, and S. Jutzi, "Livestock Production Systems in Developing Countries: Status, Drivers, Trends," *Revue Scientifique et Technique (International Office of Epizootics)* 25, no. 2 (August 2006): 505–16.

26. Conway, *One Billion Hungry*.

27. Ian Scoones, "New Challenges for Range Management in the 21st Century," *Outlook on Agriculture* 25, no. 4 (December 1996): 253–56, https://doi.org/10.1177/003072709602500407; R. H. Behnke and Ian Scoones, "Rethinking Range Ecology: Implications for Rangeland Management in Africa," (Commonwealth Secretariat Technical Meeting on Savanna Development and Pasture Production, Woburn, UK: IIED, ODI, 1992), http://pubs.iied.org/pdfs/7282IIED.pdf; Toulmin, "Tracking through Drought: Options for Destocking and Restocking," in *Living with Uncertainty: New Directions in Pastoral Development in Africa*, ed. Ian Scoones (Rugby, Warwickshire, UK: Practical Action Publishing, 1995), https://doi.org/10.3362/9781780445335; Scoones, "Wetlands in Drylands."

28. H. Schiere and L. Kater, "Mixed Crop-Livestock Farming: A Review of Traditional Technologies Based on Literature and Field Experience," FAO Animal Production and Health Paper 152 (2001), http://agris.fao.org/agris-search/search.do?recordID=XF2003410307; H. van Keulen and J. B. Schiere, "Crop-Livestock Systems: Old Wine in New Bottles," 2004, http://library.wur.nl/WebQuery/wurpubs/337607.

29. Schiere and Kater, "Mixed Crop-Livestock Farming."

30. Keulen and Schiere, "Crop-Livestock Systems."

31. Christie P. Peacock, *Improving Goat Production in the Tropics: A Manual for Development Workers* (Oxford: Oxfam [u.a.], 1996).

32. "Goats—Undervalued Assets in Asia," in *APHCA-ILRI Regional Workshop on Goat Production Systems and Markets* (Luang Prabang, Lao PDR: Animal Production and Health Commission for Asia and the Pacific, International Livestock Research Institute, 2008), http://cdn.aphca.org/dmdocuments/APHCA%20Publications/ilri_-_goats_book.pdf.

33. Conway, *One Billion Hungry*.

34. David Tilman et al., "Agricultural Sustainability and Intensive Production Practices," *Nature* 418, no. 6898 (August 8, 2002): 671–77, https://doi.org/10.1038/nature01014.

35. Ibid.

36. Ibid.

37. Akira S. Mori, Takuya Furukawa, and Takehiro Sasaki, "Response Diversity Determines the Resilience of Ecosystems to Environmental Change: Response Diversity and Ecosystem Resilience," *Biological Reviews* 88, no. 2 (May 2013): 349–64, https://doi.org/10.1111/brv.12004.

38. FAO, "What Is Happening to Agrobiodiversity?," accessed October 11, 2018, http://www.fao.org/docrep/007/y5609e/y5609e02.htm.

39. Ibid.

40. Claire Kremen and Albie Miles, "Ecosystem Services in Biologically Diversified versus Conventional Farming Systems: Benefits, Externalities, and Trade-Offs," *Ecology and Society* 17, no. 4 (2012), https://doi.org/10.5751/ES-05035-170440.

41. Agriculture for Impact, "Diversification," Sustainable Intensification Database, accessed April 26, 2019, https://ag4impact.org/sid/ecological-intensification/diversification/.

42. Wei Zhang et al., "Ecosystem Services and Dis-Services to Agriculture," *Ecological Economics* 64, no. 2 (December 2007): 253–60, https://doi.org/10.1016/j.ecolecon.2007.02.024; C. Shennan, "Biotic Interactions, Ecological Knowledge and Agriculture," *Philosophical Transactions of the Royal Society B: Biological Sciences* 363, no. 1492 (February 27, 2008): 717–39, https://doi.org/10.1098/rstb.2007.2180.

43. Michael Begon, Colin R. Townsend, and John L. Harper, *Ecology: From Individuals to Ecosystems*, 4th ed (Malden, MA: Blackwell, 2006); A. R. Ives and S. R. Carpenter,

"Stability and Diversity of Ecosystems," *Science* 317, no. 5834 (July 6, 2007): 58–62, https://doi.org/10.1126/science.1133258.

44. Agriculture for Impact, "Diversification."

45. World Agroforestry Centre, "Faidherbia Albida: Keystone of Evergreen Agriculture in Africa," accessed May 25, 2018, http://www.worldagroforestry.org/sites/default/files/F.a_keystone_of_Ev_Ag.pdf.

46. Otto Soemarwoto and Gordon R. Conway, "The Javanese Homegarden," *Journal of Farming Systems Research and Extension* 2 (1991): 95–118.

47. FAO, "Household Food Security and Community Nutrition: Improving Nutrition through Home Gardening," Nutrition and consumer protection, 2010, http://www.fao.org/ag/agn/nutrition/household_gardens_en.stm.

48. Malabo Montpellier Panel, "Nourished: How Africa Can Build a Future Free from Hunger and Malnutrition" (Dakar: Malabo Montpellier Panel, 2017), https://www.mamopanel.org/media/uploads/files/RPT_2017_MaMo_web_v01.pdf.

49. Fabrice A. J. Declerck et al., "Ecological Approaches to Human Nutrition," *Food and Nutrition Bulletin* 32, no. 1, suppl. 1 (March 2011): S41–50, https://doi.org/10.1177/15648265110321S106.

50. Jessica Fanzo et al., eds., *Diversifying Food and Diets: Using Agricultural Biodiversity to Improve Nutrition and Health*, 1st ed., Issues in Agricultural Biodiversity (London: Routledge, 2013).

51. European Commission, "Organic Farming," Agriculture and Rural Development, July 29, 2014, https://ec.europa.eu/agriculture/glossary/organic-farming_en_en.

52. Conway, *One Billion Hungry.*

53. Christine M. Williams, "Nutritional Quality of Organic Food: Shades of Grey or Shades of Green?," *Proceedings of the Nutrition Society* 61, no. 1 (February 2002): 19–24.

54. P. Barberi, "Weed Management in Organic Agriculture: Are We Addressing the Right Issues?," *Weed Research* 42, no. 3 (June 2002): 177–93, https://doi.org/10.1046/j.1365-3180.2002.00277.x.

55. Conway, *One Billion Hungry.*

56. Helga Willer and Julia Lernoud, "Organic Agriculture Worldwide 2017: Current Statistics" (February 15, 2017), http://orgprints.org/31197/1/willer-lernoud-2017-global-data-biofach.pdf; Helga Willer and Julia Lernoud, eds., *The World of Organic Agriculture—Statistics and Emerging Trends 2017*, Version 1.3 (Frick, Switzerland: Research Institute of Organic Agriculture [FiBL] and IFOAM—Organics International, 2017).

57. Rachel Hine and Jules Pretty, "Organic Agriculture and Food Security in East Africa," in *Capacity Building Study 3* (Promoting production and trading opportunities for organic agricultural products in East Africa, Geneva, Switzerland and Nairobi, Kenya: United Nations Conference on Trade and Development [UNCTAD] and United Nations Environment Programme (UNEP), 2005).

58. Joyce Thamaga-Chitja and Sheryl L. Hendriks, "Emerging Issues in Smallholder Organic Production and Marketing in South Africa," *Development Southern Africa* 25, no. 3 (September 2008): 317–26, https://doi.org/10.1080/03768350802212113.

59. Joelle Katto-Andrighetto, "Participatory Guarantee Systems in East Africa: Case Studies from Kenya, Tanzania and Uganda" (Bonn, Germany: IFOAM, 2013), https://www.ifoam.bio/sites/default/files/page/files/pgs_in_east_africa.pdf.

60. Willer and Lernoud, *The World of Organic Agriculture.*

61. Camilla Toulmin and Ian Scoones, "Policies for Soil Fertility Management in Africa: A Report Prepared for the Department for International Development" (London: UK Department for International Development, 1999), http://pubs.iied.org/7407IIED/.

7. THE NEW GENETICS

1. Gordon Conway, *One Billion Hungry: Can We Feed the World?* (Ithaca: Comstock Publishing Associates, 2012).

2. Shawn McGuire and Louise Sperling, "Seed Systems Smallholder Farmers Use," *Food Security* 8, no. 1 (February 2016): 179–95, https://doi.org/10.1007/s12571-015-0528-8.

3. Michael Halewood and I. Lapena, "Farmers' Varieties and Farmers' Rights: Challenges at the Crossroads of Agriculture, Taxonomy and Law," in *Farmers' Crop Varieties and Farmers' Rights: Challenges in Taxonomy and Law*, ed. Michael Halewood (London: Routledge, 2017), https://ccafs.cgiar.org/publications/farmers-varieties-and-farmers-rights-challenges-crossroads-agriculture-taxonomy-and-law.

4. Ibid.

5. Devra I. Jarvis et al., "An Heuristic Framework for Identifying Multiple Ways of Supporting the Conservation and Use of Traditional Crop Varieties within the Agricultural Production System," *Critical Reviews in Plant Sciences* 30, no. 1–2 (January 2011): 125–76, https://doi.org/10.1080/07352689.2011.554358.

6. Halewood and Lapena, "Farmers' Varieties and Farmers' Rights."

7. R. M. Hassan, M. Mekuria, and W. Mwangi, "Maize Breeding Research in Eastern and Southern Africa: Current Status and Impacts of Past Investments Made by the Public and Private Sectors, 1966–97" (Mexico, DF: CIMMYT, January 4, 2012), https://ispc.cgiar.org/maize-breeding-research-eastern-and-southern-africa-current-status-and-impacts-past-investments-made.

8. Kevin Pixley and Marianne Bänziger, "Open-Pollinated Maize Varieties: A Backward Step or Valuable Option for Farmers?," in *Integrated Approaches to Higher Maize Productivity in the New Millennium* (Seventh Eastern and Southern Africa Regional Maize Conference, Nairobi, Kenya: CIMMYT, 2001), 22–28.

9. Noel Kingsbury, *Hybrid: The History and Science of Plant Breeding* (Chicago: University of Chicago Press, 2009), http://www.press.uchicago.edu/ucp/books/book/chicago/H/bo5387732.html.

10. M. D. Gale and S. Youssefian, "Dwarfing Genes in Wheat," in *Progress in Plant Breeding–1* (Amsterdam: Elsevier, 1985), 1–35, https://doi.org/10.1016/B978-0-407-00780-2.50005-9.

11. African Agricultural Technology Foundation, "Hybrid Rice: Breeding by Design Project" (Nairobi, Kenya: African Agricultural Technology Foundation), accessed May 2, 2018, https://www.aatf-africa.org/files/hybrid-rice.pdf.

12. Papa Abdoulaye Seck et al., "Crops That Feed the World 7: Rice," *Food Security* 4, no. 1 (March 2012): 7–24, https://doi.org/10.1007/s12571-012-0168-1.

13. Gordon Conway, *The Doubly Green Revolution: Food for All in the Twenty-First Century* (Ithaca: Comstock Publishing Associates, 1998).

14. Yuan Longping and China National Hybrid Rice Research and Development Center, "Hybrid Rice Technology for Food Security in the World," in *FAO Rice Conference, Rome, Italy, 12–13 February 2004* (FAO Rice Conference, Rome: FAO, 2004), 3.

15. Jiming Li, Yeyun Xin, and Longping Yuan, "Hybrid Rice Technology Development: Ensuring China's Food Security," IFPRI Discussion Paper (Washington, DC: IFPRI, 2009), http://ebrary.ifpri.org/cdm/ref/collection/p15738coll2/id/23379.

16. Raafat El-Namaky et al., "Putting Plant Genetic Diversity and Variability at Work for Breeding: Hybrid Rice Suitability in West Africa," *Diversity* 9, no. 3 (July 10, 2017): 27, https://doi.org/10.3390/d9030027.

17. Kingsbury, *Hybrid: The History and Science of Plant Breeding*.

18. D. N. Duvick, "Heterosis: Feeding People and Protecting Natural Resources," in *The Genetics and Exploitation of Heterosis in Crops* (Madison, WI: ACSESS: Alliance of Crop,

Soil, and Environmental Science Societies, 1999), 19–29, https://dl.sciencesocieties.org/publications/books/abstracts/acsesspublicati/thegeneticsande/19?access=0&view=pdf.

19. James F. Crow, "90 Years Ago: The Beginning of Hybrid Maize," *Genetics* 148, no. 3 (March 1, 1998): 923–28, http://www.genetics.org/content/148/3/923.

20. Richard Crabb, *The Hybrid-Corn Makers: Prophets of Plenty* / (New Brunswick, NJ: Rutgers University Press, 1947), http://hdl.handle.net/2027/coo.31924003501131.

21. Pixley and Bänziger, "Open-Pollinated Maize Varieties."

22. Chris Lyddon, "Mexico," World-Grain.com, July 6, 2016, http://www.world-grain.com/Departments/Country-Focus/Country-Focus-Home/Mexico-2016.aspx?cck=1.

23. "CIMMYT 1999–2000 World Maize Facts and Trends. Meeting World Maize Needs: Technological Opportunities and Priorities for the Public Sector" (Mexico, DF: CIMMYT, 2001), https://ageconsearch.umn.edu/bitstream/23727/1/fa01pi01.pdf.

24. Edward P. Cunningham and O. Syrstad, *Crossbreeding Bos Indicus and Bos Taurus for Milk Production in the Tropics*, FAO Animal Production and Health Paper 68 (Rome, 1987).

25. Ola Syrstad, "The Role and Mechanisms of Genetic Improvement in Production Systems Constrained by Nutritional and Environmental Factors," in *Expert Consultation*, ed. Andrew Speedy and Rene Sansoucy, vol. 86 (FAO Animal Production and Health Paper, Bangkok, Thailand: FAO, 1989), 48–55, http://www.fao.org/ag/aga/agap/frg/AHPP86/Syrstad.pdf.

26. O. Syrstad, "Dairy Cattle Crossbreeding in the Tropics: Choice of Crossbreeding Strategy," *Tropical Animal Health and Production* 28, no. 3 (August 1996): 223–29.

27. W. Thorpe, C. A. Morris, and P. Kang'ethe, "Crossbreeding of Ayrshire, Brown Swiss, and Sahiwal Cattle for Annual and Lifetime Milk Yield in the Lowland Tropics of Kenya," *Journal of Dairy Science* 77, no. 8 (August 1994): 2415–27, https://doi.org/10.3168/jds.S0022-0302(94)77184-8.

28. Conway, *Doubly Green Revolution*.

29. Bruce G. Cook et al., "Tropical Forages: An Interactive Selection Tool," 2005, http://www.tropicalforages.info/.

30. Liana Jank et al., "The Value of Improved Pastures to Brazilian Beef Production," *Crop and Pasture Science* 65, no. 11 (2014): 1132, https://doi.org/10.1071/CP13319.

31. CIAT, "Tropical Forages: A Multipurpose Genetic Resource," *CIAT in Focus: Crop Commitments*, n.d., 9, http://ciat-library.ciat.cgiar.org/articulos_ciat/ciatinfocus/foragesfocus.pdf.

32. C. S McSweeney et al., "The Application of Rumen Biotechnology to Improve the Nutritive Value of Fibrous Feedstuffs: Pre- and Post-Ingestion," *Livestock Production Science* 59, no. 2–3 (June 1999): 265–83, https://doi.org/10.1016/S0301-6226(99)00032-9.

33. Ming Tien and Chen-Pei D. Tu, "Cloning and Sequencing of a CDNA for a Ligninase from Phanerochaete Chrysosporium," *Nature* 326, no. 6112 (April 1987): 520–23, https://doi.org/10.1038/326520a0.

34. Conway, *One Billion Hungry*.

35. H. T. Stalker, ed., "Plant Breeding in the 1990s," in *Symposium on Plant Breeding in the 1990s* (North Carolina State University, Raleigh, NC: CAB International, 1991).

36. Conway, *One Billion Hungry*.

37. J. Ruane and A. Sonnino, "Marker-Assisted Selection as a Tool for Genetic Improvement of Crops, Livestock, Forestry and Fish in Developing Countries: An Overview of the Issues," in *Marker-Assisted Selection. Current Status and Future Perspectives in Crops, Livestock, Forestry and Fish*, E. P. Guimaraes et al. (Rome: FAO, 2007), 3–13, http://agris.fao.org/agris-search/search.do?recordID=XF2007431989.

38. Grace Abalo et al., "A Comparative Analysis of Conventional and Marker-Assisted Selection Methods in Breeding Maize Streak Virus Resistance in Maize," *Crop Science* 49, no. 2 (2009): 509, https://doi.org/10.2135/cropsci2008.03.0162.

39. O. E. V. Magenya, J. Mueke, and C. Omwega, "Significance and Transmission of Maize Streak Virus Disease in Africa and Options for Management: A Review," *African Journal of Biotechnology* 7, no. 25 (January 1, 2008), https://www.ajol.info/index.php/ajb/article/view/59697.

40. Gordon Conway and Jeff Waage, *Science and Innovation for Development* (London: UK Collaborative on Development Sciences, 2010).

41. Conway, *One Billion Hungry*.

42. Michael Peel D., "A Basic Primer on Biotechnology," 1219 (Fargo, ND: North Dakota State University, 2001), https://www.ag.ndsu.edu/publications/crops/a-basic-primer-on-biotechnology/a1219.pdf.

43. *Global Status of Commercialized Biotech/GM Crops: 2016*, ISAAA Briefs no. 52 (Ithaca: ISAAA, 2016), https://www.isaaa.org/resources/publications/briefs/52/download/isaaa-brief-52-2016.pdf.

44. *Global Status of Commercialized Biotech/GM Crops in 2017: Biotech Crop Adoption Surges as Economic Benefits Accumulate in 22 Years*, ISAAA Briefs no. 53 (Ithaca: ISAAA, 2017), http://www.isaaa.org/resources/publications/briefs/53/download/isaaa-brief-53-2017.pdf.

45. Ibid.

46. Wilhelm Klümper and Matin Qaim, "A Meta-Analysis of the Impacts of Genetically Modified Crops," ed. Emidio Albertini, *PLOS ONE* 9, no. 11 (November 3, 2014): e111629, https://doi.org/10.1371/journal.pone.0111629.

47. Jennifer A. Doudna and Samuel H. Sternberg, *A Crack in Creation: Gene Editing and the Unthinkable Power to Control Evolution* (Boston: Houghton Mifflin Harcourt, 2017).

48. Ibid.

49. Conway, *One Billion Hungry*.

50. "Mutant Foods Create Risks We Can't Yet Guess," *New York Times*, June 16, 1992, sec. Opinion, https://www.nytimes.com/1992/06/16/opinion/l-mutant-foods-create-risks-we-can-t-yet-guess-330092.html.

51. Peggy G. Lemaux, "Genetically Engineered Plants and Foods: A Scientist's Analysis of the Issues (Part I)," *Annual Review of Plant Biology* 59, no. 1 (June 2008): 771–812, https://doi.org/10.1146/annurev.arplant.58.032806.103840.

52. Franziska Achterberg, "Gene-Editing of Plants—GM through the Back Door?," Policy Briefing (Brussels: Greenpeace, November 30, 2015), http://www.greenpeace.org/eu-unit/Global/eu-unit/reports-briefings/2015/Greenpeace_Gene-editing_30112015%20-%202.pdf.

53. Conway, *One Billion Hungry*.

54. "Essential Amino Acid," *Wikipedia*, April 21, 2018, https://en.wikipedia.org/w/index.php?title=Essential_amino_acid&oldid=837542237.

55. University of California San Diego, "Organic Farming," Bacillus thuringiensis, accessed May 3, 2018, http://www.bt.ucsd.edu/organic_farming.html.

56. Clive James, *Global Status of Commercialized Biotech/GM Crops, 2006*, ISAAA Briefs no. 35 (Ithaca: ISAAA, 2006), https://www.isaaa.org/resources/publications/briefs/35/download/isaaa-brief-35-2006.pdf.

57. Bruce E. Tabashnik et al., "Insect Resistance to Bt Crops: Evidence versus Theory," *Nature Biotechnology* 26, no. 2 (February 2008): 199–202, https://doi.org/10.1038/nbt1382.

58. Bruce E. Tabashnik et al., "Insect Resistance to Transgenic Bt Crops: Lessons from the Laboratory and Field," *Journal of Economic Entomology* 96, no. 4 (August 1, 2003): 1031–38, https://doi.org/10.1603/0022-0493-96.4.1031.

59. International Plant Biotechnology Outreach, "Maize in Africa," Fact Series (Gent, Belgium: IPBO, 2017), http://www.vib.be/en/about-vib/plant-biotech-news/Documents/VIB_MaizeInAfrica_EN_2017.pdf.

60. Hugo De Groote et al., "Identifying Farmers' Preferences for New Maize Varieties in Eastern Africa," in *Quantitative Analysis of Data from Participatory Methods in Plant Breeding*, ed. M. Bellon and J. Reeves (Mexico, DF: CIMMYT, 2002), 82–102, https://cgspace.cgiar.org/handle/10568/76948.

61. CIMMYT and IITA, "Drought Tolerant Maize for Africa Initiative," DTMA: The Drought Tolerant Maize for Africa Initiative, 2015, http://dtma.cimmyt.org/; Tsedeke Abate, *A New Generation of Maize for Africa*, 2015, http://dtma.cimmyt.org/index.php/publications/doc_view/196-a-new-generation-of-maize-for-africa.

62. Monica Fisher et al., "Drought Tolerant Maize for Farmer Adaptation to Drought in Sub-Saharan Africa: Determinants of Adoption in Eastern and Southern Africa," *Climatic Change* 133, no. 2 (November 2015): 283–99, https://doi.org/10.1007/s10584-015-1459-2.

63. African Agricultural Technology Foundation, "Water Efficient Maize for Africa (WEMA)," 2012, https://wema.aatf-africa.org/; Margaret Zeigler and Ann Steensland, "Case Study for Water Efficient Maize for Africa: Zambia," in *2015 GAP Report*, Global Agricultural Productivity Report (Washington, DC: Global Harvest Initiative, 2015), http://www.globalharvestinitiative.org/wp-content/uploads/2017/06/WEMA-Cast-Study.pdf.

64. Stephen P. Long and Donald R. Ort, "More than Taking the Heat: Crops and Global Change," *Current Opinion in Plant Biology* 13, no. 3 (June 2010): 240–47, https://doi.org/10.1016/j.pbi.2010.04.008.

65. P. Castiglioni et al., "Bacterial RNA Chaperones Confer Abiotic Stress Tolerance in Plants and Improved Grain Yield in Maize under Water-Limited Conditions," *Plant Physiology* 147, no. 2 (April 11, 2008): 446–55, https://doi.org/10.1104/pp.108.118828.

66. Ken E. Giller et al., "Soyabeans and Sustainable Agriculture in Southern Africa," *International Journal of Agricultural Sustainability* 9, no. 1 (February 1, 2011): 50–58, https://doi.org/10.3763/ijas.2010.0548.

67. Ray Dixon and Daniel Kahn, "Genetic Regulation of Biological Nitrogen Fixation," *Nature Reviews Microbiology* 2, no. 8 (August 2004): 621–31, https://doi.org/10.1038/nrmicro954.

68. Ibid.

8. VALUE CHAINS

1. Gordon Conway, personal communication, and AGRA, 2013, AGRA in Ghana, http://www.agra.org/AGRA/en/where-we-work/agra-in-ghana/.

2. Montpellier Panel, "Sustainable Intensification: A New Paradigm for African Agriculture" (London: Agriculture for Impact, 2013), https://www.mamopanel.org/media/uploads/files/SUSTAINABLE_INTENSIFICATION-_A_NEW_PARADIGM_FOR_AFRICAN_AGRICULTURE_2013.pdf.

3. Ibid.

4. Carlo Borzaga and Giulia Galera, "The Potential of the Social Economy for Local Development in Africa: An Exploratory Report" (Brussels: European Union, May 2014), http://www.euricse.eu/wp-content/uploads/2015/03/EXPO-DEVE_ET2014433787_EN.pdf.

5. John Aglionby, "Africa's Banks Lag behind on Innovation in Financial Services," *Financial Times*, March 7, 2018, sec. African economy, https://www.ft.com/content/68788cbc-221f-11e8-9a70-08f715791301.

6. Sizwe sama Yende, "Brisk Banking at Village Bank," News24, January 22, 2003, https://www.news24.com/SouthAfrica/News/Brisk-banking-at-village-bank-20030122.

7. Lauren Hendricks and Sybil Chidiac, "Village Savings and Loans: A Pathway to Financial Inclusion for Africa's Poorest Households," *Enterprise Development and Microfinance* 22, no. 2 (June 2011): 134–46, https://doi.org/10.3362/1755-1986.2011.016.

8. CARE, "25 Years of VSLAs: Putting Power in Women's Hands," CARE, October 21, 2016, https://www.careinternational.org.uk/stories/25-years-vslas-putting-power-womens-hands.

9. "Rochdale Society of Equitable Pioneers," *Wikipedia*, April 22, 2018, https://en.wikipedia.org/w/index.php?title=Rochdale_Society_of_Equitable_Pioneers&oldid=837660646.

10. Jos Bijman et al., "Support for Farmers' Cooperatives" (Waginen, The Netherlands: European Commission, 2012).

11. "Amul," *Wikipedia*, May 21, 2018, https://en.wikipedia.org/w/index.php?title=Amul&oldid=842303074.

12. Patrick Develtere, "Cooperative Development in Africa up to the 1990s," in *Cooperating out of Poverty: The Renaissance of the African Cooperative Movement*, ed. Patrick Develtere et al. (Geneva: ILO, 2008), 1–37.

13. Frederick O. Wanyama, "The Qualitative and Quantitative Growth of the Cooperative Movement in Kenya," in *Cooperating out of Poverty: The Renaissance of the African Cooperative Movement*, ed. Patrick Develtere et al. (Geneva: ILO, 2008), 91–127.

14. Rui M. S. Benfica, David L. Tschirley, and Liria Sambo, "The Impact of Alternative Agro-Industrial Investments on Poverty Reduction in Rural Mozambique," Food Security Collaborative Working Papers (Michigan State University, Department of Agricultural, Food, and Resource Economics, 2002), https://ideas.repec.org/p/ags/midcwp/56055.html.

15. Nigel Poole and Annabel de Frece, "A Review of Existing Organisational Forms of Smallholder Farmers' Associations and Their Contractual Relationships with Other Market Participants in the East and Southern African ACP Region," AAACP Paper Series (Rome, Italy: FAO, January 2010), http://www.fao.org/fileadmin/templates/est/AAACP/eastafrica/FAO_AAACP_Paper_Series_No_11_1_.pdf.

16. Wilberforce Kisamba-Mugerwa and Terefe Ademetegn Lemma, "Developing Contract Farming Systems in Uganda" *World Agriculture*, January 4, 2011, http://www.world-agriculture.net/article/developing-contract-farming-systems-in-uganda.

17. Poole and de Frece, "Review of Existing Organisational Forms."

18. Ousmane Badiane, "The Twenty-First Century Agricultural Cooperative: Increasing the Business Credibility of Smallholders," *African Farmers in the Digital Age: How Digital Solutions Can Enable Rural Development*, February 2016, http://ebrary.ifpri.org/cdm/ref/collection/p15738coll5/id/5234.

19. Ibid.

20. Ibid.

21. Ibid.

22. Ibid.

23. Calestous Juma et al., "Innovation for Sustainable Intensification in Africa," Briefing Paper (London: Montpellier Panel, Agriculture for Impact, 2013), https://www.mamopanel.org/media/uploads/files/INNOVATION_FOR_SUSTAINABLE_INTENSIFICATION_IN_AFRICA_2013.pdf.

24. African Technology Policy Studies Network, *The African Manifesto for Science, Technology and Innovation*, ed. Kevin Urama and Science, Ethics and Technological Responsibilities in Developing and Emerging Countries Project (Nairobi, Kenya: African Technology Policy Studies Network, 2010), https://atpsnet.org/wp-content/uploads/2017/05/the_african_manifesto_for_sti.pdf.

25. Philip G. Pardey et al., "Returns to Food and Agricultural R&D Investments in Sub-Saharan Africa, 1975–2014," *Food Policy* 65 (December 2016): 1–8, https://doi.org/10.1016/j.foodpol.2016.09.009.

26. Colin Thirtle, Lin Lin, and Jenifer Piesse, "The Impact of Research-Led Agricultural Productivity Growth on Poverty Reduction in Africa, Asia and Latin America," *World Development* 31, no. 12 (December 2003): 1959–75, https://doi.org/10.1016/j.worlddev.2003.07.001; Luc Christiaensen, Lionel Demery, and Jesper Kuhl, "The Role of Agriculture in Poverty Reduction: An Empirical Perspective," Policy Research Working Papers (Washington, DC: World Bank, September 27, 2006), https://doi.org/10.1596/1813-9450-4013; Pardey et al., "Returns to Food and Agricultural R&D Investments."

27. Juma et al., "Innovation for Sustainable Intensification in Africa."

28. Agriculture for Impact, "8 Views for the G8: Business Solutions for African Smallholder Farmers to Address Food Security and Nutrition" (London: Agriculture for Impact, 2013), https://www.mamopanel.org/resources/reports-and-briefings/8-views-g8-business-solutions-african-smallholder-/.

29. OECD, "Fostering Productivity and Competitiveness in Agriculture" (Paris: OECD, November 25, 2011), https://www.oecd-ilibrary.org/agriculture-and-food/fostering-productivity-and-competitiveness-in-agriculture_9789264166820-en.

30. T. S. Jayne, Jordan Chamberlin, and Derek D. Headey, "Land Pressures, the Evolution of Farming Systems, and Development Strategies in Africa: A Synthesis," in Boserup and Beyond: Mounting Land Pressures and Development Strategies in Africa, special issue, *Food Policy* 48 (October 1, 2014): 1–17, https://doi.org/10.1016/j.foodpol.2014.05.014.

31. Lorenzo Cotula, ed., *Changes in "Customary" Land Tenure Systems in Africa*, Land Tenure and Resource Access in Africa (London: IIED, 2007), http://pubs.iied.org/12537IIED/.

32. Nicholas J. Sitko and T. S. Jayne, "Exploitative Briefcase Businessmen, Parasites, and Other Myths and Legends: Assembly Traders and the Performance of Maize Markets in Eastern and Southern Africa," *World Development* 54 (February 2014): 56–67, https://doi.org/10.1016/j.worlddev.2013.07.008.

33. Stein T. Holden and Keijiro Otsuka, "The Roles of Land Tenure Reforms and Land Markets in the Context of Population Growth and Land Use Intensification in Africa," *Food Policy* 48 (October 1, 2014): 88–97, https://doi.org/10.1016/j.foodpol.2014.03.005.

34. Jeffrey Ira Herbst, *States and Power in Africa: Comparative Lessons in Authority and Control*, 2nd ed., Princeton Studies in International History and Politics (Princeton, NJ: Princeton University Press, 2014).

35. Holden and Otsuka, "The Roles of Land Tenure Reforms and Land Markets."

36. GIM International, "Improving Land Tenure Security with Low-Cost Technologies," March 30, 2017, https://www.gim-international.com/content/article/improving-land-tenure-security-with-low-cost-technologies.

37. Jayne, Chamberlin, and Headey, "Land Pressures, the Evolution of Farming Systems, and Development Strategies in Africa."

38. Ibid.

39. Thomas S. Jayne et al., "Is the Scramble for Land in Africa Foreclosing a Smallholder Agricultural Expansion Strategy?," *Journal of International Affairs* 67, no. 2 (2014): 35–53, http://www.jstor.org/stable/24461734.

40. Serge G. Adjognon, Lenis Saweda O. Liverpool-Tasie, and Thomas A. Reardon, "Agricultural Input Credit in Sub-Saharan Africa: Telling Myth from Facts," *Food Policy* 67 (February 2017): 93–105, https://doi.org/10.1016/j.foodpol.2016.09.014.

41. Akinwumi A. Adesina, "Africa's Pathway Out of Poverty" (speech, October 20, 2017), https://www.afdb.org/en/news-and-events/africas-pathway-out-of-poverty-by-dr-akinwumi-a-adesina-president-of-the-african-development-bank-world-food-prize-laureate-luncheon-october-20–2017-in-des-moines-iowa-17468/.

42. Gordon Conway et al., "Creating Resilient Value Chains for Smallholder Farmers," in *Africa Agriculture Status Report 2017: The Business of Smallholder Agriculture in Sub-Saharan Africa* (Kigali, Rwanda: AGRA, 2017), https://agra.org/aasr2017/chapter-5/.

43. Central Bank of Nigeria and Federal Ministry of Agriculture and Water Resources, "Guidelines for Commercial Agriculture Credit Scheme (CACS)" (Central Bank of Nigeria, 2009), https://www.cbn.gov.ng/OUT/CIRCULARS/DFD/2009/GUIDELINES%20FOR%20UTILISATION%20AND%20ACCESS%20TO%20COMMERCIAL%20AGRICULTURE%20CREDIT%20SCHEME%20(CACS).PDF.

44. International Bank for Reconstruction and Development / World Bank, "Agricultural Insurance," Primer Series on Insurance (Washington, DC: World Bank, November 1, 2009), http://siteresources.worldbank.org/FINANCIALSECTOR/Resources/Primer12_Agricultural_Insurance.pdf.

45. Ibid.

46. Marc Sadler and Olivier Mahul, "Weather Index-Based Crop Insurance in Malawi: Facilitating Farmers' Access to Agricultural Credit" (World Bank, March 1, 2012), http://documents.worldbank.org/curated/en/734611467986308477/Weather-index-based-crop-insurance-in-Malawi-facilitating-farmers-access-to-agricultural-credit.

47. SwissRe, "Successful Kenya Livestock Insurance Program Scheme Scales Up," accessed May 23, 2018, http://www.swissre.com/reinsurance/successful_Kenya_livestock_insurance_program_scheme_scales_up.html.

48. Susan MacMillan, "Record Payouts Being Made by Kenya Government and Insurers to Protect Herders Facing Historic Drought," *ILRI News* (blog), February 21, 2017, https://news.ilri.org/2017/02/21/record-payouts-being-made-by-kenya-government-and-insurers-to-protect-herders-facing-historic-drought/.

49. Conway et al., "Creating Resilient Value Chains for Smallholder Farmers."

50. WINnERS Project, "WINnERS," accessed May 23, 2018, http://winners-project.org/.

51. Victoria Seeds Limited, "Victoria Seeds Limited," n.d., http://www.victoriaseeds.com/.

52. Gordon Conway, personal communication.

53. Lulu Akaki, "Why Farmers Need to Use ARM Mavuno Fertilizer," *HapaKenya* (blog), November 17, 2014, https://hapakenya.com/2014/11/17/farmers-need-use-arm-mavuno-fertilizer/.

54. Seneshaw Tamru et al., "The Rapid Expansion of Herbicide Use in Smallholder Agriculture in Ethiopia: Patterns, Drivers, and Implications," ESSP II (Washington DC: IFPRI and Addis Ababa, Ethiopia: Ethiopian Development Research Institute, 2016), http://ebrary.ifpri.org/cdm/ref/collection/p15738coll2/id/130716.

55. International Fertilizer Development Center, "Extending Agro-Dealer Networks in Africa," press release, March 9, 2012, https://ifdc.org/2012/03/09/extending-agro-dealer-networks-in-africa-2/.

56. Brian Lipinski et al., "Reducing Food Loss and Waste," Working Paper, Creating a Sustainable Food Future (Washington, DC: World Resources Institute, 2013), https://www.wri.org/sites/default/files/reducing_food_loss_and_waste.pdf.

57. Hippolyte Affognon et al., "Unpacking Postharvest Losses in Sub-Saharan Africa: A Meta-Analysis," *World Development* 66 (February 2015): 49–68, https://doi.org/10.1016/j.worlddev.2014.08.002.

58. Jonathan Kaminski and Luc Christiaensen, "Post-Harvest Loss in Sub-Saharan Africa—What Do Farmers Say?," *Global Food Security* 3, nos. 3–4 (November 2014): 149–58, https://doi.org/10.1016/j.gfs.2014.10.002.

59. Gordon Conway, "Investing for the Future with Home Grown School Feeding," *HuffPost UK* (blog), February 8, 2012, http://www.huffingtonpost.co.uk/professor-sir-gordon-conway/home-grown-school-feeding-investing-for-the-future-_b_1259452.html.

60. Jason Snyder et al., "Local Response to the Rapid Rise in Demand for Processed and Perishable Foods: Results of an Inventory of Processed Food Products in Dar Es Salaam," Feed the Future Innovation Lab for Food Security Policy, Policy Research Brief 6 (East Lansing: Michigan State University, May 1, 2015), 5, http://foodsecuritypolicy.msu.edu/uploads/resources/Policy_Brief_6.pdf.

61. Thomas Anthony Reardon et al., "Transformation of African Agrifood Systems in the New Era of Rapid Urbanization and the Emergence of a Middle Class," in *Beyond a Middle Income Africa: Transforming African Economies for Sustained Growth with Rising Employment and Incomes* by Ousmane Badiane and Tsitsi Makombe (Washington, DC: IFPRI, 2015), 62–74, http://ebrary.ifpri.org/cdm/ref/collection/p15738coll2/id/130005.

62. David Tschirley et al., "Engaging the Agribusiness Sector in Inclusive Value Chain Development: Opportunities and Challenges," in *Africa Agriculture Status Report 2017: The Business of Smallholder Agriculture in Sub-Saharan Africa* (Nairobi, Kenya: AGRA, 2017), https://agra.org/aasr2017/chapter-3/.

63. T. S. Jayne, Jordan Chamberlin, and Rui Benfica, "Africa's Unfolding Economic Transformation," *Journal of Development Studies* 54, no. 5 (May 4, 2018): 777–87, https://doi.org/10.1080/00220388.2018.1430774; T. S. Jayne, Ousmane Badiane, and Xinshen Diao, "Africa's Unfolding Agricultural Transformation," July 30, 2018, https://www.canr.msu.edu/fsp/outreach/presentations/Jayne-Badiane-Diao-ICAE-July%2027%20-%20Thom%20Jayne.pdf.

64. Frank Hollinger and John Staatz, eds., *Agricultural Growth in West Africa: Market and Policy Drivers* (Rome: African Development Bank and FAO, 2015), http://www.fao.org/3/a-i4337e.pdf.

65. Gordon Conway, personal communication from Samrat Singh Imperial College

66. Andrew Dorward, "Integrating Contested Aspirations, Processes and Policy: Development as Hanging In, Stepping Up and Stepping Out," *Development Policy Review* 27, no. 2 (March 2009): 131–46, https://doi.org/10.1111/j.1467-7679.2009.00439.x.

9. DIGITAL FARMERS

1. Reproduced from Sandy Andelman, Peter Seligmann, and Mohamed Bakarr, "Peace of Mind: Digital Information Reduces Uncertainty for Farmers in the Face of Climate Change," in "African Farmers in the Digital Age: Overcoming Isolation, Speeding up Change and Taking Success to Scale," ed. Kofi Annan, Gordon Conway, and Sam Dryden, special issue, *Foreign Affairs* (2016): 118–24, https://files.foreignaffairs.com/pdf/sponsored-anthology/2016/african_farmers_in_the_digital_age_final.pdf.

2. Ibid.

3. "Foreword: Digital Thinking to Transform Africa's Food System," in "African Farmers in the Digital Age: Overcoming Isolation, Speeding up Change and Taking Success to Scale," ed. Kofi Annan, Gordon Conway, and Sam Dryden, special issue, *Foreign Affairs* (2016): viii–xi, https://files.foreignaffairs.com/pdf/sponsored-anthology/2016/african_farmers_in_the_digital_age_final.pdf.

4. Strive Masiyiwa, "Mobile Revolution 2.0: Lessons for a Sustainable Green Revolution in Africa," in "African Farmers in the Digital Age: Overcoming Isolation, Speeding up Change and Taking Success to Scale," ed. Kofi Annan, Gordon Conway, and Sam Dryden, special issue, *Foreign Affairs* (2016): 93–99, https://files.foreignaffairs.com/pdf/sponsored-anthology/2016/african_farmers_in_the_digital_age_final.pdf.

5. Ericsson, "Ericsson Mobility Report June 2017" (Stockholm: Ericsson, June 2017).

6. "Foreword: Digital Thinking to Transform Africa's Food System."

7. Sam Dryden, "What's Unique About Unique IDs: Delivering on the Promise of Digital Solutions for Smallholders," in "African Farmers in the Digital Age: Overcoming Isolation, Speeding up Change and Taking Success to Scale," ed. Kofi Annan, Gordon

Conway, and Sam Dryden, special issue, *Foreign Affairs* (2016): 132–37, https://files. foreignaffairs.com/pdf/sponsored-anthology/2016/african_farmers_in_the_digital_age_ final.pdf.

8. Ethiopian Agricultural Transformation Agency, "8028 Hotline," *ATA* (blog), accessed June 11, 2018, https://www.ata.gov.et/highlighted-deliverables/8028-agricultural-hotline/.

9. Tinishu Solomon, "Ethiopia: Massive Success for Agricultural Hotline," *Strategic Thinking on East Africa* (blog), June 17, 2015, http://www.strathink.net/ethiopia/ ethiopia-massive-success-for-agricultural-hotline/.

10. Dryden, "What's Unique About Unique IDs."

11. Ibid.

12. Ibid.

13. Ibid.

14. Bill Gates, "The Secret Decoder Ring: How Cell Phones Let Farmers, Governments, and Markets Talk to Each Other," in "African Farmers in the Digital Age: Overcoming Isolation, Speeding up Change and Taking Success to Scale," ed. Kofi Annan, Gordon Conway, and Sam Dryden, special issue, *Foreign Affairs* (2016): 87–92, https:// files.foreignaffairs.com/pdf/sponsored-anthology/2016/african_farmers_in_the_digital_ age_final.pdf.

15. Ibid.

16. "M-KOPA Solar," *M-KOPA Solar* (blog), accessed May 25, 2018, http://www.m-kopa.com/.

17. Masiyiwa, "Mobile Revolution 2.0."

18. EcoCash, "FAQs—EcoCash," EcoCash, accessed May 25, 2018, https://www.eco cash.co.zw/faqs.

19. Masiyiwa, "Mobile Revolution 2.0."

20. "About Us—EcoCash," accessed April 26, 2019, https://www.ecocash.co.zw/ about.

21. EcoFarmer, "Ecofarmer: Expert Farming Advice Delivered by SMS," accessed May 25, 2018, https://www.ecofarmer.co.zw/.

22. Masiyiwa, "Mobile Revolution 2.0."

23. Rikin Gandhi, "Building Community at a Global Scale: Using Video to Improve Extension and Create Farmer Networks," in "African Farmers in the Digital Age: Overcoming Isolation, Speeding up Change and Taking Success to Scale," ed. Kofi Annan, Gordon Conway, and Sam Dryden, special issue, *Foreign Affairs* (2016): 125–31, https:// files.foreignaffairs.com/pdf/sponsored-anthology/2016/african_farmers_in_the_digital_ age_final.pdf.

24. Digital Green, "Digital Green Annual Report 2013" (New Delhi: Digital Green, 2013), https://www.scribd.com/document/271434390/Digital-Green-Annual-Report-2013.

25. Ibid.

26. Akinwumi A. Adesina, "Agriculture as a Business: Approaching Agriculture as an Investment Opportunity," in "African Farmers in the Digital Age: Overcoming Isolation, Speeding up Change and Taking Success to Scale," ed. Kofi Annan, Gordon Conway, and Sam Dryden, special issue, *Foreign Affairs* (2016): 58–63, https://files.foreignaffairs.com/ pdf/sponsored-anthology/2016/african_farmers_in_the_digital_age_final.pdf.

27. Ibid.

28. "August 2017," *Cellulant* (blog), August 2017, https://cellulant.blog/2017/08/.

29. Ibid.

30. "Barn Raising: Nigeria 2015, Agriculture Interview," Business Year, accessed October 31, 2018, https://www.thebusinessyear.com/nigeria-2015/barn-raising/interview.

31. "Company Profile: Cellulant Nigeria Limited," accessed May 25, 2018, http://cel lulant.com.ng/company-profile.html.

32. Cellulant, "Made in Africa Goes Global," *Cellulant* (blog), August 11, 2017, https://medium.com/@cellulant/made-in-africa-to-the-world-nigerias-e-wallet-agritech-being-adopted-in-afghanistan-2ee91e3ab8a6.

33. Brian Clegg, *Big Data: How the Information Revolution Is Transforming Our Lives* (London: Icon Books, 2017).

34. Khalid Bomba, "Learn As You Go: The Ethiopian Example of Agricultural Transformation in Action," in "African Farmers in the Digital Age: Overcoming Isolation, Speeding up Change and Taking Success to Scale," ed. Kofi Annan, Gordon Conway, and Sam Dryden, special issue, *Foreign Affairs* (2016): 17–24, https://files.foreignaffairs.com/pdf/sponsored-anthology/2016/african_farmers_in_the_digital_age_final.pdf.

35. Ethiopian Agricultural Transformation Agency, "EthioSIS," *ATA* (blog), accessed May 25, 2018, https://www.ata.gov.et/highlighted-deliverables/ethiosis/.

36. J. T. Overpeck et al., "Climate Data Challenges in the 21st Century," *Science* 331, no. 6018 (February 11, 2011): 700–702, https://doi.org/10.1126/science.1197869.

37. Erik Chavez et al., "An End-to-End Assessment of Extreme Weather Impacts on Food Security," *Nature Climate Change* 5, no. 11 (November 2015): 997–1001, https://doi.org/10.1038/nclimate2747.

38. Overpeck, "Climate Data Challenges in the 21st Century."

39. "Genome News Network," 2004, http://www.genomenewsnetwork.org/.

40. ICRISAT, "Pearl Millet Genome Reveals How This Cereal Survives Temperatures over 42 Degrees Celsius," September 2017, https://www.icrisat.org/pearl-millet-genome-reveals-how-this-cereal-survives-temperatures-over-42-degrees-celsius/.

41. Xinan Yue et al., "Space Weather Observations by GNSS Radio Occultation: From FORMOSAT-3/COSMIC to FORMOSAT-7/COSMIC-2," *Space Weather* 12, no. 11 (November 2014): 616–21, https://doi.org/10.1002/2014SW001133.

42. Hunglung A. Huang, "GeoMetWatch-STORM: Global Constellation of Next-Generation Ultraspectral Geostationary Observatories," in *Imaging and Applied Optics (2011), Paper HTuC1* (Hyperspectral Imaging and Sounding of the Environment, Optical Society of America, 2011), https://doi.org/10.1364/HISE.2011.HTuC1.

43. "Machine Learning," in *Wikipedia*, May 24, 2018, https://en.wikipedia.org/w/index.php?title=Machine_learning&oldid=842769070.

44. Nicola Jones, "Computer Science: The Learning Machines," *Nature News* 505, no. 7482 (January 9, 2014): 146, https://doi.org/10.1038/505146a.

45. Nicola Jones, "How Machine Learning Could Help to Improve Climate Forecasts," *Nature News* 548, no. 7668 (August 24, 2017): 379, https://doi.org/10.1038/548379a.

46. Yunjie Liu et al., "Application of Deep Convolutional Neural Networks for Detecting Extreme Weather in Climate Datasets," *ArXiv:1605.01156 [Cs]*, May 4, 2016, http://arxiv.org/abs/1605.01156.

47. Provenance, "Blockchain: The Solution for Supply Chain Transparency," accessed May 25, 2018, https://www.provenance.org/whitepaper.

48. Ibid.

49. Melanie Swan, *Blockchain: Blueprint for a New Economy* (Sebastopol, CA: O'Reilly Media, 2015).

50. IPF UK, "Intelligent Precision Farming," accessed May 25, 2018, http://www.ipf-uk.com/.

10. TRANSFORMING AGRICULTURE

1. Steve Wiggins, "Can the Smallholder Model Deliver Poverty Reduction and Food Security for a Rapidly Growing Population in Africa?," FAC Working Paper No. 8 (How to Feed the World in 2050, Rome: Institute of Development Studies, 2009), 25.

2. Ibid.

3. Ousmane Badiane and Julia Collins, "Agricultural Growth and Productivity in Africa: Recent Trends and Future Outlook," in *Agricultural Research in Africa: Investing in Future Harvests*, John Lynam et al. (Washington, DC: IFPRI, 2016), 3–30, http://ebrary.ifpri.org/cdm/ref/collection/p15738coll2/id/130570.

4. "Comprehensive Africa Agriculture Development Programme (CAADP)," Office of the Special Adviser on Africa, OSAA, accessed October 30, 2018, http://www.un.org/en/africa/osaa/peace/caadp.shtml.

5. L. Fulginiti, R. Perrin, and B. Yu, "Institutions and Agricultural Productivity in Sub-Saharan Africa," *Agricultural Economics* 31, no. 2–3 (December 2004): 169–80, https://doi.org/10.1016/j.agecon.2004.09.005; Carlos Ludena et al., "Productivity Growth and Convergence in Crop, Ruminant and Non-Ruminant Production: Measurement and Forecasts," *GTAP Working Papers* 37 (November 29, 2006): 1–17, https://docs.lib.purdue.edu/gtapwp/33; Alejandro Nin-Pratt and Bingxin Yu, "An Updated Look at the Recovery of Agricultural Productivity in Sub-Saharan Africa," IFPRI Discussion Paper (Washington, DC: IFPRI, 2008), http://ebrary.ifpri.org/cdm/ref/collection/p15738coll2/id/13130; Arega D. Alene, "Productivity Growth and the Effects of R&D in African Agriculture," *Agricultural Economics* 41, no. 3–4 (May 2010): 223–38, https://doi.org/10.1111/j.1574-0862.2010.00450.x; Samuel Benin et al., "Trends and Spatial Patterns in Agricultural Productivity in Africa, 1961–2010," ReSAKSS Annual Trends and Outlook Report (Washington, DC: IFPRI, 2011), http://ebrary.ifpri.org/cdm/ref/collection/p15738coll2/id/127142.

6. Badiane and Collins, "Agricultural Growth and Productivity in Africa."

7. Ibid.

8. Antoine Bouët, David Laborde Debucquet, and Lauren Deason, "Global Trade Patterns, Competitiveness, and Growth Outlook," in *Promoting Agricultural Trade to Enhance Resilience in Africa: ReSAKSS Annual Trends and Outlook Report 2013*, ed. Ousmane Badiane, Tsitsi Makombe, and Godfrey Bahiigwa (Washington, DC: IFPRI, 2014), 4–17, http://ebrary.ifpri.org/cdm/ref/collection/p15738coll2/id/128849.

9. Badiane and Collins, "Agricultural Growth and Productivity in Africa."

10. Ibid.

11. World Bank, *PovcalNet: An Online Analysis Tool for Global Poverty Monitoring* (Washington, DC: World Bank, 2018), http://iresearch.worldbank.org/PovcalNet/home.aspx.

12. World Bank and International Monetary Fund, *Global Monitoring Report 2015/2016: Development Goals in an Era of Demographic Change* (Washington, DC: World Bank, 2016), https://openknowledge.worldbank.org/handle/10986/22547.

13. MDG Monitor, "MDG 1—Eradicate Extreme Poverty and Hunger," *Millennium Development Goals* (blog), May 15, 2017, http://www.mdgmonitor.org/mdg-1-eradicate-poverty-hunger/.

14. Badiane and Collins, "Agricultural Growth and Productivity in Africa."

15. "Chart of the Week: The Potential for Growth and Africa's Informal Economy," *IMF Blog* (blog), August 8, 2017, https://blogs.imf.org/2017/08/08/chart-of-the-week-the-potential-for-growth-and-africas-informal-economy/.

16. Godfrey Bahiigwa et al., "Tracking Key CAADP Indicators and Implementation," in *Promoting Agricultural Trade to Enhance Resilience in Africa: ReSAKSS Annual Trends and Outlook Report 2013*, ed. Ousmane Badiane, Tsitsi Makombe, and Godfrey Bahiigwa (Washington, DC: IFPRI, 2014), 70–81, http://ebrary.ifpri.org/cdm/ref/collection/p15738coll2/id/128853.

17. Thomas Anthony Reardon et al., "Transformation of African Agrifood Systems in the New Era of Rapid Urbanization and the Emergence of a Middle Class," in Ousmane Badiane and Tsitsi Makombe, *Beyond a Middle Income Africa: Transforming African*

Economies for Sustained Growth with Rising Employment and Incomes (Washington, DC: IFPRI, 2015), 62–74, http://ebrary.ifpri.org/cdm/ref/collection/p15738coll2/id/130005.

18. UNFPA—United Nations Population Fund, "Data," UNFPA—United Nations Population Fund, accessed May 30, 2018, https://www.unfpa.org/data.

19. David Tschirley, Steven Haggblade, and Thomas Reardon, eds., *Africa's Emerging Food System Transformation—Eastern and Southern Africa* (East Lansing, MI: Global Center for Food Systems Innovation [GCFSI], Michigan State University, 2014), http://gcfsi.isp.msu.edu/files/7214/6229/3434/w1.pdf.

20. Frank Hollinger and John Staatz, eds., *Agricultural Growth in West Africa: Market and Policy Drivers* (Rome: African Development Bank and FAO, 2015), http://www.fao.org/3/a-i4337e.pdf.

21. Steven Haggblade, "Modernizing African Agribusiness: Reflections for the Future," *Journal of Agribusiness in Developing and Emerging Economies* 1, no. 1 (June 3, 2011): 10–30, https://doi.org/10.1108/20440831111131532.

22. M. Dolislager, David Tschirley, and Thomas Reardon, "Consumption Patterns in Eastern and Southern Africa," Report to United States Agency for International Development (East Lansing, MI: Michigan State University, Innovation Lab for Food Security Policy, 2015); Hollinger and Staatz, *Agricultural Growth in West Africa*.

23. Mthuli Ncube, Charles Leyeka Lufumpa, and Kayizzi-Mugerwa Steve, "The Middle of the Pyramid: Dynamics of the Middle Class in Africa," *Market Brief*, April 20, 2011, https://www.afdb.org/fileadmin/uploads/afdb/Documents/Publications/The%20Middle%20of%20the%20Pyramid_The%20Middle%20of%20the%20Pyramid.pdf.

24. NEPAD, "CAADP Pillar II Framework for Improving Rural Infrastructure and Trade Related Capacities for Market Access (FIMA)" (CAADP, April 2009), http://nepad.org/resource/framework-improving-rural-infrastructure-and-trade-related-capacities-market-access.

25. T. Sonobe and K. Otsuka, *Cluster-Based Industrial Development—A Comparative Study of Asia and Africa* (London: Palgrave Macmillan UK, 2011), //www.palgrave.com/gb/book/9780230280182.

11. LEADERSHIP AND PERFORMANCE

1. Ousmane Badiane et al., "Economic Recovery in Africa and Its Determinants," in *Beyond a Middle Income Africa: Transforming African Economies for Sustained Growth with Rising Employment and Incomes: ReSAKSS Annual Trends and Outlook Report 2014*, Ousmane Badiane and Tsitsi Makombe (Washington, DC: IFPRI, 2015), http://ebrary.ifpri.org/cdm/ref/collection/p15738coll2/id/130006.

2. Ademola Oyejide, "The Effects of Trade and Exchange Rate Policies on Agriculture in Nigeria" (Washington, DC: IFPRI, October 1986), http://ageconsearch.umn.edu/bitstream/42598/2/rr55.pdf; Tshikala B. Tshibaka, "The Effects of Trade and Exchange Rate Policies on Agriculture in Zaire" (Washington DC: IFPRI, 1986), http://ebrary.ifpri.org/cdm/ref/collection/p15738coll2/id/126070; OusmaneKinteh Badiane, "Trade Pessimism and Regionalism in African Countries: The Case of Groundnut Exporters" (Washington DC: IFPRI, 1994), http://ebrary.ifpri.org/cdm/ref/collection/p15738coll2/id/125536.

3. Bruce F. Johnston and John W. Mellor, "The Role of Agriculture in Economic Development," *American Economic Review* 51, no. 4 (1961): 566–93, http://www.jstor.org/stable/1812786.

4. Montague Yudelman, "Agriculture in Integrated Rural Development," *Food Policy* 1, no. 5 (November 1976): 367–81, https://doi.org/10.1016/0306-9192(76)90072-5; Carl K. Eicher and John M. Staatz, *Agricultural Development in the Third World* (Baltimore: Johns Hopkins University Press, 1990).

5. Hans P. Binswanger, "Agricultural and Rural Development: Painful Lessons," *Agrekon* 33, no. 4 (December 1994): 165–74, https://doi.org/10.1080/03031853.1994.95 24781.

6. G. A. Cornia, "Economic Decline and Human Welfare in the First Half of the 1980s," in *Adjustment with a Human Face: Protecting the Vulnerable and Promoting Growth*, ed. G. A. Cornia, Richard Jolly, and Frances Stewart, vol. 1 (Oxford: Clarendon Press, 1987), 11–47, https://www.popline.org/node/370036.

7. International Monetary Fund, "Sub-Saharan Africa: Time for a Policy Reset," IMF Regional Economic Outlook (REO) (Washington, DC: International Monetary Fund, April 2016), https://www.imf.org/en/Publications/REO/SSA/Issues/2016/04/05/Time-for-a-Policy-Reset.

8. Mylène Kherallah et al., *The Road Half Traveled: Agricultural Market Reform in Sub-Saharan Africa* (Washington, DC: IFPRI, 2000); T. S. Jayne et al., "False Promise or False Premise? The Experience of Food and Input Market Reform in Eastern and Southern Africa," *World Development* 30, no. 11 (November 2002): 1967–85, https://doi.org/10.1016/S0305-750X(02)00115-8.

9. Christopher B. Barrett and Michael R. Carter, "Microeconomically Coherent Agricultural Policy Reform in Africa," in *African Economies in Transition*, Studies on the African Economies (London: Palgrave Macmillan, 1999), 288–347, https://doi.org/10.1007/978-1-349-27483-3_7.

10. World Bank Group, "Comprehensive Development Framework," Archive, World Bank, 2008, http://web.worldbank.org/archive/website01013/WEB/0__PAG-2.HTM.

11. Organization of African Unity, *Lagos Plan of Action for the Economic Development of Africa, 1980–2000* (Addis Ababa, Ethiopia: Organization of African Unity, 1985), https://catalog.hathitrust.org/Record/007522154.

12. Moeletsi Mbeki, "The African Renaissance," *Issues in South African Foreign Policy*, Spring Issue, 2, no. 2 (March 2000): 76–81, https://doi.org/10.1080/10999940009362215.

13. Abdoulaye Wade, "OMEGA Plan for Africa: Prepared by H. E. Mr. Abdoulaye WADE, President of the Republic of Senegal" (Algiers: Southern African Regional Poverty Network, 2001).

14. African Union Commission, "New Partnership for Africa's Development (NEPAD)," African Union, 2001, https://au.int/en/organs/nepad.

15. Ousmane Badiane, Samuel Benin, and Tsitsi Makombe, "Strengthening the Continental Agricultural Agenda and Accountability Framework—The Road from Maputo to Malabo," in *Africa Agriculture Status Report 2016: Progress towards Agricultural Transformation in Africa* (Nairobi, Kenya: AGRA, 2016), http://ebrary.ifpri.org/cdm/ref/collection/p15738coll5/id/5519.

16. Fleur Stephanie Wouterse and Alemayehu Seyoum Taffesse, "Boosting Growth to End Hunger by 2025: The Role of Social Protection" (Washington, DC: IFPRI, 2018), https://doi.org/10.2499/9780896295988.

17. Samuel Benin, "From Maputo to Malabo: How Has CAADP Fared?" (PowerPoint, July 25, 2017), http://www.iced-eval.org/evidence-action-conference-accra-ghana/.

18. Badiane, Benin, and Makombe, "Strengthening the Continental Agricultural Agenda."

19. James F. Oehmke et al., "The Behavioral-Economics Basis of Mutual Accountability to Achieve Food Security: Mutual Accountability to Food Security," *Politics and Policy* 46, no. 1 (February 2018): 32–57, https://doi.org/10.1111/polp.12244.

Author Biographies

Sir Gordon Conway is professor of international development at Imperial College London. In a career of over fifty years he has worked in north Borneo (Sabah), Thailand, India, Nepal, Pakistan, Egypt, and the Sudan and in several countries of sub-Saharan Africa. He was formerly the chief scientist for the UK Department for International Development, president of the Rockefeller Foundation, and vice-chancellor of Sussex University. Most recently he was chair of the Montpellier Panel. He is the author of *A Doubly Green Revolution* and *One Billion Hungry*.

Dr. Ousmane Badiane is Africa director for the International Food Policy Research Institute (IFPRI). In this role he oversees the institute's two regional offices for West and Central Africa in Dakar and Eastern and Southern Africa in Addis Ababa. He coordinates IFPRI's work program in the areas of food policy research, capacity strengthening, and policy communications in Africa. He is also in charge of IFPRI's partnerships with African institutions dealing with the above areas. As an advisor to the New Partnership for Africa's Development secretariat from 2004 to 2007, he was instrumental in developing and guiding the implementation of the Comprehensive Africa Agriculture Development Programme. He was formerly lead specialist for food and agricultural policy for the Africa region at the World Bank. He is chair of the African Agricultural Technology Foundation and co-chair of the new Malabo Montpellier Panel.

Dr. Katrin Glatzel is program head of the Malabo Montpellier Panel program at the International Food Policy Research Institute, based in Dakar, Senegal. Since 2016 she has led the research and writing of the panel's reports and briefing papers. She also works with the panel to ensure strategically delivered expert advice to African and European governments on their approach to agricultural transformation and growth. Previously, she worked as a policy and research officer with the Montpellier Panel based at Imperial College, London, where she continues to be a visiting researcher. She holds a PhD in environmental research from Imperial College London and an MSc in public management and governance from the London School of Economics and Political Science.

Index

CPSIA information can be obtained
at www.ICGtesting.com
Printed in the USA
FSHW011947031019
62554FS